"After the River Thames has left Tower Bridge on its journey towards the sea, it passes through a sprawl of docks, wharfs and riverside factories before it widens into marshes and finally divides the glitter of Southend on the north bank from the desolate reaches and flats of Sheppey on the south. In the thickest part of the dock area the river makes an enormous U-bend, and as it straightens out on its eastward course it runs through the old town of Woolwich, now hard to separate from its neighbouring boroughs. Woolwich docks occupy most of the north bank; the people with their shops and cinemas occupy the south bank, together with more works and factories, including the famous Woolwich Arsenal.

"In the western part of Woolwich, just south of the main road and the railway that runs beside it, the ground is shaped like a bowl, although the houses and buildings that cover it hide its contours. In this bowl, unexpectedly, is a patch of green. It is a football ground, and it is called The Valley..."

Anthony Bristowe, 1949

Rick Everitt was born in Plumstead in 1963, but until 2007 lived mostly in Welling and Sidcup. He attended Chislehurst & Sidcup Grammar School and the University of Reading, receiving an honours degree in politics, before joining the Home Office as a computer programmer in 1986. He saw his first Charlton match in 1969, launched the *Voice of The Valley* fanzine in 1988, and began contributing to the *South East London & Kentish Mercury* the following year, eventually becoming sports editor. He was secretary of Charlton Athletic Supporters' Club from 1991 until 1998, when he joined the football club as communications manager.

As well as being the author and publisher of *Battle for The Valley* (1991, 2014), Rick assisted late club historian and statistician Colin Cameron with *The Valiant 500* (1991) and was both editor and co-publisher of the latter's *Home & Away with Charlton Athletic 1920-2004*. While working at the football club he oversaw publication of Chick Fowles' *Welling to Wembley* (1998) and Charlie Connelly's *Many Miles...* (2001), as well as Keith Peacock's *No Substitute* (2004), on which he collaborated extensively. In 2005 he was credited as producer of the club's *Centenary History* DVD.

Rick served as a Labour councillor for East Wickham ward in Bexley from 2002-06, and was the party's parliamentary candidate for the Old Bexley and Sidcup constituency in the 2010 general election. Since 2011 he has been a member of both Ramsgate Town Council and Thanet District Council, on which he is the current cabinet member for finance and estates. He and his partner Corinna, who is also a local councillor, have a 15-year-old daughter, Natasha.

Let battle commence: the author on the pitch at The Valley on September 21st, 1985

Battle for The Valley

RICK EVERITT

First published in 1991 by Voice of The Valley
This revised and updated edition published 2014 by Voice of The Valley
Website: www.votvonline.com
Email: sales@votvonline.com

Copyright © Rick Everitt 1991, 2014

The moral right of the author has been asserted

Typeset by Rick Everitt
Printed in Great Britain by Charlesworth Press, WF2 9LP

ISBN 978-0-9518125-4-9

Introduction

With the publication of this new edition, more than 22 years after the first, *Battle for The Valley* finally has its happy ending. The fact that it ever appeared without that conclusion was fitting in its way, given the twists and turns of the saga, but it was never satisfactory.

This version had to be compiled completely anew, but it is generally faithful to the original. I have mostly resisted the temptation to revise judgements that I made nearly a quarter-century ago when many of the events were fresh in my mind, except where my original conclusions were obviously dated by the last two decades. I have also made some minor additions arising from information that has subsequently come to light, and of course introduced the extra chapters to extend the story to that tear-jerking, spine-tingling afternoon when the team ran out to *The Red, Red Robin* in SE7 again.

It would be surprising if the intervening years had not added new perspective, but if anything the passing of time has further vindicated the campaign, since within a decade of Charlton coming home three sides of the stadium had been completely rebuilt. It is hard to avoid the observation that by 2001 the ground bore a considerable resemblance to the scheme rejected by the council in 1990. Success did return on the field with promotion to the Premier League in 1998, the crowds did come back on a regular basis and The Valley was once more able to accommodate them.

Nevertheless, it would be easy to forget that there were voices of dissent in the 1980s, including some who argued that a move to Selhurst Park was necessary, sensible, or a reasonable exchange for top-flight football. Or simply that the men who owned the club were entitled to make such decisions and the only choice for fans was to accept them or walk away. Those who took a contrary position were stuck in the past, foolishly sentimental or just in denial about the hard economic facts of the Thatcher era. Football, like the railways, was in permanent decline. It would have to cut its cloth accordingly. And, anyway, ground-sharing was common on the continent. Why not here?

There have been echoes of some of these arguments in more recent debates about whether Charlton should yet again abandon The Valley, this time in favour of the Greenwich Peninsula. Yet if our history teaches us anything it is that directors and owners, however well intentioned, do not always know best, and that what supporters think and do can influence what happens positively.

English football is steeped in tradition and nostalgia, and the past plays a vital role in defining each club's identity. Charlton's history helped to provide a resilience that enabled it to survive seven years of exile and win the battle for The Valley, while their replacement tenants at Selhurst Park, Wimbledon, have had to take a more circuitous route. Yet still they have achieved much. Brighton & Hove Albion opened their new stadium in 2011 after 14 years of making do elsewhere. Indeed, since 1991 many English clubs have successfully made the transition to new homes. Tradition has often been compromised for practicality and profitability, and most would see it as a fair exchange. Even Fulham spent 2002/03 and 2003/04 at Queen Park Rangers' Loftus Road, during which the future of Craven Cottage was unclear.

But Charlton were the first to announce their intention to share permanently with local rivals and there has been nothing to match the remarkable campaign to return home that followed. What's more the battle did not just recover The Valley, it transformed the club and its prospects by demonstrating what was possible when supporters and directors were fully engaged in a common cause. In 2014 the modern 27,000-seater stadium is a monument to what was achieved by working together.

Neither clubs nor individuals can live on past glories indefinitely, but that is no reason why these should not continue to be recognised and celebrated. Many people have reason to be proud of the part they played in the battle for The Valley, and inevitably not all will find their role fully acknowledged here.

Others made their substantial contribution once the club had returned home and were instrumental in the work that enabled the team to win promotion to the Premier League six years later and enjoy eight seasons at that level. But there was also continuity among those who served and I have little doubt that it was the transformation of the club as a consequence of the fight to return that carried it forward subsequently. This leads me on to the once heretical conclusion that our traumatic experience in 1985 was ultimately a good thing.

There was also a tragic context. The twin disasters that year at Bradford and the Heysel Stadium were themselves a trigger for the abandonment of The Valley and brought the game to a new low, not just in public esteem but also in terms of post-war attendances. Football did not significantly reinvent itself until after the Hillsborough disaster of 1989, but at Charlton the struggle had already begun to galvanise the club's supporters. It was the 14,838 votes for the Valley Party in 1990, not Gazza's tears in the World Cup semi-final a couple of months later, which provided the watershed in South East London.

If supporters could organise and fight a local election that changed Greenwich Council's position, and then contribute to the development as well as the financial success of the Valley Investment Plan to bridge the funding shortfall, why could they not bring the same breadth and depth of expertise and determination to rebuilding the club once it had got home?

Thus the Valley Party and its fellow travellers first took over the official supporters' club and subsequently assumed key roles within the football club. Charlton became, in the 1990s and long afterwards, a club run by and for its supporters. It was this phenomenon that led Simon Inglis to write in the 1996 edition of his *Football Grounds of Great Britain*: "Once they were just another struggling club. Now, and possibly for all time, they are special."

Much of the credit for this belongs to directors and later chairmen Richard Murray and Martin Simons, who delivered the return to The Valley and subsequently assumed leadership of the board, although their role in the reopening of the ground has often been undervalued. I have tried to redress that here, because I was close enough to events to recognise that it would not have happened without them.

This is not to argue that Roger Alwen, who had pointed the way in 1989 and was still chairman in 1992, does not deserve his place in public esteem, simply acknowledgement that others on the board played crucial parts too.

Murray and Simons set the tone for the following years, with fellow directors

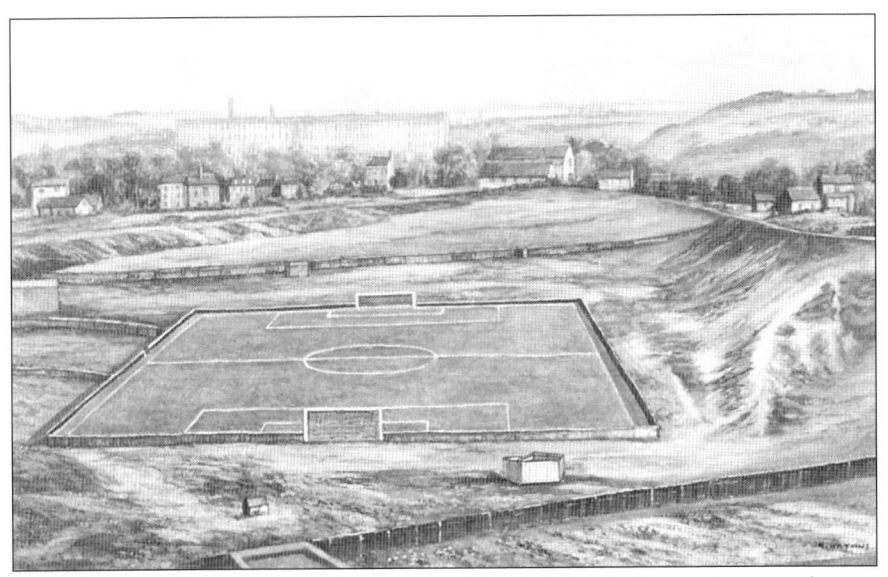

Battle field: an illustration of the newly laid out Valley in its pre-League days as shown in the *Athletic News* in 1921

contributing not just hard cash and loan guarantees but also an open and inclusive leadership style that fostered the sense of common purpose. The fact that Simons would meet fans in the local pubs in the 1990s was never an affectation. He was at home there. Murray, genial if not as reliably convivial, was a departure from his predecessors because he listened to others' ideas and could be relied upon to respond positively to sensible arguments.

What happened after 1992 is for another book, but it is relevant to note here the extent to which individual lives were changed by the Valley Party, in particular. Three 1990 candidates, Steve Clarke, Craig Norris and Wendy Perfect, went on to become elected members of the board as a result of the Valley Investment Plan. They were all still active in advising the club how to build attendances through the Target 40,000 committee as late as 2012.

Wendy was employed by the supporters' club in 1994 and subsequently by the football club from 2004 to 2012, while another candidate, Dave Archer, was taken on, initially to run the club's conference and banqueting set-up in the enlarged facilities, in 1997. He stayed for 16 years.

Steve Dixon and Roy King, the Valley Party agent, had made the switch from supporters' club to positions within the football club as early as 1991. Mark Mansfield ran the official Clubcall line, as well as becoming a familiar Charlton voice on local radio. Darren Risby joined the communications team in 1999. Paul Ellis became a long-serving member of the club's administrative team. Ben Tegg, influential in the Valley Party even though he was too young to stand in 1990, joined the staff a decade later to manage community relations.

Mick Everett, Peter Varney and Ian Cartwright may not have been Valley Party

The long march: fans leave Woolwich for The Valley on December 5th, 1992, a symbolic reversal of the route taken on foot before council planning meetings

candidates, but they all had strong supporters' club credentials from the early 1990s onwards and as fans assuming various important roles within the football club they continued the cultural transformation. So too did elected directors Mick Gebbett, Sue Townsend and Ben Hayes. Many more supporters were recruited to the staff as the years went on and for all of these people their involvement was much more than a job or pastime. It was a passion. The board became swollen with wealthier supporters chipping in financially.

Was Charlton, then, in the hands of enthusiasts who lacked the necessary competence? Hardly. The outcomes do not support the argument that the club was less professional or failed to achieve its potential as a consequence of involving so many supporters, and there were many others who contributed substantially to its success without being fans, including most significantly of all the first-team manager, Alan Curbishley, who continued in charge until 2006.

At the time *Battle for The Valley* was first published I had recently taken over as secretary of the supporters' club, as well as being editor and publisher of *Voice of The Valley*. I continued to write about Charlton in the *Mercury* for seven more years, succeeding Peter Cordwell as sports editor soon after the return home. Those were happy years for me and I was badly torn in 1998 when Varney, as managing director, invited me to establish and oversee the club's new communications set-up.

After a period in the doldrums, the *Mercury* had been reinvigorated in 1996 following its acquisition by Trinity Mirror, which already owned the rival *South London Press*. With Cordwell soon installed as de facto editor of the Greenwich, Lewisham and Bexley editions, and the strong support of group editor Rob Bowden,

I was able to extend the Charlton coverage significantly and thus already had the relationship with the club that I wanted, including since 1995 managing its official website on a voluntary basis.

Eventually, however, I decided that the insecurity of the local newspaper business, combined with the opportunity to implement my own ideas about the way the club should handle its publications and communication with supporters, meant that I could not turn the offer down.

I missed journalism, but I have no doubt that I made the right decision. The press was in decline in 1998 and that continued apace. The *Mercury* still exists, but with a much smaller distribution and limited sports coverage. Working on *Battle for The Valley* again after all these years was a reminder of how influential the local papers had once been, and this may be regarded with scepticism by some younger readers who have grown up with Sky Sports and the internet, never mind social media.

I remained on the Charlton staff in various roles for 14 eventful years, an experience for which I will always be grateful to Varney, as I am to Cordwell for giving me his unorthodox invitation to become a reporter in 1989. Together they gave me the chance to earn my living for 25 years in the realm of my childhood dreams. Who wouldn't relish that?

I have also served as a councillor and on the planning committees of Bexley and Thanet for a combined seven years, a more improbable appetite whetted by the campaign experience.

Voice of The Valley ceased publication in 2001, conflicted by my employment with the club and marginalised by the team's success. But in 2013 it was reborn and I am its editor again, with Dixon once more a prolific contributor. So too is Matt Wright, also a fan, whom I appointed my assistant communications manager in 2000 and who succeeded me as programme editor in 2003.

Another Valley Party candidate and former supporters' club treasurer, Steve Perfect, can be found selling the magazine most matchdays, as can my partner Corinna Huxley, occasionally joined by our 15-year-old daughter, Natasha. Corinna and I met through the campaign and, as she is often at pains to point out, she was already a supporter too.

But we are just a few of the people whose lives were changed and enriched by the battle to bring Charlton home and our experiences are just examples of the way The Valley became a hub for so many relationships and events, as well as the stage for a new generation of football heroes. I am proud to have played a part in that, of the enduring friendships I share with so many fellow combatants, and privileged to be able to relate the story anew.

For once the club seemed to have no future. And what we now call the *Battle for The Valley* was beyond our wildest imagination.

Rick Everitt, Ramsgate (May 2014)

MESSAGE TO OUR SUPPORTERS

It is with regret that we must announce that we will be obliged to leave The Valley the home of Charlton Athletic Football Club for 66 years.

Recent events have forced this unhappy decision upon us. On 1st July the owners of the land behind the West Stand gave notice terminating our right to use or occupy the land. Court proceedings were commenced to evict and we have been obliged to agree to go by the end of September.

On 6th August 1984, the Greenwich Magistrates ordered that the East Terrace be closed as work was required to the concrete steps and crush barriers. We were not informed of defects to the crush barriers when we were given an opportunity to take a lease of The Valley literally two hours before we appeared before the High Court Judge in March 1984 to obtain consent for the arrangements to save the Club.

The facilities at The Valley for the safe and orderly entrance and segregation of fans and accommodation for spectators and car parking have been so drastically curtailed by the effect of the two sets of court proceedings that we have had no alternative but to make other arrangements.

With effect from 5th October, the home matches of Charlton Athletic Football Club will be held at Selhurst Park which will be in future home for both Charlton and Crystal Palace who will keep their separate identities. We are delighted with this arrangement and the big welcome Crystal Palace Directors are giving us.

HOW TO GET THERE

BY BUS

No. 75. From Charlton Village to Selhurst/Norwood Junction (every fifteen minutes) — journey 50 minutes.

BY TRAIN

Charlton to Norwood Junction.
Change at London Bridge.
Charlton to London Bridge 2 trains every hour journey time 14 minutes.
London Bridge to Norwood Junction 3 trains every hour journey time 20 minutes.

The shaded part of the drawing below shows the land we cannot use as from 30th September 1985.

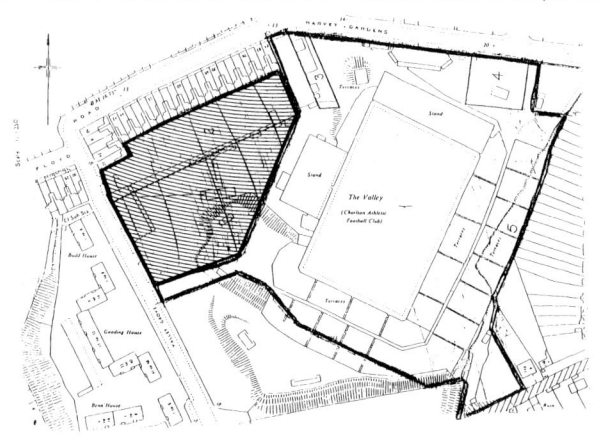

In the crisis we endeavoured to find a home in the London Borough of Greenwich, but although the Council was most helpful, to find even merely adequate facilities was impossible. Our players will continue to train locally at Charlton Park and our South Eastern Counties League matches will continue to be played at Meridan Sports Ground. It is still uncertain where we will play our home Football Combination Matches. It is our firm intention to make Charlton Athletic a First Division Club and we are delighted with such a good start to the season. Our big worry is the inconvenience which will affect you, our supporters, practically and emotionally. Like most of you I have been a supporter of Charlton Athletic for many, many years and feel very sad indeed at the prospect of football no longer being played at The "Valley", but delighted with our prospects at Selhurst Park.

We wanted you, our supporters to be the first to know. To help supporters who find it impossible to get to Selhurst Park we are prepared in the interim to provide a number of coaches. Please contact the Secretary if you wish to travel this way.

Season Ticket Holders will be offered the best seats in the house, with enormous regret, a refund, if they do not wish or cannot carry on supporting Charlton Athletic. We expect to be able to make special discount arrangements for people who wish to watch both Charlton and Crystal Palace first team games. A letter will be sent out soon to all season ticket holders.

Some compensation is that facilities at Selhurst Park are superior to those at "The Valley" and the playing field is in first class condition too.

Lets give the lads a bigger cheer this afternoon and encourage them to provide a result to take us nearer Division One.

JOHN FRYER

Chapter One

"The next programme is unsuitable for Charlton fans."
Mercury picture caption (September 19th, 1985)

They chose a warm September afternoon in 1985 for the announcement of the end of the world. I can't say that it came as a complete surprise, but the timing was especially cruel. So too was the way the news was broken.

Some heard it on car radios as they drove to The Valley for the match with Crystal Palace, a few who lived near the ground picked it up from television. But for most it came as the rudest of awakenings, on a single printed sheet distributed outside the turnstiles.

I was one of those ambushed at the gates, my only intimation a snippet of conversation overheard on the way down Charlton Lane. It was as I walked through The Valley's main entrance, on the corner of Floyd Road, that I was handed that single piece of paper, headed simply "Message To Our Supporters". Written in the semi-literate style so characteristic of the club, its import was quite startling. For Charlton Athletic, at least, tomorrow had been cancelled.

Of course, they didn't put it quite like that. The Palace game, we were told, was to be the penultimate match staged at The Valley. And by the neatest of ironies the future venue would be Selhurst Park, the home of the visitors. Details of how to get there were helpfully appended, their very inclusion an indication of just how foreign the new ground was to Charlton fans. Further down chairman John Fryer, managing director of building giant Sunley Holdings, blithely told supporters that one compensation would be the first-class condition of the Palace pitch. Presumably he thought the one at The Valley, relaid that summer by veteran groundsman Maurice Banham, resembled a ploughed field.

Charlton won that afternoon, 3-1, but even though victory was duly celebrated, most of the home supporters were in a state of shock. Many saw the whole exercise as a stunt to wrest ownership of the ground from a previous chairman, Michael Gliksten, while others just shrugged their shoulders and walked away, unable to take the idea seriously. Only a few dozen stayed behind after the match to question officials.

I watched the game from the Covered End, still reeling from the blow. Supporting Charlton had been in my blood since, at the age of six, I had finally persuaded my father that I could be trusted to watch the football, rather than spend the afternoon stopping him from doing so. For some reason he didn't feel the spectacle would hold my attention, but he needn't have worried. On December 13th, 1969, I found an addiction that I thought would last a lifetime. Charlton beat Norwich City 3-0 and from the moment the referee blew his whistle for the action to start, I was hooked.

Of course, my interest fluctuated with the team's fortunes like that of anyone else. But perhaps because I never had the distraction of being able to kick a ball straight myself, I didn't so much fall in love with the game as with Charlton Athletic in particular. It was an attachment that showed no sign of loosening as I grew older, or not on my part at least. Charlton, on the other hand, behaved with increasing

1

Here is the news: Ron Noades (left) and John Fryer announce to the press that Charlton are moving to Selhurst Park

eccentricity. I came to regard them rather as one might a beloved elderly relative growing steadily more confused with the passing years. I worried about them and occasionally lost my temper with them, but always knew that I couldn't abandon them.

And now this. It did seem like the end of the world. It would surely be the end of Charlton. And, what was more, everyone seemed to agree that it just couldn't be done. Everyone, apparently, except the men who had the power to stop the mistake being made. The local papers were besieged with letters. One fan appealed to the players to remove their shirts before leaving the field for the last time in the final match against Stoke City, while others vowed they would never make the trip.

Charlton too received many letters, although Fryer was to claim in the club programme that most, although sad about what was happening, supported the board. If true, it remains a mystery who wrote them. Certainly, the overwhelming balance of mail received by the local press was bitterly opposed to the move, with even those who reluctantly accepted it expressing serious reservations about its practicality. Only 100 season-ticket holders returned their books in disgust, it was claimed, but that still represented ten per cent of the total.

Two former chairmen also raised their voices in protest. One of them was landlord Michael Gliksten, indignant at being portrayed as the villain of the piece.

"It is not me who has blown the whistle," he insisted, while his ill-fated successor Mark Hulyer warned: "Moving to Crystal Palace is not the answer. It makes every game an away game." But the club sailed resolutely on into the storm, apparently impervious to the spiralling clamour of discontent.

It came to a head, inevitably, on the afternoon of the last match. In the days leading up to the game, fans broke into the ground overnight and daubed slogans on the terraces and buildings, attacking both Gliksten and Fryer. But still the plaintive plea, "Keep football here!", went unheeded.

And so, on September 21st, 1985, The Valley's 66-year career as the home of Charlton Athletic Football Club came, apparently, to an end. The ground had seen many great occasions, and certainly far better matches, but it had never known a more poisonous atmosphere. Anger, sadness and above all bewilderment hung obstinately in the air. A pre-match ceremony introducing some of the club's most famous sons coincided with the first of many pitch invasions, this one culminating in the laying of wreaths on the centre circle. The football itself proved so marginal to proceedings that it's doubtful many people would have noticed if the teams had stayed in the dressing rooms.

Later it would be said by some that the protests were muted, but it would be more accurate to say that they were not organised. In this respect the supporters' club failed its members lamentably, because as a body the fans might quite easily have prevented the match from taking place. They could have watched proceedings in stony silence. They could even have sat down in the roads around the ground and refused to enter. However, no one seemed prepared to take the lead, so instead there was only a shambles of discontent.

But protests there were. Before the kick-off, a group of a hundred or so fans in their twenties invaded the East Terrace, which had been closed by the Greater London Council, and sat down in the middle of it until they were gently but firmly shepherded away by police. Throughout the match a large section of the 8,858 crowd persisted in explaining to Fryer precisely where he could stick his Selhurst Park. And dotted around the stands were banners, big and small, but all with the same urgent message.

The next pitch invasion came during the half-time interval, delaying the resumption of play by nearly ten minutes. Wave after wave of young men clambered over the low railing in front of the terrace that divided the main stand from the popular Covered End, appealing by gesture as they did for the fans behind the goal to join them. The sheer weight of their numbers overwhelmed the efforts of the police to restrain them, but the more conservative patrons of the seats declined the invitation to join in, perhaps because they were prevented from doing so by a rather more formidable fence. Instead they showed their support by applauding, and chanting "We're proud of you, Charlton", the traditional hymn of approval to the team.

Soon there were hundreds in the centre circle but once there they seemed uncertain what to do next. Some sat, others shook their fists at the empty directors' box. Finally, they advanced to shout their anger from the front of the main stand. As the minutes ticked away, and with the players ready to re-emerge, manager Lennie Lawrence came out to ask them to allow the game to continue and some of the crowd also indicated that they felt the point had been made. Gradually, the demonstration crumbled. Later Fryer would claim that the invaders had been booed, but in fact they were warmly received. Only at the very end when a small group sought to snap a

Pitch battle: the half-time protest gets under way during the Stoke City game

crossbar did the crowd turn against them. It was testimony, in the teeth of the most dire provocation, to the Valley faithful's enduring sense of fair play.

When the pitch had finally been cleared the game resumed, but still the crowd chanted its slogans. "We hate Palace!" echoed round and round the old ground, a reminder that the directors had further compounded the folly of leaving by choosing the wrong alternative venue. The lone placard, "Don't let the Sunley go down on The Valley", waved defiantly amid it all from the packed bank of low terracing. Dick Ayers, a 46-year-old fan from Shooters Hill, was making his point too.

Twice Charlton scored, only briefly breaking through the increasingly ugly mood, yet fittingly giving Robert Lee, a former turnstile operator at The Valley, the honour of scoring the club's last goal there.

When the final, final whistle went, the players and officials fled as if for their lives and now the fans, old and young, poured onto the pitch and the protest began in earnest. But it was much, much too late. The directors had left their places ten minutes earlier to take refuge inside the stand and the chants of the angry crowd were directed only at empty seats. Even now there was confusion, as some fans clambered onto the East Terrace for a last look at the view, while others sat in front of the main stand, some of them, male and female, in tears. Few left the ground; those that did not choose to join the throng on the pitch remaining in the stands to see what would happen next. For more than an hour they lingered, unwilling, unable to say goodbye. Some clutched lumps of turf hewn from the pitch with penknives.

As one fan scaled a floodlight and others pulled down the boards at the top of the East Terrace that announced the backing of Sunley Holdings, I climbed the steps of that huge bank one final time and looked down again on the great concrete bowl of which I had so many happy memories. No one could ever take them away, but the directors were doing something far worse. They were destroying our dreams. Supporting Charlton had always been dependent on a suspension of disbelief, allowing you to hope for better days ahead against all the evidence to the contrary. That summer just gone, all those years of thwarted ambition had finally been rewarded. The fans now believed, correctly, that they at last had a team capable of rejoining the elite. But without The Valley, what did it matter?

My mind, like the crowd, was a confusion of emotions. Most of all, however, I was simply frustrated that the directors could not, or would not, see what was blatantly obvious to everyone else. Namely that what they were proposing to do simply could not work. It would fail not just because the chaotic South London traffic system could not accommodate the thousands who would need to make the trip, or because the rail journey involved travelling into central London and out again. It would fail because Charlton Athletic and The Valley were one and the same thing. It was playing in Floyd Road, SE7, that gave the club its identity and the team its legitimacy in the eyes of the supporters. Take that away and eventually you would have nothing but a gang of mercenaries in red shirts.

And the past did matter. For there had once been a time, a fleeting span of perhaps 15 years, when Charlton were a more fashionable, successful club. Few of the people who made their protest that afternoon ever knew those days, but the memory was part of their Charlton nonetheless. Passed on in so many cases by fathers and

We shall not be moved! Thousands demonstrate in vain at the final whistle

Turfed out: fans carve souvenirs out of the famous Valley pitch

grandfathers, the club's history provided the context in which all the modern dramas took place. More than that, the past was why The Valley was what it was. And why Charlton could never quite be reduced to the status of an Orient or a Millwall, despite the best efforts of the board.

It was true, of course, that the flood tide of people which once swept along the Woolwich Road and over Shooters Hill from Kent had long since receded. There had been too many grey winter afternoons on that mountainous bank of terracing, looking down on second-rate footballers hired by third-rate directors. So sparse were the crowds in the last years, strangers were given funny looks. Battling against relegation year in, year out, we were laughed at by football's commuters as they sped past on the nearby North Kent railway line, brandishing their season tickets for White Hart Lane and Highbury. We skulked in the shadows when Millwall came to call.

And as the crowds declined, so had parts of the ground fallen into dereliction. By the mid-1970s, The Valley was a ramshackle, decaying mess of a stadium. The toilets were a disgrace, the terracing was crumbling; all the facilities were wretchedly inadequate for a club with ambitions to play again at the highest level. Yet how we loved it, gloried in it even. For its very scale was an unspoken boast of better days long gone.

Then, at last, had come the changes: a new roof for the main stand; a bright new cover at the Heights end; and seats behind both goals, the last unpopular but undeniably lending an air of modernity. The old girl had entered the 1980s in more respectable shape; enough indeed to convince Simon Inglis to write in the first edition of his *Football Grounds of England and Wales* that "at least The Valley now has a future".

And now, suddenly, it didn't. It was nearly six o'clock when I walked out onto

Harvey Gardens for the last time, the ground all but empty, cleared by police who feared an arson attack on the wooden-floored main stand. And still I couldn't believe what was happening.

To those who saw groundsharing and mergers as the inevitable consequence of dwindling attendances and decaying stadia, the scenes in London SE7 that afternoon may have seemed no more than false sentimentality. In fact, they were much, much more as the experience of the ensuing years would prove. For even as those corporate undertakers, the property developers, were mentally measuring up The Valley, the seeds of an extraordinary revolt were being sown.

Supporter Phil Martin takes the post-match protest to new heights

Battle for The Valley

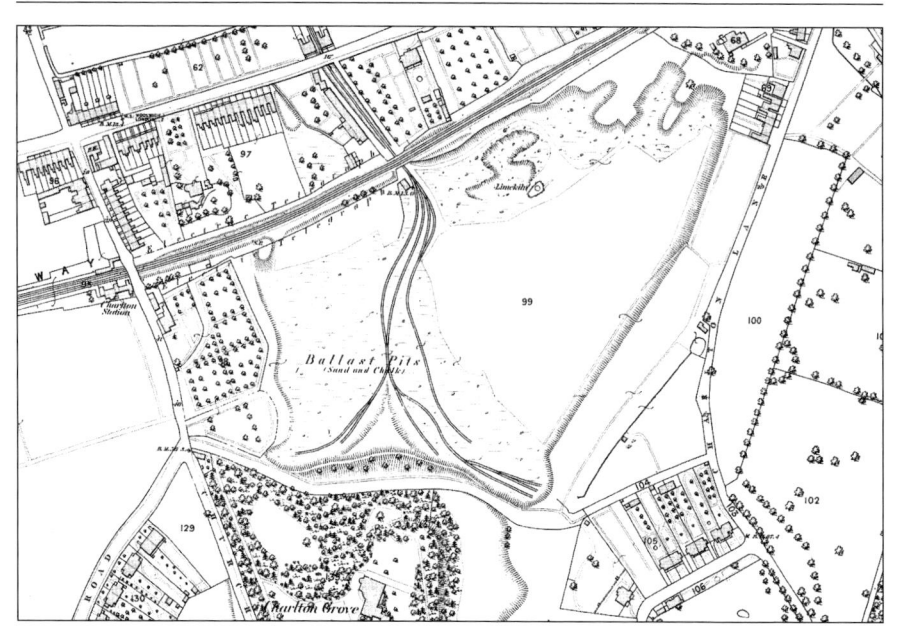

The location of The Valley in 1867, with narrow gauge railway lines running through what is now Ransom Walk underpass and down towards the Thames

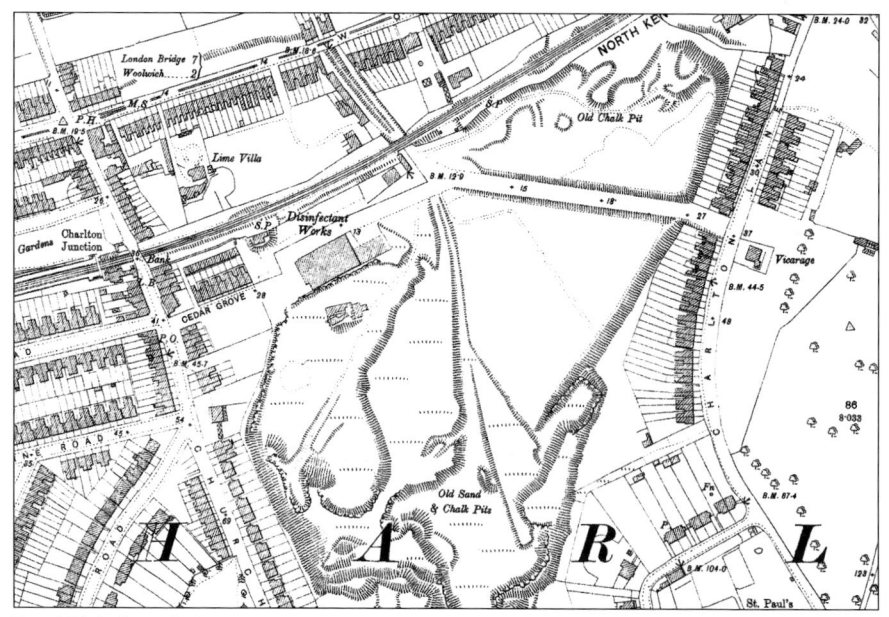

By 1894 the pit has been extended south and housing has now taken hold, although Floyd Road does not yet exist and Harvey Gardens is just a track

Chapter Two

"To lose one football club may be regarded as a misfortune. To lose two looks like carelessness."

With apologies to Oscar Wilde

This is not a history of Charlton Athletic, but it is impossible to understand the story of the move from The Valley without appreciating its context. Other clubs have left their grounds; indeed, in the case of Arsenal, who originally played in nearby Plumstead, it is strongly arguable that such a move led to the very survival and growth of Charlton. But no club has abandoned such established roots in a more dramatic and foolhardy fashion. It is worth considering, therefore, what it was that Charlton left behind. And it is important to remember that they made the mistake not once, but twice.

For the battle for The Valley did not begin on September 7th, 1985, when the club's owners made public their "impertinent assumption" that the supporters would follow the team eight miles across South London to Selhurst Park. Nor, as a cynic might suggest, did it finally commence a little over a year later, when the unsuspecting sports editor of the local paper unleashed a torrent of emotion by devoting his back page to a petition on the subject.

Rather it began on a foggy Sunday morning around the beginning of 1919, when Fred Barned, Frank Cross, Harry Gritton, Bert "Fatty" Heath and Archie Watt, all members of the then amateur club's committee, strolled up the path that is now Lansdowne Mews and surveyed a deep and derelict chalk and sand quarry, known

The pioneers: volunteers dig out The Valley in the summer of 1919

Battle for The Valley

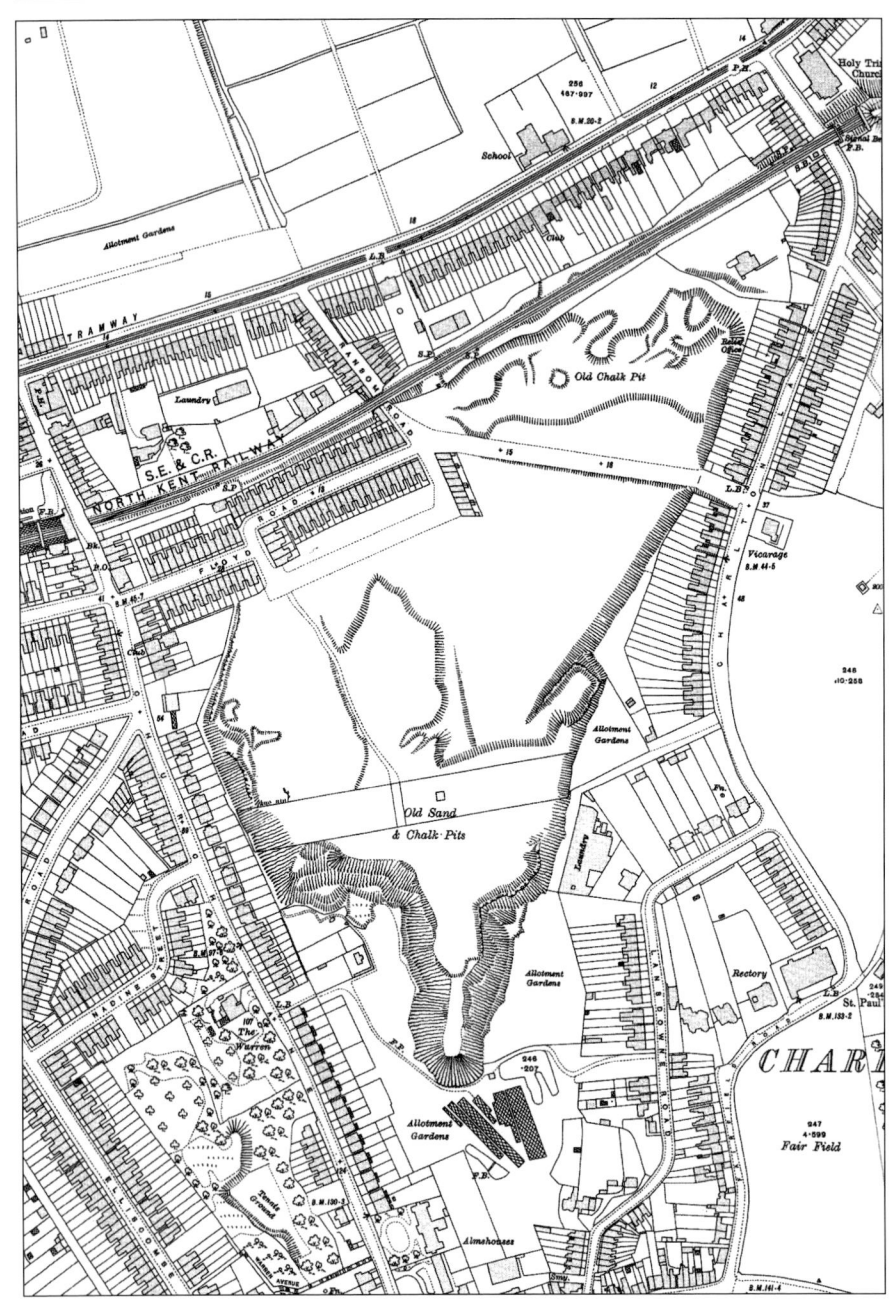

Ready and waiting: the site of The Valley in 1914, with Floyd Road now built up and a laundry in place near what would later become the Bartram Gate

Another group of willing workers break off for a team photograph in 1919

locally as "The Swamps". Perhaps, in view of the financial mess that would result from the club's attempts to build a first-class stadium there, its name was not inappropriate.

The quarry had been operated since the middle of the 19th century by the Glenton Sand and Ballast Company and there is some evidence that Charlton's interest in the site predates the First World War. In a 1927 issue of the *Supporters' Club Gazette*, Heath, a key figure in the immediate pre-League days, claimed that the possibility of playing there was seriously considered as early as 1911, but ultimately discarded in favour of Horn Lane, where they set up home two years later.

In fact, Charlton's roots were north of the main Woolwich Road, close to the banks of the River Thames. The club was founded in 1905 by teenage boys from East Street, West Street and Hardens Manorway. In their first season, they played only friendly matches, using Siemens Meadow, hard by the river, as a pitch. The wasteland site was a favourite spot for dumping rubbish and following a year in the Lewisham League, it was decided in 1907 that this problem and the unsatisfactory state of the playing surface were sufficient reasons to decamp to Woolwich Common.

Here they found conditions more acceptable, even if the goalposts did have to be carried from East Street and the players were forced to change behind a shop in what is now Frances Street. Charlton were now members of the Woolwich League as well, but their tenure at the Common was to be even more fleeting, lasting just one season. This time the move was born out of tragedy. Having scored a vital Lewisham League goal on Good Friday, Bill Pirie drowned two days later on the Thames. A benefit match was arranged for April 30th against Bostall Heath Athletic on a private ground at Pound Park and so impressed were the Charlton players that they successfully

Battle for The Valley

negotiated to use the enclosure the following season.

Here, despite a notoriously sloping pitch, the club would remain for five seasons. Surrounded by a hedge, it was the first of Charlton's venues which could accurately be described as a ground and not just a pitch. It was even possible to pass round a collecting box, and soon to charge admission.

Significantly, it was also very close indeed to The Valley, on land developed in the 1920s to become Wolfe Crescent, Coxmount Road, Hasted Road and Pound Park School. The club used the Royal Oak pub in adjacent Charlton Lane as a base.

The decision to abandon Pound Park was necessitated by the phenomenal progress on the field. Just eight years old, Charlton graduated to senior amateur status in 1913, entering the South Suburban League and the London League. The new venue they chose was the Angerstein Athletic Ground, off Horn Lane and near the Blackwall Peninsula. It was alleged to have a capacity of 4,000 and Charlton moved in to share with South Suburban League rivals Deptford Invicta. Palace chairman Ron Noades would surely have approved.

However, world events were fast overtaking football, which was deemed unpatriotic in wartime, and in April 1915 the club closed down for the duration. It was reformed in 1918, but by then the Horn Lane ground had been requisitioned as a petrol dump and Charlton were forced to play their 1918/19 programme of friendly fixtures at Charlton Park and Rectory Field.

So it was that a sub-committee had been set up that winter with the task of finding a new home. They had looked at several sites, including that which became the Stones sports ground, opposite The Valley on the north side of the Woolwich Road. Now, as Heath related, they had come to inspect the most promising one.

No terracing in this pre-League view from behind The Valley's south goal

It was soon apparent that the base area of the quarry was insufficient to accommodate a full-size playing pitch and that it would be necessary to dig into the walls if one was to be laid. A number of small ponds would also have to be filled in. Nonetheless, a meeting was arranged at the Mission Hall in Troughton Road to secure public support. The *Kentish Independent* reported: "The special meeting held on Tuesday, January 21st was well-attended, a large number of old faces being present in addition to the many members who have joined during the past 12 months. Enthusiasm was the keynote of proceedings and it was unanimously decided to make the necessary arrangements for the club to re-occupy the high position held in amateur football circles before the war. The question of the ground naturally occupied a deal of time and discussion and it was eventually decided to apply for a site situated between Charlton Lane and Church Lane."

A five-year lease was duly secured from Boyd Estates at a rent of £5 per annum and Charlton had arrived at The Valley, although that name did not immediately come into use. The *KI* reported on May 2nd that negotiations had now been completed and commented that "the ground was in a most suitable position, being easy of access by tram, train and omnibus", a judgement that in time would be called into serious question.

The work necessary to turn the quarry into a football ground took place during the summer of 1919, largely carried out by volunteers under the foremanship of Sam Budden and with the aid of a steamroller loaned by the local council. Extra gravel and earth was brought from a nearby hospital excavation and is said to have been full of old bones. But the raising of funds proved a difficult task. The more affluent locals tended to favour rugby, leaving the enthusiasts to scramble together what cash they could through a variety of public meetings and other events.

Another early match at The Valley, around 1920, looking towards the north goal

Another pre-League view of the undeveloped Valley, again looking north

One such venture was a stopwatch competition, with entrants paying 2d to purchase the second at which, if they were lucky, the mechanism would cease to function. The watch, a 9ct Waltham lever, was placed in a sealed box which was entrusted to the safekeeping of Mr F Lamley on July 29th. It ran for eight hours, 56 minutes and 39 seconds with the winner judged to be Mr E Hatman of Blue Anchor Lane, Peckham, who had overestimated by 27 seconds.

Also in July, it was reported that the "first cheque for the erection and supply of fencing had seriously depleted the club's exchequer and an earnest appeal is made to all sportsmen of the district to come forward and give their financial assistance". It was not to be the last such plea that would be heard. Fortunately, the local Conservative MP Sir Ion Hamilton Benn, who became president of the club, agreed to act as guarantor for a £700 loan which, even though it was never taken up, did provide the venture with a little security.

By the start of the new season, work was sufficiently advanced for the opening game to take place, a South Suburban League fixture against Summerstown. Charlton's "A" team won 2-0, with the ground's first goal being scored by Fred Jamieson before a thousand enthusiastic spectators, who saw a "splendid exhibition". Yet the pitch had not been seeded, the enclosing fence required by the lease not erected and the only changing accommodation was a house in Ransom Road. The *KI* therefore advised: "As the contractors have been unable to complete the enclosing, no charge can be made for admission but collecting boxes will be on the ground to which it is hoped supporters will subscribe as liberally as possible."

The first team made their debut appearance on October 25th when they defeated Chatham in the Kent League with Mr T Jenning's renowned brass band in attendance, but the match ended in controversy when the visitors disputed the legitimacy of Charlton's late winner and refused to complete.

Ironically, in view of later events, the first FA Cup match played at The Valley was a preliminary round tie with neighbours Catford Southend on September 25th, 1920, which Charlton won 6-0.

The club's progress was to continue apace. They spent their first season at The Valley in the Kent League, having failed to gain entry to the Isthmian, but by February had resolved to turn professional and in August 1920 joined the Southern League. Just one year later, on the expansion of the Football League to four divisions, they became members of the senior competition itself.

With this ambition in view it had been decided in January 1921 to form a company with a share capital of £10,000 in order to secure the purchase of the ground. A registered office was established at 25 Church Lane and large and enthusiastic public meetings were held in the town halls at both Woolwich and Greenwich to encourage investment.

In February, a popular journal of the day, *Athletic News*, even proclaimed that The Valley was "a prospective venue for FA Cup Finals" and a "suitable site for the Football Association to construct a national home", which can have done the club's League membership application no harm at all. Nor can the prospects of election to the Third Division (South) have been hindered by the fact that a proliferation of Welsh clubs formed the competition for the two available places. Aberaman and Bridgend having withdrawn, Charlton were required to see off the challenge of Aberdare, Pontypridd, Abertillery and Barry from the principality, with Bath their only rivals from England.

The man chosen to speak in support of the application at the League's annual general meeting was director Edwin Radford, a prominent figure in local public life and evidently a formidable sportsman in his youth, who had previously been involved with Woolwich Arsenal. By 1923, he would be president of the Woolwich Chamber of Commerce and have raised the huge sum of £122,000 for the War Memorial Hospital, close to Charlton at Shooters Hill, where he became superintendent.

Radford told the gathering of clubs' representatives, held in the Connaught Rooms at Holborn on May 30th, that Charlton were the rightful successors to Arsenal. There was a population of a million in the immediately surrounding districts and over the previous season, despite the lack of a stand, they had collected £8,000 from a 9d gate. The ground could be extended to accommodate 150,000 and by the opening of the new season they would already be able to house 50,000 in comfort.

He added that he held in his hand financial backing from certain directors and other local gentlemen to a "very considerable sum – far more than would be necessary to carry out any obligations for the next year".

Whether the last was true or not, his arguments proved sufficient to convince the members of the League, who elected Charlton to their ranks with 30 votes, eight fewer than Aberdare but 18 more than nearest rivals Bath. Pontypridd, Abertillery and Barry managed just five, four and one respectively.

Arrangements were immediately made to acquire the freehold of The Valley from Messrs BH Mansergh for £3,000, which was "hardly more than is being asked for a six-roomed house". But despite Radford's boasts, the share issue remained poorly subscribed – only £2,997-worth had been taken up mid-1923 – and even this modest expenditure was to prove beyond the means of the club. The initial deposit of £300 was paid with a loan from the chairman Douglas Oliver, a Croydon timber merchant and former director of Croydon Common FC. But when the public failed to respond in sufficient numbers to the team's election, the agreement was eventually taken over by the club's building contractors, Humphreys Limited, who added it to their bill, in the meantime charging Charlton a rent of £180 per annum.

Another problem relating to the purchase was uncertainty over the ground's boundaries on the eastern side of the pitch. At first, it was unclear whether the giant sandbank that was to become The Valley's most characteristic feature actually formed part of the site and the directors were anxious to avoid being held responsible for its safety if it was outside their property. On the other hand, if it was included in the ground, they held the vendor to account for the condition of the rear fences of the Charlton Lane properties which abutted the border.

The position was further complicated by the fact that the London County Council had a sewer on the southern edge of the site, the stench from which was sufficiently powerful in October 1921 for the club to bring it to the attention of Greenwich Borough Council's medical officer. This led to the discovery that the LCC, which had a legal right of way between the existing sewer and Ransom Road on the opposite side of The Valley, was planning to build a further storm overflow sewer across the eastern part of the ground. Accordingly, it was decided to leave the matter of the boundary in abeyance for the time being. However, Charlton did benefit from the work on the new sewer, charging the LCC a fee of £500 for tipping the material removed during construction and reaching an agreement to have the right of way diverted to their satisfaction.

Tommy Dowling, scorer of The Valley's first League goal

Around the same time a proposal to have the Ransom Road railway arch opened up to ease access to the ground was discussed with the South Eastern and Chatham Railway Company, who indicated their willingness to cooperate on condition that they did not have to pay for the work. However, the borough engineer advised that this could not be done without considerable expense and for the present such an outlay by the club could not be justified.

Indeed, Charlton were struggling just to pay Humphreys, whose commitment to The Valley was to oblige them to play a leading role in the club's survival during the financially turbulent decade of the 1920s. The Knightsbridge firm had initially been contracted to build a main stand on the west side of the pitch but, partly due to delays in obtaining permission for the structure from the LCC, it was not ready for the start of the club's League career, a 1-0 home win over Exeter City on August 27th. In the meantime, they agreed to supply a temporary wooden and canvas stand to seat 300-400 for the opening matches at no additional cost.

Such was the optimism at the beginning of the season that only three days before the club made its bow, the directors arranged for an extra 20 rows of terracing, additional to the 20 in the original contract, to be built on the east, north and west sides of the pitch at an added cost of £1,250. But it seems the south side was left undeveloped, with only the vantage points created by the original excavations from which to watch the game. An indication of how basic was the early spectator accommodation at The Valley can be drawn from the fact that not until October 1921 were Humphreys given instructions to build any public lavatories!

Charlton immediately fell behind with their payments to the company. The first instalment of £1,000 was due on September 22nd, but not paid until a month later, and then only courtesy of a loan from director Thomas Sullivan, the landlord of the Prince of Wales pub in West Street. The second was deferred from October 1st until November 1st in acknowledgement of the loss of revenue caused by late completion, but still could not be met when it fell due.

In January, with Humphreys threatening legal action that would have led to closure, the board was obliged to sell forward Scotty Kingsley to Fulham to raise the money. The player had been one of the pioneers of football at The Valley and did not want to move, but at length he was persuaded that unless he did so the club would die. Kingsley thus gained the dubious distinction of being the first in a long line of Charlton stars sacrificed to satisfy impatient creditors.

The £14,000 bill for the stand eventually rose to £19,937 4s 6d, a millstone that would hang around the directors' necks for more than a decade. In addition, the club had to pay £181 3s for huts as temporary changing accommodation and a further £101 18s for other items, including a horse to help in the construction work. Another extra was the sum of £35 for lining the two large baths in the new dressing rooms with white glazed bricks.

The escalating building costs were to prove quite beyond a small club still finding its feet in the senior ranks. Effectively, Charlton were caught in a trap. Such expenditure with no knowledge of what attendances League football might attract was a huge gamble. Yet they had to cater for the enlarged crowds without which the venture could not succeed. They also had to bear in mind that visiting teams would soon draw the line at the more primitive of the existing arrangements, a point well illustrated by a reference in the autobiography of Jimmy Seed, who was manager of the club from 1933 to 1956: "I recall how dreary The Valley was in 1920 when I played there for the first time in a Spurs reserve team against Charlton in a friendly game," he wrote. "After a cold, wet and thoroughly miserable day we were unable to take a bath or a shower, but had to stroll to a nearby hut so that we could change back into our dry clothes."

The stand was eventually completed in time for the 2-1 home defeat by Portsmouth on February 18th, 1922. Just 60 yards long and perched in isolation on

A section of the 11,000 crowd, behind the north goal, for Exeter's visit in 1922

the halfway line, it was a tall, proud structure, lent some authority by the flat land that surrounded it. There were said to be 2,500 seats in all, with a paddock at the front that could accommodate 1,500 standing customers. The elegant multi-span roof was an abbreviated version of the one on Arsenal's East Stand at Highbury, which was demolished as early as 1936. It is a significant comment on the relative ambition of the two clubs that the one at The Valley survived for another 43 years.

The architect was probably the celebrated Archibald Leitch, who had designed the similar building at Arsenal and later worked with Humphreys on Crystal Palace's Selhurst Park. His comments about The Valley and its great potential appear in a September 1921 edition of the *Football Special*.

By Leitch's standards, however, this was a modest enterprise. Inside the stand there was little room for the club's administration with the result that as the commercial aspects of the game grew more and more important over the years, the land behind it became littered with a succession of makeshift buildings and wooden huts necessary to accommodate the increasing number of staff.

Nor was the stand even remotely adequate by the time the club reached the First Division some 15 years after joining the League. The share prospectus had promised that it would be capable of extension at either end to provide additional seating as required and in 1936 there was even talk of building a replacement if Charlton had a successful inaugural season in the top flight, but nothing happened on either count. Even after the paddock area had been seated in the summer of 1950, the total of 2,900 seats for sale was simply not enough for the vast crowds that attended many of the matches. Yet this was to remain the only reserved accommodation available at The Valley right through until the ground's eventual closure in 1985.

However, the inadequacy of the stand was hardly the problem that troubled the Charlton directors as they took their first faltering steps in the Football League. Their concern was to pay for it. Despite the team finishing a modest 16th in the table, the average crowd in the first season was a respectable 8,011. But by March it was estimated that outgoings exceeded income by £100 every week and the club eventually lost £7,096 18s 2d over its debut campaign.

In a bid to raise extra funds, several events were arranged at The Valley for the summer of 1922. The supporters' association had to abandon plans to stage open-air dancing because of the need to prepare the pitch for the new season. However, the go-ahead was given for a series of boxing entertainments, organised by a Joseph Smith. The board even gave instructions for a Charlton Athletic Boxing Account to be opened with Barclays Bank in Woolwich.

But such ventures made little impact. The major problem was the lack of wealthy backers, to play the role that would eventually be filled by the Gliksten brothers. At this stage, the heavy expenditure on the ground was being underwritten by men of only modest means. One was Arthur Bryan, the local fishmonger who had reputedly inspired the club's "Addicks" nickname in the summer of 1908 by providing the players with haddock and chips suppers and attending matches with a similar fish nailed to a stick. Bryan had been granted the catering concession for The Valley during the first League season – in April he had been warned that his boys were not to go round the pitch during play – but by August 1922 he was asking to be released

Fishmonger Arthur Bryan (left), who inspired the club's nickname, with Tom Sullivan, a local pub landlord and member of the Charlton board from 1921-24

as one of the club's guarantors at the bank. Later his relations with the directors deteriorated and he applied in vain to be appointed to the board.

Disappointingly, the Third Division crowds declined in Charlton's second League campaign, despite the remarkable achievement of reaching the last eight in the FA Cup. The "Babes" knocked out no less than three First Division sides in successive rounds, beginning with Manchester City at Hyde Road and then the previous season's beaten finalists Preston North End at The Valley.

The ground record, variously estimated at 16,000-18,000 people for Millwall's Third Division visit in February 1922, was broken three times in succession. Preston drew 22,490, encouraging Charlton to lay extra terracing in time for the meeting with third-round opponents West Bromwich Albion, which pulled in 31,489. When the Addicks finally lost their fourth-round tie against another First Division side, eventual finalists Bolton, there were 42,033 in attendance at The Valley.

Yet each time gates for Third Division fixtures tailed away again immediately following the Cup matches. A week after the Bolton game the visit of Aberdare attracted just 7,095. The only League fixture to lure in excess of 10,000 that season was the derby with Millwall and the average fell to 6,175. Over the campaign the club lost £6,388 5s 7d and this despite an estimated profit of £3,000 from the Cup run.

One complication was that some of the proceeds from the Bolton match were swallowed up in compensation payments. Weight of numbers had caused the low railing around the pitch to collapse in at least two places during the afternoon, demonstrating the inadequacy of the ground for such a crowd. The most serious incident came behind the north goal in the 37th minute as fans struggled to get a better view of a promising Charlton attack. A number of people were injured and play had to be suspended while they were helped away by police and St John's Ambulance men.

In October, these problems were aired at Woolwich County Court, which heard the case of James Clinch, from Ilford, who had been off work for seven weeks after the incident. A surveyor who had inspected the ground in June said that in his opinion the railings were not substantial enough to withstand the pressure of a 40,000 crowd. But manager Walter Rayner insisted that the ground was actually capable of holding another 10,000 people. There had been 70 policemen and 42 stewards to control the crowd and the problem was the tendency to congregate on the halfway line where the plaintiff had been standing. Had spectators obeyed police and stewards' instructions to go where there was more room, the railings would have held.

Clinch had demanded £50, but was awarded only £12 plus costs, as was George Cox, a boy living at Eglinton Road, Plumstead. However, the club was still dealing with claims arising from the incidents more than a year after the event, including some from Bolton supporters.

The financial situation was hardly improved by the extraordinary number of people who were now choosing to spend matchdays working in the allotments on the south-west side of the ground which just happened to command an excellent view of the pitch. This was to remain a problem until the mid-1930s when the club erected a high wooden fence to eliminate the free view.

No one who reads the minutes of the board meetings in those early seasons can fail to be touched by the predicament of the directors. Almost every page is marked by news of another tradesman or benefactor anxious to receive an outstanding sum.

Chelsea and Hull City football clubs repeatedly applied in vain for unpaid transfer fees. Even the suppliers of the club's typewriter wrote demanding £23. One can reasonably assume they reclaimed their goods because shortly afterwards the minutes become handwritten!

The prestigious Radford had resigned from the board in dismay at the "absence of financial policy" as early as November 1921. He was followed just under a year

How the *Kentish Independent* saw Charlton's 1923 tie with West Bromwich Albion

later by the secretary and pre-League chairman Arthur Brandon, who found the directors unable to meet any of the liabilities that they had incurred and stated that he was personally embarrassed as a result of loans that he had made to the club.

Matters finally came to a head in the spring of 1923 when Humphreys again ran out of patience. On April 5th, their representatives Messrs Jacks and Freeman attended a special board meeting at the ground for the purpose of assessing the position.

The minutes describe proceedings thus: "Mr Jacks, on behalf of the firm, then gave a detailed explanation of the exact position between the club and the firm. He pointed out that it was with some misgivings that they had entered into the contract having in mind the experience of a previous first-class club in the district, which was only dispelled by the unbounded optimism of the directors and their genuine belief that the district would support the directors' efforts in accordance with their promise at the mass meeting held at Woolwich Town Hall.

"In spite of the fine performances of a really good team, the public had failed in their promise. This only pointed out that the district either could or would not support first-class football. Having this in mind, the directors of Messrs Humphreys were getting very anxious and it was with great reluctance that they had instructed their solicitors to write to each of the guarantors giving ten days' notice for them to pay what monies were due to the firm or an alternative of submitting a concrete proposal which would satisfy the firm that their position was secured."

Understandably, the directors were now frightened men. They had already dug deep into their modest pockets to support an enterprise that at best now looked foolhardy and they were facing personal ruin. Small wonder then that in their desperation they were ready to clutch at any straw. But what a bizarre one it turned out to be.

The district had already lost Arsenal ten years earlier through poor support, a move that had so outraged the *KI* that it ran a series of cartoons attacking the decision and took to referring to the

Chairman Douglas Oliver

Gunners as Highbury-Arsenal to differentiate them from a new Woolwich club that was formed in their stead. Now the Charlton directors resolved to abandon The Valley and merge with the amateurs of Catford Southend, decamping to the latter's home, four miles to the south-west in the neighbouring borough of Lewisham.

The public justification for this move was that the new location would offer better support. In this respect, the club was to be bitterly disappointed. But in fact it does not seem likely that it was the prospect of success in Catford that decided the Charlton board's complicity at all. It is more likely that what obliged them to move was the certainty of imminent disaster if they did not leave The Valley, or find some other dramatic solution to the company's chronic insolvency. And in that situation, who could blame them for taking what must have appeared to be a promising path?

Although a successful amateur club between their foundation in 1894 and the outbreak of the First World War in 1914, Catford Southend had been crippled by the cost of equipping their ground to an acceptable standard. With the amateur game fast being eclipsed by professionalism, it was felt that Lewisham should grasp the opportunity of having its own League club.

The *Lewisham Borough News*, which was notably enthusiastic about the merger, reported on May 2nd that the first approach had come from the Valley club's directors and that discussions had been taking place over a considerable period of time, even prior to the FA Cup run. However, the Charlton records tell a different story. As late as April 9th, director Morton Cadman told Radford and Brandon, now representatives of the shareholders and supporters' association, that the board "had no knowledge of any steps being taken to remove the club, but he personally would say there was very little truth in the rumour". Nonetheless "if it were true that anyone connected with the club was taking action they were only adopting the correct procedure in his opinion".

Four days later the board was told by its chairman that "outside influences" were at work with a view to the club's removal. "Full particulars were not in his possession but he could say that if the directors were to enter into negotiations for the proposed move, their position financially would undoubtedly be improved and much responsibility lifted from their shoulders."

At that same meeting, Humphreys' George Freeman remarked that "after very careful study he had come to the conclusion that no first-class club would ever succeed in this district. The fault of the club's failure to attract large crowds was not that of the management. In his opinion, people would always go to see a good game, but unfortunately that did not apply to the people of this district. The only alternative, therefore, would be that the club must move to a district where it would be supported. This was the first case in his experience in which a club had equipped a good ground and had received no support".

Yet had not the district already clearly demonstrated that it would support the club when, and only when, it crossed the threshold between mediocrity and success? That surely was the message of the 1923 Cup run and it would be repeated throughout Charlton's history. It was scarcely the directors' fault that they had neither the resources to buy that success immediately, nor the time to build it gradually, but it was too simplistic to pretend that the backing just did not exist.

On April 23rd the board met to consider formally the move to Catford. Significantly, the offer was explained by Rayner, nominally the team manager, but in reality more like a modern general manager, or even managing director. He would eventually depart in disgrace having burnt the accounting books and was ultimately suspended from football sine die for financial irregularities during his time at Charlton, so there is some basis to question his probity.

Rayner reported that an approach had been made "by various gentlemen of Catford" who were prepared to purchase the new ground, make arrangements with Humphreys Limited about the outstanding liabilities, introduce new capital and put up the money required for building work. The existing directors could either stay on the board or resign with the prospect of their commitment to date being reimbursed in due course. In the circumstances, it was hardly surprising that the resolution to accept the offer was carried unanimously. Three days later it was agreed to pay £500 for the assets of the existing Catford club.

The fact that Catford Southend held the whip hand financially in the merger was immediately evident from its terms. Explained the *Borough News*: "Although Charlton are in higher circles of football, Catford could claim the seniority as regards length of existence and it was made clear that any scheme propounded must be in the nature of an amalgamation; under no circumstances would any proposal be agreed to that would mean the extinction of the Catford Southend club."

Amalgamation was a strange description of this arrangement, however. Had it proceeded as originally announced, Charlton Athletic would effectively have ceased to exist. A condition of the deal was that permission should be sought as soon as possible for the combined club to play in the Catford colours of dark and light blue stripes and for the League team's name to be changed to Catford Southend. Small wonder, then, that the Catford committee agreed to the proposal and that some of those who had founded the Charlton club and seen it through to maturity dissented and pledged to set up a successor senior amateur club in Charlton with the eventual aim of taking over The Valley.

Initially, they found a sturdy ally in the *Kentish Independent*, which made no attempt to conceal its disdain of the Charlton directors' behaviour. Commented the *KI* leader writer on May 18th: "The outstanding feature of the arrangement is the complete eclipse of Charlton and the swallowing up of that club in the mediocrity of Catford Southend. There still remains much to be explained and those outside the inner counsels of the clubs concerned are very curious as to why Charlton should be giving so much and apparently receiving so little in return. What are the partners in the new concern contributing to the common assets? Charlton bring with them a famous name, wonderful prestige, a record that in all probability will never be excelled in the history of football, an organiser of victory in the person of their trainer-manager, Mr Rayner, and the players who are bound to form the backbone of the new club and the mainstay of the teams which it will put into the field.

"These constitute an overwhelming contribution by the club which, while it gives so much, puts the finishing touch to its generosity by tamely surrendering its name and colours. On the other hand, Catford Southend have been doing well in a moderate kind of way, but when the question is asked what substantial share they are contributing to the assets of the new club, echo answers what?"

In fact, the Charlton directors did make a late and lame attempt to assert their club's identity, or at least diminish Catford's. In mid-July they proposed to amend the agreement with the amateur club's committee in order to rename the "Catford Ground" as the "Ringstead Road Ground", delete the condition about adopting the Kittens' colours and drop the title "Southend" from the name. But the Catford committee threatened to withdraw their backing for the merger and the board hastily decided to accept the original wording.

One might also add that, Cup results apart, Charlton's performances hardly justified the enthusiasm with which the team was now being described.

Continued the *KI*: "Light has been thrown on many points, but we are still tantalisingly in the dark as to what is to happen to the Valley ground, which is naturally the matter that concerns us most. We are told that none of the money now being raised is 'going to meet any of the liabilities of the Charlton club at Charlton: any liabilities remaining at Charlton will be met at Charlton'. Is it not high time that we were told how this is to be done, and what is to become of that valuable asset the Valley ground? We hope the directors will see the propriety of taking the public into their confidence on this point without delay. Many rumours are afloat, but in the absence of any authoritative statement from the directors it is impossible to winnow the wheat from the chaff. Something must be going on behind the scenes – what is it?"

Manager Walter Rayner

Quite clearly, there was concern that some of the existing debt would be met by the sale of The Valley. Rayner had already been quoted as saying: "You can take it from me that if the Charlton Athletic football club is moved, there will be no more football played on the Valley ground at Charlton." Indeed, he told the first formal meeting with the Catford men that the agreement of Millwall to the merger was conditional on no more football being played at Charlton. Presumably there were fears that the Lions might complain to the League about the new club being formed on their doorstep.

Yet at an extraordinary general meeting of shareholders convened on May 7th, Oliver gave a different response when asked by Radford if "the directors would dispose of the present ground to an amateur club in appreciation of the efforts of old members of the club. The chairman replied that there was no objection to football being played on the ground so far as the directors were concerned, but it must be

Preparing The Mount: work gets under way at Catford in 1923

borne in mind that the company were not the freeholders".

In any event, the formation of "Old Charlton" was announced in late May and a successful application was made to the London League for the following season. Among those chosen to form the committee at a meeting held in the Antigallican Hotel at the junction of Woolwich Road and Charlton Church Lane, were Frank Cross (chairman), William Manchester (vice chairman), Fred Barned, Bert Heath (secretary) and Sam Budden. Heath had previously been secretary and later honorary secretary of Charlton Athletic from 1908 until 1921 and all had been key figures in the club's original establishment at The Valley.

Their intentions in setting up Old Charlton were quite clear. The *KI* reported that at a second meeting in the Antigallican on June 21st, it was stated that "the old committee felt it was up to them to see that something was done for the continuance of football in the district". Among the rules was "a very definite one" which prevented the new club ever being diverted from its amateur status – another past bone of contention – or being taken from their midst. Committee member Frank Pritchard received vocal backing when he inferred that the new club might one day take the name "Charlton Athletic". Heath agreed, stating that their one aim was to return to The Valley and resurrect the established name. Furthermore, the new team would play in the Athletic's colours of red and white.

At first there seemed to be no animosity between the two Charlton clubs. The

Battle for The Valley

Humphreys' Catford workers stop for the photographer in the summer of 1923

sponsors of Old Charlton clearly believed that they would have the first option on taking over The Valley, as soon as their finances would allow it. In the meantime, they secured an agreement to play on a sports ground in Morley Road owned by GA Harvey Limited, a metal company that later built and gave its name to Harvey Gardens, the housing estate behind The Valley's north stand. An Old Charlton Supporters' Association was established to raise money for the cost of dressing-room accommodation at Morley Road and the purchase of kit. Budden, who had overseen the development of The Valley in 1919, was appointed groundsman and E Griffiths team manager.

On August 17th, the *KI* reported another meeting of Old Charlton at the Antigallican, at which a list of players who had been secured for the following season was announced, including Messrs E Llewellyn, Kimpton and "Snowy" Marshall, who had all formerly played for Charlton Athletic.

Cross told the assembled company that they should not run away with the idea that this was a new club. It was really a continuation of the one founded in 1905 and which, he said, had taken a "wrong turning". There had been no idea of forming this new club until the Charlton directors had announced they were moving to Catford.

But now the situation was further confused by the announcement that Charlton Athletic would field a Kent League side at The Valley after the first team and reserves had departed. This couldn't be before early November because of the work necessary at Catford's Ringstead Road ground, which had now been renamed "The Mount".

The Kent League team would alternate at The Valley with local amateurs Bostall Heath of the London League, raising the intriguing, but apparently unfulfilled, prospect of Old Charlton visiting the ground as an away club. In the event, the Heathens did not play at The Valley until January. While the Third Division side were still in the district, the new team would have a preponderance of away fixtures, with any home matches being played at Bostall Heath's existing ground in Abbey Wood.

It can be surmised that the idea of fielding a Kent League team was Rayner's way of countering the threat to the existing support posed by Old Charlton. Announcing it on August 24th, the *KI* also stated: "To allay many rumours that are afloat, it may be stated that the Valley ground is the property of the directors of Charlton Athletic, although it is mortgaged to Messrs Humphreys, the contractors, and there is no question of it being surrendered for any other interests."

It can be no coincidence that the same edition of the *KI* carried news of a complete breakdown in the relationship between the old and new clubs. At a meeting held at the Antigallican that Tuesday, Heath and other members of the Old Charlton committee had revealed that they had received the following letter from the secretary of Charlton Athletic.

Abraham Goodman, scorer of the first Charlton goal at The Mount

"I am instructed by my directors to inform you that the question of life membership conferred upon you by the company has been under consideration and after very careful deliberation they are of the opinion that your actions are prejudicial to the interests of the company. Therefore, in accordance with the minutes of the company dated August 19th, 1921, they have directed me to inform you that they intend withdrawing the privileges of life membership conferred upon you."

Heath said that he had been the secretary of Charlton Athletic FC on the date to which the letter referred and that no such provision had been included in the minutes. It might have been added since, but if so it was without his knowledge. Life membership for certain individuals had been part of the agreement that transferred the club into the company and furthermore each of them were also due the sum of £1 which had never been paid. However, the surviving version of the minutes does include the provision for life membership to be rescinded in such circumstances and there is no evidence of the document having been amended.

Vice-chairman Manchester had also received a copy of the letter and said it was a "dirty trick" done for the sole purpose of undermining Old Charlton. He had issued a writ over the matter and since the Charlton Athletic directors were claiming to own The Valley, it was time to make public the fact that the club had never been paid for. He and others intended to sue Charlton Athletic for past loans that had never been repaid and for work they had done.

Possibly the Charlton pioneers would have been further enraged had they known that the same meeting which decided to remove their privileges extended same to the retiring Catford Southend committee, who had already contributed three new directors to the Charlton Athletic board: Dr J Jackson, EB Bateman and Harry Isaacs. Of these the most important was unquestionably Isaacs, the proprietor of the Dartmouth Hotel, Catford, who acquired the freehold of the adjacent ground and leased it to the football club at a rent of £300 per annum for 21 years.

An army of labourers spent the summer and autumn progressing preparation of The Mount at the expense of another massive sum, £17,334. Substantial alterations were necessary, including the relocation of the pitch and the construction of terraces, initially to accommodate 30,000-40,000 spectators, but which it was thought might ultimately house up to 80,000. Unlike The Valley, this was no natural ampitheatre, however, and 44,000 tons of earth had to be dug out and raked into position to form new banking. It was hoped eventually to transport the recently completed stand from Floyd Road, at a cost estimated to be £5,000, but for the present a small temporary building was erected, the existing one having been demolished to make way for the new playing area.

One of several obstacles to Charlton's arrival was the fact that during the war parts of the Ringstead Road ground had been let to allotment holders, one of whom, a Mr Pinnion, had written to Rayner in threatening terms. An angry meeting took place at the Dartmouth Hotel before it was eventually agreed that the club would pay minimum compensation of £3 per ten-rod plot.

The board now decided to increase the £10,000 share capital of the company to £25,000 to cover the new liabilities, with specific appeal being made to Lewisham people to support the venture. The Mayor of Lewisham had presided over a meeting to announce the merger at the town hall in Catford on May 15th and it is evident that there was a fair measure of civic pride involved in the affair.

Oliver told those assembled that they should take a personal interest and feel that it was their club and their team. The registered office had already been removed to Lewisham – to 25 Bromley Road, Catford, in fact – and some £5,000 had been subscribed towards the ground improvements. Another carrot for the Lewisham public was the claim that the local unemployed would be specifically assigned the work necessitated by Charlton's arrival in the district.

Yet the club's identity crisis evidently continued, for in August even the *Lewisham Borough News* was referring to "Charlton Athletic's ground" at Ringstead Road. It was not until well into November that the paper began to refer to the team as the "Kittens", the Catford club's old nickname, culminating in the audacious headline of

"Kittens come home" in late December. The *KI*, on the other hand, virtually ignored the development of The Mount and while its attitude softened to the extent of wishing the team well, it never considered them to be anything other than Charlton Athletic.

It had been clear from the outset that the club would have to start the new season at The Valley and this was one reason given for the retention of the old name. Another was that Charlton, unlike Catford Southend, were exempt from the qualifying rounds of the FA Cup. But it is also likely that the League would have taken a very dim view of what would have amounted to one club handing its place over to another, albeit with players and manager as part of the package.

The question of colours is less clear cut. Charlton started the season in their usual red and white – the *Borough News* even called them "the Reds" – but this cannot have been enforced by the authorities because on September 15th at Merthyr they turned out for the first time in Catford's colours and soon appeared in them at The Valley, too. Perhaps this was an attempt to lure more followers from the Lewisham area since, not surprisingly in the circumstances, the opening matches at The Valley had been very poorly supported, with that against Southend United attracting less than 4,000 people. Meanwhile, Catford Southend had ceased to function and transport was laid on to The Valley from the Dartmouth Hotel on matchdays.

Despite the optimistic talk of playing there in November, The Mount was not ready until the last Saturday before Christmas and by then Isaacs had had to surrender the freehold of the ground to bankers Barclay, Perkins and Company in order to secure a £6,000 loan with which to pay Humphreys for their work.

Even then tragedy struck with the death of a workman eight days before the opening game. It had been necessary to level a large slope by means of excavating machines and during this process labourer George Miller from Deptford was buried by a sudden and heavy fall of clay which broke his back. The club met the funeral expenses and opened a subscription list to assist the widow, which they headed with a donation of ten shillings. The unfortunate Jessie Miller was not satisfied, however, and she tried unsuccessfully to sue Humphreys for compensation the following May at Greenwich County Court.

The first visitors to The Mount were Northampton and they attracted a crowd estimated to be around 8,000. Charlton again turned out in the Kittens' former colours, but they did not bring them much luck as the game ended without a goal.

The Catford ground's capacity was now claimed to be approximately 20,000 but the biggest crowd it would house for a Charlton match was the estimated 10,000 who turned out to see Queens Park Rangers on Boxing Day – and the *KI* reported then that this was as many as it could take. Indeed, seating accommodation in the temporary stand was so inadequate that special permission had to be sought to stage February's FA Cup match against Wolverhampton Wanderers at The Valley. As in the previous campaign, the knockout competition produced the season's best gate, 20,057, but this time Charlton drew 0-0 and were eliminated by the eventual champions of the Third Division (North) in the replay.

One rumour at the time of the move's announcement had been that Millwall would take over The Valley and in January a letter arrived from the New Cross club enquiring as to the ground's future. The Charlton directors decided not to reply for the present, although it is possible the Lions were simply concerned about The

Valley's use affecting their own Third Division attendances at The Den.

Meanwhile, the site continued to serve other profitable purposes. In February, Rayner gave permission to Messrs Kinnear, Moody and Company of Victoria Street, London SW1, to use it as a tip. Two large holes were filled in with Charlton receiving £62 10s for their cooperation. As late as April 1924 the club offered to sell The Valley, minus the stand, to former director Radford for £6,000. When he failed to take up the offer, manager Rayner was instructed to lease the ground at an annual rent of not less than £700 and at the beginning of May there was again talk of Old Charlton moving in as tenants.

But attendances at The Mount had slumped to barely four figures and the promises of financial support had not been fulfilled either, with less than £2,000 of the new share capital subscribed by February. Speculation about the future was clearly rampant and on May 7th the *Lewisham Borough News* was obliged to insist: "It may definitely be stated that Charlton are not leaving Catford and Charlton are not leaving the English League."

Less than a fortnight later, however, the Catford adventure was over. The *KI* reported that the club had been advised it would cost £10,000-12,000 to build a stand at The Mount, expenditure which could not easily be justified. The crisis came to a head at a board meeting on May 20th, 1924, when the directors were invited to consider a letter from Radford, as chairman of the supporters' association, asking them to ponder "the serious advisability of returning to Charlton for the future". More significant was the news that Humphreys, who were keeping the club afloat, had agreed to advance a further £500 but only on condition it reverted to The Valley. Reluctantly, the board resolved to do just that.

"Walking mascot" Tom Swift, who made the journey to Charlton's first round FA Cup clash with Accrington in 1924 on foot. He left the Dartmouth Hotel the previous Sunday afternoon carrying two black kittens for luck and was rewarded with a goalless draw

A mere 13 first-team games had been completed at the Catford ground, Exeter City having been obliged to visit twice because their first fixture was abandoned due to torrential rain. Only QPR, Exeter and Brentford had been beaten there in the 12 Third Division matches and discounting the unfinished game just 22 League goals had been seen, these being divided equally between the home side and their visitors. Charlton had failed to score on five occasions.

Abraham Goodman claimed the distinction of recording the first goal at The Mount, in the 3-0 win over Rangers, and also the last there for Charlton, on May 3rd against lowly Bournemouth and Boscombe Athletic, who won 2-1.

Coincidentally, those games attracted the biggest and smallest crowds, that against Bournemouth being described as around 1,000. Bad weather, simmering resentment among some of the old supporters and a modest season on the field – the team finished 14th, six points above bottom club QPR – had not helped the venture, but it was apparent to most concerned that it could not continue.

In the meantime, the new Kent League side had been showing outstanding form, both before and after their arrival at The Valley on November 17th, when they entertained Gillingham. The "Junior Reds", as they were dubbed, quite overshadowed Old Charlton's exploits in the London League and didn't even concede a goal until December 8th. It was Boxing Day before they suffered their first defeat, when Erith and Belvedere won 2-1 at The Valley.

The third team would finish champions by a comfortable margin, losing only twice and drawing three of their 30 games, one of which, oddly, was played at The Mount. A record of 79 goals scored and only 19 against perhaps explains why their matches at The Valley attracted considerable public interest, notwithstanding the weather, to the embarrassing extent that by the end of the season they were allegedly getting bigger gates than the League side!

With hindsight the Catford expedition looked foolhardy, but it had at least staved off the impending financial disaster of the previous summer. Even so, over the season the club lost £11,369 16s 6d, and this despite a surplus of £2,770 on transfers. Fortunately, Isaacs, who with Oliver had acted as guarantor for the Catford expenditure, took over the lease of The Mount and the burden of finding the £9,500 that had already been paid to Humphreys for work on the ground, as well as half the £8,000 still outstanding.

Several weeks of utter confusion followed, marked by considerable bad feeling from old Southend committee men and allotment-holders alike. The former felt that Charlton had not given the enterprise their full enthusiasm, and reserved particular venom for the "rabbit hutch" temporary stand. The latter wanted to know who was going to pay their compensation.

Eventually the Kittens reformed and entered the Kent League in Charlton's place, sharing The Mount with rivals Catford Athletic. The local branch of the Charlton supporters' association felt that their recent donation of £25 should now be returned, but the Charlton directors countered by demanding the balance of the association's funds. A compromise was eventually reached whereby the latter was paid to the new Catford Southend, and then partly used to recompense a member of their committee who had loaned money to Charlton.

It did the amateur club little good, however. Their revival proved to be brief and they folded, mid-season, in January 1927. Today The Mount is the south-west corner of Mountsfield Park and all that remains of the ground is a little terracing, concealed by bushes.

In spite of this, Lewisham does boast a professional football club, provided four decades later by the whims of those responsible for local government reorganisation. Millwall originated across the Thames on the Isle of Dogs, but had played in South East London at The Den since 1910. The New Cross ground was swept into Lewisham when that borough swallowed its former neighbour Deptford in 1965.

Maybe it is an irony that Harry Isaacs would have appreciated, had he been alive to toast the boundary commissioners in the bar at the Dartmouth Hotel.

Chapter Three

"Never look back wishing."
  Lennie Lawrence – Charlton programme v Stoke City (September 21st, 1985)

So Charlton were back at The Valley but at first there were grave doubts that the club would be able to continue at all. Edwin Radford rejoined the board and the Old Charlton committee pledged their renewed support, but there was still no cash in the kitty. There was difficulty providing even basic equipment such as training balls and the players' recall was delayed because the directors could not afford to pay their outstanding wages. In August came an enquiry from the Football League management committee as to whether the club would be able to fulfil its fixture obligations in the coming season.

The board replied that a scheme of financial reconstruction was under discussion but even they seemed to have genuine doubt that they would be able to carry on. Prior to the transfer of the Catford lease and debts to Harry Isaacs, Charlton's liabilities amounted to £57,249 and their assets – the two grounds plus the players' registrations – to just £17,000. Humphreys was owed almost £30,000, while the directors' loans to the club now amounted to £23,000 with the remainder outstanding to tradesmen and employees. Among those flourishing unpaid bills was the *Kentish Mercury*, who agreed to accept an issue of debentures in lieu of payment for the time being.

As preferential creditors and debenture holders, Humphreys continued to intervene in the club's affairs, advancing further sums of money on increasingly stringent conditions. However, the board's conduct of matters showed no sign of improving the overall situation. In November, Humphreys finally forced the resignation of the old directors and the formation of a committee of management, consisting of Radford, Douglas Oliver and two directors appointed only in September, Joseph Hocking and Ernest West, respectively a builder and decorator and the landlord of the Antigallican pub. Eventually, the Knightsbridge firm agreed to accept a further issue of debentures with David Clark, who had supervised the company's work at The Valley from the outset, joining the board to represent its interests. Such was his involvement in the club that he would remain a director until November 1969, then serving as president up to his death in 1971.

Understandably, given the financial situation, little major work was carried out at The Valley in the summer of 1924, although various turnstiles were repositioned and pay boxes replaced. Perhaps with the problems at the Bolton Cup tie in mind, a small concrete wall was erected to strengthen the fencing in front of the terracing and the familiar low railing installed on top. A quantity of corrugated iron fencing and four sets of iron exit gates were also removed from Catford for use at Charlton.

The other innovation was a scoreboard with enamel number plates provided free of charge by the *News of the World*, situated in a central position at the back of the east terracing. The same paper was given permission to advertise on the side of the stand which faced the Ransom Road entrance for an annual rent of £10, although the latter arrangement soon fell foul of a London County Council bye-law.

The influential Walter Rayner was sacked in May 1925 and with the merging of

Fans seek a vantage point on the cliff for the local derby with Millwall in 1927

the posts of secretary and manager in the person of Alex Macfarlane, a former Scotland international, the club at last began to make a trading profit. For the first time since turning professional, running expenses were now less than income, even though the cost of servicing the existing debt remained prohibitive and overall losses continued on an annual basis.

What Charlton badly needed was success in the League and they would have to wait until their eighth season in the Third Division before it was forthcoming. In 1926, they suffered the indignity of having to apply for re-election and it was 1928 before they finished in the top half of the table. Even then, they were 11th out of 22. But surprisingly, the following year they pipped Crystal Palace for the championship on goal average and thus took the only promotion place.

Still more remarkably, considering the prevailing financial climate, this was the signal for further major work to be carried out at The Valley by Humphreys. In anticipation of larger crowds, improvements were made to the stand, toilet facilities and terracing, which together with alterations to the pitch cost the extraordinary total of £2,687 16s. The terracing was certainly extended and the expenditure of such an amount, apparently without any major structure being erected, suggests that the original earthen steps, supported by timber, may have been concreted.

The directors also approved the widening of the playing surface to 112 x 73 yards and the laying of a perimeter track. And they managed to secure a 14-year option on the purchase of 1.5 acres of land behind the stand at a price of £500. By the time they took it up, shortly after the outbreak of war, the value of the plot to the club was very much greater.

That Charlton could not really afford the new work done at The Valley is underlined by the fact that in October 1929, long before Humphreys' bill was presented, the board was unable to find the cash to pay the interest due on debentures. The directors even suggested that the holders should exchange them for ones of a lower nominal value in order to help keep the club afloat. Yet 12 months later improved financial results led Radford to make a bold prediction at the company's ninth annual general meeting, held at The Warren in Church Lane.

"It has been proved that first-class football can be made to pay at Charlton," he announced. "Now that the financial tangle has been straightened out, the club should be able to keep going and if finances are carefully watched, the company will ultimately be free of debt and possess its own freehold ground."

Radford was right, but slightly premature. It was not until Clark introduced the wealthy Gliksten family to the club the following year that it was really placed on a sound footing. In December 1931, the old company went into voluntary liquidation and a new one was formed with a capital of £1,000 in 20,000 shares. Two months later, the four directors resigned en bloc and a new board was formed with Albert Gliksten as chairman, the immediate situation being stabilised by an injection of the timber merchants' cash. As part of the deal, Humphreys agreed to transfer the freehold of The Valley back to the club, in the form of the new company, in exchange for £65,000 of non-interest bearing debentures, redeemable in 1956.

Since 1927/28 the average home attendance had always been better than that away and in the first full season under the new regime it reached 15,000. The potential was obviously there but if the club was ever to run at a profit more spectators had to be attracted and that could only be done by offering them a higher grade of football.

Disappointingly, despite the Glikstens' expenditure of £25,000 on new players in their first few months in charge, Charlton were relegated back to the Third Division in 1933. It was not until the inspirational appointment of Jimmy Seed as secretary-manager in September that year that they found success on the field, finishing a promising fifth at the end of his initial season. The campaign also included a fixture against the first of many foreign teams to visit The Valley for a friendly match, French club Nice Olympique.

Meanwhile, there was now some money for further developments off the field. A small gymnasium was built under the main stand in August 1933 and fitted out with punch balls, rowing machines and other contemporary exercise equipment. That same month the board authorised the purchase and erection of 102 feet of new fencing in the south-east corner of the ground. Perhaps they were concerned about the number of people who were getting in without paying. In January that year an inspection of the fence running the length of the LCC right of way "clearly showed that unscrupulous free entry was obtained to the ground on matchdays".

However, the major project came during the spring of 1934 when the north terracing received its low, basic roof at an estimated cost of £3,514 17s. By contrast with the time taken over more modern developments, the work was scheduled to last just three weeks and the 243-foot long stand was officially opened on Good Friday,

March 30th, at a match against Reading. Apparently, the Gliksens had been dismayed by the rapid exodus from the ground following a cloudburst during a fixture against Bristol Rovers.

The erection of this stand was portrayed as a magnanimous gesture by the owners and an example of their ambition. The following notice appeared in the club programme in August 1934: "Messrs Albert and Stanley Gliksten have put Charlton on the football map and while they guide the destinies of the club, supporters need not fear of any lack of enterprise. Let the club receive the measure of support it rightly deserves and the next move will come from the boardroom. Last season great improvements were made at the Valley ground, including the erection of a covered enclosure which will house 10,000 of our 'bob' supporters under cover. Other big moves are on the taps, but first the supporters must show their appreciation of what has already been done before further enterprise is warranted."

A fly on the wall at a board meeting held in May that year, just six weeks after the Covered End's opening, might have told a rather different story. Clark reported the necessity of repainting the roof of the main stand, both underneath and at the back. The total cost would have been £83. Instead, the board decided for the present to have the top of the roof painted only, thus saving the club £53.

Meanwhile, there were several opportunities to buy more land. One abortive plan was to purchase former director Joseph Hocking's property, a house and builders' yard which jutted into The Valley opposite Ransom Road. The club's solicitors were authorised to bid up to £650 at an auction in October 1934, but in the event it was

Another view of the cliff, around 1929, with fans perched only on the right

Battle for The Valley

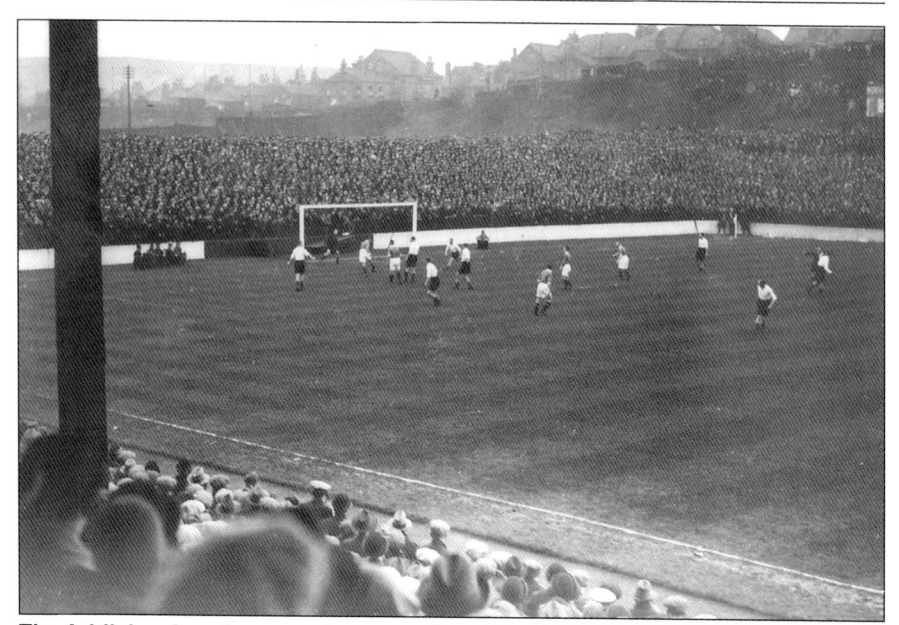

The Addicks close in on goal as seen from The Valley's main stand around 1930

acquired by Harvey's to service their growing housing stock. It would be four more decades before the land was finally obtained and integrated into the site, despite repeated attempts over the years to buy it. In the meantime, Charlton had to share their main entrance with Harvey's, who gained access to the yard by means of a doorway just inside the Valley gates. The house fronting the road was to become the main club office in 1977 and it was subsequently refurbished and extended in 1990 to include a souvenir shop.

When Charlton did enlarge the ground back in the 1930s, in December 1935, it was by purchasing the "triangular pieces of land heading the cliff on the eastern boundary", which it can reasonably be assumed refers to the area which became the Bartram Gate. This had been offered to them "subject to restrictions" at a price of £300. Messrs S Clifford, Tee and Gale were authorised to accept on the club's behalf, on condition that the restrictions did not preclude building access, including a stepway, to the existing Charlton property.

Earlier that year, in July, the club had been approached by Greenwich Borough Council, which wanted to buy a 100-foot strip of The Valley fronting Floyd Road. Mr Tee advised the board that the transaction might generate £2,500, but the new boundary line would have cut across the existing practice pitch and "shooting-in gallery" and the directors decided that they were not prepared to sell.

The same month, Charlton ordered five tons of red granules from the English Red Brick Company to surface the running track around the pitch. Thus, it seems, was originated the track's distinctive colour and texture, an enduring Valley feature.

That season just ended, 1934/35, Charlton had won the Third Division championship and gates were beginning to climb. Back in the Second they first reached an average of 20,000, then more as the team mounted a realistic promotion challenge. Unbeaten at home, a distinction they shared that year only with Gateshead, the club set a new ground record of 46,860 with the visit of Tottenham Hotspur, just three games from the end of the season.

The fact that the accommodation was still inadequate for such a crowd was apparent. Afterwards, according to the *KI*: "Portions of the bank looked like they had been subject to a heavy artillery bombardment. Broken and twisted railings were everywhere and there were gaps in the ground where the posts had been torn from their sockets. The pressure had been so great behind the top goal that iron railings were distorted into shapeless bars and the concrete walling was cracked. Had these supports given way, there would probably have been a heavy list of casualties." Charlton also received numerous complaints from spectators, some demanding damages for torn clothing. The claimants were referred to the club's insurance brokers, WR Ponting Limited.

Attendances had now risen 130 per cent in the short time the Gliksten brothers had been involved. A rumour had even gone round in March that Charlton didn't want promotion to the First Division because the facilities and administration couldn't keep pace with the progress of the team. But it was not only the club which could not cope. There was a great deal of chaos at Charlton railway station, which was simply inadequate and by common consent in need of replacement. Another complaint was about the state of the surrounding roads, which were muddy and full of potholes due to work on the new housing estate to the north of the ground – Harvey Gardens.

Nevertheless, at the climax of the campaign, some 27,943 turned up at The Valley for Port Vale's visit, which was to prove the last Second Division game to be played there for 21 years. Charlton grabbed a vital point and top grade football thus returned

Another large crowd in the period before the north stand was built in 1934

to SE London for the first time since Woolwich Arsenal had abandoned the district in 1913. The Addicks had become the only team ever to climb from the Third Division to the First in consecutive seasons, a distinction that they would retain until 1968 when Queens Park Rangers repeated the feat. The Mayor of Greenwich even held a civic reception to mark the achievement.

As long ago as September 1932, the programme had promised: "You will no doubt have read in the London papers during the last week that the brothers Gliksten have in contemplation extensive improvements at The Valley. So soon as the attendance will warrant it, a start will be made on the scheme which has as its object: The Valley, the finest football ground in London. If all the improvements contemplated are put in hand, the cost will run into many thousands of pounds, but, as I have already stated, it all depends on you. With the population of the surrounding district, we should reasonably expect for the League side gates averaging 20,000."

From 1935 to 1958, Charlton's average attendance never once fell below that figure. Indeed, after the war, it reached double the target set by the 1932 programme. The public kept their part of the bargain, but the Glikstens did not keep theirs. Instead, having surpassed their stated aim in season 1935/36, when the average was 22,153, the brothers announced: "When Charlton ascend into the First Division they will move up with the knowledge that they possess a ground with unlimited possibilities in the matter of housing capacity. There is no ground in the country of such size if the full extent in the matter of layout was taken advantage of than The Valley, but to

Goalkeeper Sam Bartram lends a hand with the close-season work in 1936

do that would cost a tremendous sum of money and for the time being the Charlton directors are going to make sure of consolidation of the team in the First Division before providing seating accommodation that might never be required."

Even this wasn't the truth, since money was spent on the ground rather than players that summer, but short-sightedly it was invested in extra standing room rather than additional seats. The marginal cost of terrace places was obviously much lower, but in fact both were necessary and even an extension of the existing stand would have been profitable, because the present accommodation was now totally inadequate. Instead, the Gliksfens arranged for new terracing to be constructed on the east and south sides of the pitch at a cost of £5,000 and new turnstiles to be installed to cope with the enlarged crowds.

By far the most significant undertaking was the concreting over of the huge sandbank opposite the main stand. This had always been a precarious vantage point because of falls of sand, although fortunately there had been no major accidents. The East Terrace, sometimes known as "The Mound", became quite the largest viewing platform at any football ground in Europe, some 132 steps in height and claimed to be capable of holding 45,000-50,000 people. Its construction was an even bigger job than it sounds, since underneath it ran that 1921 sewer belonging to the LCC. Early progress was hampered by heavy rain and another obstacle was a large bulge in the sandbank which had to be levelled off, the enterprise providing work for 200 well into August.

"To avoid unemployed men making fruitless journeys to the Valley ground in connexion with the ground extension scheme, we are asked to state that all applications should be made in the first place to local labour exchanges," advised the *KI*, a poignant reminder of the depressed state of the country.

For all its ambition, however, the project was flawed. In August, the *Mercury* reported: "To carry out the reconstruction of the bank a concrete framework was sunk into it to form the basis of the steps upon which the spectators will stand. The steps themselves will be filled with sand and ballast which will gradually sink as more weight is put upon it. As this ballast sinks, more men will level it again and once more the public will do its share of the work by standing on the bank and so hardening it. In the end, the whole structure will be as firm as a rock."

Some hope! What it meant was that no proper foundations were being laid. Over the years the concrete steps subsided alarmingly, weakening and twisting the crush barriers. The lower section was no more stable, having been built over the original timber terracing, which rotted away creating voids. Together these defects would eventually attract the attention of the safety inspectorate of the LCC's successor body, the Greater London Council.

The new banking also extended round behind the south goal, giving The Valley a notional capacity of 80,000, and using the land acquired that winter an additional entrance was constructed near the laundry at the top of Charlton Lane. This was the Bartram Gate, eventually named after long-serving goalkeeper Sam, whose career was then in its infancy. Work was also put in hand to improve the track that led to the new turnstiles into a road, with the club contributing part of the cost. This became Lansdowne Mews.

Now the Southern Railway chipped in by electrifying a siding outside Charlton station that could accommodate up to half a dozen trains, allowing a three-and-a-half-minute service until the crowds were clear. This was a compromise solution only, however, for earlier that year there had been some talk of building a new station adjacent to the railway crossing in Charlton Lane.

Even the local authority did its bit. "The Greenwich Borough Council is proving most helpful in its efforts to improve the ground approaches and work is already in hand for the provision of a circular stretch of road from Charlton Lane to Floyd Road," reported the *KI* on July 10th, presumably referring to Harvey Gardens. "This will be a distinct improvement on the old cinder track which has masqueraded under the name of a road for several years."

So now the ground was ready to house First Division crowds – providing only that they didn't expect to sit down. It was not a moment too soon. On the afternoon of Saturday, October 17th, 1936, Arsenal arrived for their first professional engagement in the district since April 26th, 1913. The official attendance was recorded as 68,136, although the gates were closed 15 minutes before kick-off and many more got in by scaling the fences, a familiar problem at The Valley owing to the difficulty of policing such an extensive boundary.

It was said afterwards that if the loudspeaker system had not broken down, preventing officials from packing the crowd effectively, Seed's contention that the ground could take 80,000 would have been borne out. However, reliable sources, including skipper Don Welsh, later insisted that the real attendance figure had been concealed and was actually 79,000. Certainly all the stand seats, none costing more than half a crown, had sold out on September 2nd, prior even to the first home game of the season, against Liverpool. Whatever the true size, it was then comfortably the biggest assembly to have gathered at The Valley.

The club was not alone in benefiting from the team's extraordinary success. A flourishing industry quickly grew up among local residents who hired out their back yards as bicycle parks and there was a big increase in stalls and stands selling refreshments and favours in the streets around the ground. The *Mercury* dramatically increased its coverage of club affairs in a bid to cash in on the huge public interest, even sending a reporter to cover away matches.

Charlton lost the Arsenal game, their first defeat on the ground for nearly two years, but in general they were enjoying an astonishing debut among the elite. When they had topped the League after four matches it had been easily dismissed as a fluke, yet they regained the summit on December 12th after beating Everton. New Year saw them placed fourth, but still level on points with the leaders and by mid-February they had knocked the Gunners back into second place and were once again making the running. Only after a bad defeat at Derby County in late March did eventual champions Manchester City steal the leadership and thereafter they had to produce some irresistible form to retain it.

So the Addicks had to be content with the runners-up position and, had they but known it, the chance of the ultimate domestic prize ever coming south of the River Thames was probably gone forever. They did at least have the not inconsiderable satisfaction of knowing that at last the club was on a sound financial footing. Yet it

Jimmy Seed (left) and Stanley Gliksten survey The Valley's newly laid terracing from behind the south goal

was at this zenith in Charlton's fortunes that the fundamental mistake was made. Although they went on to finish fourth and third in the remaining two seasons before the outbreak of war, no further improvements of substance were made to the ground.

That the money existed is not in doubt. In 1937/38 Charlton made a gross profit of £14,724 and after interest on debentures a net sum of £5,826, a record and an improvement of more than £600 on the previous year. In general, the club would even make a profit during the war. As Anthony Bristowe wrote in 1949: "The average gates were now 30,000, which was high enough to enable the club to go on making a profit and at the same time indulge in some more capital expenditure." Yet the projects he then cites approvingly, such as improvements to the dressing rooms and the excavation of the pitch to discover two large concrete slabs that were preventing effective drainage, are trivial.

The three fifth-round FA Cup matches against Aston Villa in February 1938 alone were watched by more than 200,000 people in aggregate, with that at The Valley attracting the club's official record crowd of 75,031. Even that figure was disputed, being initially announced and widely reported as 76,031. Among English League clubs, only Spurs, Sunderland, Aston Villa, Manchester United, Everton and Manchester City can beat the former number and just the last four the latter. Only City, with a record of 84,569 set in 1934, can surpass the 79,000 claimed for Arsenal's visit two years earlier.

It was hardly as if Seed was a profligate manager, either. As far as was possible he retained the players he had recruited for the Third Division days and where

Other priorities: spectators stand among the weeds on the East Terrace for the first game of the 1944/45 season, a wartime fixture Charlton lost 8-2 to Reading

replacements became necessary he sought to discover them through an extensive and highly effective network of scouts. Whereas in the four-year period prior to his arrival, the club had spent £11,000 more on transfers than it received, Seed eventually claimed a profit of no less than £115,000 during his 23-year period in charge.

As he wrote in his autobiography, the Glikstens "had put plenty of cash into launching the new-look Charlton, but with costs mounting it was soon made clear to me there wouldn't be a cheque-book spree. They quite rightly wanted the cash they had put into the club to be paid back as soon as conveniently possible and when it was all returned they did not want to finance the club again". But the situation was never that simple. Had the Glikstens reinvested anything like the profits the club was making, they would have succeeded only in multiplying their return. It wasn't a question of them going into debt again, more of sensible forward planning.

Later in his book Seed virtually admits as much: "Charlton made a mistake in 1937 after reaching the First Division. I raised the question of building a new stand. Albert Gliksten came back quickly: 'Will you guarantee to keep us in the First Division for three seasons?'

"I have never been a super-optimist... and wouldn't feel justified in sticking out my chin by offering a guarantee that no manager in the country could make unless he was a born gambler. I'm not. 'Right,' said the chairman, 'There'll be no new stand at The Valley.'"

Gliksten later reminded Seed of this exchange on the outbreak of war and the latter agreed that his chairman had been right. However, the post-war acceleration in the price of materials and labour changed his mind: "One of the reasons for the poor gates at Charlton could be put down to the inadequate stand accommodation. When we were riding on the crest of the waves, I'm sure we lost many potential season-ticket holders through lack of covered and seated accommodation.

"It is easy to be wise afterwards, but Charlton could have become the Arsenal of South East London if the Glikstens had retained the same enthusiasm as when they took over. If Charlton had built a second stand and had improved the accommodation not only for fans but visiting directors and officials, they may well have staged international games like Arsenal and Tottenham."

Still, if the club's owners lacked enterprise, they could always rely on their neighbours. In September 1947, Dr John Montgomery complained to his fellow directors about the number of people erecting private grandstands in their back gardens at the top of the East Terrace and proposed the erection of advertising hoardings to block the view.

One ground improvement over which Charlton had little choice had come in April 1937, when Clark informed the board that the local council had "insisted upon the provision of proper brick-built lavatory accommodation, with WCs for men and women". The cost was estimated at around £500 and the work was put in hand immediately. Evidently the new facilities were inadequate, however, for a decade later the subject came up again following a complaint from a female supporter. Once more it was decided to erect new structures, although after discussions with medical man Montgomery it was agreed that a dry closet would suffice.

Surprisingly, considering its proximity to Woolwich Arsenal and the docks, the war left The Valley largely unscathed. A small roof fire in the main stand in 1941 and slight bomb damage to the north stand were the limit of the problems caused, although four bombs fell on the terraces and two more on the pitch. There was also a direct hit on an ambulance hut. It had been feared the ground might be taken over for an ARP and decontamination centre, but in the event only a small area was used for military purposes. As war damage, the cost of repairing the Covered End roof was met by the government, although the section that had been replaced was easily distinguishable even 40 years later.

The Glikstens were largely pre-occupied with the war work brought them by their timber business, but they did find time to take up that long-standing option on the land behind the main stand, later to become the car park.

A "fitness for service" physical training programme for the public had been held at the ground in the summer of 1939 and a similar exercise took place the following year. Fixtures in the emergency regional league, meanwhile, were poorly attended and frequently interrupted by air raids, despite a belated official sanction for the use of spotters to avoid needless stoppages. In December 1940, the increasingly meaningless action was suspended.

Play resumed the following season, however, and two years later Charlton were joined at The Valley by neighbours Millwall. The Addicks' reserves switched to The

Den, where the wooden main stand had been destroyed by fire on the last day of the 1942/43 campaign. It was a tragedy for the New Cross club, yet one caused not by the war at all, but probably by a discarded match or cigarette at the London Senior Cup Final between Dulwich Hamlet and Tooting. The Lions' brief visit to SE7 was groundsharing of a sort, with Charlton even appearing as visitors at The Valley in November, but due to fixture clashes Millwall also played twice at Selhurst Park and once at Upton Park during their exile. By the end of February, they had tired of the inconvenience and decided to return to their damaged Den.

Charlton did well in wartime football, twice reaching Wembley, and emerged from the conflict a confirmed power in the game. Yet their successes on the field were still not reflected off it. Among the minor projects that never proceeded was the idea of purchasing two out of the small row of shops in Floyd Road to improve access to the ground. Discussions reached board level in April 1946, but as usual nothing materialised. Ironically, in March 1951 one of these retail units became a sports shop run by goalkeeper Sam Bartram.

The necessity of doing some work on The Valley was even acknowledged by the chairman Albert Gliksten, who told a board meeting in October 1948 that a "large sum of money was required to renovate the ground to arrest further deterioration". But he felt it necessary to substantially reduce the size of the second debenture before such works could be entertained.

However, if the Glikstens were conservative in their expenditure, they were less so in some aspects of their thinking. An even more fanciful idea than the relocations attempted by his predecessors and successors was the chairman's apparently serious contemplation of moving Charlton to South Africa, revealed in Seed's autobiography. The manager built up a strong tradition of recruiting Springboks, but it is difficult to understand how an English League club of even Charlton's eccentricity could have been effectively transplanted abroad.

Another colourful but foolhardy venture was the staging of midget car racing at The Valley, billed as "100 thrills a minute at 100 miles per hour", in May 1948. Organised by an American millionaire and his film star wife Lana Turner, the event was a complete flop and caused extensive damage to the playing surface.

More conventionally, the previous year had seen the ground become the first other than Wembley to stage an FA Cup tie that was also televised live. Blackburn Rovers' fifth-round visit was notable for little else, however, except that it marked another hurdle on the way to what transpired to be the club's greatest achievement, with skipper Welsh lifting the trophy at the Empire Stadium after a 1-0 win over Burnley. Seed's men had lost out to Derby County in the final 12 months earlier.

His initial investment thus handsomely rewarded, Albert Gliksten died suddenly in December 1951, succumbing to a heart attack while on a business trip to British Honduras. He was succeeded as chairman by his brother Stanley. The only substantial work that the pair had authorised since the war was the seating of the main stand's former paddock in June 1950. The nine-row extension was accomplished at an estimated cost of £2,757, plus £1,068 for the 750 new wooden tip-up seats. Additionally, the existing ones in the main body of the stand were replaced by those of a tip-up variety at a price of £3,000. The first plastic seats would not arrive until

Snow clearing at The Valley during the bitter winter of 1946/47

1977, and then they were donated by the supporters' club.

The extra seating caused a further problem, however, because it was discovered that the line of sight would be broken by fans using the terraces to either side. Accordingly, it was decided to excavate and rebuild the sections causing the obstruction and hence the subsequently very low level of the front steps of these small banks in relation to the pitch.

Oddly, despite the fact that the seats in the former paddock area were necessarily more exposed to the elements than those behind and offered an inferior view, Charlton charged a higher price to sit in them in the 1950/51 campaign than for those in the body of the stand. Admission was eight shillings and sixpence against six shillings – itself a shilling rise – and eight guineas against six guineas for a season ticket. This policy was obviously not successful, however, since the next year they reverted to a standard price throughout of six shillings per match and six guineas for seasons.

Following the stand extension, the police set a new capacity figure in December 1950 of 73,500. This comprised 26,000 behind the south goal at one shilling and threepence, 32,000 on the East Terrace at one and six, and 12,600 behind the north goal and on the terracing adjacent to the stand at two shillings, plus the 2,900 seats.

Subsequently, the limit fell to 67,000, but because other large grounds were developed in the decades after the war and Charlton's remained unchanged, it eventually boasted the biggest capacity in the League.

It was a hollow boast, however, because The Valley was clearly unable to cope adequately with special occasions, or even the club's own more attractive matches. For this the elder Gliksten brothers must bear the full brunt of any criticism. Perhaps one small point should be made in their defence, however. Charlton had enjoyed a miraculous rise and despite the vast crowds that attended some fixtures, a little consolidation was

An unusual view of The Valley in the 1950s, showing the north stand repairs and the skyline as seen from The Heights behind the south goal

not that unreasonable, given the company's chequered financial history. Later experience would show that clubs which rose through the divisions quickly, such as Northampton Town and Swansea City, sometimes slid back again just as fast.

Had Seed's success continued for another few years the board might quite possibly have seen the common sense of further investment, but the opportunity was denied them by the outbreak of war in 1939. By the time the post-war austerity of the Attlee government was over, so too were the days of big crowds at The Valley. Charlton's gates reached a peak of 40,216 in 1948/49, but thereafter always remained below the divisional average until they were eventually relegated in 1957. Indeed, on only five occasions between 1950 and 1991 did they exceed the average for their section, in all cases the result of a promotion challenge.

Although the ageing squad had lifted the FA Cup in 1947, the club would never again aspire to the pre-war heights in the League. For most of the early 1950s, First Division survival appeared to be success enough for the directors and the fans drifted away. Between December 1951 and February 1962, the period of Stanley Gliksten's chairmanship, just six players were purchased, at a total cost of £16,925. By contrast 22 were sold, raising £107,932.

According to a national newspaper report in 1960, the club was losing £15,000 a year. But the Gliksten timber business had just generated an annual profit of £1,246,059. "I cannot even remember the money I have put into Charlton in the past 30 years," Stanley told the reporter. Neither could the fans, unless they had long memories.

48

"I keep on because everything in my business life in the past has been successful. But success at Charlton has eluded me," he continued. "This club would have been fine but for the war."

His 22-year-old son Michael went one better, blaming not Hitler but the supporters themselves. "It's a heartbreaking disgrace," he said of a Second Division attendance at The Valley which had fallen below 8,000 while Fourth Division Palace were drawing 19,000 to Selhurst Park. "What sort of a club can you run on those gates. It cannot go on. But for my father the club would have had to close six years ago. No man can or would want to go on subsidising the local population like that."

Yet it was only 20 months since a fourth-round FA Cup tie with Everton had pulled in a Valley crowd of 44,094. And as recently as 1956, a 2-0 defeat by Arsenal in the fifth round had attracted a mind-boggling 71,767. The fans were still out there and given a glamorous fixture they would come in their thousands. But year in, year out, the Glikstens offered only mediocrity. If they lost money as a result, there was no one really to blame but themselves.

Seed had gone as manager at the start of the relegation year and after one last flicker of hope, the team going close to regaining its former status at the first attempt, gates had declined drastically over the next few seasons. The general average was between 12,000-16,000, with the exceptions the two relatively successful campaigns of 1963/64 and 1968/69 when the figure went a couple of thousand higher.

Of course, attendances were in decline across the country, but the significant point is that Charlton's fell faster and further than the general trend. From being the 12th best-supported English League club in 1949, one of only 15 ever to average 40,000 plus, the Addicks plummeted to occupy 64th position by 1974. The performances on the field were the major factor, but they were not the only problem. Another was the

No sale: the Charlton players resist Bartram's Floyd Road bargains in 1954

The charming but rather dated main stand roof at The Valley forms the backdrop to this goalmouth incident against Plymouth Argyle in 1963

poor location of The Valley. Unlike the homes of most other London clubs, the ground was not served by the Underground, so anyone wanting to make the trip into the unfashionable south-eastern suburbs from the centre of the capital was largely dependent on what was now the Southern Region of British Rail. It was far easier for people living elsewhere in London to travel to Highbury, White Hart Lane or Stamford Bridge than trek down to Charing Cross to pick up the appropriate train.

Arsenal, in particular, were also a drain on local backing. Forty years after the Gunners had abandoned the district, their Woolwich roots still marked them out as direct competitors for support. Commented the Charlton programme in August 1953: "Last season was one of the poorest on record for attendances at Charlton. The main reason for it, and we are firmly convinced on this point, was the clash of our home fixtures with Arsenal. This season, we are happy to report, our home fixtures alternate with Arsenal. With this handicap removed, a more satisfactory state of affairs in regard to attendances at The Valley is confidently expected."

In evidence, average gates ended three-and-a-half thousand higher, despite a dip in League position from fifth to ninth. But the improvement was short-lived. Not only did the team's fortunes continue to decline, but the abolition of the trams, which had provided an efficient shuttle service to the ground from surrounding suburbs, complicated matters further.

The transport problem, together with the physical and psychological barrier of the River Thames and the other not inconsiderable rival attraction of neighbours

Millwall, whose fans were densely concentrated in the inner South London boroughs of Bermondsey, Camberwell, Deptford and Lewisham, plus for historical reasons the Isle of Dogs, meant that Charlton's support was substantially drawn from the southeastern side of the ground.

A survey conducted in 1972, by which time the old metropolitan boroughs of Greenwich and Woolwich had been merged into one, found that 37.5 per cent of the crowd came from Kent addresses, with 47 per cent from Greenwich and the adjacent parts of Lewisham. But by the mid-1980s, the club claimed that a majority of season-ticket holders came from the outer London boroughs of Bexley and Bromley and their Kentish neighbour Dartford. This trend was partly the product of a general population drift out of London, intensified in the Greenwich area by the closure of the surprising number of industrial firms in the district. Many of these had been based in Charlton itself and their Saturday morning shifts had provided a bedrock of local support. The demographic changes were reflected in the closure of the nearby Charlton greyhound stadium in September 1971.

Genuine attempts were made to overcome the problems by courting London Transport and arranging for special buses on matchdays. British Rail co-operated by stopping coast trains at Charlton and laying on extra local services. But without the lure of top-class football and the former sparkle of success, it was all to no avail.

For 40 years after the club reached the First Division, little or nothing seemed to change at the ground. Indeed, the only major development between 1936 and 1978 was the installation of floodlights in 1961. Much of the £20,000 cost was raised by the Charlton Athletic Supporters' Development Association (CASDA), formed at the club's instigation in 1958 with Bill Jenner, a data-processing manager, as its chairman. Jenner was subsequently a director of the club for 14 years from November 1968. By 1962 the organisation had 5,000 members, operated a highly successful weekly tote and had its own premises in Valley Grove, known as Sawyer's Lodge. This was named after a founder member, Albert Sawyer, who had sadly died in April 1960. The development association became the Charlton Athletic Fund Raising Organisation (CAFRO) in 1969.

The new floodlights made their debut at a fixture against Rotherham United in September, yet the possibility of erecting them had first been discussed at a board meeting as long ago as 1953. The cost of putting in a substation at the corner of Church Lane and the Woolwich Road then was estimated to be £10,000, some of which would have been paid by the London Electricity Board. But Stanley Gliksten deferred action on the basis that attendances were down and the club had more urgent commitments in respect of ground repairs.

Perhaps it was true, but a club that erected lights in the early 1950s would certainly have benefited from the novelty value. Many did, initially using them for training purposes and charity matches. Although Wembley did not install floodlights until 1955 and their general use in competitive games was not freely allowed until 1958, it was humiliating that Second Division Charlton were among the last clubs to have them. The advent of the League Cup may have been the final spur. The Addicks had to go into their first-ever tie, at West Ham United in September 1960, knowing that in the event of a draw they would have to concede home advantage in the replay.

Presumably because of the structural uncertainties of the East Terrace, the two 120-foot towers on that side of the pitch were built right at its foot instead of being set higher up where more modest pylons might have sufficed. As part of the project, a substation was erected behind the main stand which incorporated a transformer and a 60hp diesel alternator for use in case the mains supply failed. Various improvements were made to the lights over the years. Six extra bulbs were added to each pylon in 1966, bringing the total to 30, but more significant was the installation of powerful tungsten lamps in 1977. As club photographer Tom Morris would readily confirm, the Valley floodlights were clearly superior to those at many grounds, including The Den, but markedly inferior to those which greeted Charlton on their arrival at Selhurst Park.

After the team left home in 1985, the pylons continued to poke defiantly above the surrounding houses for four years, clearly visible from the adjacent railway and a somewhat poignant reminder of the absurdity of Charlton's situation. Ironically, six months after they were eventually dismantled and sold to Biggleswade Town FC in the summer of 1989, the club came to rue its decision because plans for more sophisticated replacements had to be put on ice.

The development fund continued to do well for many years and during the close season of 1966 improvements were made to the pitch to aid drainage and to the toilets, no doubt to similar effect. In 1968 a new heating system was installed in the dressing rooms.

During season 1967/68 one-and-a-half acres of land at the rear of the Heights end terrace was sold to the council for £34,500 and the following summer the vast bank at that end was slightly truncated and a new boundary wall erected. Six years later,

A Charlton attack against Manchester City in 1964 shows the south terrace to good effect, prior to the sale of land at the rear

Battle for The Valley

The popular but rather basic Valley Club under construction in 1969

plans were finally announced for a 17-storey tower block, eventually to be called Valiant House in acknowledgement of the nickname adopted by the club – but not the fans – in the 1960s. Together with seven town houses, The Valley's imposing new neighbour would form Sam Bartram Close, named in honour of the club's greatest player who had kept goal 623 times between 1934 and 1956.

It was not until late 1975 that Valiant House was ready for occupation, but once finished it did provide the tenants with a superb bird's-eye view of the action. This was apparently in breach of a covenant between Greenwich and the club, causing general manager Rodney Stone to remark sarcastically: "No doubt the council will hire out deckchairs for the matches." Residents did indeed appear on the balconies in the early days, but their free view was short-lived. After the construction of a new south stand in 1979, the flats' outlook on the near goal was totally obscured.

Another spectator that evaded the turnstile operators was a stray black kitten which wandered into the ground at the start of the 1968/69 season. Since no one claimed it, the cat was given the name Lucky and seemed to live up to it as the team briefly climbed to the top of the Second Division. The feline intruder would stay for 15 years before staging a farewell pitch invasion during a game with Derby County in 1983 and almost immediately succumbing to old age.

The summer of 1969 saw the opening of a single-storey prefabricated building behind the Covered End that was intended to be the club's new social centre. Erected at a cost of £25,000, the Valley Club had its own access on to Harvey Gardens

The much-loved Covered End behind The Valley's north goal

adjacent to the north exit of the East Terrace. Fully licensed, it had a large hall and a smaller games room. It soon became a popular local rendezvous, especially after the appointment of manager Ray Donn the following year, but later there was little effort to encourage Charlton fans to patronise it. Quite the reverse, in fact.

Although it eventually became both run-down and rather tatty, the club was a financial success in its early days and after Charlton abandoned The Valley in 1985 it was for four years the only sign of life at the ground. At the time of the move the lease had recently been taken over by former skipper and manager Mike Bailey, together with his business partner Ken Hunt. The supporters' club loyally continued to use the building for their functions and meetings despite the evident decline in its custom and decoration over many years.

The social club's fortunes were not dissimilar to those of the team. A succession of managers arrived and departed through the 1960s and 70s, none of them able to arrest the slide on the resources allowed them by Stanley Gliksten's son Michael. He had become the League's youngest chairman at 23 following his father's death in 1962. His brother David Gliksten also continued as a director for some time but showed little interest in the club and eventually surrendered his 10,000 shares to Michael in October 1977, giving the latter control of all but one – and that was held by his son Nigel.

Even worse was to come on the playing side. In 1972, after years of narrow escapes, Charlton slipped back into the Third Division. Attendances immediately halved to 5,000 or worse and on one occasion, in March 1973, only 3,015 arrived for the visit of Halifax Town. On such an evening, The Valley was a forlorn place, the echoing shouts of the players a mockery of the great roars from the crowds of former times.

The club now seemed in the grip of a terminal decline and matters were not helped by the continuing silence from the boardroom. In May 1974, the *KI* published a front-page editorial complaining that not once in all the time that he had been chairman had Michael Gliksten consented to give the paper an interview. Instead, Charlton's main spokesman seemed to be Stone, a marketing consultant who had been appointed general manager in 1970. One of his proposals for bringing in much needed funds was to make more efficient use of the ground, but two years of discussions with Greenwich Council about the development of a £2.5m sports centre ended in disappointment in December 1972. Ironically, the Labour leader of the council was John Cartwright, later MP for Woolwich and an active supporter who, with fellow councillor Dick Neve, presented the pre-match record requests over the Valley tannoy.

Under the scheme, the building of a sports hall, sauna and squash courts would have been financed by Charlton, in conjunction with the Sports Council, and the centre leased to Greenwich on a long-term basis. Instead, the council announced that it planned to develop facilities at nearby Charlton Park, a decision Cartwright later attributed to left-wing members' reluctance to countenance any form of partnership with a private company. The club gathered a 5,000-name petition among fans in protest but to no avail.

Relations with the council became frostier still in the spring of 1973 when the authority blocked plans to hold a weekly market of 200 stalls in the Valley car park. Opposition came from local shopkeepers and also the market traders of Woolwich whose royal charter gave them the power to object. Greenwich Council upheld their

Despite its scale, the proximity of terraces and pitch made The Valley an intimate ground as this picture of a Mike Kenning cross in 1971 demonstrates

Pop goes The Valley: the outlook from the stage in 1974

complaints, although the market did trade briefly, making use of a legal anomaly.

Frustrated by these setbacks, Stone gave a notorious interview to the *KI*'s Peter Burrowes in April 1973, in which he claimed that following the clashes with Greenwich, the club had been approached by "a progressive Midlands borough" with a view to relocating there. His remarks caused a storm of protest from fans, just as he had intended, but according to Stone they unexpectedly also led to serious discussions with Milton Keynes officials about the practicality of such a move. The club programme was obliged to insist: "There is no possibility of Charlton Athletic leaving The Valley unless we are forced out by the attitude of Greenwich Council."

Even more controversial, although not with the fans, were two major pop concerts which the general manager arranged at the ground in the summers of 1974 and 1976. The Who, Bad Company, Humble Pie, Lou Reed, Lindisfarne and Maggie Bell appeared at the first, attended by a crowd estimated to be around 80,000. A 10,000-watt sound system was erected on two 15-foot towers either side of the temporary stage, while extra toilets and refreshment kiosks were hired to cope with the enormous crowd. The event was pronounced a great success by the organisers but not by the local residents and the council, who objected to the noise levels, litter, inadequate toilets, lack of food hygiene and poor crowd control.

Nonetheless, The Who returned in 1976, albeit in front of a smaller audience. This time, however, the concert was also marred by indiscriminate bottle-throwing. An application to stage a third event in 1978 was successfully thwarted by a combination of objections from Greenwich and a residents' protest to the licensing authority, the Greater London Council. Meetings staged at The Valley by Jehovah's

Night sight: the floodlights reveal the massive crowd at the 1974 pop concert

Witness groups in the 1970s met with noticeably less opposition.

In 1973, Charlton finished 11th in the Third Division, just one place above halfway; the following year they were 14th. The prospects for a revival looked gloomy. Yet the appointment of Gillingham boss Andy Nelson as manager in the summer of 1974 had just such an effect. Simply by reorganising the team assembled by his sacked predecessor, Theo Foley, he won promotion at the first attempt. Attendances went through the roof for the vital games, nearly 25,000 paying to get in for the clincher against Preston North End in April and hundreds more being manhandled over the turnstiles by police anxious to relieve the dangerous congestion outside.

A vital part of Nelson's success in attracting the fans back was his team's swashbuckling attacking style, with many encounters being won by the odd goal in five or even seven, and an unusual proportion of floodlit evening matches, the brightness of the lights somehow adding lustre to the occasion.

The significance of his arrival for The Valley was twofold. Firstly, his stated aim was to build a First Division club and that necessarily entailed major ground improvements. Secondly, by winning promotion the club became subject to the provisions of the Safety of Sports Grounds Act 1975, and The Valley was designated in 1979, which meant it had to be licensed as safe by the local authority, initially the Greater London Council. This new legislation was the government's response to the fatalities at Ibrox in January 1971 when 66 people were crushed and suffocated due to a badly designed stairway. It was the first of four major disasters in the space of 20 years that would all have a significant impact on The Valley's future.

The act, which came into force in January 1980, required the strengthening of all

Battle for The Valley

The main stand in 1975, four years before the roof was replaced

terraces and railings, improved crush barriers, turnstiles and exits and that all seats be 12 inches apart. At least £300,000 needed to be spent on the ground just to keep it open. In the event, Charlton would make great strides to satisfy the law, much aided by the chairman's guarantee on a £250,000 loan and a large grant from the Football Grounds Improvements Trust, a body funded from the takings of the pools companies' Spot The Ball competition. But the completion of the work, particularly that due on the East Terrace, always looked beyond them.

Nonetheless, plans were drawn up to construct a new stand on the uncovered terrace behind the south goal. Originally intended to be complete in time for the start of the 1978/79 season, it was much delayed by the backlog in meeting orders of steel and was eventually finished during the close season of 1979. In the intervening period, the terrace had to be kept closed during matches, resulting in a disconcertingly unusual atmosphere.

Built at a cost of only £120,000, all raised by the now flourishing lottery that had grown out of CAFRO under the control of commercial manager Tom Enefer, this bright modern construction was some 212ft wide at the front, 152ft across at the rear and 84ft deep. The cantilever roof had a single central prop and thus provided a reasonably unobstructed view. In reality, it was little more than a covered frame erected on the existing bank, although the terracing was completely renewed. Indeed so cheap and sensible was the project that it rather begged the question of why it had not been undertaken ten or 15 years earlier. At least now another 8,000 fans would be able to watch the game sheltered from the elements.

Also in the summer of 1979, the distinctive, but now rather dated, multi-span roof

Battle for The Valley

of the main stand was removed and replaced with a similar construction to that on the south stand. Otherwise the existing building was retained, ending many years of internal debate as to whether the club would be better off demolishing the whole structure and starting again. Having established that the base was sound, the directors decided in favour of refurbishment rather than replacement. In the light of the serious fire at Bradford City's Valley Parade ground in 1985, they probably made the wrong decision, because the wooden floors continued to be a major hazard. However, the cantilever roof, this time without the central prop, did give a superb view of the pitch, making it all the more poignant that it was to see just six years of service.

Finally that summer, work commenced on the construction of an eight-foot high perimeter fence which eventually extended to all three fully-terraced sides of the ground. This innovation, partly inspired by a pitch invasion during a League Cup tie with Stoke City the previous season, was both deeply resented and largely unnecessary.

Prior to the full security fence going up, Charlton had compromised in 1976 by erecting a new continuous crush barrier inside the existing low perimeter fence and joined to it by a sheet of almost horizontal steel netting. This followed a spate of quite innocent final-whistle pitch invasions which led to the club raising the junior price of admission by 5p to 40p. The assumption seemed to be that this barrier would make it a more cumbersome process to reach the pitch and thus allow police the extra seconds required to repel invaders. It was erected only on the end terraces and the small bank adjacent to the main stand in the south-western corner of the pitch.

The fans were given even more cause for complaint when it was revealed that the new south stand, the first major development at the ground for 43 years, was to be reserved for the use of visiting supporters. This was a typical example of Charlton's ability to turn even the most obvious benefit against themselves, but there was also a certain logic to it. The more vocal home supporters had long congregated in the old Covered End and the visiting fans on the south terrace. Even so, the new Jimmy Seed Stand, as it was eventually named, was acoustically far superior and allowed small numbers of visiting fans to make a disproportionate amount of noise. For this reason, it would have made good sense to reverse the traditional arrangements.

Fortunately, segregation was rarely enforced strictly. Whereas Millwall's Den had been closed by the FA following serious crowd trouble on no less than five occasions by the late 1970s, hooliganism was comparatively rare at The Valley. When it did occur, it was almost invariably confined to visiting supporters, such as on Easter Monday 1977 when Chelsea fans lit bonfires beneath the Covered End, home players were coined and windows in surrounding streets smashed as a consequence of Charlton's 4-0 victory.

Like most others, the club always had a fringe of vocal youngsters but anyone with serious hooligan ambitions was almost certain to soon turn their attentions to poor old Millwall. On the rare occasions that Charlton supporters were involved in incidents it was usually with followers of Queens Park Rangers, Crystal Palace and, later, Wimbledon, all of whom were of similar lowly status in the unofficial league table of thuggery. When the bigger London clubs came to The Valley the people who had so much to say during games with lesser opposition were usually notable by their absence, or at least their low profile.

One reason why the lack of trouble must have owed more to the nature of the supporters than to efficient crowd control is that effective segregation was virtually impossible to accomplish anyway, due to The Valley's size and layout. Even so, the police did attempt to control the movement between the four sides of the ground when necessary. Steel fencing with access gates was built on either side of the Covered End and between the East Terrace and south stand in the 1979 close season.

The police's apparently arbitrary opening and closure of the gate providing access from the terrace to the new stand drew much criticism from fans, particularly in wet weather or when there were few away supporters. By the third League match of the season, Charlton were already holding meetings with the force to discuss complaints about the away restrictions. But it should be noted that unrestricted movement between the four sides was a modern phenomenon. As implied above, in the past there had been differential pricing and charges for transfers.

One of the more ludicrous fences

A tall, wire-mesh fence with a gate was also added between the main stand and the Harvey Gardens turnstiles, effectively making it possible to stop people crossing from one end to the other on this side too. Unfortunately, this barrier also restricted access to a major toilet block resulting in some chaos behind the Covered End, where only limited facilities were available, and several arrests for indecent exposure!

Lateral fencing, which became the fashion as a means of dividing large areas of terracing into more manageable portions, was almost impossible on the East Terrace due to its extraordinary height. Nonetheless various attempts were made to accommodate visitors there during the time the south terrace was closed, and after it became all-seated in 1981. This involved either temporary wooden stake fences or a barrier which consisted of a single strip of tape. Both these forms of enclosure were highly inefficient to police and, on the whole, rather a waste of time.

Typically, the radical changes to the ground in 1979 coincided with another season of struggle, culminating in relegation. After three reasonably successful campaigns, Nelson's team had become dangerously erratic and in both 1977/78 and 1978/79 Charlton were lucky not to succumb. In 1979/80 they remained in a lowly position throughout, winning just six games all season. Shortly before their fate became mathematically certain, the manager was sacked to make way for his chief coach, Mike Bailey. But unfortunately, although relegation provided a timely release from the now rather eccentric stewardship of Mr Nelson, it did not exempt the club from the increasingly urgent requirements of the Safety of Sports Grounds Act and the new season would provide the first intimations of the crisis to come. Not that this was in any way foreshadowed by the 1980/81 handbook, in which Jenner announced bold plans for the construction of two wings on the main stand which would have extended it the full length of the pitch. The first of these would have been built on the south side and incorporated new dressing rooms, a medical room, a laundry and a players' lounge. This would have released space for an executive club and restaurant on the first floor of the existing stand and enabled the administrative staff currently working in the temporary buildings to move in below.

The second stage of the new scheme was to level the unacceptably steep rear steps of the East Terrace into a wide walkway, provide limited car parking at the Bartram Gate and construct a north wing on the main stand. Finally, the Covered End would be replaced by a double-decker stand, with seating on the upper tier and a roof to match the existing stands. This element in particular, said to be in only embryonic phase at the time, always appeared to be pure fantasy.

It was perhaps more significant that Jenner also referred to a scheme to move the Valley Grove turnstiles up to the south stand and thus isolate visiting fans in a narrow corridor. This would have been precisely the effect of Michael Gliksten's controversial efforts to reclaim two acres of land in 1985, which were cited as a reason for leaving. It would also have eliminated an enduring oddity of The Valley, namely that to gain access to the main stand it always remained necessary to go through two sets of turnstiles because it had no street entrance of its own.

Before the season was a few months old, all the optimism about the future was swept away. The local press reported that the GLC was on the brink of slashing the

Gladys Dutton, Jimmy Seed's daughter, opens the new south stand in August 1981. Former players, Matt Busby and (extreme left) Michael Gliksten look on

A modern-looking Valley at last, with Valiant House visible in the background

ground's capacity to just 13,000. There was work needed on exits, fire-proofing and crush barriers. But above all, time – and the safety authorities – had at last caught up with the East Terrace. Overall, the safety work necessary was put at £500,000, but Charlton declined to comment, insisting they were still discussing the matter with the council.

When they did emerge from their bunker, in January, it was to announce an extraordinary and unpopular plan to convert the ground into an all-seater stadium. Some 7,000 seats were to be installed behind the two goals, with 18,000 more to follow on the big side. When finished, the club estimated it would have 36,000 seats and the most modern stadium in the English League.

Work began almost immediately on the Covered End, to the utter disgust of most of its regulars. Many decamped to the low bank next to the main stand never to return. Some made a break of a more permanent kind, correctly foreseeing that the changes would destroy the ground's little remaining atmosphere. At least the terracing was relaid to a more suitable raking for seats, although in the case of the south stand this was the second time the job had been done in the space of two years.

As for the scheme to put "all-weather" seats on the East Terrace, the fans were entitled to wonder whether the directors had taken leave of their senses. Even if they were to be forced to sit down, people were hardly going to take kindly to seats which would inevitably on occasion be soaking wet. Moreover the money to accomplish this mammoth enterprise simply didn't exist, which prompts a vague suspicion that it may have been no more than a means of buying time from the GLC. In the interim, Charlton were finally allowed a temporary capacity of 20,000, with a 10,000 limit on the East Terrace, on the promise that the work would be carried out. However, even this decision was against the advice of the council officers, who were overruled by the politicians.

Notwithstanding the hindsight that the Taylor Report into the 1989 Hillsborough disaster would supply, the decision to install seats behind the goals was a major mistake. Had the lottery money been spent instead on renewing a limited amount of terracing, beginning with that in the Covered End, the claim made in 1985 that the ground's capacity without the East Terrace was insufficient to continue would have been even more obviously invalid.

The last significant changes made to The Valley were the installation of a police observation box on the south-west floodlight pylon in the summer of 1981 and the construction of eight executive boxes at the back of the main stand, opened at the start of the 1982/83 season. Plans to stage the northern game of rugby league were also mooted, following its apparently successful establishment at Fulham.

However, that June Gliksten suddenly sold the club to a mysterious Wilmington businessman, Mark Hulyer, but retained ownership of the ground through his company, Adelong. Although the new chairman promised to get at least some of the north stand seats removed, it was too late. Little as we suspected it then, time was running out on The Valley and the vultures were hovering overhead.

Chapter Four

"Some compensation is that facilities at Selhurst Park are better than those at The Valley and the playing field is in first-class condition too."
John Fryer – Message To Our Supporters (September 7th, 1985)

Mark Hulyer was 28 years old when he took over Charlton Athletic in June 1982. Like his predecessor, he was the youngest chairman in the Football League at the time of his appointment. But in every other respect he was utterly different.

A member of Charlton's executive club, Hulyer had arrived on the scene the previous year with a high-profile sponsorship scheme. Indeed, most matches in the 1981/82 season were sponsored by Marman, "an international company in the field of chemicals and commodity foodstuffs". Before long the company's logo appeared on the fascia of the main stand, welcoming supporters to the ground.

It was not until the tenth game of that campaign, all sponsored by this hitherto mysterious organisation, that supporters learned of the reason behind it all. Hulyer, "chairman and founder of the Marman group of companies", revealed himself as a lifelong fan who wanted "to contribute towards getting the club back into the First Division". In fact, he had made an unannounced appearance in the programme for the previous match, pictured among a group of executive supporters.

A less generous account of his arrival is given by team manager Alan Mullery, who recalls Hulyer breezing into the ground with a cheque for £50,000 to pay for five years' stand advertising, and thereafter becoming a regular companion of the players. Mullery, appointed to replace the departed Mike Bailey, resigned after just one mediocre season in charge – on the day that it became clear Gliksten was handing over the chair.

Hulyer's reign was to be short, but it would have devastating consequences for the club. It started with many fine words about a new era and ambitious plans for strengthening the playing staff. The cynics ridiculed an abortive attempt to sign former England captain Kevin Keegan, but were silenced when he landed ex-European Footballer of the Year Allan Simonsen instead.

Unfortunately, the new chairman had neither the money to finance his ambitions, nor the judgement to restrict his promises to those he could keep. When the crowds failed to respond sufficiently to his gamble with Simonsen because the team continued to struggle, he fell into increasing difficulties, eventually incurring a punitive penalty clause for failing to keep up payments due to Gliksten. His problems were complex, but at their root, inevitably, was the deal he had agreed on the ground.

The shares in the football club had changed hands for a token £1,000. But first Gliksten had separately acquired its principal asset, The Valley, through his company Adelong Limited for £414,000. Hulyer then signed a 30-year lease on the site and the recently developed training facilities at Valley Leisure in New Eltham for a rent of £110,000 per annum. An additional £300,000 was loaned to the club by Gliksten to cover half the existing overdraft, which the former chairman had guaranteed, and the remainder of which he now paid off. The outstanding amounts, plus the interest on the loan, were to be repaid over four years in quarterly instalments at a fixed rate of interest.

Charlton's new team: Bill Jenner, Peter Crystal, Richard Collins, Mark Hulyer, Malcolm Stanley and Michael Gliksten. All but two would soon be gone

Initially, the new landlord remained on the board, one of only three of the existing seven directors to survive the upheaval. Another was the diminutive Richard Collins, a 40-year-old chartered surveyor who had once lived in Lansdowne Lane behind the ground. He had joined the board the previous summer and now became managing director. The final man to provide continuity was the faithful fundraiser, Bill Jenner.

Apart from Hulyer, numbers were swollen by Peter Crystal, a solicitor, and Malcolm Stanley, chairman of the FADS chain of DIY stores which had become the club's first shirt sponsors the previous year. Builder Alan Ward also joined at the start of the season.

But the new board soon disintegrated. Jenner went in November, unable to answer Hulyer's appeal for funds, and Gliksten followed a month later, ending half a century of family representation. Stanley also quit at the same time, taking his sponsorship deal with him, while Ward and Crystal lasted until March. Now the increasingly beleaguered Hulyer found himself with only two colleagues, Collins and Chief Francis Arthur Nzeribe, the Nigerian chairman of arms supply company Fanz International, who had replaced Jenner.

The reason for the spate of departures soon became clear. There was deep internal unhappiness over the way the club was being run. The Simonsen transfer had been a financial disaster, because although the player proved a success, scoring nine times in his 17 games, and the home matches saw an increase in attendances of some 40 per cent, it wasn't nearly enough to meet the combined bill for his wages and the transfer fee. The deal had also been the subject of a drawn-out wrangle with his previous club Barcelona, who wanted binding guarantees of Charlton's ability to pay the reported £324,000 fee. The row had reduced Hulyer's credibility and by the time Simonsen left in March for his former club Vejle in a damage limitation exercise, the storm clouds were gathering. A promising young central defender, Paul Elliott, had to be sold to Luton Town at a knock-down price in order to meet the wage bill.

Then Gliksten struck, gaining a summary judgement in the High Court for repayment of his loan, plus the interest for the full period of four years, a total figure of £420,000. The only money he had ever received was that for the shares and the first quarterly instalment. But Hulyer argued that since the deal had not been signed until November and it was now March, only one instalment of £54,000 had been missed. And that, he claimed, had been the consequence of Stanley withdrawing his sponsorship. He also professed puzzlement at Gliksten's pursuit of him through the courts, although he must have known of the penalty he might face for falling behind.

In the ensuing confusion, two sympathetic businessmen, neither of them Charlton supporters, separately tried to save the situation by acquiring The Valley on Hulyer's behalf in order to act as more benevolent landlords. Millionaire Ron Billings was the 80-year-old founder and chairman of an extraordinary Southern League club, Corinthians, based near Fawkham in Kent, which sought to play the game according to civilised values. He despised the professional game, but was nonetheless willing to help Charlton and he offered Gliksten £750,000 for his remaining assets. However, talks broke down because he was unwilling to meet the loan debt.

Gliksten now obtained a bankruptcy order against Hulyer, which he refrained from serving while he saw how matters developed. Billings resurfaced with an offer of £700,000 plus a further £300,000 in respect of the loan. Again, Gliksten said no, apparently because he wanted the full interest of £120,000 which would have accrued over four years as specified in the original contract. Not surprisingly, Billings refused and this time he withdrew from the scene permanently.

Frustrated at Charlton's failure to pay the £35,000 balance of the £180,000 fee for winger Carl Harris, who had been the first of new manager Ken Craggs' signings the previous summer, Leeds United made history by becoming the first club ever to seek a winding-up order against a fellow League member. Gliksten joined the action and so too did the Inland Revenue, chasing arrears of £145,000. The case was adjourned until July 25th, and then October 7th to give Charlton time to find the money. On that date the Revenue reached a settlement, only to be replaced as chief creditor by Gliksten, now claiming to be owed some £573,000.

By the following month, no less than 14 other creditors had emerged. Another white knight, in the shape of textile businessman Leslie Wise, a 57-year-old Arsenal supporter, arrived on the scene with a new offer of £850,000 for The Valley plus the New Eltham training ground Valley Leisure, which had never been in the ownership of the football club. But his bid was less than the second amount offered by Billings, and Gliksten was now said to want £1.25m, comprising £250,000 for the training ground, £420,000 for The Valley and £580,000 in respect of the original loan and unpaid rent plus interest.

Battle for The Valley

Come fly with me: director Malcolm Stanley takes Allan Simonsen to Carlisle

Hulyer briefly stood down as chairman in October 1983, hoping to revive potential investors' confidence and Collins succeeded him, but two months later he was back in the chair. Frustrated at the failure of all his efforts to secure a successful takeover, his successor quit the board, saying only that people would have to draw their own conclusions as to who was to blame for him drawing a blank.

Now there were only two directors, of whom one was the obscure Chief Nzeribe. And within weeks he too had quit. But by then Hulyer had hit upon a wheeze for obstructing the relentless progress through the courts. In November, he started legal action of his own against Gliksten for alleged offences under section 42 of the

Companies Act 1981, relating to the sale of The Valley. It would earn the club a four-month breathing space.

And now at last the fans, thus far no more than extras in this extraordinary soap opera, began to respond. A "Save Charlton Action Committee" was formed, chaired by Clive Franklin, a Bexleyheath company director, and including prominent behind-the-scenes figures like Colin Cameron, the club historian; his close friend, Alan Honey; *Kentish Times* sports editor Tony Flood; and supporters' club chairman Jack Linsdell.

Its major contribution was to raise part of a transfer fee outstanding to Rotherham United for striker Ronnie Moore. Charlton had been called before a League inquiry to explain themselves over the matter and there were fears that points would be deducted. It would have been a shattering blow to the efforts of yet another new manager, Lennie Lawrence, who had somehow hoisted the troubled club to the fringe of the Second Division promotion race. Fans were issued with certificates in exchange for their donations, collected in buckets by volunteers, and a cheque for £8,000 was presented direct to the Yorkshire club.

There was also talk of setting up a company with the aim of selling £10 shares in order to raise up to £100,000 and buy an equity interest in the football club. But quite clearly the supporters' club, whose tiny membership of 250 more than trebled during the crisis, simply lacked the financial muscle to make a serious impact.

Charlton's still considerable potential was underlined on the last Saturday in January when an unexpectedly large crowd turned out for the fourth-round FA Cup tie against First Division, but hardly glamorous, opposition in the shape of Watford. The attendance was given as 22,392, of which at most 7,000 came to support the Hertfordshire club. Strictly speaking, in fact, the gate was narrowly above The Valley's official safety limit, something which was conveniently overlooked. The home side lost 2-0, although some consolation was the club's share of The Valley's record receipts, which totalled £70,423.

Just two days later, however, they were back in court, where the Inland Revenue was now demanding £108,554, of which it would take at least £70,000 to buy a stay of execution. Hulyer turned to Greenwich Council for short-term help, but wisely the authority refused. For any such insignificant sum injected into the now terminally insolvent company would have been money wasted. Charlton were given a fortnight's reprieve and when the court reassembled on February 13th it was told that the mysterious Nzeribe was trying to mount a rescue operation through his Flintgrange company, which was sufficient to earn a further two-week respite.

But Hulyer rejected this deal, the details of which were never made clear, and when on February 27th he offered the Revenue a solution of his own, involving three payments of £30,000 paid through Marman's Swiss bank account and dependent upon the progress of a quantity of rubber from Bangkok, Judge Mervyn Davies concluded that he had heard enough. He reluctantly gave instructions for Charlton Athletic to be formally wound up.

For 24 desperate hours, it seemed the club would die, the most substantial English League outfit ever to go to the wall, leaving The Valley, however briefly, a decaying monument to the mismanagement of a generation. But behind the scenes Collins had been hard at work. From an apparent multiplicity of potential consortia, including one involving Anton Johnson, a former Valley season-ticket holder whose activities at Rotherham and Southend United had led to a League investigation, he had found the club's saviours. Together with the hitherto unknown Michael Norris, an Eltham chartered surveyor and property developer, Collins had interested John Fryer, managing director of the giant Sunley building conglomerate, in acquiring the ground from Gliksten. Their plans had been laid months earlier, but only now that Hulyer and the hopelessly debt-ridden old company were leaving the scene could they afford to come forward. And it meant that they had to act desperately quickly, because the Football League was demanding to know whether the club could fulfil its fixtures.

Even now Hulyer wanted to fight on. It wasn't until two days later that he finally gave up hope of appealing against the winding-up order. In the meantime, the gates of The Valley were locked by the official receiver and the players and staff exiled to the neighbouring Valley Club to wait, with the fans, for news of Charlton's fate. Hard-won new signing Moore was even thrown out of the Clarendon Hotel at Blackheath because of fears that the bill would not be paid.

Initially it seemed that the consortium of Collins, Norris, Fryer and former director Stanley would take control of a new company on March 1st. But the official receiver wanted more time. That in itself might have spelled the end of Charlton, but as the following day wore on the League gave them a stay of execution by agreeing to postpone the weekend fixture at Blackburn Rovers. The news came as a relief to the anxious players, who were in no mood to face the long journey north. But it was

Time's up: Lennie Lawrence waits anxiously at The Valley for news of a reprieve

Heroes and villains: directors John Fryer, Michael Norris and Richard Collins celebrating the club's survival before the Grimsby game on March 10th, 1984

received with disappointment at Ewood Park, where there was some concern as to whether they would be able to cancel the matchday order of pies. Charlton, meanwhile, were back in court on the Monday, then Tuesday, and finally Thursday, with the League's deadline now just hours away.

Fryer, as he soon had good reason to stress, was a Charlton fan, who claimed to have seen his first match at The Valley at Christmas 1927. But as the saga dragged on and on, and the probable cost to his company rose, it is unlikely that he would have proceeded had it not been for the encouragement of his partner John Sunley, whose main sporting interest was horse-racing rather than football. In the closing stages of the negotiations, it was Sunley who persuaded Fryer to indulge himself by saving the club.

The original plan had been for the building company to purchase the freehold of The Valley for a mammoth £1,075,000 and put just £50,000 into the Charlton company itself. But the League's demand for financial guarantees had ruled out the idea of Sunley's becoming simply benevolent landlords, recouping their investment by the development of a sports complex. All creditors had to get 60 per cent of the money due to them, with other clubs receiving 70 per cent and the Inland Revenue paid in full.

These were the same terms which had been imposed on the other member clubs that had come back from the dead. But they were an awesome burden on the hopeful consortium, given the total debt of over £1.5m, and they led to the departure of Malcolm Stanley, who angrily accused the League of wanting Charlton to die. The

Debutant Robert Lee scores the second Charlton goal in the 3-3 draw against Grimsby before a relieved crowd of 7,626

other members of the consortium promptly dissociated themselves from his remarks for fear of losing Lytham St Annes' goodwill in the vital days that followed. But the truth was that they simply did not have the money. It had to come from Sunley's. The firm consequently became the owner of the football club, with Fryer, not Norris as had been intended, chairman.

A valuable intervention now came from Greenwich Council, which had turned a deaf ear to all Hulyer's pleas and even rejected a plan for a market at The Valley which might have helped him. It agreed to inject £250,000 into the new company over five years in return for benefits to the community and a seat on the board.

Still more fundamental to the rescue operation was an agreement between the warring parties of Gliksten and Hulyer to waive the debts incurred by the old company and drop the legal actions against each other. The former had been woken at 5am in Australia to be told the news of the winding-up and hurried back to England. Hulyer had made various claims about the money Marman had put in, but a figure of around £300,000 was put before the court. Only at the last possible moment, as the hearing began at 3pm on Thursday, March 8th, was this vital agreement reached.

When the parties arrived in court to seek the judge's approval, they had to stand in the aisles because the public gallery was choked with anxious fans. It was just before 3.30 when the news finally came that Charlton were safe. And even then there was a desperate dash to the London offices of the League to satisfy them that the new company, Charlton Athletic (1984) Limited, could meet the obligations that had been set down for them before they would be accepted to run the club.

Council leader John Austin-Walker explains Greenwich's role in the rescue

Charlton had literally been within minutes of becoming the Accrington Stanley of their generation. There was, above all else, monumental and justifiable relief. The new directors emerged to tumultuous and deserved acclaim at the following Saturday's home game with Grimsby Town. But ownership of the ground and club remained divided. For Gliksten had rejected Sunley's offer for The Valley. Instead, the consortium had secured a ten-year lease at a reduced rent of £70,000 per annum with a view to an eventual purchase. That division was to be the crucial factor in all that followed. Yet it is worth noting that even if the original deal had gone through, and Sunley's bought the ground but not the club, the separation of ownership would still have existed. And who is to say what path history might have taken then?

For just over a year, all seemed to be well. Three new directors were added to the board, two of them with a usefully intimate knowledge of the game. Derek Ufton was a former club captain and the first ex-player to return as a director and with him came Cllr Bill Strong, a stalwart supporter and member of Greenwich Council since 1953. The third was Jimmy Hill, the controversial Coventry City manager and chairman turned television pundit, who when at the Professional Footballers' Association had negotiated the abolition of the maximum wage. Almost immediately, he became acting chairman for six months while the ailing Fryer recuperated from surgery. And it was he who would lay the way for an extraordinary revival of fortunes on the field.

Charlton had an uninspiring time in 1984/85, the highlight being another "illegal" attendance, claimed to be 21,409, for a much-postponed third-round FA Cup replay with Tottenham Hotspur after the First Division leaders had been held to a momentous draw at White Hart Lane. The season also saw the beginning of a highly successful tie-up with new sponsors, the Woolwich Building Society, that was to become one of the longest-running partnerships of its kind in the League. And American football made a hesitant debut at The Valley on Easter Sunday, April l4th, when the fledgling Greenwich Rams went down to the highly-rated Milton Keynes Bucks 42-0. Wet weather nearly caused a postponement and kept the crowd down to 1,346, despite the doubtful bonus of an Easter bonnet competition.

But it was the events at the end of the campaign which sparked the most interest. Having settled the outstanding debts, and with attendances plummeting as low as 3,500, the new owners granted manager Lawrence a modest budget of £300,000 to strengthen the team. He bought wisely and, of seven new faces, six would slot instantly into an obviously much-improved side. That summer the fans began to talk cautiously of promotion. But now around them a fresh storm was breaking. First, the Greater London Council obtained a closure order on the giant East Terrace. Then, a fortnight into the season, the club let it become known that Gliksten was reclaiming a part of the ground.

The seeds of the latter disaster had been sown at the time of the winding-up order. For it was now disclosed that the new lease did not include two acres of land behind the west stand, for reasons which became the subject of much dispute. Charlton appeared to claim that the area had been excluded in 1984 at the former chairman's demand and that he would not have reached a settlement that would satisfy the court unless they remained at his disposal.

Significantly, however, the notoriously reticent Gliksten vigorously rebutted this allegation in a statement issued just before the final game at The Valley. According to him, the exclusion had been at the specific suggestion of Collins, who proposed that he could use this redundant part of the ground to recoup the losses he had incurred in his dealings with Hulyer. "At the meeting where the deal was struck, it was the club who produced a drawing showing the boundaries of the land they required and the two acres were outside it," he insisted. "It is totally untrue that I refused to agree a lease unless this land was left."

Clearly, Gliksten was outraged and it seems certain he was telling the truth. Later, when London Weekend Television claimed in an edition of their *London Programme* that he had forced the club out of The Valley, he successfully sued them for undisclosed damages, which he donated to charity. The magazine *Football Monthly* was also obliged to apologise in similar circumstances.

What was never disputed is that the two acres were not included in the lease and that in August 1985 Gliksten had duly demanded them back. The club professed to be baffled, although they agreed, through solicitors, to vacate the land after a summons was issued against them for a court hearing to be held on August 27th. Fryer told the *Kentish Times* of September 5th: "I understand that Mr Gliksten hoped to sell the two acres for building and has now got a buyer for it."

Remarkably, however, that was the last anyone ever heard of the former chairman's ambitions to develop the area. It was to remain derelict and overgrown for several years to come and in that time no planning application was received by Greenwich Council in respect of it. So Gliksten's intentions remain a mystery, if one illuminated by the plans his friend and fellow director Jenner had outlined in the 1980 handbook. For the effect of the land's exclusion from the ground would have been precisely that described there, namely to confine visiting supporters to a narrow corridor leading from Valley Grove to the south stand.

Fryer would subsequently claim that the loss of the land, and the 23 turnstiles which gave access onto it from the road, made effective segregation impossible and would have rendered the ground unacceptable to the police. But it simply wasn't true. The two acres reclaimed still allowed more than adequate access to the south stand. Indeed, it was strongly arguable that the new arrangements would actually have improved segregation, since visiting fans could for the first time have been effectively contained in that part of the ground. True, the turnstiles would probably have had to be resited – and some would have been lost – but Charlton hardly needed 23 there anyway.

Car parking was a thornier question, but since there were only 110 spaces in the ground anyway, it is hard to believe that some alternative arrangement could not have been made to replace them elsewhere if only the will to do so had existed.

Details of Gliksten's actions emerged publicly only days, four in fact, before the announcement of the move to Selhurst Park itself. They were leaked, apparently on an unattributable basis, to the *South London Press*, and two days later the story also appeared in the *Kentish Times*, with comment by Fryer. But Charlton had surely known all along that he would reclaim the land, and that he wanted to do so in the immediate future since at least mid-August. Yet only now, when a scapegoat was required for a deal that was already done, did they choose to reveal it. There seems no doubt that, in this respect at least, Gliksten was cruelly used.

But if the issue of the two acres was a smokescreen, what of developments on the other side of The Valley? Here the GLC had by now successfully applied for a closure order on the East Terrace, thus reducing what had until five years earlier been the ground with the largest capacity in the League to one of the smallest, with a limit of

Unfit for human habitation: the empty East Terrace at the Liverpool friendly

just 10,500. Here, too, there was allegation and counter-allegation.

What is not in question is that the terrace was in a parlous state and had been for many years. Even to the naked eye, its undulations were apparent and some of the rear steps were so steep they posed an obvious safety hazard. The concrete was flaking badly in places and the exits could not easily have coped with its theoretical capacity. But there was the rub. The Valley was now rarely patronised by anything above 10,000 people as a whole and the terrace was already under a restriction of that number anyway. The average attendance in season 1984/85 had been a miserly 5,039, of which at most half would have congregated on that vast slope. And to crowds of that size there was little danger of any kind, save perhaps of catching pneumonia from exposure to the elements.

The GLC, however, did not see it that way, particularly in the light of the disaster at Heysel Stadium, Brussels, in May that year when a charge by Liverpool supporters across similarly antiquated terracing had led to the collapse of a poorly maintained wall and the death of 38 fans. That, and the fire which gutted the main stand at Bradford City's Valley Parade ground on the last day of the 1984/85 season, killing 56, had justifiably led to a new safety-consciousness among local authorities. The GLC said they had found all the other London clubs cooperative, but Charlton had proved an exception.

Like so much else, however, the circumstances of the closure order are obscured by dispute. Just days after the last game at The Valley, David Chambers, head of the GLC's ground-safety team which first visited the site on July 3rd, told the *Mercury*'s Peter Cordwell: "We would have bent over backwards to keep football at The Valley but they refused to meet and discuss the problem. I can only conclude they already knew of the possibility of moving to Crystal Palace."

According to Chambers, he wrote to Collins on July 15th asking for a discussion at the ground, but heard nothing until ten days later, when the Charlton director phoned to say that the club was not prepared to do anything about the state of the East Terrace. Then, on August 2nd, Collins phoned again to say that they would be using it for a pre-season friendly against Liverpool. It was this that prompted the GLC to seek a court order from Greenwich Magistrates on August 6th, the day before the match, closing it permanently.

Collins retorted that the GLC was running scared because it didn't like being held responsible for the move and claimed part of the problem was a lack of communication within the council, with Mike Allsop of the architects' department writing to the club on July 1st, just two days before Chambers' original inspection, stating that they had a year to resolve the problem. In his version of the July 15th phone call, he offered Chambers a compromise, to be outlined in detail in a comprehensive report. But according to the GLC official, that document only arrived on the morning of the hearing and reached him as it was about to start.

In court, Charlton asked for a new temporary limit of 3,000 people to be set, pointing out that the terrace could hold 26,500 and that the GLC had itself accepted a limit of 10,000 only four-and-a-half years previously. But the GLC's Jan Korff, who had confirmed the findings of the council's safety team after making his own site visit on July 10th, refused to commit himself to a figure of even 1,000.

Director Jimmy Hill and Labour leader Neil Kinnock share a joke at one of the last Valley matches, against Middlesbrough at the beginning of the 1985/86 season

Counsel for the GLC, Miss Patricia Scotland, argued that the 1981 agreement didn't mean that the council had been satisfied with the state of the terrace even then. "Repairs were attempts to cover up defects and were not of a remedial nature," she said. "Nine out of ten crush barriers tested in a random sample were not up to standard."

Despite an unexplained plea by Collins for the GLC to "wait six or eight weeks", magistrate Pamela Long found for the council under section ten of the Safety of Sports Grounds Act. It meant the closure of the East Terrace, by law, until such time as repairs were effected.

In the end just 7,902 turned up for the glamorous friendly with Liverpool; a respectable enough gate for a meaningless match, but hardly a safety hazard. In fact, had it not been for the Heysel Stadium tragedy, it's unlikely that Charlton would have been playing Liverpool at all, so it was doubly ironic that the fixture should aggravate the dispute. The Merseyside club was unable to play any continental friendlies because of the European ban imposed after the disaster. And so, unusually for them, they embarked on a series of domestic warm-up matches. According to new manager Kenny Dalglish, they had approached the Addicks because of the reputation of the Valley pitch.

So now it seemed that Charlton were in trouble on two fronts and they were faced with expensive work to make good a ground owned by an apparently uncooperative landlord. But just how expensive is another moot point. Once the decision had been made to move to Selhurst, it was always in Charlton's interest to exaggerate the cost of repairing The Valley, which had initially been put at £250,000. That figure had trebled by the time of the announcement and it went on rising, reaching a peak at the end of September when secretary Graham Hortop told *The Observer* that the work plus the purchase of the ground might reach the incredible total of £5m.

What was certainly true was that Fryer was not prepared to spend any money on The Valley while it remained in Gliksten's ownership, if indeed he was prepared to spend it under any circumstances. And there is no doubt that his always lukewarm enthusiasm for getting involved with Charlton was by now fading fast. Gliksten, meanwhile, was not prepared to sell the freehold to anyone who he thought had ambitions to redevelop the site for profit and it hardly took a suspicious mind to put Fryer into that category.

It was into this web of confusion and distrust that the Crystal Palace chairman Ron Noades now entered. He had long been an enthusiast for groundsharing and had already seen tentative plans to move Wimbledon, of whom he had previously been chairman, and Chelsea into Selhurst Park thwarted. By contrast Charlton must have appeared ripe for the plucking. According to Noades, the first approach came from Fryer, but even if it did it was in the full knowledge of the Palace chairman's enthusiasm for such a venture. From the Eagles' point of view, the idea seemed to have few drawbacks. Their fans need hardly be aware of Charlton's presence, yet costs for the upkeep of the stadium would be halved.

Not that Noades put it like that, of course. He was one of a new breed of high-profile chairmen, in tune with the Thatcherite mood of the times. Ruthless at exploiting commercial opportunities, he was personally highly ambitious and frequently made himself very unpopular with the fans on the terraces. He would eventually lead Palace into what appeared a new golden age, including their first Wembley appearance, but not without making many enemies, among them a few thousand Charlton supporters.

His successes cannot be denied, but nor should his failures be forgotten. Also in 1985, jealous of the revenue pools companies derived from the use of the football fixtures, he helped set up a new pool run by the clubs themselves. Called Top Score, it proved a disastrous flop. Ironically, his new partners Charlton were one of the few clubs that refused to get involved in it. He was also heavily implicated in the establishment that year of a third major cup competition, originally titled the Full Members' Cup, which staggered along for seven seasons despite being held in obvious contempt by the football public.

For Noades, the groundsharing scheme was a giant leap forward for the game, with Charlton as pioneers in a new dawn of economic realism. "I believe that we will see groundsharing by six more teams – even in the next year. It will always work," he claimed at the time. "I know how supporters feel. This move will upset many of them. But I believe they will eventually see the light."

Five years later there were indeed three more cases of groundsharing, but all were partnerships forged in desperation, involving smaller League clubs making a temporary home at non-League grounds. And in every case the tenant club was making attempts to build a new stadium of its own. Noades' prophecy was to prove utterly false and as for Charlton fans seeing the light, he could hardly have been more wrong.

At the press conference announcing the move, Fryer claimed that Charlton had also had discussions about sharing with West Ham United, who had turned them down, and Arsenal, who were thinking it over. However, it was neighbours Millwall

Battle for The Valley

Two of The Valley's less celebrated features, pictured in September 1985. Above: the ladies' toilet behind the west stand. Patrons reported that it was rather less than a convenience.
Below: the supporters' club's matchday premises

who were the most obvious partners in terms of geography. According to Fryer, the New Cross club was not interested. But the Lions have always denied that they were ever approached and there seems no obvious reason why they should lie about it. Indeed, the Cold Blow Lane outfit's then chairman Alan Thorne had gone on record during the winding-up crisis 18 months earlier as saying that they would be happy to provide Charlton with a home at The Den if it ever became necessary.

It would certainly have been a more popular choice. And had Charlton moved to Millwall, they would probably have retained many of the fans they lost. For although there were a great number who refused to accept that Charlton could play anywhere else and still retain their identity, there were many thousands more who were deterred from supporting what they continued to regard as their local club by the horrendous transport complications of reaching London SE25. Selhurst was closer to the minority of fans on the north-west Kent fringe of the Charlton catchment area, closer even than The Valley, but it was an hour or more's drive through Saturday shopping traffic from the Bexley, Greenwich and north Kent heartland of the club's support and the journey took still longer by bus. Rail passengers had to travel into central London, to London Bridge, and then back out again to Norwood Junction or Selhurst.

No such logistical difficulties existed in relation to The Den, which was served by the same railway lines and bus routes as The Valley, and was a relatively short trip by road. Less tangibly, but equally importantly, it was also a part of the same working-class South East London environment, even if a substantially less prosperous one. Selhurst, on the other hand, seemed to many to be surrounded by a rootless suburbia, its alien nature symbolised by the fact that for months many people could not find their way there without the aid of a map.

But the Charlton chairman seemed to be under the delusion that the fans would follow the club round the South Circular Road, or else if they did not that the team's success would attract new followers to replace them. "Selhurst has a capacity of 38,000. We will need that if we are to get into the First Division next year," said Fryer. Not only did the owners believe that they required a stadium capable of housing big crowds, but one with further money-spinning commercial facilities such as restaurants and executive boxes, and here John Sunley may have been a powerful influence. A man with little exposure to the traditions of the game, he appears to have discounted the identity of the club against the belief that better facilities would act as a magnet to the public.

In this respect there could hardly have been a less suitable venue than The Den. And it was tainted, too, by the hooligan reputation of the Millwall fans and the tight network of forbidding, crumbling streets which hemmed it in. Selhurst Park, on the other hand, had modern facilities in abundance for the entertainment of businessmen, the so-called "executive" supporters whom many clubs had by now convinced themselves represented the salvation of the game. Its bright, modern appearance was in sharp contrast to the threatening ambience of The Den. Yet with a supermarket dominating one end, it was, in the words of an improbable but welcome *Guardian* leader, "an efficiently soulless ground, a concrete monument of the *Clockwork Orange* era".

Fortuitously, or otherwise, Charlton met Palace three times in the opening weeks of the 1985/86 season, beginning with the latter's visit to The Valley for a Milk Cup

The surprisingly sumptuous Valley boardroom, with its wood panelling

first-round, first-leg match on August 20th. From there, it isn't hard to piece together events. Charlton went to Selhurst for the return on September 3rd, the day of the story in the *South London Press* about the loss of the two acres behind the stand. When Palace returned to The Valley four days later for the third engagement, the wedding was announced.

According to contemporary sources, the whole thing had been arranged in that week, but there is evidence to the contrary. For a start, it is known that two directors, Hill and Ufton, were earlier summoned by Fryer to a meeting in central London and told that he had agreed the deal with Noades. Both were aghast and endeavoured to talk him out of it, with apparent success. Indeed, Ufton was on holiday on September 7th and was startled to learn the news that it was going ahead from the radio. Hill, on the other hand, was party to talks with Greenwich Council leader John Austin-Walker and Fryer some ten days earlier, in which they told the councillor they were "having discussions with other clubs regarding possible groundsharing". So either he had had a dramatic change of mind, or else some considerable time had elapsed from the previous conversation.

Neither Hill nor Ufton emerged with much credit from the affair, with both defending the move publicly and Ufton, in particular, taking the part of propagandist with an emotional piece in the programme for the last match which made the improbable claim that the ghosts of heroes past, including the hugely revered Sam Bartram, would be waiting to greet fans at Selhurst Park. But it was Collins who

Mark Stuart leads a first-half attack during the final game, against Stoke City

appeared to take on the role of spokesman, even emerging to explain the situation to those fans who waited behind after the game on the day of the announcement.

Bill Strong, Greenwich's nominated director, only learned the news at a board meeting two-and-a-half hours before the Palace match kicked off. He said at the time: "I would have thought that any proposals to move would have been put to a board meeting to be discussed and voted upon. Instead the directors were called to a meeting and told by chairman John Fryer that Charlton were moving. I think it was wrong to go about it that way. For all I know the plan may have been hatched months before. Some of the other members of the board knew in advance. I am not suggesting that there have been meetings behind my back but there must have been discussions."

The one director who never said a word publicly for the whole period of the move was Norris and it seems likely that he, like Strong, was kept in the dark until the last moment. Norris was furious, perhaps about the failure to consult as much as the fact of the move, and his initial reaction was to walk out, but he was eventually persuaded that he could serve Charlton better by continuing as a member of the board. At least no one could later accuse him of the hypocrisy of having defended the decision. But had he, or any other director, declared openly for the opposition it would have gone much of the way to destroying the board's credibility. Instead, they presented a united front and would continue to do so for some time to come.

The reaction of the fans to the announcement was one of utter bewilderment. Suddenly, the heroes of 1984 had turned into even bigger villains than their

Kept in the dark: Cllr Bill Strong, Greenwich's man on the board

predecessors. There had long been a feeling of impending doom about the club and some had feared for the future of the crumbling Valley, but now the terrible reality of the situation left them numbed. There followed an awful crisis of leadership, which with hindsight is eloquent testimony to the run-down state of the club and the cynicism engendered by the years of neglect. Briefly, it seemed the supporters' club, chaired by veteran Jack Linsdell, would mount a protest. Journalist and supporter Colin Cameron, who had covered Charlton's home matches for the *Exchange Telegraph* news agency for nearly 30 years and was widely regarded as the greatest living authority on the club, drafted a statement to which Linsdell agreed to put his name. It was widely picked up by the national press and amounted to a condemnation of Gliksten and a demand for urgent talks with the board.

An immediate response came from an established Selhurst Park pressure group, the Palace Action Campaign, whose members Noades appeared to be under the delusion he had successfully banned from the ground. Their chairman, Chris Wright, called the groundsharing scheme "football piracy" and pledged to unite with Charlton supporters to defeat it. However, Wright was a maverick character who was distrusted by many Palace fans. He went on to fight a south-coast parliamentary seat unsuccessfully for Labour in the 1987 general election, but three years later became a target for the tabloid press over his alleged role in organising a march which led to an outbreak of hooliganism during the World Cup finals in Italy.

In his efforts to organise against Noades he faced an unexpected and insuperable handicap. For where were the Charlton supporters to join him? When a TV crew was sent to The Valley to cover the story, only Wright was featured as an opponent. Linsdell had now recanted his opposition. He told reporter Mick Dennis, then writing for *The Sun* but later to become a hate-figure for fans on the *Evening Standard*: "After meeting with club officials we realise that there is no alternative. Financially the move makes sense and we should be thankful to those in charge for keeping the club alive when it came close to folding a year ago."

In fact, it was only the massive goodwill that Sunley's had earned by saving Charlton in 1984 and more recently investing in players that was preventing the directors being publicly lynched. Fans recognised that they were still deeply in their debt and for that reason were reluctant to believe that they could be really be the party responsible for this nightmare scenario. But it was to the utter discredit of the leadership of the supporters' club that they would continue to peddle Linsdell's new line for years to come, even after the case for Selhurst had been totally destroyed by events and the fans had turned overwhelmingly against the board.

It ought to be said at once in mitigation that those running CASC at the time were basically well-meaning people who were hopelessly ill-equipped to take on the role which circumstances now demanded of them. They had joined the committee to run coaches to away games and sell lottery tickets, not front a bitter political campaign. But there was a desperate need for some or other faction to take that lead. And it still seems incredible that no one did. It was hardly as if the supporters were incapable of organising themselves, as they would eventually prove. Rather it was a disastrous act of collective cowardice for which all the most vehement critics must take their share of the blame.

Instead, the major focus of opposition became the local press. Like most of the smaller London clubs, Charlton received scant attention from the capital's sole surviving evening newspaper, the *Standard*, and had always been heavily dependent

Dick Ayers' lone placard waves above the packed north-west terracing

on the plethora of weekly titles in the surrounding suburbs for publicity. Even their number had declined with the general contraction in the industry and by a cruel twist of fate the summer just past had seen the closure of the paper most closely associated with Charlton, the Woolwich-based *Kentish Independent*. The *KI* had been notoriously supportive of the club and it seems doubtful that it would have come out strongly against the move, except that its offices and switchboard would undoubtedly have been completely swamped by anxious supporters.

Without it, the fans were left with three other titles through which to vent their fury. Two, the *Kentish Times* and the *South London Press*, largely sat on the fence. even though *KT* sports editor Tony Flood was a fan and had actually been on the Save Charlton Action Committee a year earlier. "FURY AS CHARLTON MOVE TO PALACE" roared the back page, but his editorial comment was curiously inane and the paper seemed content to blame Gliksten.

The *South London Press*, although much more marginal to the area in which most supporters actually lived, was popular with Charlton fans because it came out twice a week and on different days to its rivals. However, it was famously reluctant to express an opinion about anything in its sports pages. Even so, its reports of the affair reflected an underlying scepticism, particularly in the case of Brian Stater's summary of the last match, which explained how one man, told by Hill that it would cost £3m to stay at The Valley, replied that in that case it would be better to let the club die. Wrote Stater: "While Charlton's directors point to their balance sheets, the fans treasure their traditions, and the man who rebuked Jimmy Hill got it just about right. The club may be moving to Selhurst, but for many, many honest supporters, Saturday's game was not only The Valley's last match, but Charlton's too."

In at the beginning: Peter Cordwell (right) monitors the view on the terraces

Last goal: Robert Lee makes history by beating Stoke keeper Peter Fox

Ironically, the paper that would rise to the challenge of events was that most distrusted by the fans, the *South East London and Kentish Mercury*, the capital's oldest local newspaper. The *Mercury* had genuine claims to be Charlton's main paper, and indeed had been for many years. When the club won the FA Cup in 1947, it was the *Mercury* that devoted most of its front page to the news, not the traditionally sober *KI*, in which sporting events then rated little coverage. But times and fashions had changed, as the Woolwich paper had lately discovered to its cost. Run down over many years by its Kentish parent company, the much-loved *KI* had proved unable to compete with the *Mercury*'s decision to counter a rapidly falling circulation by opting for free distribution.

Charlton fans were largely oblivious to all this, but what they had detected was the fact that the surviving paper's sports editor, Arsenal follower Maurice Woolf, had no great affection for their club. Millwall, and even Palace, who had lately been easily the most successful of the three teams covered but were on the periphery of the circulation area, appeared to receive more favourable attention. And for that reason, many Charlton supporters did not like the *Mercury*.

Yet now it was to prove their most valuable ally. And again fate had intervened. Just days before the season began, the elderly and diminutive Woolf surrendered the sports editor's chair to a very different kind of journalist, the 38-year-old Peter Cordwell, a local man who had variously been a Communist, a Lewisham Council press officer, a professional footballer in Finland and, 15 years earlier, a remarkably young sports editor of the *KI*. Cordwell was by no means a Charlton fan, indeed he professed to support West Ham where he had failed to make the grade as a youngster, but he instantly endeared himself to followers of both Millwall and Charlton by expelling Palace once and for all from the sports pages. And the issue of The Valley might have been made for him.

Loud, opinionated and irrepressible, he projected his forceful personality brilliantly into the coverage, battering at the wall of silence erected by the Charlton directors week after week in a way no football club had ever been attacked by its local paper. And, in doing so, he caught the mood of the ordinary fan. The *Mercury* now made little pretence of reporting the minutiae of the team's affairs, beyond the obligatory match reports, then written, incredibly enough, by a former Moscow correspondent of the *Morning Star*, Terry Bushell. Instead it launched wave after wave of attack on the club, and always with an inescapable tone of high moral indignation.

The onslaught began on September 12th. While its competitors were still discussing the details of the arrangement, Cordwell took the young sons of his friend Tim Sellick, a genuine Charlton fan, down to The Valley for a photocall and led the front page with the simple headline, "Why us?", capturing the essentially human issue that was being lost in the debate about who owned which piece of land and how many crush barriers might or might not be defective. The following week, two days before the last game, he focused on one old aged pensioner, a fan for 60 years but unable to contemplate the awful journey to Selhurst, as he prepared to watch his beloved Charlton for the very last time. It was vivid, crusading journalism, although even Cordwell could hardly have realised that he was embarking on the single biggest story in the newspaper's entire history.

All that still lay ahead, however, and for the moment, no one was moved. And so the awful day dawned and Charlton Athletic bade a tearful farewell to their home of 66 years, give or take the odd expedition to Catford.

That, as far as most of the media were concerned, was that and Charlton's ground was now Selhurst Park. But, on the contrary, the real drama was only just beginning.

Sign of the times: a fan makes off with a special souvenir after the last game

Chapter Five

"We shall never, never return there. It is not going to happen."
John Fryer – Croydon Advertiser (May 1986)

If the story of the move from The Valley is one with many villains, it has, at least, one undisputed hero. No one could ever have imagined that Robin Michael Lawrence would become manager of Charlton Athletic, but it was hugely to the club's good fortune that he did.

By 1985, Lawrence had already earned a secure place in the fans' affections by hauling the team clear of relegation in 1983, and then the following year mounting a remarkable promotion challenge which was vital in maintaining morale during the spiralling financial crisis. Had the players instead succumbed to the pressures created by the doubts about their futures and the club plummeted towards the Third Division, it might have been that much more difficult to persuade the prospective purchasers that there was anything left worth saving.

Yet the former Downham schoolteacher, universally known as "Lennie", had never played League football, enjoying only an undistinguished career as a centre-half with Sutton United, Carshalton Athletic and Croydon. He found his way into the senior game at Plymouth Argyle in 1977 when manager Mike Kelly, whom he had met on an FA coaching course, appointed him as his assistant, later serving as caretaker boss at Home Park and under Malcolm Allison before moving on to Lincoln City to work for Colin Murphy. It was in the summer of 1982 that he successfully answered the advertisement for a reserve-team manager at Charlton under new boss Ken Craggs. Lawrence thus had nominal charge of the reserve game that finally launched Allan Simonsen's career at The Valley that October. But within a fortnight Craggs was gone, made the scapegoat for a run of poor results which culminated in a 5-1 home defeat by eventually relegated Rotherham United.

There were impressive candidates to succeed him. Among the favourites was Leighton Phillips, the skipper, whose career was ending because of injury worries, while Ernst Netuka, the Dane responsible for Simonsen's arrival, was another strong contender. Gillingham manager Keith Peacock, a former Charlton skipper second only to Sam Bartram in the number of appearances he had made for the club, would also have been a popular choice. Former Bolton Wanderers and Oxford United boss Ian Greaves rejected an offer, as did Luton Town's David Pleat. And instead Mark Hulyer opted for the unassuming 34-year-old Lawrence as caretaker. He was popular with the players but otherwise almost entirely unknown, yet it was to prove the luckless chairman's one stroke of genius.

Lawrence made his managerial debut at Shrewsbury Town, where his side earned a 0-0 draw, and was then given a seven-match trial. But in the next three outings Charlton won twice, beating Newcastle United and Barnsley at The Valley. Even though they also went down 4-1 at Bolton, it was enough to convince Hulyer of his caretaker's abilities and four games early, at the staff Christmas party, Lawrence was confirmed in his post until the end of the season. He went on to justify that faith immediately, even though the relegation struggle went to the final match, which by

Mark Hulyer presents Lennie Lawrence with a new contract in January 1984

coincidence produced an exact reverse of the scoreline at Burnden Park, condemning the Lancashire side to the Third Division in Charlton's stead.

However, it was the events of the following season that first thrust Lawrence onto a wider stage and made the fans take him to their hearts. Few will ever forget the image of the young boss waiting anxiously by the phone at the Valley Club to hear whether or not he still had a job, or his nervous appearances on national television to discuss the crisis. But if Lawrence lacked self-confidence among the lights and cameras, he soon became a popular figure with the press. A cynic might suggest that this derived from reporters' appreciation of his uncanny ability to throw out a serviceable quote. But many football writers genuinely respected him for his candour, and above all his unfailing honesty. That was to prove both a strength and a weakness, because later when the Addicks were struggling, the fans soon became weary of what seemed to them an endless stream of pessimism.

Lawrence was certainly no Brian Clough or Ron Atkinson. But then their undoubted talents would probably have been ill-suited to Charlton's predicament in the 1980s. The job needed someone who was willing to get his head down and graft, who was prepared to be knocked down time and again by factors outside his control, yet would still keep getting up to try again. Perhaps initially because he knew that this was his one opportunity to make his name at the top level, Lawrence was just such a man.

Battle for The Valley

He also had personal qualities unusual in a football manager, of which a key one was loyalty. That, too, would make him unpopular when it was tested by the move to Selhurst Park. But otherwise it was part of a fundamental decency which struck a chord with the Charlton public. Another factor in his success, no doubt, was his grasp of the skills of man management, which he had picked up during his training as a teacher. These were tested for the first time in January 1984 when he had to deal with an awkward outburst from the hugely popular captain Derek Hales over the proposed signing of former player Mike Flanagan. The two had exchanged punches while teammates in an FA Cup match five years earlier. But Lawrence soon had them back in harness together.

In the summer of 1985, he had appeared poised for success. Temporarily released from the budgetary restraints of the Hulyer era, he had acquired seven new players in a matter of months and a struggling side had apparently been transformed into one ready to challenge for promotion. Now, suddenly, the ground was literally cut from under him. If he wanted to remain manager, he could hardly have done other than toe the party line. However, Lawrence went further than that, emerging after the angry scenes at the final game to defend his absent chairman. The move was the result of 30 years of neglect, he argued, and the blame for that could not be laid at the feet of John Fryer. Otherwise his approach was purely professional, insisting that if the team was good enough, it wouldn't matter where it played. But in his programme notes that last day at The Valley, he did offer the embittered fans a few crumbs of sympathy. And loyalty figured here, too.

Welcome to the future: the players salute the crowd at the first Selhurst game

"The harsh reality is that all the staff and players are paid employees and their job has moved to Selhurst Park. I expect everybody to come to terms with that quickly and positively," he wrote. "In my mind, after today, there is no room for sentiment or emotional excuses about what went before; we must look to the future and hopefully a bright and successful future for this club. In short, never look back wishing, a motto all employees would do well to heed.

"However, loyal supporters of Charlton FC, at The Valley over many years, do have my utmost sympathy, especially those who will find it difficult to travel to Selhurst Park. 'Loyalty' is a word that is often abused in football in this day and age. Players and managers often move around considerably to further their careers and give themselves financial security, and loyalty is hardly a word that can be applied to most people in this profession. Perhaps only supporters can lay claim to real loyalty, especially if they have supported a club for 10, 20 or 30 years or even longer, through good times and bad times, and perhaps in Charlton's case the good times have been rather thin on the ground.

"To those people goes my greatest sympathy and appreciation, and there will be many in the crowd today. I hope that you can see your way clear to continuing that support at Selhurst Park."

And hope was all he and Charlton could do, since the move to Selhurst amounted to an enormous leap into the dark. No one, least of all the directors, truly knew who would follow the club round the South Circular Road. But it was always obvious that the best hope of long-term survival lay, as indeed it did at The Valley, in First Division football. And the burden of providing that fell on Lawrence. His team had already made the best start to a season of any in the club's 64-year League history, but how would it be affected by the drama unfolding around it?

The answer, as far as one could reasonably tell, was not at all. Presumably the fact that the side contained so many newcomers made the sudden departure less of a wrench. Charlton won their first match at Selhurst Park and were beaten only twice in the remainder of the Second Division fixtures there that season, several of which had to be moved to a Tuesday night to avoid a scheduled clash with Palace.

Of more urgent interest were the attendance figures. The first game was fortuitously against well-supported Sunderland, who brought around 1,500 people with them, boosting the gate to a respectable 5,552. Doomsday predictions of only 1,500 home fans were thus confounded, helped by the provision of 12 free coaches which ran from all parts of the traditional catchment area. But the journey took many people an hour and the crowd contained many sightseers. The real test would surely come later.

At least that Sunderland game ended in victory, Mark Reid scoring the club's first "home" goal at Selhurst from the penalty spot just past the half-hour and Mark Stuart turning in the winner eight minutes from time after Eric Gates had equalised early in the second half. It was a warm, sunny afternoon and there was no repeat of the protest at The Valley, despite elaborate police precautions, including the stationing of their latest crowd-control toy, the "Hoolivan", at the corner of the pitch. The atmosphere was sullen rather than angry, but the team was well-received.

Afterwards, Lawrence made fresh enemies by remarking that the atmosphere with a small crowd was better at Selhurst than at The Valley. It was true enough, since the roof of the Arthur Wait Stand provided a better class of echo than the mountainous East Terrace and low Covered End had allowed. But it was hardly diplomatic. The Palace ground could have been as well-equipped as Old Trafford or as awesome as the San Siro and it would have made no difference to the disgruntled, displaced fans. It wasn't home.

To be fair, Selhurst Park was not a bad stadium, if one undermined by the supermarket which had engulfed the large, open Whitehorse Lane end and the car park behind it in the early 1980s. The truncated terrace which was rebuilt could hold only 3,000 and was backed by a sheer brick wall. There were worse end terraces in the Football League, notably at Notts County and Hull City, but its effect was much exaggerated at Charlton's opening games by the need to keep it empty. One of the conditions of the planning permission granted to Sainsbury's had been that the giant store would close on Saturday afternoons when Palace were at home, thus helping to limit local traffic congestion and parking problems. However, no one drawing up the agreement had taken into account the possible arrival of a second League team and therefore no provision had been made to deal with it. So Sainsbury's continued to open, and since the terrace provided the store's emergency exit, Charlton were forced to play in a three-sided ground.

Most of the new "home" fans congregated in the paddock of the large Arthur Wait Stand, with its impressive acoustics. Completed in 1969 as Palace reached Division One for the first time in their history, the stand took its name from the club's chairman

Grounded Sunderland keeper Bob Bolder can't keep out Mark Stuart's winner

of the day. Spartan in construction, it had none of the proliferation of facilities in its older counterpart opposite, but the standing area at least afforded an excellent view of the pitch. Ground season-ticket holders, who had formerly been able to choose between a seat in the Covered End or a spot on the East Terrace, were sweetened by the offer of access to the seats behind. But an early promise that movement would be allowed between the two sections, as it had been at The Valley, was quietly set aside. Another grievance was that Charlton adopted Palace's admission prices, which meant that on top of the cost of the journey, fans using the Wait enclosure faced a 40p price rise.

In their preference for the Arthur Wait, Charlton fans were notably different from their Palace counterparts, for whom the vast open bank behind the Holmesdale Road goal was the traditional home. In 1985, its capacity was put at 17,000. The Palace faithful had been much offended when a corner of it was reserved for away fans following the redevelopment of the Whitehorse Lane end, but they had always resisted the club's attempts to move them into the Wait paddock.

The new stand and the modern Sainsbury's terrace gave the ground a misleading appearance of recent construction. In fact, Palace had moved there only five years after Charlton had arrived at The Valley and the main stand, now designated the members' stand, dated back to 1924, although its paddock had been seated much more recently. Also built by Humphreys Limited and designed by the celebrated architect Archibald Leitch, it nonetheless revealed its age upon close examination. The propped roof intrudes upon the view, not least from the executive boxes which run along behind the rear seats.

The reader may reasonably assume that the author is biased against Selhurst, so I quote Simon Inglis for evidence of its lack of aesthetic appeal. The Arthur Wait, he wrote, "is rather a dull stand, like a loading bay of a warehouse... Notice how many different colours are used at Selhurst Park, from the garish tones inside the foyer to the blue stanchions and orange nets on each set of goals. Consequently, there is no unity, no indication of who plays here and in what colours. Selhurst Park was underdeveloped for so many years, and now it has been improved it still does not look modern".

The ground's transformation was indeed recent, but then that owed much to the unremarkable fortunes of its home team. Palace, who with Millwall were elected to the League in 1920, one year before Charlton, had led a spectacularly unsuccessful career until the mid-1960s. Apart from the Third Division (South) championship in their debut season, they had never won anything at all, and until finishing runners-up in the Third Division in 1964 had spent just four seasons above that level in 44 years. In 1958 they were founder members of the League's Fourth Division, again along with Millwall.

The club's first major success had been reaching the First Division under Bert Head in 1969, a season that uniquely saw all three South East London sides battling for promotion from the Second. Millwall faded, but Palace eventually finished runners-up to Derby County, with Charlton third, six points behind. Sadly, in those days only two clubs were promoted, although Charlton did have the consolation of knocking Palace out of the FA Cup in a third-round replay at Selhurst Park. The crowd that night, at 39,404 a record for the fixture, sorely tested the capacity, with many

Empty Selhurst seats form the backdrop as Mike Flanagan scores against Hull

sliding down the mud slopes which then topped the terracing. The ground record was set ten years later when 51,482 saw Palace claim the Second Division championship with a 2-0 win over Burnley.

At least Palace still owned their own ground in 1985, although even this ceased to be true under a complex piece of trading a year later which effectively made them tenants of a separate company, Altonwood Limited, in which Ron Noades had a substantial shareholding. Charlton were also to be tenants, although another of the many oddities of the move is that initially Fryer seemed set to purchase half the freehold. Indeed, one boast he made several times was that Charlton and Palace would be equal partners as joint owners of the stadium and it is a matter of record that a company, Selhurst Valley Limited, was set up and registered at Companies House. However, from the very beginning Noades denied to the *Croydon Advertiser* that Charlton would share the ownership and it never happened, something for which both sets of supporters have considerable cause to be grateful.

Instead, the Addicks contracted to hand over ten per cent of their gate receipts, plus half the cost of maintenance and safety work. The new arrivals thus prudently protected themselves to some extent against poor attendances, although there were to be many rueful comments from the terraces every time Charlton had a good gate that now Palace would be able to buy another player.

Charlton's arrival was marked by the appearance of three newly-constructed Portakabins on the corner of the Holmesdale Road terracing, which became the club offices, although the telephones were only connected two days before the first fixture. However, the administration staff were all that ever moved to SE25, despite the sprinkling of hastily erected red and white signs insisting that "Charlton Athletic welcome you to Selhurst Park" which greeted curious onlookers at the opening game. Lawrence and his small coaching staff instead set up home at the club's borrowed training ground in Sparrows Lane, New Eltham.

Damning evidence of Charlton's new vulnerability came with the second "home" match, ten days after the first, against Bradford City. It was watched by a miserly 3,141, the club's record low for a Second Division match. Secretary Graham Hortop blamed the fact that it was an evening kick-off, which was undoubtedly a problem because fans working in London were largely unable to go home before the game, forcing them to come straight down to Selhurst and make the awkward return journey by rail. Younger supporters, too, faced a late night since they could not expect to be at home before ten o'clock, although against this the traffic congestion was much reduced, at least after the game.

But if the evening kick-off was a factor, the next home League match, against Shrewsbury on a Saturday afternoon, was little better supported, with a crowd of 3,233. And before the start the pitch was invaded by several demonstrators waving placards demanding that the directors "Give us back The Valley". They were gently ejected but not arrested, although the continuing bad feeling found voice in the fans' new anthem, sung home and away: "We should have stayed at The Valley."

The imponderable question, of course, was how much bigger the crowds would have been had Charlton done just that. Attendances there in recent years had been little better. But now the team was building a realistic and consistent promotion challenge. After the Shrewsbury game, they went second in the table, something unknown since that ultimately ill-fated tussle with Palace 17 years earlier.

For many people, including Lennie Lawrence, the Carlisle United game on November 30th would be the acid test. The club again recorded its lowest post-war crowd for a Second Division fixture, 3,059, and now the alarm bells were ringing. But the following week came the first evidence that the resisting fans could be lured back by success, when 7,121 turned out for a crunch game with promotion rivals Sheffield United. Then a fortnight later it was back to 3,525 for Grimsby Town's visit.

In these early days at Selhurst, the club would grudgingly admit that it had lost 1,000 regular fans by moving, but the situation was actually more complex than that. Since attendances were already in a trough at The Valley, it is reasonable to assume that there were several thousand who would otherwise have been attracted back by the team's success fairly easily. Many people associated with the club suspect that the trickle back would have become a flood as winter turned to spring. It had happened that way 11 years earlier, when Andy Nelson revived Charlton's Third Division fortunes and the evidence that the support was still out there had been provided by that unexpectedly large crowd of 22,000-plus for Watford's visit the previous January.

Equally, at Selhurst, Charlton were unquestionably attracting a few hundred floaters from the Croydon area and adjacent parts of Bromley, among them some Palace fans. If the old catchment area was proving difficult to tap, the directors' hope had to be that they could recruit replacements locally. In this ambition, Charlton received splendid support from the dominant local paper, the *Croydon Advertiser*. This in turn provoked a storm of protest from its Palace readers, for whom it traditionally provided a comprehensive service.

The paper justified its decision to extend coverage to Charlton on the grounds that the latter were now a Croydon club, but in reality it looked like commercial opportunism. For Charlton were now all but abandoned by the *Kentish Times*, where hostile management took the opportunity to slash the paper's coverage, in spite of the efforts of sports editor Tony Flood. Effectively, the decision cut the club off from its many thousands of passive supporters in Bexley, Bromley and Dartford, a serious blow indeed. The *Kentish Independent* was dead, and the *South London Press* remote. And the *Mercury*, then only in Greenwich and Lewisham, was ploughing a furrow all of its own.

Unknown to the readers, sports editor Peter Cordwell came close to axeing Charlton too. The paper's resources were stretched by having two League clubs in its area and Charlton's departure appeared to offer a solution. The credit for dissuading him goes to Kevin Nolan, a personal friend who was a lifelong Addicks fan and then beginning to write about boxing in the paper. At the end of the season, Nolan would take over the match reports, earning wide acclaim for his descriptive powers and world-weary wit, but for now his contribution was to keep the flame burning. However, no one could pretend that the *Mercury*'s coverage of team affairs in this period was good. On the contrary, it was a shambles and it doesn't take much imagination to work out that comment is cheaper than fact. But whatever his motives, week after week Cordwell continued to hammer away, in the process fuelling the smouldering discontent, which incredibly still found no other expression.

First in the firing line was Greenwich Council, an apparently innocent party in the move, but one committed to paying Charlton, now based miles outside the borough boundary, £250,000 over a five-year period. Oddly, despite the fact that the deal had only been reached at the end of the 1983/84 season, it was several times reported that three payments, totalling £150,000, had already been made. Council leader John Austin-Walker's initial view was that the club was able to maintain its obligations under the agreement, which were basically to make its ground available and develop coaching schemes with local schools. But Selhurst Park was too far away to be of much use to the local community, and the

Charlton's John Pender has a word with one of the neighbours

links with schools, at first obstructed by a long-running teachers' dispute, never materialised.

A commitment to offer free matchday admission to children in care, the elderly and the disabled was clearly meaningless in view of the difficulty and expense that would inevitably be incurred in making the longer journey. "£250,000 for WHAT?" demanded Cordwell across his back page and the rest of the grant was soon cancelled.

A week after this story appeared, a fire at The Valley, the first of many, slightly damaged the main stand. There was no security and the gates had been left wide open when the staff quit on September 27th, almost an invitation to local vandals and arsonists. "Valley left to rot," screamed the *Mercury*. Warming to his theme, Cordwell next week demolished Charlton's cosy matchday programme note that legendary Valley groundsman Maurice Banham had taken early retirement, under the headline: "I was sacked."

Axed: Maurice Banham takes down the Valley goalnets for the last time

Thus far the club's relationship with Palace had appeared an amicable one, although Charlton's arrival had already been marked by an obscure dispute about the erection of a sign on the back of the main stand. Now events took a more serious turn when the kick-off in a Full Members' Cup match was delayed by 20 minutes because of a floodlight failure. Lawrence lost his temper and told the press that his club were "poor relations" at Selhurst Park. A faulty timer eventually proved to be responsible for the immediate problem, but the Charlton boss complained: "I guarantee that if Palace had been playing here this week it would not have happened." However, the lack of lights had little effect on Charlton fans, who numbered barely a quarter of the tiny 3,714 crowd which had turned up to see the club's home debut in the fledgling competition, against First Division Chelsea.

More significant was Lawrence's other revelation, that since the Sunderland game Palace would not allow his players to train on the unfamiliar pitch before a match. Asked who had stopped them doing so, he replied: "Who do you think? Palace say they do not train on the pitch. I don't care a damn what they do." But Noades later said that this had been a part of the two clubs' agreement in order to preserve the pitch in good condition. The row was eventually smoothed over, with Charlton escaping a possible League fine for the late kick-off by producing a letter from the electricity board admitting responsibility.

Nonetheless it was a humiliating illustration of the extent of the club's new dependence on their neighbours. And events took a further turn for the worse the very next evening, when none of the Charlton directors turned up for their traditional guest appearance at the supporters' club AGM, held at the Valley Club. Even now and in spite of all the furore, the attendance was only 100, but that was still three times the norm. Just 37 of them raised their hands to back the unopposed re-election of the officers and, much to the committee's dismay, member Richard Hunt successfully proposed a motion from the floor expressing the meeting's disgust that the directors "should all have found engagements more pressing than the club".

The one man who emerged with credit, inevitably, was Lawrence who faced a barrage of questions, to most of which, understandably, he was unable to offer answers. Veteran supporters' club chairman Jack Linsdell resigned the following week, taking his wife Doris, the treasurer, with him, although that seemed to those present to have more to do with accusations about free travel to away games than the main issue. Whatever the cause, it was splendid ammunition for Cordwell, whose fourth consecutive "exclusive" centred on some transparently daft allegations by Linsdell that "some of these people joined the supporters' club solely to use it as a platform to air their views and stir up the rabble". Digging furiously at his own grave, he went on: "We did our best to get the directors along, but we must remember that they are businessmen." However, it was certainly untrue, as Flood later claimed in the *Kentish Times*, that Linsdell "had been hounded out of office by abusive, disillusioned supporters".

His successor was 53-year-old Bill Treadgold, from Bromley, the long-standing travel officer, who immediately nailed his identical colours to the mast by appealing to fans to end the demonstrations and get behind the team. The supporters' club's one concession to events was to stipulate that the money they raised should not be used towards ground improvements at Palace. "Nobody is happy about the move to Selhurst Park but there is not a lot we can do about it," claimed secretary Roy King.

The supporters' club's dilemma was twofold. In the first place, many of those involved were simply incapable of running an effective campaign against the club's situation and they were temperamentally disinclined to do so anyway. Secondly, they needed facilities from which to run the only away travel service that Charlton had. If they took up arms against the directors, their base in the Selhurst club shop would surely be taken away. Travel was the only reason most people bothered to join the supporters' club in the first place. But in fact they could have built a mass membership simply by campaigning for a return to The Valley. That was something which nobody seemed to understand.

Had Charlton struggled on the field at Selhurst, there might have been no need for a campaign anyway. Attendances would surely have dwindled to nothing, forcing an early rethink. But the team's success left the stay-away fans in a quandary. Many of the less committed were deterred by the journey, but the prospect of promotion was a cruel temptation to those former regulars who were not attending on principle. The position was rendered all the more absurd by the fact that a number of them continued to travel to away matches. Slowly, grudgingly, some of them began to make the trip. In March, there were 3,767 for Oldham Athletic. Three weeks later, there were 4,143 for Huddersfield Town. And as the season reached its climax, 5,766 turned up on the penultimate Saturday to see Charlton beat Blackburn Rovers. It was 28 years to the day that a 4-3 Valley defeat at the hands of the same opposition had seen Charlton miss an instant First Division return by a single point. And then the crowd had been 56,435.

In between these run-of-the-mill matches, of course, there were better gates for more attractive opposition. Portsmouth were Charlton's main rivals for promotion and when they visited a week before Oldham, the five-figure barrier was broken for a League match at Selhurst for the first time, with a crowd of 10,132. The arrival of eventual champions Norwich City on Easter Monday brought in 8,458. But these were still meagre to what might have been expected at The Valley. And when West Ham United, then chasing the League championship, came for a third-round FA Cup tie in January, talk of a 32,000 crowd was proved ridiculous by the actual attendance of 13,037. The match was being covered live by BBC TV's *Match of the Day*, but the gate suggested to many that Charlton could never hope to lure their passive support to Selhurst.

The team's progress was remarkably consistent throughout the campaign and they never looked likely to drop out of promotion contention. Using the six-foot tall John Pearson, recruited from Sheffield Wednesday for £100,000 the previous summer, as a target man, they rattled in the goals. Led from midfield by the skipper Mark Aizlewood, and bolstered by the newly-acquired attacking full-backs Mark Reid and John Humphrey, from Celtic and Wolverhampton Wanderers respectively, the side was obviously the club's best for 20 years at least. No one was more influential than the veteran Mike Flanagan, now 33 and in his last full season of League action. Up front the youthful partnership of Robert Lee and Mark Stuart, who had contributed the goals in The Valley's final match, yielded 20 in total.

Charlton's only stumbles before their own fans were against Hull in November and in the crunch game with Portsmouth. But they bounced back from the latter by winning at Bradford City, also homeless after the terrible fire and obliged to stage

New boy Jim Melrose celebrates Charlton's first goal at Craven Cottage in April

the game at the cavernous Odsal stadium, the ground of Bradford Northern rugby league club. And there were other important victories at Sunderland, Middlesbrough, Huddersfield, Brighton & Hove Albion and Leeds United.

Lawrence had already bought well, but in March with 11 games remaining, he produced a stroke of genius, recruiting the much-travelled Scottish striker Jim Melrose from Manchester City for £45,000. Melrose scored on his debut at The Den against Millwall and added four more priceless goals on the run-in.

As the race entered the final furlong, there were three main contenders for the two remaining promotion places, Norwich being runaway leaders despite their 1-0 defeat by Charlton at Selhurst Park. The others were Portsmouth and South London neighbours Wimbledon, even more improbable candidates than Charlton with their tiny ground at Plough Lane, poor support and brief League history.

The breakthrough came in April, five games from the end, on a Tuesday evening that found Charlton at Craven Cottage, playing in a one-sided match which confirmed Fulham's relegation. The Addicks were fourth, on 64 points, one point behind Wimbledon who also had five games to play. Portsmouth, second, were five points ahead on 69, but had only three games left.

Visiting fans made up the vast majority of the 5,587 crowd, and they were in buoyant mood as Charlton easily shrugged the Second Division's bottom club aside, with two second-half goals from Stuart adding to Pearson's opener. But it was the news that came over the tannoy at half-time that set the supporters dancing at the Putney end. Portsmouth were a goal down at Stoke City. When the final whistle went there were long anxious minutes before the Charlton fans left the ground, waiting ouside the Cottage itself for that crucial scoreline. And when, eventually, it filtered through, there was disbelief and jubilation. Pompey had lost 2-0. Now even if they won their last two fixtures, nine points from Charlton's four would see the Addicks home. And three of those games were at Selhurst, with the fourth at struggling Carlisle. Only the last match, a deliberately rearranged fixture with fellow challengers Wimbledon, appeared to offer a test.

After so many grindingly mediocre years, the end of the club's long exile from the top flight was in sight at last. At the following Saturday's final whistle and with their side comfortable 3-0 winners over Blackburn, the crowd chanted in vain, time and time again for news of Portsmouth. "What's the score at Bramall Lane?" they sang. But the announcer, apparently oblivious, had no news to give. It wasn't until the fans got back into their cars to make the tedious journey home that they heard confirmation. Pompey had drawn 0-0 with Sheffield United and the margin of Charlton's victory meant that three points from the midweek return game with Fulham would all but send the Addicks up.

And now, at last, the supporters came out in appreciable numbers. A crowd of 9,393 turned up to witness at first hand what had for so long seemed impossible. It was hardly massive and not even Charlton's largest at Selhurst, but it was comfortably the biggest contingent of their own fans to make the awkward journey. Poor Fulham had only a couple of hundred loyalists in tow, one of whom brought a coffin to protest at the plight of their club.

But this was a different Fulham side from that beaten so easily at Craven Cottage,

John Pearson (second left) breaks the deadlock against Fulham at Selhurst, effectively ending Charlton's 29-year exile from the top flight

The celebrations begin: fans pour on to the Selhurst pitch after the game to salute the team's amazing success, but still they chant for The Valley

and it was a difference made largely by the inclusion of one player, defender Paul Parker, who would later play for England. Try as they might, Charlton could not get past him. In goal, Gerry Peyton was also in marvellous form, tipping over Aizlewood's free-kick and Melrose's bicycle-kick. As the minutes ticked away it seemed that even now the dream might be shattered at the last.

Then on came Lee, a player fated, it seemed, for a special significance in Charlton history. On 69 minutes, he finally got the ball past Parker on the right side of the penalty area, made for the byline and cut it back. No Charlton player could supply the touch at the near post, but nor could any defender clear it. And there, lurking on the other side of the goal, was the lanky Pearson. His mis-hit shot went in off a defender on the line.

The roar was long and lingering. It was tinged with every kind of emotion, but most of all relief, and it seemed to go on forever. The whole crowd was dancing now, the bitterness that had stained all that had gone before forgotten in the excitement of the moment. Three minutes from time, Lee went down the right again and crossed for Pearson, but before the ball could reach him, Fulham defender John Marshall had sliced it into his own goal. "Armageddon apart", as the *Mercury* put it, Charlton were back in the First Division after 29 years.

The few fans who prematurely invaded the pitch were urged off by their peers, anxious that nothing should spoil the moment. They were massed on the touchline now, and at the whistle the playing area was swamped by delirious supporters, only a handful of whom were old enough to have seen their heroes leave the First Division stage all those long seasons ago.

Inside the stand, the naturally cautious Lawrence took some persuading to join the celebrations. If Charlton lost their last two games and Portsmouth beat Bradford by a combined margin of nine goals, they might still be overtaken, he insisted. But nobody out on the pitch believed that a possibility. And now that the match was won, the fans remembered their grievance. A solitary placard waved in the middle of the throng with its defiant messages, "Division One at The Valley", and "10,000 at The Valley" on the back. If anything, the latter seemed a modest assessment. And up went the chant again: "Bring back, bring back, bring back The Valley to us, to us!"

Yet still it was not over, for Carlisle, Charlton's penultimate Second Division opponents, were in desperate need of points to stay up. They shocked the 1,500 visiting fans by scoring twice in the opening 23 minutes through defender Wes Saunders. When news filtered through that Pompey were 1-0 up at home to Bradford, suddenly Lawrence's nightmare scenario did not seem so remote. It took a freak incident five minutes before the break to steady Charlton nerves. Under little pressure, Carlisle's Jim Tolmie turned and swung his boot at a back pass fully 30 yards from goal. Keeper Scott Endersby was clearly caught unawares but he seemed to make up ground, only for the ball to strike the near post and roll along the goalline, going in on the far side.

It was the break Charlton needed, and they rallied strongly in the second half, although it was the 70th minute before Mark Stuart knocked in the equaliser. Ten minutes from time skipper Mark Aizlewood beat Paul Haigh on the edge of the area and slotted the ball home from 15 yards. Now there could be no more doubt, Charlton

Battle for The Valley

George Shipley, Steve Thompson, Mark Aizlewood, Robert Lee and John Pender celebrate the winner at Carlisle, while (below) John Fryer joins the crowded bench ready for the final-whistle pitch invasion

Lennie Lawrence is shouldered high by delirious fans at Brunton Park

were up and for the second time in five years the promotion had been sealed at Brunton Park, the most distant ground in the League. It was rough on the many people who could not make the long journey, but few who were there were complaining.

This time even Lawrence was celebrating and the hundred or so supporters who got onto the pitch at the final whistle chaired him across to the visitors' enclosure. Grinning sheepishly, the manager nervously saluted the fans, perhaps concerned that he might experience a sudden fall to earth. Fryer approached and was given the same treatment. The response from the terrace was similarly generous, even if in his case there were a few dissenters.

So now the Selhurst experiment was to be tested to the limit. For if the fans would not turn out for First Division football, then clearly it was never going to work. Misleading evidence to the contrary was provided by the crowd of 13,214 at the club's final game of the season, against Wimbledon, who brought at most 3,000.

The Dons had also earned their place in the top flight, by winning at Huddersfield, and the match was academic, except that it could decide who picked up £7,500 from League sponsors Canon for finishing second. In the end, it did no such thing, since although it was fiercely competitive it ended in a goalless draw. Perhaps the only memorable moment was the teams' arrival together on the pitch, led by their respective managers and warmly received by the two sets of fans. The result left Wimbledon to claim the runners-up spot by winning at Bradford two days later, but this they failed to do, instead drawing 1-1.

John Fryer, enjoying his moment of triumph, on the coach home from Carlisle

Any lingering hopes among the Charlton supporters that the success would open the way for a fairytale return to The Valley were immediately quashed by the chairman. "We shall never, never return there," he insisted, as the fans once again danced on the Palace turf, although this time with little response from inside the stand. "It is not going to happen. It would cost £3m to put things right at The Valley. Here at Selhurst Park we have the use of the best stadium in South London. Mr Noades has made considerable developments to the ground which we could never have done at The Valley. Our future is here and now that we are in the First Division we shall try to make sure that we stay there."

They were bold, defiant words. But they were also completely empty ones.

Chapter Six

"It was not supposed to be like this."
Patrick Collins – *The Mail on Sunday (August 1986)*

Charlton's achievement of gaining promotion in spite of the upheaval of leaving The Valley was a remarkable one. However, its major effect was simply to postpone judgement on the groundsharing scheme. The much larger crowds for the final two home games of the season had created the illusion that support might yet dramatically improve, and prompted manager Lennie Lawrence to appeal for 5,000 people to buy season tickets to provide funding for him to strengthen the team.

But despite early claims of a tenfold increase in orders, there were still just 1,600 season-ticket holders by the opening game, only a few hundred more than the previous year. And the gate for Charlton's first appearance in the top flight since 1957 was a bitter disappointment, too. At just 8,501, it was easily the lowest crowd in the First Division that day and fewer than seven in the Second. Perhaps opponents Sheffield Wednesday were not the most attractive opposition – "a bit like going on a blind date with Hilda Ogden", Patrick Collins called it in *The Mail on Sunday* – but it was still something of an anti-climax after a summer of keen anticipation.

Money worries had also disrupted pre-season preparations. At the root of the problem was a lucrative bonus scheme established the previous year by director Jimmy Hill. It had been instrumental in luring the key players to the club, but chairman John Fryer had foolishly refused to insure against promotion. Having been obliged to pay out large amounts, claimed to total up to £250,000, as a consequence, he was now disinclined to fork out again for a First Division wage structure. Accordingly, he instructed that there were to be no pay increases.

Led by their increasingly outspoken skipper Mark Aizlewood, the players went into open revolt. "None of the playing staff, including the manager, are getting a penny rise for taking the club into the First Division. I have told our boss Lennie Lawrence that I want to go if the situation remains the same and I expect other players will do likewise," he said. Another to make a formal transfer request was full-back Mark Reid, while lion-hearted central defender Steve Thompson and goalkeeper Nicky Johns were said to be unhappy.

Lawrence was caught in the middle, although he was naturally concerned at the thought of his successful squad being broken up or their team spirit being undermined. He was even linked with leaving himself, to take over at First Division rivals Luton Town, but eventually a compromise was reached in the wages dispute, with the players accepting another generous bonus scheme in lieu of increased basic payments.

The exception was Johns, who claimed that the club had promised him a two-year extension to his current contract but was now unwilling to commit to it. He demanded to go on the transfer list. Perhaps not by chance, the row coincided with the £20,000-signing of Sunderland goalkeeper Bob Bolder, Johns' former deputy Tony Lange having already left for Aldershot along with young midfielder Darren Anderson.

Robert Lee (7) celebrates the first Division One goal with the Selhurst crowd

For Bolder, born in Dover, it was something of a homecoming. Rejected by Charlton at the age of 17, he had been spotted by Sheffield Wednesday manager Len Ashurst and gone on to make nearly 200 League appearances for the Owls, before moving to Liverpool, where he spent three frustrating seasons unable to break into the team. Two dozen games for the Roker Park outfit had followed and a loan spell at Luton as cover, but at 27 he was still waiting to make his First Division bow.

Two more players who left that summer were veteran central defender Les Berry and the influential Mike Flanagan. Clearly, the higher grade was beyond the ambitions of the loyal and long-serving Berry and he moved to Brighton & Hove Albion on a free transfer. However, Flanagan's departure, like his first seven years earlier, was an angry one. He was keen to join the coaching staff, but unwilling to accept new terms that would have reflected that position rather than his continued registration as a player. He eventually joined Cambridge United, where he would appear in only a handful of games before a knee injury finished his League career. Instead, Lawrence recruited Colin Clarke, a former Oxford United defender and Kettering Town player-manager with whom he had worked during his time at Plymouth Argyle, as youth-team coach.

But it was the last acquisition, ironically a £125,000 signing from first top-flight opponents Sheffield Wednesday, who was to have the most impact. Yorkshireman Peter Shirtliff was 25, a commanding central defender with leadership qualities that would develop sharply as the season progressed.

The campaign began well, if not spectacularly, with a 1-1 draw. Yet again Robert Lee was the man to claim the historic goal, running on to Thompson's kick upfield to slot the ball between advancing keeper Martin Hodge's legs eight minutes after half-time. Before the game members of the Junior Reds, the club's flourishing children's section set up in the last summer at The Valley, paraded around the field wearing the colours of the 22 First Division teams. In front of the supermarket end, now open for the exclusive use of those who had joined the newly-instituted membership scheme, American-style cheerleaders performed with ludicrous irrelevance. Yet what should have been a special day somehow fell flat.

Just as he had when the team made its final appearance in SE7, Collins articulated the feelings of the long-standing supporters best. Under the defiant headline "No grounds for celebration" and a picture of the overgrown Valley, he told his readers: "In a ground devoid of atmosphere and a match devoid of charm, Charlton Athletic returned to the First Division after an absence of 29 years.

"It was not supposed to be like this. Those of us who had waited, hoped and thrown in the odd desperate prayer for such an event, had imagined an occasion awash with joyful nostalgia. It would be one of The Valley's most memorable days.

"But The Valley is no more than a derelict monument, with vandalised stands, decaying terraces and a pitch ablaze with towering weeds. Charlton slipped away from Charlton 11 months ago and their traditions died with the move... Football has changed, Charlton have changed. And not, I fear, for the better."

So Fryer's brave new world still showed no sign of appearing. Collins' sentiments were an accurate reflection of many letters that had appeared in the local papers during the summer, demonstrating that for some Charlton's success had only served to make the club's absence from The Valley more painful still.

Among them was 20-year-old Steve Dixon, from Eltham, who had written to the *Mercury* to complain about a comment by Kevin Nolan in his Carlisle United match report that on that day some fans seemed ready to forgive the chairman anything. "I would like to inform Mr Fryer, and for future reference your paper also, that some Charlton supporters will never forgive him for his actions," he wrote.

It was significant because Dixon was now to become the bridgehead for a far more militant attitude within the supporters' club. Impeccably middle class, he was a somewhat improbable leader for the disenchanted masses on the terraces, who often mistook his characteristic earnestness for a lack of humour. Brought up in a family of Charlton supporters, he had a personal grudge against the club in that his mother had been responsible for the executive-box catering at The Valley and had been a victim of the same abrupt termination as many of the others who gave their services behind the scenes.

Dixon had joined the supporters' club committee immediately after the move to Selhurst Park, but he came to prominence with the launch of a CASC newsletter in August 1986. The first edition of the season was an unremarkable eight pages of notices and travel information, but from the second Dixon began to contribute editorial that took an increasingly hostile attitude to the football club's situation. It was to mean that at last the fans had a method of communicating with each other and sharing their discontent. Before long, that smouldering ill-feeling would explode into a brilliant inferno of protest.

As yet, however, the team was still taking its hesitant initial steps in the top flight.

First blood: Mark Stuart's sensational winner at Old Trafford

They were thrashed 4-0 in their first away game, against a Nottingham Forest side whose superiority left Lawrence shell-shocked, but then followed it up with a truly astonishing single-goal victory over Manchester United at Old Trafford.

Charlton could hardly have chosen a more glamorous venue to record their first win and the 2,000 or so travelling fans looked on in mounting disbelief as the minutes ticked away after Mark Stuart had shot them into a second-half lead. Time after time it seemed that the Manchester men must equalise, but on each occasion the situation was dramatically retrieved. It was true that United had already started the season with two defeats and manager Ron Atkinson was on the way out, yet it was still a momentous and memorable day for fans and players alike, and one that Charlton would struggle to match however long they stayed in the top flight.

But again it provided evidence of the club's impossible position. For the following Tuesday they entertained Wimbledon and drew a crowd of just 6,531, less than half the attendance for the two sides' promotion party four months earlier and inevitably Charlton's lowest-ever First Division gate. Just to make matters worse, the Dons took the points with a Dennis Wise goal three minutes from time and went to the top of the League in the process.

The comparison with Wimbledon was to remain a particularly galling one. Both from South London, promoted together and with similarly low gates – even if Charlton's were always slightly the better of the two – it was an obvious temptation to the media to bracket the clubs together. Closer examination revealed that the similarities were more superficial than real, however. The Dons played a long-ball game based on physical strength and a continuous aerial bombardment, gaining an early and justified reputation as the division's bad boys. Charlton, on the other hand, used an increasingly sophisticated passing game and often relied heavily on their ability to soak up pressure and score on the break. Unfortunately, for them and the game in general, it was a distinction that was reflected in terms of results, with Wimbledon's shock tactics much the more successful.

The reasons for the clubs' poor crowds were also very different. The Dons, as was proved when they reached Wembley in the 1988 FA Cup, beating Liverpool in the final, simply didn't have many supporters. Their lack of League tradition had denied them the opportunity to build up the large passive following to which Charlton could lay claim, much good though it did them at Selhurst Park.

Finally, Wimbledon's ground at Plough Lane had barely been developed since its Southern League days and was not really capable of staging First Division football, something which was hardly true of Selhurst Park or, if refurbished, The Valley.

The proof that Charlton needed to strengthen the side further in order to compete with the elite was provided when the fourth fixture, against Second Division champions Norwich City, ended in another defeat, 2-1. This time the winning goal came five minutes from time, but more significantly the tannoy announcement of the derisory attendance of 5,312 was greeted with great hilarity by the travelling Norwich fans and chants of "You're in the wrong division!". It was the last time for some years that the attendance was announced at a Charlton home match, suggesting at least that someone within the club retained a sense of shame.

Lawrence's response was to move into the transfer market to bolster the midfield, bringing in Nottingham Forest's Colin Walsh for £125,000 and Grimsby Town's Andy Peake for £75,000. Walsh, a 24-year-old Scot, was to add some necessary guile to the side and soon become famous for his conversion of free-kicks. Peake brought with him a reputation made on a 1980 *Match of the Day* programme when he had twice scored from distance in the same match for his former club Leicester City. Dubbed "Peakie's Rocket", his powerful shot became something of a running joke as he notched only one goal in his first four seasons, against Spurs. And even that took a deflection.

The two faced making their debuts at Anfield, of all places, and Walsh's was complicated by a freak injury to Reid after 20 minutes when the left-back collided with the dugout. It meant the new signing playing in his injured countryman's position for the rest of the game. Despite this setback, Charlton hung on for 55 minutes before Jan Molby converted a disputed penalty, awarded for handball against Aizlewood, and although Ian Rush added a second 12 minutes from time, the visitors were far from disgraced.

In fact, the Forest game excepted, the newcomers had made a sound start in the top flight, if one which had yielded few points. It was a pattern which was to become all too familiar. A crowd of 5,587 now saw them outplay Coventry at Selhurst, but gift the visitors a point courtesy of an Aizlewood own goal three minutes from time.

The following Tuesday's Littlewoods Cup game with Lincoln City ended in a 3-1 win, but attracted only 2,319, the lowest crowd for any first-class fixture since the exile at Catford, more than 60 years before. Watching from the stand was the *Mercury*'s Peter Cordwell, a rare visitor to matches, who decided that enough was enough. "Only an emperor with a penchant for parading around starkers would fail to see that Charlton have no real future at Selhurst Park. It can't go on like this," he wrote in his match report. It was almost exactly a year since the club had played at The Valley. And now, at long, long last, someone decided to do something about it.

The next Thursday, October 2nd, Cordwell picked up an idea from Reg King, a fan from Kidbrooke, and devoted the entire back page of the *Mercury* to a petition form, under the heading: "Our HOME is The VALLEY." Inside, he offered readers this challenge: "Who cares, and how much? They're the questions behind the petition for Charlton fans on the back page this week. Stick your name down – and get others to sign, too – if you believe that Charlton should return to The Valley from Crystal Palace's ground, Selhurst Park. It's your chance, if nothing else, to voice your frustrations at being stranded miles from home.

"Hardly a day goes by without *Mercury Sport* receiving a phone call or a letter pleading the case for a planned return to The Valley or a new site in Greenwich. Talk among fans at Selhurst Park always gets round to The Valley. A banner opposite the press box always carries the same, poignant message. Chants of 'Back to The Valley' echo eerily around Norwood Junction railway station.

"We know for a fact that Greenwich Council would be impressed by a massive response to the *Mercury* petition. If you Charlton fans really care, you'll go to great lengths to prove it. We're talking sackloads."

He needn't have worried. The response was immediate, enthusiastic and enormous. By the time the paper went to press the following Wednesday it had already received 4,000 names. A week later the total had topped 10,000. And three days further on, little more than a fortnight after the form had first appeared in the paper, 15,000 signatures had been put to the petition. Easily the biggest postbag in the *Mercury*'s 153-year history, it amounted to an extraordinary sociological phenomenon, as if some great psychological dam which had been holding back this torrent of emotion had suddenly been opened.

The response was all the more remarkable when it is considered that properly speaking the paper covered just the boroughs of Greenwich and Lewisham, which were together home to only between 30-40 per cent of Charlton supporters. Of course, many fans from Bexley and elsewhere still read the *Mercury* and signed the petition, but not nearly as many, it is reasonable to assume, as might have if the paper had been distributed in the outer boroughs and north Kent too. Post after post after post they came, and many with heartfelt thanks for the initiative. One man sent a poem. And in that first week, just two letters arrived criticising the paper for what it had done.

But now that the petition had been gathered, how should it be presented? Fatefully, the opportunity presented itself straight away, even if it took a little prompting on my own part to point it out. Although I had written to all the local papers numerous times in the previous year, thus far I'd been as much to blame as everyone else for the inaction. Apart from half-heartedly distributing a single-sheet *Voice of The Valley* newsletter at the opening Selhurst game, against Sunderland, I'd done nothing to organise the campaign which I had always felt certain would be unstoppable.

Nor, to be honest, was it my intention to do anything much now, except point out that the pending supporters' club AGM was just the occasion for the presentation.

However, Cordwell, with whom I had never met or spoken at the time, chose to interpret the letter I sent him as an invitation from a member of the CASC committee. "We'll be there!" screamed the back page on October 16th, just four days before the meeting, together with a story encouraging everybody else to come along, too. I couldn't really complain, since a massive demonstration was exactly what I'd wanted, but the conservative supporters' club officials were aghast.

Vainly, they tried to mitigate the effect. But it was too late. Events were now developing a momentum of their own and the tannoy announcements at Saturday's game with Leicester City that the meeting was for members only fell on deaf ears. In any case, many of the people most likely to turn up weren't at Selhurst anyway by definition.

The Sunday papers, too, had got to hear of the size of the petition and for them it provided a nice contrast to another dismal gate. Then, on the Monday morning, the controversy was fuelled by a story in the *Daily Express* which quoted Aizlewood as backing the fans' campaign: "Even the players who never played at The Valley want to go back," he was alleged to have said. "It's a joke, all the players are nursing hopes that the club will somehow be able to move back. We only go to Selhurst Park just before the kick-offs. That's all we see of the ground. If the traffic was re-routed, I would get lost going to games."

The venue for the AGM, as ever, was the Valley Club, which could cope with an attendance of about 400. Prudently, I got there early, to be greeted by a worried-looking Bill Treadgold and registration secretary Paul Ellis, whom I knew slightly. But it soon became evident that there was no chance of proceeding with the meeting

Former goalkeeper and Valley favourite Charlie Wright signs the petition

as normal. Hundreds of people were streaming in by the minute. Eventually, with the hall now seriously overcrowded, the doors were locked, but sympathetic fans already in simply opened the fire exit to admit those still outside. Before long, the police had to be called to disperse the hundreds still arriving.

There were now up to a thousand people in the Valley Club. Notoriously stuffy anyway, the atmosphere had become hot and sticky to an unprecedented degree and the doors couldn't be opened for ventilation lest still more people tried to force their way inside. Matters weren't helped by the fact that the directors weren't due to arrive until halfway through the abandoned proceedings. Manager Mike Bailey wasn't complaining since he was doing a roaring trade behind the bar, but supporters' club committee members were left to try in vain to explain their own position to the largely hostile, although still good-humoured, crowd.

At last, the official party arrived – directors Michael Norris and Derek Ufton, new chief executive Tony Shaw and, surprisingly, Aizlewood. The last was a shrewd move on the club's part because the already popular player had achieved hero status with his comments to the *Express*, even though he now backed away from them. Norris and Ufton, however, were roundly jeered and were clearly badly shaken by the intensity of feeling.

Penned into the stage area by a wall of bodies, they bravely tried to answer questions from the floor but the sound system was of such poor quality and the temptation to heckle such that little could be heard. When the audience did briefly fall silent, it was to be told that the two directors had no authority to answer questions about finance, couldn't say how long Charlton could survive on their present gates and didn't know whether the club would be prepared to buy The Valley from Michael Gliksten if he was prepared to sell. It was hardly a message calculated to impress, although Norris did claim that gates at Selhurst would rise to an 11,000 average by the end of the season.

Before they could make their escape, however, council leader John Austin-Walker arrived to make a few points of his own. He promised that while Greenwich could not compulsorily purchase The Valley, it could and would refuse planning permission for the site to be developed while Charlton remained in exile. "They owe that club to this borough," he announced to rousing cheers and demanded that the directors hold a fact-finding meeting with the council and fans to discuss ways of coming back. It was an offer that Ufton and Norris were hardly in a position to refuse.

The petition, contained in a black plastic sack, was duly handed over and thus ended one of the most extraordinary nights in Charlton's history. The supporters' club officials were deeply unhappy about having their AGM hijacked, as they saw it, by the *Mercury*, but they seemed to miss the point. The people who attended the Valley Club that night were not intruders at a private function, but the very supporters whose views they should have been representing all along. It was their failure to do that which had made the angry demonstration necessary.

For the first time, the Charlton directors had had to confront the people whose opinions they had hitherto been able to discount. Dignified it wasn't, but then neither had the treatment of fans over the move to Selhurst been in the first place. And the national publicity that the meeting earned – the *Express* led its back page with the

Mike Norris loses his cool as the temperature rises at the CASC AGM

headline "Rumpus at The Valley" – had placed the issue back on the agenda for the first time in 12 months. Even the *Standard*, which soon became notoriously hostile to the campaign, splashed the story across the back page the following day.

Ironically, the discontent had surfaced anew as Charlton were enjoying their best spell of the season, winning six consecutive matches, four of them in the First Division. The dramatic change in their fortunes had begun with a 1-0 success at Chelsea, followed by a memorable 3-2 win over eventual champions Everton at Selhurst Park. Jim Melrose struck a hat-trick as Charlton claimed their first victory in the top flight at Selhurst, before a crowd of 10,564. Only 5,779 were back for the 2-0 win over Leicester seven days later, but those who made the shorter trip to West Ham United the next week were rewarded with a 3-1 win. This time Melrose scored in just nine seconds, the fastest goal in the club's history. With this result, Charlton went 13th in the League, which was to prove their zenith for the season.

It was the Littlewoods Cup win over Queens Park Rangers which created controversy, however, with the Selhurst floodlights failing 14 minutes into the second half, almost a year to the day that the kick-off had been delayed against Chelsea because of a similar problem. This time it was the main fuse that had blown, but had the 20-minute delay been extended by just two more minutes it would have reached referee Mike James' deadline and the game would have been abandoned.

In the interim, Charlton fans in the Arthur Wait Stand gave vent to their fury with a deafening chorus of "We should have stayed at The Valley" and "What a poxy ground this is!". Just to reinforce the point, the enclosure had been closed to all but season-ticket holders for building work, forcing the crowd into the seats behind. In the event, the Addicks won more comfortably than the 1-0 scoreline suggested, but

Lawrence receives his Bell's Manager of the Month award for October 1986

one man particularly grateful that the game had been finished was Steve Thompson, by coincidence a qualified electrician himself. The goal was his first and as it proved only one for Charlton.

An indication of the club's internal discomfiture over events off the pitch came with the refusal to allow Thames Television to film the match for their *Midweek Sports Special* slot. A bewildered Thames spokesman was quoted as saying: "Their chairman John Fryer said they simply do not like the media. It's all to do with the press reports about the fans wanting the club to leave Selhurst Park."

More cause for dissatisfaction came just three days later when the visit of Arsenal attracted 19,614, Charlton's biggest League crowd for more than seven years but still the lowest ever for the fixture. At least half of those who attended came to support the visitors and the semi-closure of the Arthur Wait terrace led to dangerous overcrowding behind the Holmesdale Road goal, where Charlton fans had also to be accommodated. Together with the membership scheme, which had been demanded by the government but effectively ensured that two sides of the ground were kept half-empty, it meant that many people were either locked out or were unable to obtain a view of the pitch.

Just to make matters worse, it was a wet afternoon and Charlton lost 2-0, despite Lawrence receiving the Manager of the Month award for his team's unbeaten October before the kick-off. It was hardly the best way to welcome back those Charlton supporters attending the most glamorous fixture the club had yet staged at Selhurst

Park. The disgruntled "home" fans were further antagonised by the police's eventual decision to relieve overcrowding in the Arsenal pen by allowing a thousand or so Gunners fans to move into the supposedly closed enclosure.

A new voice had been added to the Valley campaign a week earlier, that of the club's former player Billy Bonds, then well into the veteran stage of his apparently unending career at Upton Park. Woolwich-born and a Charlton supporter before he signed for the Addicks as an apprentice in his youth, Bonds admitted in the West Ham programme that the move to Selhurst Park had destroyed any feelings he had for his old team. "The Valley is Charlton to me and always will be," he wrote. "That is where all my memories are. I appreciate the reasons which forced them out and am delighted they are back in the First Division because I think Lennie Lawrence has done a marvellous job. It is just that some of the magic has gone and for me this is just another League game."

The credibility of the supporters' club had sunk so low, meanwhile, that they were no longer trusted to represent popular opinion, and six "unofficial" fans were recruited to attend the meeting with councillors and Charlton directors alongside the CASC officials. But one thing that had been appreciated for the first time, even by the supporters' club, was the extent of Fryer's authority. By their answers at the AGM, Ufton and Norris had made this clear. Treadgold was now quoted as saying: "There must be someone from the club's owners, Sunley's, at the meeting. It would be unsatisfactory if it was just Mr Ufton and Mr Norris again."

In the event, it proved to be Ufton, Norris and Collins, although this time they stressed that they had full authority to speak for the board. Their discussions had been given added point two days earlier when a double dose of Ron Noades – the Full Members' Cup and groundsharing – combined to produce a ridiculous attendance of 821 for the visit of Birmingham City. As if to underline that it was no fluke, four less would come to the next round's tie with Bradford City, providing easily the lowest gates in the club's history. Even so, they were only 150 less than Millwall had managed at The Den for their first-round match against West Bromwich Albion in the same competition.

But the news from the meeting, such as it was, appeared good. Indeed, in the context of what had gone before it was spectacularly so. The Titanic, if not turned, appeared to have at least been brought to a shuddering halt short of the iceberg. Cllr Austin-Walker emerged from a two-hour session in committee room number five to read an agreed statement to the 100 or so fans who had spent the evening waiting patiently outside.

It said: "The representatives of the board and Greenwich Council expressed their wish for Charlton Athletic to return to the borough at the earliest opportunity. Both sides accept that a return to The Valley does not appear to be a viable proposition. The council and the directors are anxious to explore the possibility of the development of a New Valley stadium at a location in the borough. The council will do all in its power to assist the board in exploring that possibility and agree to reconvene tonight's meeting with representatives of supporters on January 15th to give a progress report."

Recently appointed vice-chairman of the club, Collins took the opportunity to appeal for an end to the boycott of games at Selhurst Park. But that was always a vain hope, since it depended upon the largely erroneous assumption that the absent fans were motivated by politics and not convenience. And to many it seemed that it was only the low gates which were bringing Charlton back to the negotiating table. As for the acceptance that The Valley was now a dead duck, that was very far from the case. A return there was exactly what most people were seeking, while a new ground seemed a remote and fantastic possibility.

Nonetheless, with a dispute over the outstanding years of the lease on The Valley still pending but apparently no nearer coming to court, it was towards the building of a new stadium elsewhere in the borough that everyone, including the *Mercury*, now turned their attention. Even before the town hall meeting, Cordwell had announced the launch of a trust fund with the hugely ambitious target of raising £1m towards a new ground. The council, claimed the sports editor, was hinting heavily that it would match any sum that was contributed.

Unfortunately, the idea was flawed by a serious credibility problem. In order to be persuaded to donate, people had to believe that raising the necessary money was a realistic ambition. And in order to persuade them of that, the paper clearly had to demonstrate that the cash was indeed coming in. It was a classic Catch 22 situation. But even if that could have been overcome, the £1m target would have required every signatory to the Valley petition to contribute an average of £67, which was optimistic to say the least, given that not all of them were Charlton supporters.

In the end, the fund would raise the paltry sum of £5,800, despite a plethora of fundraising initiatives which at least gave fans the satisfaction of doing something constructive about the club's situation. Four supporters – Billy King, Mark Andrews, Ken Swain and Ian McLaren – completed a sponsored walk from The Valley to the

The fans who walked to Southampton to raise funds for the Mercury Trust Fund

away match at Southampton. Deptford punk Paul "Gonad" Harley organised a concert at the Tramshed Theatre in Woolwich which was wrecked, bizarrely, by a fight between rival generations of Charlton hooligans. And there were numerous other sponsored events, all well-meant but unfortunately with little impact.

For whatever small chance the trust fund might have had was destroyed by the subsequent lack of developments between club and council. The meeting promised for January 15th was postponed, allegedly because negotiations had reached a delicate stage, although no one even bothered to tell Treadgold, who found out by accident the previous day. Despite talk of rearranging it for a few weeks later, it would never take place. From the council, there was only embarrassed silence, while the club simply deflected all enquiries in the former's direction. And, incredibly, once again the issue seemed to slip off the agenda.

Charlton, meanwhile, had even more pressing worries on the field, where their six straight wins in October had been followed by the same number of consecutive defeats in November. Bolder had come into the team for the first time after Johns was taken out by Mark Falco in a 4-1 defeat at Watford, but he had a nightmare debut at Maine Road, gifting Manchester City their winning goal as Charlton lost 2-1. Three days later he started his second game by conceding an own goal from Peake as the team went out of the Littlewoods Cup at Highbury. Johns duly returned but in the very next game was sent off for committing a professional foul in the 3-1 home defeat by Southampton. Thereafter Bolder never looked back, and was even voted player of the year.

When the first three games of December all ended in draws, fans began to wonder if the team was aiming to set some kind of record. The last of these, and the most creditable, was a goalless encounter with mighty Liverpool on the Saturday before Christmas. Charlton might just have sneaked it, too, had Lee not been forced to go off on the hour with a twisted ankle. Steve Thompson having already been replaced at half-time after colliding with a temporary advertising hoarding, the home side were obliged to complete the game with ten men. Memorable it certainly was, although not quite to the extent suggested by the sub-editor at the *Today* newspaper, who added the strap "Ten men hold Liverpool to historic draw at The Valley" to his paper's match report.

The sequence of results was finally broken on Boxing Day, with a 2-0 defeat at Aston Villa, but two days later Addicks fans got some seasonal cheer in the shape of a 5-0 win over fellow strugglers Manchester City at a wet and muddy Selhurst Park. It was to be Charlton's biggest victory during their stay in the First Division and it also lifted them back off the bottom of the table where they had been deposited 24 hours earlier.

The new year brought their biggest crowd at Sehurst yet, 19,744 for the holiday game with Tottenham Hotspur. It was lost 2-0, but two days later there was much controversy surrounding a 1-1 draw at Norwich. The visitors had gone ahead early in the game through Stuart and when referee David Axcell signalled an equaliser 15 minutes from time it provoked a furious response from the Charlton players, who were convinced that Wayne Biggins' shot had been cleared by Reid before it crossed the line. A pack of them set off after the official, who collided with Reid as he tried to make his escape in the direction of the centre circle. Aizlewood tried to help him to his feet only for the official to black out as he rose, prompting claims from several newspapers that he had been hit.

Fortunately, Axcell later went to great pains to absolve the Charlton players of blame, but as a result of TV evidence Reid was subsequently charged with bringing the game into disrepute. An FA hearing eventually found him not guilty. Ironically, the film also confirmed that the ball had not crossed the line, a view allegedly expressed at the time by Axcell's replacement, linesman Paul Healy, who was unable to overrule the original referee's decision.

The game's drama had not ended there, however, because in the dying seconds Melrose had chipped the ball into the net for what might have been the winner, only to be called back by Healy who had given a free-kick to Charlton for a foul which the Scot had shrugged off en route to goal.

January also brought an early and embarrassing exit from the FA Cup, at the hands of Third Division Walsall. They

The remarkable Ralph Milne

won 2-1 at Selhurst Park despite Stuart's opening goal before a 4,541 crowd, Charlton's lowest in the competition since 3,875 had seen Merthyr Town's visit to The Valley in November 1927. It was followed by the smallest First Division crowd so far that season anywhere, 5,050, for what had looked an attractive visit from Brian Clough's Nottingham Forest.

It was an inauspicious debut for a man who would prove to be one of Lawrence's least auspicious signings. Dundee United right winger Ralph Milne had arrived for £125,000 in midweek looking suspiciously overweight. Departed for Leeds United were promotion heroes John Pearson and Aizlewood for £72,000 and £200,000 respectively. Despite his goalscoring exploits the previous year, Pearson had found it difficult to adjust to the more sophisticated defences of the top flight and had scored only once, an extraordinary effort at West Ham. Welsh international skipper Aizlewood was allegedly sold to raise money for team rebuilding, specifically a striker, but it is likely his frequently outspoken behaviour was also a factor.

Lawrence's plans were immediately wrecked by an injury crisis. Central defender John Pender, a regular member of the promotion team who had missed the start of the season with a long-term injury problem, damaged a knee on his comeback in the 2-0 defeat at Wimbledon. Shirtliff suffered a similar blow in the same game, leaving only Thompson to play in the middle of the defence. The manager's response was to buy Spurs' vastly experienced defender Paul Miller, then 27, for £130,000.

Miller, a director of a company which supplied fresh fruit and vegetables to top London hotels, had appeared at Wembley no less than seven times during his days at White Hart Lane, but he could hardly have expected to return there with Charlton.

Nor could the Addicks fans have anticipated such a twist given the farcical start they had made in their Full Members' Cup campaign. Yet that is exactly what happened.

The turning point came when they survived an impossible looking away draw to Everton by winning a penalty shoot-out after extra-time. Only a single coachload of supporters had bothered to make the trip, yet they were handsomely rewarded when Miller headed a second equaliser in the 72nd minute to make it 2-2 and set up the dramatic finale. It still took 16 penalties to divide the sides, with each missing two of their initial five. Finally, Neil Pointon shot wide and Stuart stepped up to earn an improbable victory and a semi-final contest against Norwich at Selhurst.

That came just seven days later, on March 10th, and the prospect of a Wembley place for the first time since 1947 was enough to lure 5,321 round the South Circular Road. They went home happy, but only just. The 90 minutes were already at an end when Robert Rosario took advantage of a mistake by Bolder to prod the ball into an empty net and apparently seal the match. And yet, somehow, Charlton managed to equalise, Walsh's shot creeping home at the far post with the Norwich defence in hot pursuit. Then, three minutes into extra-time, John Humphrey's 25-yard effort was deflected past keeper Bryan Gunn by Ian Butterworth.

So the Addicks were at Wembley, but Lawrence was quick to stress that although the occasion provided a nice diversion, the game was insignificant compared to the battle to stay in the First Division. It looked at first as if Charlton would have to play their scheduled League match the day before the final, a home fixture against Chelsea. But with the help of Noades, a member of the League management committee, they succeeded in getting it postponed.

Their opponents at Wembley were to be Blackburn Rovers, then enjoying an undistinguished season in the lower reaches of the Second Division. Rovers were another poorly supported team and critics of the Full Members' Cup took the opportunity to predict that an embarrassingly low crowd at Wembley would result in the competition's demise. In the event, they were wrong, although a clear majority of the 40,000 who did turn up came from Blackburn. The Charlton contingent was estimated at just 15,000, but even this was as many Addicks fans as had attended any one match for a decade.

This poor turnout came despite the fact that the event did attract much interest in South East London, where it was the talk of the pubs in the week leading up to the game. One reason, perhaps, why this failed to harden into more substantial backing on the day was the lamentable failure to make tickets available in the proper place. Despite requests, Charlton refused on grounds of security to sell them at the Valley Club, meaning that fans had either to buy them at the midweek fixture with Oxford United, five days earlier, or make an extra awkward and time-consuming journey to Selhurst Park. When the ticket office there opened especially on the Sunday before the match, the club took £30,000 in four hours. Of course, there was nothing to stop supporters paying on the day, or buying tickets direct from Wembley, but there is no doubt that some people were deterred from going and it provided yet another example of the club's incompetence.

Ticket sales were the reason given for another embarrassing incident on the evening of the Oxford game, when Charlton officials failed to announce the attendance, claiming that staff were too busy to work it out. A few miles away at Plough Lane,

Wembley woe, but these Charlton fans looked happy enough before the game

neighbours Wimbledon were playing FA Cup semi-finalists, and eventual winners, Coventry City in front of 4,370. Theirs would have been the lowest First Division crowd since the war, had Charlton not shamefacedly admitted the following day that they had done even worse. The official attendance at Selhurst was just 4,205, and this despite the fact that the evening provided the sole opportunity for most to buy Wembley tickets. Otherwise the Oxford game, a goalless draw, was notable only for the debut appearance of 19-year-old striker Carl Leaburn, as a substitute.

In the event, the Blackburn match was also a forgettable affair, culminating in a late winner scored four minutes from time for the Lancashire side by defender Colin Hendry. But it was, at least, a memorable day out for the fans of both sides, neither of whom could look forward to an early return in a more glamorous competition. It was a fitting reward, too, for players like Thompson, captain for the day in the absence of the injured Shirtliff, and George Shipley, an industrious and popular midfielder now on the transfer list after failing to secure a regular First Division place. No one had really cared who won the trophy, the prize had been the Wembley final and with it a lucrative and welcome cash bonus. Afterwards, the Charlton party drowned their sorrows at the White Elephant Club, which seemed to many highly appropriate.

In the aftermath, however, there was a sense of anti-climax in the air, not only because of the result but due also to the extent to which the Charlton fans had been outnumbered. And everyone was now only too aware how vulnerable the club would be if relegation to the Second Division became a reality in the remaining nine games

The first Charlton team to appear at Wembley for 40 years pose for the camera

of the season. The position was further complicated by the League's decision to reduce the size of the top flight to 20 sides. It meant that as well as the usual three relegation places, the side finishing fourth from bottom would go into a knock-out play-off competition with the teams finishing third, fourth and fifth in Division Two.

Predictably, Charlton's 4-3 win over Watford the following week, in which the long-serving Steve Gritt powered home his first Divison One goal, left them occupying just that controversial 19th spot. It was always on the cards that this was where they would finish. Before that, however, they tested the faith of their followers almost to the limit. In three consecutive London derbies, all difficult games admittedly, they collected only a single point, drawing 0-0 with Chelsea before unluckily succumbing at Highbury and then White Hart Lane.

Before the Chelsea game, Arnie Warren, the chief scout, took over as general manager, replacing the short-lived Shaw who had arrived from Millwall earlier in the season and now quit over a "difference of opinion". Anne Payne, from the office staff, stepped up to club secretary. Director Jimmy Hill, meanwhile, had departed for his first love Fulham, who had developed ground problems of their own. Charlton fans had found it richly ironic that he now seemed so keen to keep his old club at Craven Cottage when he had apparently done nothing to keep theirs at The Valley. "He came, he saw, he concurred," remarked Cordwell in the *Mercury*.

Just as Melrose had been a late signing the previous year, so Lawrence again secured a striker for the final run-in. This time it was the 29-year-old former

Battle for The Valley

Jim Melrose almost leaps out of frame to score the first goal at Southampton

Tottenham and Stoke City forward Garth Crooks, for whom he paid West Bromwich Albion £75,000 on transfer-deadline day, allegedly on the back of the Members' Cup run. Crooks had been cup-tied for the final and suspended for the Watford game, but had made his debut as a second-half substitute against Chelsea. His first full appearance came in the vital home game with fellow strugglers Aston Villa on Easter Monday morning after he had missed the trip to his former club, Spurs, suffering from the after-effects of flu.

The Villa game was crucial to both sides, with Charlton now in 20th place, five points behind Leicester and six adrift of 18th-placed Oxford, two clubs who would meet on the last day of the season. Both the Addicks and Villa, who were one point further behind, had to win if they were to keep their respective hopes alive. In the event, it was a task Charlton managed comfortably, all the goals in their 3-0 victory arriving by two minutes after the interval.

Southampton were the next opponents, with the intrepid walkers duly arriving in time to see Melrose shoot Charlton into a half-time lead. But the afternoon seemed set to turn sour with 20 minutes left when Humphrey, normally the embodiment of professionalism, was sent off for protesting too vehemently to the linesman about the legality or otherwise of Kevin Bond's equaliser. Within five minutes, George Lawrence's shot had been deflected past Bolder and the visitors were behind. Fortunately, Lee popped up to put Charlton level again and a precious point was saved. Now they were two behind Leicester and four adrift of Oxford with three games to play.

Then came disaster. An innocuous-looking home fixture with Luton, which Charlton had dominated, ended with Bolder picking the ball out of the net after a soft breakaway goal from Mick Harford four minutes from time. The only consolation was that fellow strugglers Leicester and Oxford had also lost. But it meant that Charlton had to travel to Newcastle United needing points to secure their chance of making the play-offs by winning the final match of the season.

Deprived of Melrose by a viral infection, Lawrence had raged at the ineptitude of his forwards in the Luton match. He had sent on young Leaburn and now for the first time selected him in the starting line-up at St James' Park. It paid off, too, when the leggy striker stooped to score his first League goal, from Walsh's cross just after the hour. By then, however, both Miller and Crooks had also scored their opening goals for the club, so it completed some kind of hat-trick. The real hero of the afternoon was little Shipley, playing for the first and only time on the ground of his heroes and savouring every minute.

Charlton might yet have escaped the torment of the play-offs had Oxford not emerged 3-2 winners of a bizarre game at Kenilworth Road the next evening. Playing on the Hatters' artificial pitch and supposedly without any support due to the home club's away-fan ban, Oxford built up a 2-0 lead, only to see it clawed back in the closing stages. But in the dying seconds they broke away to score the winner. In the process, they extinguished the Addicks' last hope of conventional survival.

Now on 41 points from 41 matches, Charlton went into their home game with QPR in possession of the vital 19th place, thanks to the superiority of their goal difference over that of Leicester. Aston Villa were already down, but the picture was complicated by the deathbed revival of Manchester City, who had previously been bottom. Their only chance, however, was if both Charlton and Leicester lost and they won at Upton Park. In the event, they lost 2-0.

Rangers, with only one win in their previous 11 games and 11 goals conceded in the last two, looked ideal visitors, and so it proved. Charlton took the lead just before half-time through a Walsh penalty, awarded for handball against Alan McDonald. It came just seconds after an equally plausible appeal against Miller at the other end and incredibly it was the Addicks' first League spot-kick of the season, and thus their first in the top flight since 1956.

When Crooks turned in Reid's cross eight minutes into the second half, it should have been all over. But instead Charlton dissolved in a jelly-legged panic that all but threw the game away after Leroy Rosenior had headed Rangers back into contention five minutes later. How Robbie James failed to equalise in the dying seconds when the ball landed at his feet four yards out is a mystery he will take to the grave. However, as it turned out it didn't matter, because Leicester had only drawn anyway.

And so to the play-offs, as every Charlton fan had half-suspected would happen ever since the decision to hold them had been taken. Competing with them for their First Division place would be Oldham Athletic, Leeds and Ipswich Town, who had respectively finished third, fourth and fifth in the Second Division. "I'll stick my neck out and say it's down to us and Leeds," predicted Lawrence. "Some things are meant to be."

He was right. Ipswich were to provide stiff semi-final opposition at Portman Road after Walsh had squandered Charlton's second penalty kick in consecutive matches, in the tenth minute, but the game ended goalless. In the second leg, Melrose killed them off with two quick headers midway through the first half. The tannoy had already given details of the next phase by the time Steve McCall grabbed a late consolation five minutes from the end. Leeds had won their first play-off match 1-0 at Elland Road but trailed 2-1 at the end of 90 minutes in the return on the Boundary Park plastic, forcing the game into extra-time. There was no further score and they qualified on the away goals rule, despite having finished seven points behind Oldham in the League.

So the stage was set for the big showdown, with the added spice of Pearson and Aizlewood returning to play against their former club. Once again Charlton demonstrated their naivety by predicting a Selhurst crowd of 30,000, despite an all-ticket requirement imposed to control the Yorkshire club's infamous hooligan following. The game was originally due to take place on the Friday night, but had to be moved to Saturday afternoon to accommodate late-night shopping at Sainsbury's. At least this time tickets were sold at the Valley Club. In the event, however, the attendance was just 16,680, and half of them were visitors.

No one had ever doubted that the matches would be close, and so it proved. Leeds had been handed an advantage – unreasonably given the clubs' relative League positions, thought Lawrence – by playing the first match away and they meant to benefit from it. Charlton battled well, but they had to wait until the dying minutes for the first-leg lead they craved. Only three remained when Walsh sent in a quick free-kick from the left and the inevitable Melrose popped up unmarked to head the ball past Mervyn Day and silence the hordes behind the Holmesdale Road end goal.

But was it enough to take into the Elland Road cauldron, where 30,000 fanatical fans would surely create an intimidating wall of noise? It was, but only just. Charlton needed all the composure and experience they had gained in their season among the elite and for this reason had cause to be grateful that Shirtliff, who had missed the previous four games, recovered to take his place in the defence alongside Miller. Indeed, it was the skipper, always willing to try his luck up front, who clipped the bar with a header in the first five minutes as Charlton attempted to catch Leeds cold.

So much was at stake for both clubs, Leeds having been out of the First Division

Peter Shirtliff is first to the ball for the vital second goal at St Andrews

since 1982, that it was never going to be a contest for the purists. More than once the challenges bordered on the vicious and as guilty as anyone was Aizlewood, booked at Selhurst for poleaxing Stuart. He earned his third caution of the play-offs with an assault on Peake.

It was Aizlewood who set up the goal which put the Yorkshire club level on aggregate eight minutes after half-time. Receiving a short corner from John Sheridan, his shot hit Shirtliff and was scrambled goalwards by Bob Taylor with Brendan Ormsby arriving to apply the final touch as the ball rolled into a vacant net in front of an exultant Kop. But try as they might, Leeds could not breach the visiting defence again. It meant a replay, at neutral St Andrews on Friday night, May 29th, and a record-breaking 57th game of the season for Charlton.

Lawrence could afford to feel satisfied with this outcome, for anywhere was better than Elland Road, but at Birmingham, too, Addicks fans would be vastly outnumbered. Less than 2,000 had made the intimidating trip to Leeds and not that many more were willing to brave the less remote but still hostile atmosphere. No local fans were given tickets, restricting the crowd to 18,000, but as the dozen Charlton coaches neared the ground, many of the natives still took the opportunity to wave their support.

Thanks to the police, however, the passengers on those coaches almost missed the kick-off. Although they reached the city in good time, the 400-strong West Midlands officers on duty were anxious to retain control of the streets around the ground and kept them waiting a mile away until just minutes before the start. The result was much bad feeling and a furious dash to get through the turnstiles before the beginning of the game.

Again, there was little to divide the teams. This time the aggression was more controlled despite an ugly fracas in the penalty area when Ian Baird went in too hard on Bolder and was brought to account by Shirtliff. Aizlewood was booked yet again, but this time it was for handball. The press had unanimously judged Charlton to be ahead on points over the first two games, and now did so again. Unfortunately, the method of settling the contest if it remained level after extra-time was somewhat less reasonable than an appeal to the journalists present. Anxious to see an end to the season, the League had sanctioned the lottery of a penalty shoot-out, an absurd way to resolve nine months' endeavour.

Lawrence had called the prospect nonsense but it loomed into view nonetheless when the 90 minutes ended without a goal and barely a clear-cut chance. Then Miller was harshly judged to have handled the ball 25 yards out. As the fans behind the other goal looked on in horror, free-kick expert Sheridan stepped up to drive the ball superbly over the wall and into the top right-hand corner of the net. Suddenly, a great chasm had opened underneath Charlton Athletic, a drop much deeper than just relegation to the Second Division and perhaps into oblivion.

Still the minutes ticked away on the giant clock at the far end of the stadium and now there were only seven left to play. The Leeds fans began to celebrate promotion, but they were hopelessly premature. A Charlton free-kick found the veteran Gritt out on the wing and his cross the feet of Stuart, inside the Leeds penalty area. With defenders blocking his way, he simply laid the ball back into the path of Shirtliff, the man whose hour had come. Clinically, the skipper sidefooted it out of Day's reach and into the corner of the net.

Behind the far goal it was the Charlton fans' turn to rejoice, but it was the hush that fell over the Leeds followers which was more dramatic. Even now the penalties beckoned, but Shirtliff had other ideas. Never before in his career had he scored twice in a match. Yet with three minutes left, Gritt dummied a free-kick, Walsh back-heeled and Peake curled in a cross that the Yorkshireman stooped low to reach before Aizlewood. Leeds were behind, their spirit was broken and incredibly, impossibly, Charlton were safe.

Unquestionably, that second goal, a move rehearsed on the training ground 24 hours earlier by coach Brian Eastick, was the most important to the club since Chris Duffy's winner in the 1947 FA Cup final. It sparked a flamboyant gesture of delight from Bolder at the final whistle and wild celebrations among the travelling fans, who were hardly able to believe what they had seen. It was as if the team had been relegated and promoted again all in the space of 20 minutes.

Though dramatic, it was not enough to call it luck. It was more than that, an achievement made possible by the great character within the team and a tribute to the spirit built up by Lawrence. Most important of all, it meant that the club had once again escaped the nightmare prospect of Second Division football at Selhurst Park.

Chapter Seven

"These people don't deserve football at all in my opinion."
Bill Treadgold – *Mercury (January 1988)*

The historic borough of Greenwich had always boasted more than its fair share of tourist attractions but it had little cause to be proud of the latest addition. By the summer of 1987, The Valley had lain abandoned and untouched for almost two years, save for the attentions of vandals and local children. Its future remained shrouded in the mystery of Charlton's departure. Allegedly, there was a legal dispute between Michael Gliksten and the club over the outstanding years of their lease. Charlton argued that they had not been aware of defects in the crush barriers when they accepted the deal at short notice in 1984, even though Richard Collins, a chartered surveyor, had then been on the board for nearly three years. But none of the arguments were ever tested in court.

Meanwhile, the old stadium was falling gradually into dereliction. Possibly, had a bulldozer done its work in those hopeless days, the campaign to return there would have ebbed away. But instead The Valley simply became overgrown and increasingly littered with debris. The area in front of the old Harvey Gardens turnstiles had become a popular local rubbish dump while inside the ground large numbers of programmes and other papers, some of them valuable memorabilia, had been abandoned by the club in the hasty departure. Many of these were looted by souvenir hunters, who

The abandoned Covered End at The Valley, damaged by the 1987 hurricane

Battle for The Valley

gained access by prising open the clumsily nailed-up turnstile doors.

Children played daily in the now wrecked house on the corner of Floyd Road which had been the club offices. However, the building most vulnerable to the vandals was the wooden-floored main stand and it was repeatedly attacked by arsonists. The other two stands were more sturdy structures, but in the autumn of 1987 southern England was hit by a freak hurricane, the most violent storm in living memory, and minor damage was done to the corrugated roof of the half-century old Covered End, leaving several gaping holes. Ironically, the fierce winds which felled so many ancient trees elsewhere otherwise served only to flatten the towering weeds which had previously flourished undisturbed on the neglected pitch and the slopes of the East Terrace.

Throughout that year, there were enduring and persistent rumours that Charlton would return. Hundreds made the tearful pilgrimage to The Valley hoping against hope for some telling indication that the stories were true. There were repeated claims that parts of the pitch had been mown, tales of men in suits inspecting the site and reports of exploratory test bores having been sunk.

In August, as the new season loomed, Peter Cordwell took the decision to close the book on the Mercury Trust Fund. Incredibly, neither the club nor the council had anything to add, it seemed, to their meeting with fans the previous November. However, others had plenty to say on the continuing silence and among the suggestions was the establishment of a rival supporters' club. The idea came from Ian McLaren, one of the four fans who had walked to Southampton in the spring.

"In almost two years nothing has been done," he wrote. "And I dare say in four years the same situation will prevail. Is the supporters' club going to become solely

Weeds were left to take over the terraces at the deserted Valley

used for functions and travel? If we wanted that in a supporters' club we would travel by British Rail. As far as I can see there is no difference between the two organisations. No wonder us fans feel let down. Why don't we set up our own supporters' club? The competition would be good for them."

In fact, the more militant wing of the existing supporters' club had begun to lose patience itself. Secretary Roy King had strongly attacked the board in the final newsletter of the previous season. "Never before can a football club have been run in such secrecy and shown such disregard for its supporters," he complained. In the absence of firm information, a strong rumour had circulated that the Addicks would move across the Thames to Orient for the 1987/88 season. Finally, the story was denied, not by the Charlton directors at all, but by Palace's Ron Noades.

Yet in spite of the apparent lack of activity, the summer of 1987 saw developments of singular significance, even if their import was not fully recognised at the time. Shortly after the play-off victory at Birmingham, John Fryer, now in increasingly ill health, stood down as chairman in favour of Richard Collins and became joint president with his business partner John Sunley. More importantly, the board was strengthened by the addition of wealthy supporter Roger Alwen, who was strongly rumoured to have become involved on the basis that Charlton endeavoured to return to The Valley.

Writing in the first issue of the supporters' club newsletter for the new season, director Derek Ufton remarked that in spite of the changes "Sunley Holdings will remain the major shareholders in the club". It was little noted at the time, but thus far they had been the sole shareholders; a progressive handover of control was therefore under way. Significantly, in view of what happened the following year, the date of the changes was June 1st.

Alwen, a Lloyds broker and farmer, had been a fan since 1949 and was already a member of the vice-presidents' club, an elite group which paid for the privilege of special facilities on matchdays. But he had been introduced to the Charlton directors as recently as the previous February when a guest of the Coventry City chairman John Poynton for the away match at Highfield Road. His arrival signalled the investment of £200,000 in a new midfield player, West Bromwich Albion's Steve MacKenzie.

Rather better value for money was the acquisition of the club's 18-acre training ground of the previous two years, the Aries Sports Ground in Sparrows Lane, New Eltham, for £250,000. Just over three miles as the crow flies from The Valley and adjacent to Adelong's Valley Leisure, it was now lavishly refurbished at the expense of a similar sum and justly earned a reputation as the best in the League, a novel distinction for anything connected with Charlton.

Not only did the training ground provide splendid facilities which could be used as bait to attract promising youngsters, but it at last provided the club with a base in the borough of Greenwich. Theories that it could one day be developed into a new stadium were soon quashed, however. Clearly, no such planning permission would ever be granted for the site; its green status was protected by planning guidelines and in any case access was grossly inadequate. Notably, too, the ownership remained with the purchasers, Alwen and Michael Norris, and not with the football club, which was instead granted a lease at a peppercorn rent.

Colin Moynihan tries out the facilities at the New Eltham training ground, watched by John Fryer, John Austin-Walker, Richard Collins and Roger Alwen

Renamed, rather obviously, the Charlton Athletic Training Ground, it was opened by sports minister, Lewisham East MP and Charlton fan Colin Moynihan on October 4th. Despite early showers the weather held off to attract a curious crowd of around 3,000. It was an impressive public relations exercise, particularly from a club which had treated its supporters so badly in the recent past, and was to prove another sign that things were changing. A few fans even wrote to the *Mercury* urging the release of the trust fund money on the strength of it, but not everyone was quite so easily impressed. Kevin Nolan commented sardonically of the children who mingled with their Saturday afternoon heroes: "Some of them were too young to realise that elsewhere in the borough of Greenwich is another football ground – dilapidated, neglected, vandalised but home, always home, to their dads and a forgotten army of fans."

Back on the foreign field, Charlton's second season in the First Division had not begun well. The team won only once and drew three times in their opening 13 games, being pinned to the foot of the 21-club table as a result. The only highlight came, improbably enough, at Anfield, where Charlton twice led the eventual champions, with goals from Garth Crooks and Colin Walsh, before eventually succumbing 3-2. New signing MacKenzie, whose £250,000 move from Palace to Manchester City as a 17-year-old prior to his League debut had made headlines in 1979, struggled to make an impact on his return to Selhurst Park and became the focus of the crowd's frustration.

But the side's more obvious deficiency was a goalscorer. Jim Melrose had netted 17 times the previous season but had been obliged to commute weekly from his home in Macclesfield because he could not afford to move south. Lennie Lawrence was unwilling to let that situation continue, and Melrose played only three times at the start of the new campaign before falling victim to an ear infection and eventually departing for Leeds in a £50,000 deal. Ironically, the man who would prove the solution to the problem made his debut in the game that marked Melrose's last appearance, at Plough Lane. He was 22-year-old Paul Williams, a £12,000 signing from non-League Woodford Town the previous season, who announced his arrival by hitting the Wimbledon post with his first touch.

In the meantime, however, Lawrence was looking to make a big-money signing and lined up former Spurs striker Mark Falco, then enjoying a brief spell with Glasgow Rangers, only for the deal to collapse because the Addicks could not afford his terms. Instead, the Charlton boss turned his attention to the Third Division's leading scorer.

Port Vale's Andy Jones signed in September for a club record fee of £350,000 after an impressive performance for Wales in a European Championship qualifier against Denmark at Ninian Park. He had scored 35 goals for the Potteries side in 1986/87 but was not to prove one of Lawrence's better buys, struggling to adapt to the pace of the First Division. He took until his fifth game, at Oxford United, to open his account, even if he did then score four times in the next six matches.

In November, defender Paul Miller, who had been at the club only nine months, was placed on the transfer list at his own request after being left out of the team. Three weeks later he was substituted in a reserve match at Reading and disciplined after swearing at coach Colin Clarke.

More woe arrived in the form of a serious injury to influential Scottish midfielder Walsh who for no apparent reason was pelted with coins, cans and bottles by Newcastle United fans as he lay prostrate in front of the Gallowgate End at St James' Park with a broken left leg.

Despite Jones' welcome goals, it was not until December and a controversial 1-0 win on a Sunday morning at White Hart Lane that Charlton began to revive. It was only their third success of the season

Andy Jones, a £350,000 record signing

Stretcher case: physiotherapist Jimmy Hendry examines Colin Walsh's leg

and came courtesy of a late goal from Northern Ireland midfielder David Campbell, signed for £75,000 from Nottingham Forest in October, after the lively Williams had nipped in to prevent Tony Parks from gathering the ball. The tackle left the unfortunate Spurs keeper with a cut lip and two broken teeth, and his manager Terry Venables fuming, but in fact it was simply a typical example of the little striker, recalled from a very successful loan spell at Brentford, using his lightning pace to good effect. Despite the disputed nature of the goal, Williams had already hit the inside of the post and Charlton fully deserved their first win on the ground for 32 years.

Part of the credit for the team's revival belonged to new coach Mike Flanagan, who had returned to the club at the beginning of October. Almost immediately, Brian Eastick left to take over as manager at Fourth Division strugglers Newport County. Although in charge of the reserves, Eastick had also worked with the first team and now, doubtless, saw his opportunities at Charlton as limited.

Whether it was due to the fact that they were bottom of the First Division, or whether some of the excitement of that debut season back among the elite had worn off, the club's attendances were even worse than the previous year. A week before the Spurs game, the visit of League champions Everton brought in just 7,208, a drop of nearly a third on the corresponding fixture in 1986/87.

Lawrence's future had been brought into doubt in early November when he refused to sign a new, three-year contract surprisingly offered to him by the Charlton directors as a token of their confidence. The failure to accept it prompted speculation that he might be thinking of leaving, but he soon explained that he simply didn't want to burden the club with such a commitment if he was unable to improve the team's fortunes. Another offshoot was a freesheet story to the effect that Charlton were about to replace him with sacked Spurs manager David Pleat, a claim which was strenuously denied.

Prior to the Everton game, Charlton took the unusual step of issuing a statement at the turnstiles denying a Kevin Moseley report in the *Daily Express* that the club was about to go under. Scrutiny of the annual accounts had revealed a paper debt of £2.2m to Sunley Holdings, accumulated since the rescue in 1984. But for tax credits, it would have reached £3m and the debt had grown by £750,000 the previous year. And that was despite an apparently modest wage bill, by First Division standards, which included just £40,000 for Lennie Lawrence and sums of between £30,000-35,000 for seven players.

In this depressing situation, fans were ready to clutch at any available straw and one had duly been offered by Moseley, a supporter himself, at the end of October under the headline "Charlton look to The Valley again". In the story he reported, accurately as it was to prove, that meetings had been held with Gliksten and that Alwen and Norris would soon emerge as kingpins of a revitalised club.

Two other clues to the future came in further newspaper articles around the same time. The *Mercury* carried a similar piece the same week headed "Valley rumours are hotly denied" reporting contact with a source describing itself as "high up at Selhurst Park". But the claims were "categorically and vehemently denied" by Norris, who added: "It's just ridiculous." Finally, the briefly revived *London Evening News* carried a short piece apparently rebutting hopes of a return to The Valley but containing an extraordinary quote from Alwen that: "If it doesn't happen in the next two years, it seems pretty certain it won't happen at all." He went on to say that at present the money to return to The Valley wasn't available. It was significant, however, because for the very first time a Charlton director was openly talking about the possibility of a return there and not to another site.

In November, relations between the board and the supporters' club reached an all-time low following some blistering criticism in *Valiants' Viewpoint*, as the latter's newsletter was to become known. Ironically, the several causes of the row were nothing to do with the ground situation at all. The first was a well-merited but dangerously libellous attack on the quality of the Charlton programme and the apparent lack of care and imagination with which it was compiled. The second was a piece criticising the lack of press coverage of the pre-season tour of Sweden, which erroneously lambasted the club's press officer Peter

New director Roger Alwen

The derelict main stand at The Valley, which was looted by supporters

Burrowes, the former sports editor of the defunct *Kentish Independent*. The third was the publication of an old bonus contract found among the debris at The Valley, which in fact referred to the promotion season.

In the first two cases, Burrowes, who was also the programme editor and a familiar figure around the club, started proceedings for defamation. The supporters' club officials took legal advice and were told that as far as their comments on the programme went they would probably win the case but that it wasn't worth the risk of defending it. On the subject of the Swedish tour, the article had simply been wrong in asserting that Burrowes had been among the party. Eventually, these two matters were resolved to mutual satisfaction by a small supporters' club donation to the Charlton youth team.

In the furore over the bonus contract, the football club had only itself to blame. If they chose to leave confidential documents lying around the derelict ground, they could hardly complain if they were recovered by inquisitive trespassers. Naturally the directors didn't see it that way, however, and they sought to punish Steve Dixon, whom they had correctly identified as a future thorn in their side. They now demanded his removal from the supporters' club committee and a ban on him writing for the newsletter, as well as the right to vet future issues before they were printed. Unfortunately for the board, in this case the offending articles had been written by CASC secretary King, who was the editor, and chairman Bill Treadgold, while the bonus contract was the former's discovery. They were simply barking up the wrong tree in pursuing Dixon, although typically they refused to accept this.

The row was essentially ridiculous, but it brought into sharp focus the fact that the supporters' club would never be free to articulate the fans' grievances fully. And fuelled by fear of what might happen if Charlton were relegated, it finally prompted me to take the plunge and launch a publication of my own.

Then working for a particularly idle section of the Home Office, I had watched the growth of the *Viewpoint* with a great deal of interest. In fact, it had done much to rehabilitate the image of the supporters' club among the dissidents, although it did not really represent the views of the CASC committee, who even under the latest provocation meekly buckled down to submit their articles for approval. Now its limitations had been made obvious, it was time to break new ground with a publication that would exist beyond the punishment of the directors, namely an independent fanzine.

The project upon which I was to embark was by no means unique. All over the country in the opening months of 1988, fans were reaching for their word processors. Some of the most famous fanzine titles such as the *Fingerpost* at West Bromwich Albion, *City Gent* at Bradford City, *The Pie* at Notts County and *Terrace Talk* at York City were well-established and the national giant *Off The Ball* and its then lesser rival *When Saturday Comes* were already widely read. *Eagle Eye*, for Crystal Palace, and *The Lion Roars*, at Millwall, first saw the light of day almost simultaneously with my own effort.

These new, cheaply-produced magazines had been anticipated more than a decade earlier by *Foul*, a general football publication which had tackled some of the issues of the day with an irreverence quite revolutionary for its time. Modelled on the successful music fanzines and exploiting the vogue for alternative comedy, epitomised by the hugely successful adult comic *Viz*, the new wave of football fanzines varied enormously in style, taste and content. Their common feature was an undying commitment to club or game and its traditions, and an unfocused but implicit loyalty to the political left and its values. Thus many were in the vanguard of grass-roots movements to stamp out racism and hooliganism on the terraces and most were extremely hostile to the Thatcher government, particularly when it was perceived to be attacking the game.

Many of the fanzines were essentially frivolous publications but others reflected the growth of consumer power in society. Football fans had traditionally been treated shabbily over facilities and accommodation, but the modern emphasis on the executive supporter had created an almost Victorian class division between rich and poor fans. At the same time, the sport's hierarchy had sought more and more ways to increase their earnings from a diminished customer base, with the multiplicity of unpopular cup competitions the obvious example. After the disaster at Heysel Stadium in 1985, Liverpool fans set up the Football Supporters' Association in an attempt to reclaim control of the game. Although worthy, the organisation never caught the public imagination to any extent and thus failed to achieve the mass membership it sought, but its aims were largely shared by the proliferating fanzines, which often publicised its activities.

Initially bewildered, some clubs enlisted the help of the police to prevent the sale of fanzines outside their grounds. In one case, at Brighton & Hove Albion, the editors were successfully pursued through the courts for defamation. Only a few clubs were openly supportive and most seemed simply to hope that the magazines would go away if ignored. It was soon obvious, however, that they would be an enduring phenomenon. By 1991, only a handful of titles had disappeared and, although the boom was certainly over, new ones were still appearing by the month.

I had some experience of such samizdat publications from my schooldays, not so many years earlier, when I'd edited a highly popular, although with hindsight embarrassingly juvenile, underground newsletter. Casting around for a name for the new publication, I at first – and only half-seriously – came up with *Left In The Dark*, in honour of the club's notorious secrecy and the two Selhurst floodlight failures, and was surprised when one contributor to the first issue remarked that it smacked of political bias. Suitably chastened, I plumped instead for *Voice of The Valley*.

There were to be all kinds of ironies in this selection. The original Voice of The Valley had been Charlton's venerable tannoy announcer of 27 years' service, Dick Neve, who died during the winding-up crisis of 1984. Neve had also served for many years as a Labour councillor and had in fact been Mayor of Greenwich in the mid-1970s, making it all the more ironic that a magazine which shared his nickname would later be drawn into a direct conflict between club and council. The Valley dispute would have undoubtedly troubled him deeply had he survived to witness it. Later, I was to meet a member of the Neve family who seemed, to my relief, rather pleased at the continuation of the title.

The magazine's name was also to upset Norris greatly, although I have to say this caused me rather less disquiet. In any case, I suspect that he soon became rather more concerned with its contents.

Going down? Mark Stuart tripped by Newcastle's David McCreery in November

In order to attract contributions for the first issue, I wrote to all the local press seeking publicity. Only two of the four papers obliged, the *Mercury*, inevitably, and the *Croydon Advertiser*. Much to my surprise, the letter published in the *Advertiser* generated an equal response to the piece in the *Mercury*. The result was 16 pages of clumsily-typed copy which I produced over the Christmas holiday. This did not meet with the printers' approval, however, so I took it to work and produced a word-processed version. In fact, I was to spend an increasing part of my supposed hours of employment preparing issues of the *Voice* over the following months. It was therefore fortunate in the extreme that I happened to have a job where work was only an occasional diversion from games of pool with an equally redundant colleague from the floor below.

That first issue bears little resemblance to those produced subsequently. It contained no pictures and was somewhat anarchic in content. Yet in putting it together, I had one flash of inspiration. It was to steal from Dixon, whom I had yet to meet, the idea of promoting a mass boycott of the Selhurst fixture with Oxford. Ever since Charlton had moved, there had been advocates of this kind of protest, but the difficulty of mobilising such a diverse group of people as a football crowd behind an idea that would require strict discipline had always prevented it happening. Nonetheless, Dixon had finally made the suggestion publicly in the December issue of the *Viewpoint* after studying the responses to a questionnaire issued the previous month. It struck a chord with me and I determined to steal it. Cordwell, of course, loved the idea and plastered the news across the back page of the *Mercury*. Thus the *Voice* gained its launch publicity and by no means incidentally we had injected some urgency back into the campaign once again.

From the moment that fellow supporter Steve Archer and I walked down the special train carrying us to Nottingham Forest that January afternoon selling the first *VOTV*, life would never be quite the same again. If memory serves, there were about 130 people on the train and we sold more copies than there were travellers. Only one man refused to buy it and he later became one of its most enthusiastic readers.

By then I had made the acquaintance of Dixon, ironically enough courtesy of a Palace fan, *Eagle Eye* editor John Ellis, who had invited us both to a Football Supporters' Association London branch committee meeting to discuss Charlton's predicament. In many ways Dixon and I could hardly have had less in common. I was working class, a trade-union activist, a Labour Party supporter and university-educated. He was none of these. But fortunately we held near-identical views about what needed to be done, even if he was more pessimistic than I was about the apathetic nature of Charlton supporters.

The response to *VOTV* proved to both our satisfaction that I had been right, and days after the Forest game we held the first of many discussion meetings in a Bexleyheath pub. Many of the dozen or so people who attended that first evening soon disappeared. Others came in after they had read the debut issue. But the inner circle quickly hardened into a committed handful who would stay with the magazine over the next few years. Their role was a vital one, even if they eventually ceased to be fellow conspirators and became instead simply unpaid matchday sellers. We soon decided to set up a rival Valley Supporters' Club for subscribers to the magazine, although it never really existed in more than name.

Even with the generous financial assistance of Neil Bellers, a supporter from Grove Park who had answered my appeal for written contributions with a cheque for £50, I had printed only 500 copies of that modest first issue. Sportspages bookshop in the Charing Cross Road, by then well on its way to becoming a mecca for the fanzine world and the new, alternative football culture, was eventually to sell 400 on its own, so an early reprint was an urgent requirement. I made my hesitant selling debut at Selhurst on a wet and windy Saturday afternoon outside Sainsbury's.

In view of the content of the magazine, the occasion could hardly have been less appropriate. It was the day of Liverpool's visit, unbeaten in the First Division and at the height of their form. The game drew a crowd extraordinary in the context of Charlton's others that season, no less than 28,095. It was comfortably the biggest since the club had left The Valley.

Officially, Charlton made no comment on the emergence of this new voice in their affairs or on the proposed boycott. From the club's perspective this was surely the correct response, because to condemn it would only have conferred credibility, although Lawrence did remark on Radio 2 that it was the last thing the players needed in the present situation.

Predictably, much stronger condemnation came from the supporters' club, with Treadgold fuming: "This boycott idea is a load of bloody rubbish. These people don't deserve football at all in my opinion. The team is in danger of relegation and needs support more than ever, not this kind of action. We support a team, not a ground. As far as I'm concerned, the boycott will get no backing whatsoever from the supporters' club."

Dixon had warned from the outset that it would be impossible to persuade the supporters' club committee to lend its backing, but he tried nonetheless. Of the officers, only social secretary Barry Nugent, a postman and Selhurst Park steward, was prepared to support him. I had anticipated that Steve would now come over to *VOTV*, but instead he chose to remain a contributor to the *Viewpoint*. This proved to be short-lived, however, because the CASC committee refused to publish several of the articles he submitted for its next edition. As well as rejecting those supporting the boycott, they also took exception to one criticising the post of sports minister, on the feeble basis that the present incumbent, Moynihan, was a friend of a Charlton director. Ironically, all the offending pieces had been seen by Derek Ufton, who had raised no objection, and the only effect of CASC's refusal to print them was that they reached a much wider audience through appearing in the second Voice.

The *Viewpoint* duly appeared, minus Dixon's offending articles but containing much condemnation of the boycott. A particularly facile contribution came from committee member Malcolm Gentry. "I can put up with going to Selhurst every other week if it means the chance to go to Old Trafford, Anfield, Goodison Park etc," he wrote, apparently oblivious to the fact that it was Charlton's tenancy of Selhurst Park which made it an absolute certainty that his visits to such illustrious venues would shortly be curtailed.

His was not the reaction we were getting on the terraces. There we found strong support for the boycott, stronger indeed than we had dared believe possible. The distribution of a leaflet at the next home game, against Wimbledon, also went well, encouraging us further.

The choice of the fixture with Oxford for the boycott had been no accident. Not only was it the weakest attraction of the League programme, as the previous year's record-low attendance had demonstrated, but it was distant enough to allow us plenty of time to organise and bring pressure to bear on the directors. The tactic of staying away was susceptible to the charge that it would undermine the team for that match, but those who took that position seemed to miss the point that unless something dramatic was done, and soon, there would be no team to rally behind.

Our second problem was what to do with the fans once we had got them to The Valley. We had preliminary discussions with the police about holding a rally in nearby Charlton Park but found to our surprise that they preferred us to mass in the streets around the ground. We now believed that we could get more people there than the club would have at Selhurst Park. The joke was that we hadn't the vaguest idea what to do once they had arrived.

Fortunately the dilemma was resolved in the most unexpected and welcome way. The first indication came with an extraordinary advertisement published in the programme for the match with Sheffield Wednesday. Under the heading "Another way to help your club" it advised: "Owing to being inundated with requests from our supporters who wish to help Charlton Athletic Football Club in some capacity or other we are now starting a register. If you wish to offer your services i.e. by supplies, builders, plumbers, electricians etc, we would love to hear from you."

The notion that dozens of fans had been ringing Charlton to offer this kind of help seemed a bizarre one. After all, the club had no premises that might require such work. Selhurst Park had its own maintenance staff and not even the Charlton directors could have been under the delusion that the fans would willingly help out there. And the new training ground had just been completely refurbished. Could it have been that someone was trying to tell the fans something? If not, it was an extraordinarily naive thing to do in the prevailing atmosphere.

A second hint that something was afoot came when we tried to hire the Valley Club for a public meeting. After initially accepting the booking, landlord Mike Bailey changed his mind, explaining that the football club wouldn't approve. But the place was obviously in need of all the business it could get, so what did it have to do with Charlton? As part of the Valley site, the freehold was in the hands of Adelong.

When an advertisement appeared in the *Daily Mail* inviting applications for the post of groundsman to a First Division club, speculation reached fever pitch. It took a devious phone call to the agency responsible, who made it clear the club was not Charlton, to restore a sense of reality.

The second issue of the *Voice* was delivered immediately prior to the fixture at Arsenal on the last Saturday in February. Foolishly, we reasoned that we might have difficulty selling it at Highbury and took only a handful of copies to the game. And it was there that the strongest rumour yet began to circulate. The following Tuesday evening, we received a tip-off that hardened it into fact. Two Charlton directors had indeed bought The Valley, as Moseley's article three months earlier had suggested they would. Obviously, we were delighted, but we were also left with 2,000 out-of-date magazines. Somewhat selfishly, we decided to keep what we knew to ourselves until the weekend in the hope of selling them.

In this we were hopelessy naive. I was about to set out for work the following morning when the phone rang. It was David Smith of the *Evening Standard*. Did I know anything about the report in that morning's *Daily Mirror* that Charlton were going home? I told him what I could. As for the magazines, we needn't have worried. They sold even better than before. In fact, the readers' main concern was that we shouldn't stop producing it just because Charlton were "going back".

But quite whether Charlton were actually going back or not was to remain a source of great confusion for some time to come. Adelong, which owned the ground, had indeed been acquired from Gliksten, who was said to be in financial difficulties, for a sum of £2.6m. But acquired by whom? After 48 hours of conflicting rumours, Charlton issued only the briefest of statements, apparently because Fryer prevented Norris from being more fulsome; hardly an indication of harmonious relations inside the club.

Mike Norris: secrecy was essential

"Following amicable negotiations, Adelong Limited, a company controlled by the Gliksten family, has been acquired by Mr Michael Norris, vice chairman of Charlton Athletic Football Club, in his personal capacity with the financial assistance of Laing Homes," it read. "It is intended that any benefit from this transaction will be for Charlton Athletic, who will continue to play at Selhurst Park while an alternative and feasible solution to play in Greenwich is finalised."

According to Norris, secrecy had been essential: "We are very sympathetic towards the supporters and very much regret that we have not been able to communicate with them as we would have liked," he said. "We had no alternative in view of the very complicated discussions with Mr Gliksten, Laing's and other people. A confidentiality clause was built into all agreements and if a word of the negotiations had come out the whole thing would have fallen through."

It was easy to see that talks would have been difficult with the fans looking over the directors' shoulders. For example, it might have encouraged the seller, Gliksten, to inflate his price. Yet many felt that this explanation was too glib and the details now being given too scanty. On the basis of them, it was difficult to see how the equation added up, and the passing years have not made it any easier.

For a start it was obvious, and admitted, that the money to buy the ground had come from Laing Homes. Norris simply didn't have it and it was notable that Alwen, who might have, was not initially mentioned at all. Indeed, the latter would play very much a back-seat role in the partnership for some time to come. There was talk of a new company having been set up, but this seems to have been a confusion resulting from the restructuring of the troubled Adelong, whose board now comprised Norris, Alwen and three directors from Laing's.

The bait for the builders was a two-year option to redevelop part or all of the site for housing at a time of a booming property market. The gamble, a disastrous one as it was to prove, was that the council would grant them planning permission even though the site was presently designated community open space in the borough plan. It would appear a curious assumption for such a large and experienced company to have made and one can only speculate what assurances they may have been given and by whom.

A similar situation applied at the training ground, where the directors had earmarked two acres of spare land for redevelopment by Laing's in order to generate further funding. It soon became clear that no suitable planning permission would ever be granted.

For The Valley, two planning applications were promised, one for a smaller stadium financed by the loss of 4.5 acres to residential use and another for a complete redevelopment. Should the club decide to return there, it seemed likely that the pitch would be turned through 90 degrees in order to better accommodate the new housing. If the more ambitious scheme was chosen, Charlton would use the profit to build a new multi-purpose stadium somewhere on the 298-acre Blackwall Peninsula, where British Gas, owners of much of the old industrial land, were about to announce a massive development scheme of their own.

This was the option preferred by Greenwich, Norris and, understandably, Laing's themselves. On BBC Radio, new council leader and member for the Charlton ward Dave Picton summarised the local authority's position thus: "The problem with The Valley is that it is totally surrounded by housing and therefore not a suitable venue for some of the other events that can take place at a major stadium. Certainly I, and most other council members, would be happier to see a stadium built on another site so that it could be used for a whole variety of purposes."

Norris later explained that he simply believed that a new beginning elsewhere would be more viable. On strictly financial criteria, it was hard to disagree. But fortunately, British Gas, sensitive to the effect of a major football stadium on house prices, were less than enthusiastic about accommodating Charlton and so began yet another period of confusion and rumour.

For the present it was cruel indeed for the fans that what had seemed like news of the longed-for return to The Valley had instead developed into something much less tangible, or even comprehensible. Most would have preferred a new ground in Greenwich to Selhurst Park, for the practical advantages were obvious, but the directors seemed to be missing the point. It was The Valley for which the fans were pining.

Nonetheless, the boycott had to be called off. Indeed, it would have been wrong to continue with it, given this startling new evidence of progress. Some fans wrote to demand that we continue until the club agreed to return specifically to The Valley, but it would have been a forlorn gesture had we tried. The mass support that the protest might have commanded would clearly now not be forthcoming. Neither Dixon nor I were particularly impressed with the prospect of a new ground, but we were equally aware of the dangers of being seen to look a gift horse in the mouth.

Paul Miller scores the vital equaliser at Stamford Bridge to keep Charlton up

One group that didn't mind where Charlton ended up as long as they left Selhurst were the residents of London SE25, who expressed their relief on the front page of the *Croydon Advertiser* under the headline "Goodbye and good riddance!" They quite reasonably complained that although they accepted and understood the nuisance of having one football club on their doorstep, the sudden imposition of a second, meaning that during the season there was a match every weekend and more often than not in midweek as well, had made life intolerable.

If the supporters were much relieved at the dramatic developments of early March, the news seemed also to have an uplifting effect on the morale of the team. Afterwards no one at the club was willing to accept that it had been a factor, but the change in playing fortunes was spectacular. One off the bottom at the time of the news and seemingly plunging to inevitable relegation, Charlton suffered only a single defeat in their next 10 games, enough to lift them into 17th place by the time they travelled to Chelsea for the final fixture.

They could not go down automatically, but were left needing a point at Stamford Bridge to avoid the torment of a second successive appearance in the play-offs, this time possibly with the cruel twist of having to face landlords Palace over two legs at Selhurst Park. And fatefully it was Chelsea themselves who would suffer the play-off torture if Charlton were successful. The Blues had made a respectable enough start to the season, but then gone 21 games without a win, plunging themselves into dire trouble.

Like Elland Road a year before, Stamford Bridge was an intimidating place to have to fight for your First Division life. The crowd of 33,701 was a hostile one in which the Charlton fans were outnumbered ten to one, but once again the team rose to the occasion. And again it was a demonstration of great character, particularly after Chelsea took the lead from a 17th-minute penalty which should never have been awarded. Video evidence was hardly necessary to confirm that Gordon Durie was a yard outside the box when John Humphrey brought him down, yet referee Darryl Reeves ruled otherwise.

Charlton's 67th-minute equaliser was a comical affair, Carl Leaburn's long throw finding Miller, whose shot was deflected off two defenders before looping over the stranded Kevin Hitchcock in the Chelsea goal. That Miller should score was richly apt, for this was to be very much his afternoon. Transfer-listed and twice disciplined during the season, the second time for swearing at a ball boy during the defeat at Norwich City, he was made for the occasion, the tone of which was set on the terraces when infiltrating Chelsea fans started fights in the away end following the first goal.

There was violence aplenty on the field, too, making it all the more amazing that only Humphrey and Reid were booked, the former for arguing about the penalty. In the worst incident, as Chelsea struggled for a winner, the giant Leaburn suddenly went down in his own penalty area, poleaxed by an unseen fist. When he came round the normally mild-mannered striker had to be physically restrained from taking his revenge.

Chelsea might still have won, had Bolder not made an amazing fingertip save from Durie's free-kick a quarter of an hour from the end. And in the dying minutes Miller appeared to foul Colin West just inside the penalty area, but referee Reeves remained unimpressed. So Charlton were safe, and Chelsea sent to Middlesbrough and ultimately Second Division oblivion in their stead. If less dramatic, it had in some ways been an even more remarkable escape than that the previous season. But now what was to become of The Valley? It would be a longer wait than anyone then conceived possible before we found out.

Chapter Eight

"I came past The Valley tonight and I found myself staring at it. All those memories! We had to go back, didn't we?"
　　　　　　　　　　Roger Alwen, Woolwich Town Hall (March 23rd, 1989)

The one thing that had upset some Charlton fans about the boycott plan had been the perception that the supporters were reduced to fighting among themselves. But in reality the argument had been remarkably free from animosity, so there were few fences to mend in the aftermath.

Stung by an observation of mine in *Voice of The Valley* that *Valiants' Viewpoint* seemed likely to disappear now it was without Steve Dixon's contributions, CASC secretary Roy King had upgraded his publication to meet the challenge. Like the Voice, its last two issues of the season were professionally printed and carried pictures, but the competition between the two remained amicable in the extreme. Indeed, we co-operated in the launching of a new petition, this time urging the council to facilitate a return to The Valley, rather than the construction of a new stadium on an alternative site.

In fact, the council was only part of the problem, as became clear when Dixon, King, Bill Treadgold and myself were invited to a meeting with Mike Norris and Derek Ufton at the former's Knightsbridge office in June. Norris and Roger Alwen had acquired the controlling shares of the football club from Sunley Holdings on the first day of the month in a £3.25m deal. However, Richard Collins remained in the chair and John Sunley was now listed as a director, suggesting that they were not yet fully extricated from the financial entanglement with the builders.

Ostensibly, the purpose of the meeting was to arbitrate between the warring factions of the supporters' club. Norris began in the tone of a headmaster admonishing naughty schoolboys, an approach he fortunately modified as soon as he realised there was no longer any quarrel to settle. Dixon and I had long recognised the futility of proceeding with a Valley Supporters' Club, which could not now hope to compete with the established organisation unless it continued the onerous business of running travel to away games. This neither of us were prepared to do.

On the other hand, we were determined to continue with *VOTV*, something to which Norris was vehemently opposed. Having failed to persuade us to abandon it or bring it under the CASC banner, he switched tack and asked us to change the title, but again we refused.

This was to prove a meaningful exchange, for it was evident that he was keen to head off any campaign against a new stadium and in favour of The Valley. He was quite candid that it was his preference that Charlton should build a new stadium on the Blackwall Peninsula, financed by the total redevelopment of the old ground. Indeed, his private position was much more clearly defined than the club's public statements had ever suggested.

One might speculate on two reasons for this. Firstly, that Alwen did not share his enthusiasm for the new site, although the latter made almost no public comment from which his views could be determined. Or, secondly, that the two of them were worried how supporters would react if they made their own preference too clear. Whatever the truth, we left the meeting extremely pessimistic about the chances of a return to The Valley.

The other revelation was Norris's hostility towards John Fryer. Indeed, it was clear that his sympathy was far more with Michael Gliksten. Further evidence of the way the latter had been misrepresented came when his libel action against London Weekend Television was heard around the same time. Counsel told the High Court that Charlton's departure had been "a great shock and a grave disappointment" to the former chairman. There was no truth whatsoever in the allegation made in the *London Programme* that he had evicted the club with a view to developing the ground for profit.

Gliksten's sensitivity on this point, coupled with the fact that he donated the damages to charity and Norris's attitude to him, were pointers to a very different picture from that successfully painted in 1985. It was even rumoured that he received regular updates on the club in which he was supposed to have lost interest from his friend and former co-director Bill Jenner, who was still an active fan.

But the former Valley landlord did bear some responsibility for the confusion created by his reticence. In particular, his failure to submit a planning application for the two acres of the ground that he had reclaimed in 1985, or indeed to do anything else with them subsequent to Charlton's departure, was simply baffling. At least Norris, by his readiness to meet us in this way, had signalled a willingness to open a channel of communication that had never previously existed between club and fans.

The Valley Supporters' Club quietly forgotten, Dixon rejoined the CASC committee as assistant secretary, with *VOTV*'s Ben Tegg, Mark Anderson and myself

Steve Dixon (left) presents the second Valley petition to Cllr Dave Picton

becoming members for the first time. Thus the lasting effect of the abortive boycott was to tilt the political make-up of CASC away from its traditional conservatism. This trend would be heightened in time as the focus of opposition switched from the directors, to whom some existing committee members were deferential to an almost comical extent, to Greenwich Council.

Yet for the present we had to play our hand carefully. We remained, defiantly, *Voice of The Valley*, but had to acknowledge the financial realities. These not only dictated that the new owners would choose the site most likely to be viable, but meant we had to acknowledge that they were our only real hope of getting the club back to Greenwich, whichever venue was chosen. Thus our petition, which eventually ran to some 4,500 names, was still presented to council leader Dave Picton, even though it seemed at the time that it was the club whom we should have been lobbying.

Norris obviously relished the commercial potential of the Blackwall Peninsula, where he hoped to build a multi-purpose arena with a capacity of 25,000-28,000 and possibly retail, as well as sporting facilities. The favourite site was that of the old South Metropolitan Gasworks, outside the boundaries of Charlton and in the eastern part of Greenwich, on the other side of the old Angerstein Athletic Ground which the club had briefly occupied before the First World War. It had the advantage of being adjacent to both Blackwall Lane, a major thoroughfare leading back onto the Woolwich Road, and the motorway which formed the Blackwall Tunnel southern approach.

Less conveniently, it was a far greater distance than was The Valley from the nearest railway station, in this case Westcombe Park. The on-off plans to extend the Underground network into that part of South London might have provided an alternative for visiting fans coming from north of the river, but it would have been irrelevant to most home supporters.

And there were several other reasons why the Metrogas site was considerably less attractive to Charlton fans. For a start, it wasn't The Valley. A major aspect of the disenchantment with the present situation centred around the loss of the identity the club derived from its former ground. A stadium which wasn't recognisably someone else's would certainly have been better than Selhurst, but it was still questionable whether the supporters would ever call it home.

In the second place, the Blackwall Peninsula was on the wrong side of the borough. The Valley was already on the fringe of the club's support area and this would take them in the opposite direction, towards Millwall's Den. It was only just over a mile's difference, but surely if Charlton were to build a new stadium it made more sense to do so in the heart of their catchment area.

And there was a third problem. The peninsula was notoriously blighted by a smell generated by Tunnel Refineries, a company based on its western side which manufactured animal feed. That and the remote and largely unfamiliar derelict industrial landscape made it a bleak and unattractive prospect.

In any case, British Gas felt much the same way about having football supporters abroad in their new development as the fans felt about going there. The government was in the process of introducing legislation to force football to adopt compulsory identity cards and with the political hostility to the game then prevailing, it's easy to surmise the effect that Charlton's presence might have had on the prices of the houses

Question time: Roy King tries to get some answers at Greenwich in September

the gas company was hoping to build. When the planning brief for the whole site was published in August, there was no mention of a football stadium.

Norris countered that it would be accommodated within 36 acres set aside by Greenwich for leisure use but that did not prove to be the case. British Gas claimed that Charlton had not followed up their initial interest, although Norris retorted that the council was supposed to be acting for them.

And all the while, the question of The Valley lingered on in the background. According to Norris, it would cost roughly the same to build his ambitious new stadium there, but since this would mean that the crucial housing development would be confined to the remainder of the site, the project would be much more difficult to finance. Since it also seemed likely that the existing pitch would have to be turned around in order to maximise the land available to the developers, the stadium would bear so little resemblance to the original that it made more sense to take advantage of the benefits of moving elsewhere.

Yet as the ensuing years were to prove, this was an oversimplification of the position. For in order to develop even part of The Valley, Charlton had to get planning permission. They had to overcome the very designation of the site by the council as community open space that had been meant to prevent the previous landlord making such an application successfully. And while councillors might have agreed to a land swap, whereby Charlton replaced that green area with another elsewhere in the borough, the politicians' subsequent behaviour suggests that it would have been unwise to assume that they would definitely have done so.

As it was, Norris arrived at a public meeting in Greenwich Borough Hall on

Head to head: Dave Picton and Lennie Lawrence at Greenwich Borough Hall

September 7th with very little to add. When we had met in June, he had promised better communication and we had taken him at his word by arranging this first confrontation with the mass of supporters since that at the Valley Club two years earlier. Understandably, given their previous experience, Norris and Ufton were nervous of how they would be received. In fact, their concern was misplaced because, like Dixon and myself, the fans wanted to give the new owners a chance.

But if Norris had little to say himself, he was given plenty to think about by the 600-strong audience, one of whom had flown in especially from the United States to attend. Many fans came to the microphone to appeal for the club to return to The Valley, but Norris refused to be drawn on whether this was possible. A more interesting response came from Picton, another who shared the packed stage. He did not think such a homecoming feasible but pledged: "If Charlton get together a deal involving The Valley, we would not stand in its way." They were words that would come back to haunt him.

The council was keen to see the football club come back as part of a new multi-purpose sports stadium in a borough, indeed a part of London, that was sadly lacking in top-class facilities. But any such development would necessarily include an athletics track, which would be deeply unpopular with the fans, to whom the proximity of pitch and terraces was the key to the special atmosphere of a British football ground. That was an objection which drew warm applause when I made it to Cllr Picton. However, neither he nor the directors would commit themselves against it.

If the meeting was unproductive in terms of information, it was a great success as a public relations exercise, not least on behalf of Lennie Lawrence who several times brought the house down during a short session on team affairs at the end. And the evening did lay the basis for a fragile trust to develop between directors and fans. There was even a tentative promise of more news before Christmas.

Meanwhile, the infighting within the supporters' club was not quite at an end. While Treadgold was largely content to leave the politics of the situation to others, he remained the obvious spokesman when the media were looking for a quote. In August he had inadvisedly told the *Kentish Times*: "I think it would be better if the new stadium was built because it would have better facilities and then they should flatten The Valley to stop any more breakaway groups wanting to return there."

They were hardly remarks in the conciliatory tone of our meeting in June. Nor were they likely to aid our efforts to rehabilitate CASC in the eyes of fans. Bill eventually claimed, somewhat unconvincingly, that he had been misquoted and King persuaded the *KT* to insert a brief disclaimer the following week stating that the chairman's comments were merely his own personal view. But they had served to harden our determination that he had to go.

Knowing our intentions, his supporters on the committee deliberately gave no public notice of the AGM, in October, at which we had persuaded *VOTV*'s Nick Tondeur to table a vote of no confidence. We countered by advertising it in the *Voice*, then encouraging Cordwell to splash the story all over the back page of the *Mercury* on the day of the meeting. Treadgold's backers retaliated by controlling admission to the extent that members whose subscriptions were not up to date were at first not admitted. After a heated debate they were reluctantly accommodated but not allowed to pay up or vote, the first known example of the supporters' club refusing to allow people to join.

The consequence was that we lost by 31 votes to 17. It was not the result that a ballot of the full membership would have produced, but we had simply misjudged the extent to which people cared who was chairman of the supporters' club. Or indeed about the supporters' club at all. In the event, they were not enough to outnumber Bill's friends and the only real winner was apathy.

The most remarkable feature of a bad-tempered evening was that the same meeting voted to back a proposal from the floor that no money should be handed over to the football club while it remained in exile, a measure that had been defeated in the past. And, just as we had planned, it was agreed that the officers, including the chairman, should have to stand for re-election annually instead of every three years, thus reversing a defensive constitutional ploy of two AGMs earlier.

Once again the focus had shifted away from the performances on the field to the political battles behind the scenes. But in fact the 1988/89 season was to be the most relaxed of the club's spell in the First Division. That is not to say that it was without its crises, but then what Charlton campaign ever was? No longer backed by the mighty financial resources of Sunley's, the team remained doomed to struggle in the lower reaches of the First Division. Success would be a good Cup run and mid-table security by April.

There had been no new signings at all in the 1988 close season, although popular central defender Steve Thompson had departed for Leicester City for £15,000.

Thommo had made a considerable contribution to the club's extraordinary return to the elite, one a Third Division defender three weeks past his 30th birthday could hardly have anticipated when Lawrence brought him to The Valley as a stopgap in 1985. But he had lost his place to Paul Miller the previous season and at 32 his days in the top flight were surely numbered.

Evidence of the gulf in resources and ambition within that section was provided by Liverpool's visit to Selhurst Park on the opening day. This time only 21,000 were in attendance, but manager Kenny Dalglish was able to keep his legendary midweek signing Ian Rush on the substitutes' bench while his lookalike John Aldridge grabbed the headlines with a hat-trick.

Charlton were to lose three of their first four games by the embarrassing margin of 3-0, even if the fourth, at Coventry, was under the quite considerable handicap of an early injury to goalkeeper Bob Bolder. It left that flexible veteran Steve Gritt, now in his 12th season with the club, to demonstrate his prowess between the posts. The second home fixture having been lost, with painful inevitability, to SE London rivals Millwall, Charlton had only a sparkling 3-1 win at eventually relegated West Ham United as consolation. There young Paul Williams struck twice, giving soon-to-be-justified grounds for optimism that goals would be easier to come by this time around.

Utility man: Steve Gritt takes over in goal during the match at Coventry City

In October, Paul Miller departed in predictably controversial fashion, joining Watford for £85,000 after being sent off for spitting at Newcastle United's Andy Thorn during a match at Selhurst Park. The incident left Lawrence fuming over a 1-0 lead that had become a 2-1 deficit before Robert Lee's face-saving late equaliser. The summer sale of Thompson now looked a mistake; certainly the player thought so and he was soon on the move again, first to Sheffield United and then to his former club, Lincoln City, where he eventually became team manager in November 1990.

Lawrence's own problems were quickly compounded by Peter Shirtliff's dismissal in a Littlewoods Cup match at Loftus Road. Colin Pates had been recruited from Chelsea as Miller's replacement for a club record fee of £430,000, but he had played only four games before he needed a hernia operation, just as Shirtliff's suspension was about to begin.

Now the Charlton boss was forced into the market for another central defender.

The one he found was Tommy Caton, a former Arsenal and Manchester City player, who at £100,000 represented something of a bargain; much better value for money, in fact, than the very capable Pates.

But despite these setbacks, confirmation that this was not to be just another season of struggle had come with an unexpected 3-1 win at Carrow Road, home of table-topping Norwich City. Two more goals from Williams and a splendid solo effort from 20-year-old Paul Mortimer allowed newly-promoted Millwall to replace the Canaries on their lofty perch.

Omitted from the side for the opening match against Liverpool, Williams was to strike 10 times in his first 13 games of the season, the most prolific spell of marksmanship at the club since the heyday of Derek Hales. His lethal combination of lightning pace and instinctive touch marked him out as a real discovery and it was not long before he was attracting transfer speculation.

There could hardly have been a greater contrast with his striking partner, the lanky Carl Leaburn. He too had become a fixture in the side but had failed to score since that timely strike on his full debut at St James' Park. Still only 19, his return of one goal from 15 appearances by the start of the season was not yet a disastrous one. But as it stretched and stretched through the opening weeks of the campaign, the fans began to wonder, and finally to lose patience with this ungainly forward.

A crucial turning point had come in the home match against Tottenham Hotspur with Charlton 2-1 ahead despite having to field the ever-versatile Gritt as a makeshift central defender. Twelve minutes from time, Leaburn squandered an obvious chance to seal victory, poking the ball against the post from five yards out when it looked easier to score. Immediately, play switched to the other end and Paul Allen netted a simple equaliser.

Yet the Leaburn situation was never clear-cut. Although he did not score himself, he was responsible for making numerous goals for Williams, a point not fully appreciated by many of his critics until they studied the season in review on video. That he was drained of confidence was proven by his performance following the Guinness Soccer Six at Manchester's G-Mex Centre in December, when he finished an improbable leading scorer in Charlton's equally unlikely triumph over all their First Division rivals. He re-emerged the following weekend at Selhurst Park to dominate the first half of the game with Queens Park Rangers.

It was that performance which finally confirmed his cult status, with his supporters arguing that his contribution to the side merited his inclusion. But the display only briefly silenced his detractors and the debate between the two camps became increasingly furious. Perhaps, too, there was an implicit hint of racism from some quarters. However, ultimately there could be no disputing the fact that strikers were supposed to score goals and Leaburn did not. Nonetheless he remained a fixture in the side until the turn of the year.

The season also marked the sharp development of two other black youngsters, each an exciting prospect. Fulham reject Mortimer, installed on the left side of midfield, began to show signs of instinctive ball control and deft touch that set him aside from even the best of his teammates. The goal he scored at Norwich was only the first of a series of spectacular efforts, even if his critics called him lazy. His form was good enough to allow Lawrence to release displaced and disgruntled left winger

Mark Stuart to Plymouth Argyle for £125,000 in early November, despite the fact that another left-sided player, Colin Walsh, had already sustained his second broken leg in less than a year during a September reserve match with Arsenal.

On the right flank, 19-year-old youth-team graduate Micky Bennett lacked some of Mortimer's delicate finesse and vision, but offered instead power and acceleration. It was never better demonstrated than in making Williams' early goal in the home game with Everton when he left the visitors' defence trailing in his wake before crossing to create an easy chance for the equally fleet-footed finisher. Bennett was named player of the tournament in the Soccer Six success, but was cut down in his prime just three days later when he damaged knee ligaments in an unnecessary third-minute challenge with QPR's former Addick Alan McDonald. It was an injury from which he never fully recovered.

Just a week earlier, at Old Trafford, another right winger had come back to haunt the club. Ralph Milne, written off and discounted to Third Division Bristol City the previous February, had done so well at Ashton Gate that he had attracted Manchester United's attention. And even as the Charlton fans taunted their old whipping boy, he responded by shooting United into the lead, courtesy of a highly fortuitous deflection.

Having reached the dizzy heights of 11th in the First Division in late October, the team suffered the now traditional November slump and by the Boxing Day defeat at the hands of Arsenal were down to 19th, just one off the bottom. The fans' depression was deepening once again and their mood was not much helped by the continuing

Robert Lee celebrates scoring Charlton's goal in the 1-1 draw at Wimbledon

success of nearest neighbours Millwall, who even now were holding their own in fourth place.

That the Lions should have won the clubs' Selhurst encounter was unremarkable, for this was the traditional outcome of the fixture. Only eight of the 47 derby matches since 1921 had ended in Charlton victories. However, the Valley fans' historic consolation had been that theirs was the bigger and more successful outfit. Now Millwall were in the First Division, and doing well.

In fact, and despite the endless rhetoric of their supporters, the gates at The Den were by no means exceptional. The Lions' debut match in the top flight attracted only 13,000, certainly less than the Addicks might have hoped for in similar circumstances at The Valley. But their attendances were still much better than those Charlton were getting at Selhurst and they provided a yardstick by which to measure the scale of the exiles' problem.

In any case, there was more lasting damage being done than simply bruised pride. For the first time, Millwall shirts and Millwall car stickers were beginning to appear not just in Greenwich, where they had long been seen, but out in Bexley, too. Population drift was partly to blame, but so was Charlton's continuing absence from the district. And who could fault the young fans now growing up in the affluent north Kent suburbs for seeing the New Cross club as their local team?

In January, the *Mercury* newspaper, so long the Charlton fans' ally, moved into Bexley as well, an area it had not served for half a century. In the early weeks its sports coverage in that borough reflected a Charlton bias not found in its Greenwich and Lewisham editions. But it also brought Millwall match reports into the locality for the first time since the war. Not even the old *Kentish Independent* had covered the Lions, in spite of its editorial concentration on Greenwich where they inevitably had many supporters.

With the *Croydon Advertiser* progressively reining back its Charlton coverage as the gates continued to demonstrate a lack of local concern, press interest in the club's traditional heartland became a persistent theme for *VOTV*. Notwithstanding the *Mercury*'s campaigning edge and the growing reputation of Kevin Nolan's match reports, surely no First Division club in history had been as poorly served as this by its local papers.

Ironically, the lack of detailed coverage, plus the poverty of the club's own publications, was surely a factor in the continuing success of the *Voice* itself. Sales had reached the 2,000 mark with the fourth issue, at the end of the previous season, and they continued to climb, nudging 2,700 by February, a year after the launch. We were now reaching the vast majority of the Selhurst crowd and were also slowly building up a base of subscribers from exiled supporters all over the country.

Thanks to our dedicated army of sellers, there was a perception that the *Voice* was the work of a large group of people, which was useful in terms of credibility. I would never belittle the part played by people like Nick and Andy Tondeur, Reed Cavanagh, Mark Sutherland, Mark and Steve Moncur and John Stickings, who without fail made themselves available on matchdays to collect the cash. But in fact the core of the operation was just two people, Dixon and myself. Since we both had full-time jobs – and my enforced idleness within the Police National Computer Unit ended with an

Director Richard Collins, who instigated the ban on the *Kentish Times*

internal transfer in February 1989 – we were working flat out.

The situation was further complicated by the fact that at no time did Dixon get involved with the final stages of planning and laying out the magazine, primarily because I had a monopoly on access to the necessary technology. He worked tirelessly to sell it, dealt with most of the correspondence and wrote more articles than anyone apart from myself, but it meant that the arduous final stages of production were all down to me. And by no means incidentally that my personality and not his was stamped all over the magazine.

Flushed by the success of the *Voice*, I had made my own small contribution to resolving the press coverage problem the previous summer by persuading the editor of the *Kentish Times*' sister freesheet *The Leader* to allow me 300 words a week to comment on Charlton's affairs, a labour of love for which I was paid the princely sum of £5. But even that arrangement briefly broke down in mid-season because the paper's accounts department did not want to pay up.

Another breakthrough came when a new and sympathetic sports editor, Richard Liston, was appointed at the *KT* that summer. He took the trouble to attend the supporters' club AGM and reinstated match reports in the paper's Bexley and Eltham editions. Indeed, Liston would have liked to have gone further and given Charlton comprehensive coverage across north Kent but he was once again constrained by hostile management. And then, fatuously, Charlton managed to fall out with the paper.

The culprit this time was the ubiquitous Collins. That he was still Charlton chairman could only have been a consequence of an arrangement with the previous owners. At functions he appeared to the supporters to be, in Bernard Ingham's splendid phrase, a "semi-detached" member of the board of directors. And it was Collins who fuelled the rampant press and public speculation about the site of Charlton's new ground.

While the gasworks option was not entirely discounted, at least by the club, new possibilities had loomed into view. Charlton would move to Sutcliffe Park, at Kidbrooke, claimed one source. Another suggested they would build a stadium just down the road near the Dover Patrol public house. The Metrogas sports ground, at Horn Lane, was mentioned and even the Isle of Dogs, north of the river and Millwall's point of origin. But the strongest rumour related to the Thames Polytechnic sports ground in the heart of Eltham.

Had this prospect hardened into reality, there seems little doubt that there would have been an enormous public outcry, not least from the clubs that presently used the pitches. The idea that Charlton could be transplanted into the heart of suburban and largely middle class Eltham always seemed a fantastic one. And one irony was that the site was just round the corner from where Dixon lived and he was notably unenthusiastic about having his beloved football club dumped on his own doorstep.

However, the prospect was evidently serious enough to provoke the sending of an anonymous letter, purporting to come from a local resident, to the *KT*. Liston believed that it was a plant from within Greenwich Council, designed to stir up local opposition. But the paper duly contacted Collins to ask for the club's view. The chairman confirmed that the polytechnic sports ground was one of a number of options and claimed that there would be a press conference in the second week of December to announce the site Charlton had chosen.

But then, according to Liston, he announced that there was an embargo on the story and the paper was not to print it. Not surprisingly, the *KT* demurred. The information had not come from Charlton and the paper therefore owed them no duty of confidentiality over it. Newspapers had a responsibility to the communities they served as well as to their local football club. So the *KT* ran the story. The next day, Collins rang to say that in future no one at Charlton would talk to them.

Thus the club had lost another ally in the fight to retain its identity. Ironically, the paper had even backed the plan to move to Eltham in an editorial. Now they dropped coverage completely. It would only be revived, in the form of a 300-word column contributed by supporter Richard Redden, the following August, by which time Liston had left and a new sports editor had been appointed.

But Collins had not finished yet. When the promised press conference failed to materialise, he popped up in *The Mail on Sunday* at the turn of the year forecasting news within two weeks of a move to a site just "a stone's throw" from The Valley. It led to rampant speculation about the derelict Stone's sports ground, literally opposite The Valley on the Woolwich Road. Yet again, no announcement came.

Frustrated by these false alarms and faced with yet another apparently endless wait, the fans began to lose patience with the directors. From within the club came not even an apology for the delay, with all enquiries, as usual, deflected in the direction of the council. Not until mid-February did the board make any comment at all and then, at the specific request of the supporters' club, the following notice appeared in the matchday programme.

"The directors of Charlton Athletic Football Club would like the supporters to know that they are continuing with the discussions concerning the plans for the club to return to the London Borough of Greenwich.

"At the supporters' meeting at Greenwich Town Hall last autumn, it was stated that an announcement would be made by Christmas last. Regretfully this was unable to take place because the proposed arrangements are taking longer to finalise than at first thought. Every effort is being made to conclude the terms and a meeting will be convened with the supporters as soon as we have something firm to report and discuss."

Meanwhile, the derelict Valley was about to gain its first tenants in three-and-a-half years. In the early hours of March 1st, three caravans arrived at the ground, the advance guard of a party of travellers evicted from Horn Lane by Greenwich Council. They gained access by breaking the locks on the main gates in Floyd Road and set up camp inside. By dawn they had been joined by 20 caravans more plus an assortment of lorries.

In retrospect, it was surprising that this kind of invasion had not happened earlier. The Valley must have seemed ideal to the travellers, offering as it did a large but enclosed adventure playground for their numerous children, plenty of space to park their vehicles and even a ready supply of scrap metal. Their spokesman Jack Collins told the *Mercury*: "The council's travellers' site manager John Grey, who came to see us, suggested that we put in a planning application for the football ground!"

Understandably, Norris was not amused: "We won't act illegally, but the travellers know they can't just go parking themselves on private property. We gave them 24 hours' notice to move on and they ignored us. Now it's up to the courts, or the police, if there's trouble."

But ironically the intruders had arrived on the scene just too late. The ground had stood empty all that time, most of which neither club nor landlord had apparently been prepared to admit responsibility for it. Had there been an earlier invasion, it would have been interesting to see which, if either, party had sought the court order necessary to evict the intruders. Now the travellers had discovered the site, it was about to be taken away from them.

For finally, in early March, a deeply frustrated Alwen stepped out of Norris's shadows and became chairman. He had at last decided to put up the money necessary to refurbish the only possible site. Behind the scenes, a whole year had been wasted in seeking the inevitable confirmation that no suitable and available land existed to build a football stadium in Greenwich bar that which the club's committee had inspected that Sunday morning in early 1919. Against all the odds, Charlton would return to The Valley.

The plan was to announce the news at a public meeting to be held on Thursday, March 23rd. In the meantime, the board's cover story was that they were about to launch a fundraising Lifeline prize subscription scheme, similar to that run highly successfully by Palace. Few people were in on the secret, but by a freak coincidence I was one of them. There were obvious sources for a leak. Woolwich Town Hall had to be booked. Planning permission had to be granted for the partial redevelopment scheme and that meant discussions with council leader Picton. And there was a

Happy hour: fans celebrate the official announcement of the Valley return

massive clue in the elevation of Alwen to chairman.

Despite having stumbled into a Civil Service backwater after leaving university, I have always been, by instinct, a reporter. And this was the biggest football story that was ever likely to fall into my hands. But there was no time to bring out a special *VOTV* and only one other place where it could be published. On the morning of Friday, March 10th, I phoned Peter Cordwell at the *Mercury*, convinced that the club must at least give out details of the meeting at the following day's home match. They didn't. There was no piece of paper on the turnstiles and nothing in the programme. No news came over the tannoy at half-time. One consequence was that Dixon was berated after the game by disappointed fans whom he had told to expect an announcement.

On the Monday, we both spoke to Cordwell again. He in turn called Arnie Warren at Selhurst Park. At first the general manager pleaded ignorance, but the *Mercury* man had already established the fact of the town hall booking with council officials. Then Warren recovered his poise and gave him the Lifeline story. But commercial manager Steve Sutherland had already told us that no such scheme would be launched while Charlton remained stuck in SE25.

The club's version of events clearly didn't add up, and Cordwell decided to run a speculative piece under the headline "Deathline!" But on Tuesday morning, I persuaded him to take a more reckless gamble. Only Cordwell would have taken the risk. Other than what I'd told him, he had nothing to go on except the fact that the town hall had been booked and the club was being secretive about the purpose. But then it was a running joke that Charlton were quite capable of being secretive about the team changes if it suited them. And if he put the story directly to anyone at the club for confirmation, he faced the possibility of the news being announced by them as a spoiling tactic long before the paper appeared on Thursday morning.

Fortunately, the sports editor of the *Mercury* was a born gambler. And his story was correct in every single respect, although what the readers would have made of the revelation that the editor of *Voice of The Valley* was the "impeccable source" who related the details is anyone's guess.

There was one last fright. As the stone subs prepared the paper for printing at High Wycombe on the Wednesday morning, Charlton press officer Peter Burrowes came on the phone. But Burrowes knew nothing, he was simply asking that since Cordwell was aware of the meeting, the story should include the fact that admission was by ticket only. And he was too late anyway.

The plan was that Charlton would make their return early in 1990. The old main stand, vandalised beyond repair, would be demolished to make way for a modern replacement that would run the length of the touchline. The capacity would be 20,000 and there were to be no alterations to the pitch.

Those were the details that appeared in the *Mercury* and also those which Alwen stood up to announce at Woolwich Town Hall seven days later. There had been no official confirmation earlier, so he was not deprived of his moment. The 600 tickets had been snapped up immediately, but another 200 who turned up without them were allowed to stand at one side of the hall. Still more waited outside in the evening drizzle, anxious for the signal that it was really true.

This was to be a quite remarkable occasion in the history of any football club, religious in its fervour and raucous in its good humour. Later Woolwich Town Hall would be the scene for other and more traumatic chapters in the same unfolding story, but here and now there was simply euphoria, even if it was to prove hopelessly premature.

In fact, the party had begun two nights before, at the midweek visit to Highbury, where a much larger than anticipated contingent of Addicks fans had packed the Clock End. Buoyed by the *Mercury* story, they had seen one of the most memorable Charlton performances of any season. It had ended 2-2, with Steve MacKenzie's determined second-half equaliser capping a brave performance against eventual champions Arsenal.

Now the same fans packed the pubs of Woolwich, then streamed along to take their places in the overcrowded hall. Only when no more could safely be admitted were the doors firmly locked and did the club officials, seven of them in all, take the stage. Each, when introduced, earned a rousing cheer, even the obscure and not obviously relevant Warren. The last chair was left vacant, ready for Picton to make a theatrical late entrance from the wings.

It was Alwen's moment, however, and he milked it unashamedly, the emotional quiver in his voice betraying both nervousness and his own deep feelings. His words were sweet music to the audience.

"During the past two-and-a-half years and particularly since the recent acquisition

Congratulations: Norris and Alwen celebrate after the announcement

of The Valley, we have had numerous meetings and lengthy conversations with various parties to enable Charlton Athletic to return to the London Borough of Greenwich and there has been much publicised speculation as to their outcome. We appreciate that many of you have felt left in the dark by the club. However, we hope that you understand that this has not been intentional and we have tried to keep you as well-informed as possible. The club has had, of course, to respect the confidential nature of these conversations."

The silence was acute. Everybody was straining to avoid missing the merest nuance of the statement. One paragraph more, and the meeting erupted.

"We have had favourable indications from the council that a planning consent may shortly be given on part of The Valley and we are therefore very happy to put in hand a major refurbishment programme which will enable Charlton Athletic Football Club to once again play football at The Valley."

The final words were drowned out. As one, the hall rose. A champagne cork popped. Families, friends and even strangers embraced. Left with little real alternative, Alwen paused. Cameras snapped, tears flowed.

At some length, the chairman managed to subdue the audience sufficiently to allow him to continue: "The work involved will be substantial and costly, but we hope that it will begin in the next few weeks and be completed early in 1990, so that for a part of next season, football can be played at The Valley.

"Following the purchase in 1987 of the training ground in New Eltham, we feel that this is another step towards helping Charlton Athletic to once again be a major force in English football. For our move back to be successful and completed on time, we need total support from every Charlton supporter and we will be looking at ways the many offers of help can be taken up. Our aim is to provide a modern stadium of which we can all be justly proud.

"Finally, we would like to thank Laing Homes Limited, for without their assistance this decision to move back to The Valley would not have been possible, and also the council and their leader, Dave Picton, for their support."

Now from outside, where the unlucky latecomers had waited so patiently, came an answering roar of triumph. And, as if on cue, in came the council leader. But before he could speak it was Norris's turn. He explained the club's plans in more detail, and responded in particular to the questions fans had written down at the prompting of the office staff on the way into the hall. Overwhelmingly, they related to the fate of the infamous Covered End seats. What luxury to be arguing again about such domestic trivia! Catching the mood, Norris agreed that they should go.

He explained that there was a choice between waiting until the new west stand was completely built or going back as soon as enough was ready for use. Predictably, the audience roared their approval for the latter option. They cheered too the news that the travellers had left the ground that morning, as suddenly as they had arrived three weeks before.

The only dissent came when the capacity of 20,000 was confirmed. "Not enough!" was the cry from several in the crowd, a familiar complaint in the months to come. The directors quite reasonably argued that the important thing was to retain the ability

Sad sight: the area behind the main stand after the travellers' short visit

Do it yourself: fans help clear the East Terrace during the Valley clean-up

to increase the limit if attendances justified doing so. It would also have been foolish to start with a larger capacity if the marginal cost of doing so was high. But the fans were surely right in thinking that with this figure the board would have been turning away vital revenue when the big clubs visited The Valley. The obvious area for expansion was the East Terrace, which we were told would be divided horizontally with the rear part possibly being sold for redevelopment, the boundary being marked by a new retaining wall.

Steve Sutherland was also given the opportunity to unveil his Valley Gold fundraising scheme, although this, as yet, was hardly more than an idea.

However, the most significant contribution came from Picton, who urged fans to write to the council in support of the forthcoming planning application for the housing part of the scheme. "Charlton have a great past and I think that now they have a great future," he enthused. "And I'm pretty sure that when the formal processes have been gone through, that future is going to be back at The Valley."

In the excitement of the moment, few realised the true import of what he had said. Instead, we put his lack of conviction down to the fact that as council leader it would have been improper for him to prejudge a planning application. In fact, his remarks were an awful and largely unheeded warning of the bitter political wrangles that lay ahead.

Armed with prior knowledge of the Woolwich meeting, *VOTV* was ready to launch into print the following week with a special issue. Comprehensively recording the night's events, its 3,500 copies soon sold out, quite easily a record. All 2,500 that we had at Selhurst for the game with Middlesbrough were instantly snapped up by the 6,696 crowd, impressive penetration indeed for a fanzine. By comparison, a

Home fire burning: the great Valley clean-up at its height

leading Arsenal title, operating within what was obviously a much larger potential market, was still struggling to sell 2,000 copies at the time.

The day after the Boro game there was a morning of sheer delight at The Valley, an occasion which generated an amount of goodwill no public relations agency could have bettered. The directors wanted urgently to clear the choking weeds and debris that had accumulated during three years of neglect, the latter particularly during the stay of the recent uninvited guests. Their inspirational solution was to ask the fans to do the job.

Sunday, April 2nd, dawned wet and miserable and it seemed at first their plans would be in ruins. But no dedicated Charlton fan was going to miss this experience. At first a trickle, then a steady flood, they jammed Floyd Road and Harvey Gardens with their cars, then swarmed all over the East Terrace, hacking away at the jungle with more enthusiasm than method. Such were the numbers that it took no more than an hour to clear the weeds. Suddenly, The Valley had begun to look like a football ground again instead of a nature reserve.

Now a bonfire raged in the centre circle, pure symbolism this in what might once have been the stadium's funeral pyre. Even *The Red, Red Robin*, the club's theme tune, echoed around the ground again courtesy of Richard Redden's tape recorder, a splendidly dotty gesture entirely in keeping with the mood of the occasion.

Their enthusiasm unquenched, fans tore into the wreck of Humphreys' 1921 grandstand, ripping seat after seat from the rotten wooden floorboards. There was danger here, in the random flinging of debris onto the pitch below and the clambering over frail timber, but the magic of the day was such that no one was hurt.

Battle for The Valley

In the midst of it all was Cordwell, who had played such an important role in fostering the campaign, first lending more practical assistance with his hands, then finding the right moment to present Alwen and Norris with the proceeds from the ill-fated Mercury Trust Fund. They could use it, he joked, to buy some grass seed.

Finally, the bedraggled army gathered in front of the stand where Alwen, Norris and a bemused looking Lawrence held an impromptu press conference. The manager had urged his players to stay away, but one, Gritt, was as much a part of this occasion as any fan and was not to be denied.

The work that the directors had envisaged taking many Sundays had substantially been accomplished in less than two hours. No one could deny the fans the chance to return the following week to tidy up, and this they did, but by their efforts on that first morning they had signalled just how important the homecoming was to them.

Crucial to its success, however, was the team's survival in the First Division. Experience suggested that at a lower level the club could expect no more Charlton supporters than presently attended the home matches at Selhurst Park. It was now more than 30 years since The Valley had last staged a top-flight game and no one could do any more than guess what crowds might attend. But it is reasonable to assume that removing the major obstacle to watching the club, South London's congested traffic and inadequate public transport, would certainly have ensured they were a lot bigger than those at Palace.

The prospects of staying up were reasonable, at least by Charlton's standards. The team's first home victory of the season, 2-1 over Sheffield Wednesday on October 29th, had been followed by a run of ten games without a win. However, a comfortable 3-0 triumph over Luton on January 14th was followed immediately by a 2-0 success against Newcastle at St James' Park. Together the results appeared to provide the platform for escape into mid-table.

The mood on the terraces was also improved by a string of fortuitous home draws in the FA Cup. First Oldham Athletic, with a last-minute Williams' goal, were eliminated, then giantkillers Kettering Town from the GM Vauxhall Conference were removed. The latter match attracted a 16,001 crowd to Selhurst, prompting wry observations that club officials had been determined the home support would not be outnumbered by the estimated 8,000 visiting fans.

Struggling West Ham, already beaten at Upton Park and held 0-0 at Selhurst in the League, appeared the ideal draw for the fifth round and an easy ticket into the sixth for the first time since 1947. But it was not to be. The Hammers survived the very harsh 44th-minute dismissal of Mark Ward to win 1-0 and Charlton's glimpse of glory was over for another season. That it was the third time in four years that the Addicks had been eliminated by West Ham did nothing to ease the disappointment.

So back to the League and comic relief in the form of Carl Leaburn's second goal, which finally arrived at Villa Park and gave the visitors a deserved 2-1 win. No one begrudged the youngster his large slice of luck, but the fact that the ball had been turned in by Aston Villa defender Derek Mountfield was difficult to deny.

However gained, the points were to prove invaluable. Charlton eventually made their escape by winning the last four home games, again prompting the suggestion that the team had been boosted by developments off the field. But it was more likely the consequence of greater determination against teams whose season was effectively over. And then there was the timely arrival of the annual penalty, awarded against Manchester United and decisively converted by Mark Reid.

The major threat came from two dismal showings at the end of April. In the first, at Loftus Road, the team performed woefully against an uninterested QPR side. Even so they peppered the goal late in the game but just could not get the breakthrough they needed and were beaten 1-0. Three days later they crashed 5-2 on the plastic pitch at fellow strugglers Luton Town as a novel attempt to combat Hatters striker Mick Harford by playing three central defenders and relegating Williams to the substitutes' bench went badly wrong. Charlton were four down by half-time, even if the third was so far offside that not only the crowd but the referee seemed to have difficulty believing his linesman.

The fact that the Addicks' two second-half goals came from substitute Andy Jones, just back from injury and recuperation on loan at former club Port Vale, did nothing to appease the legion of visiting fans who had breached the Kenilworth Road fortress. For it lent impressive weight to the arguments of the anti-Leaburn lobby. And those vociferous critics were given fresh cause for complaint the following weekend when Jones was once again left out while Leaburn returned to the side.

This time, however, their howls of protest were cut short, for it was the controversial striker who scored the only goal of the game against Wimbledon with 12 minutes gone. And on this occasion there was no disputing that it was his, a neat

Paul Williams feels a hand on his shoulder at Sheffield Wednesday in March

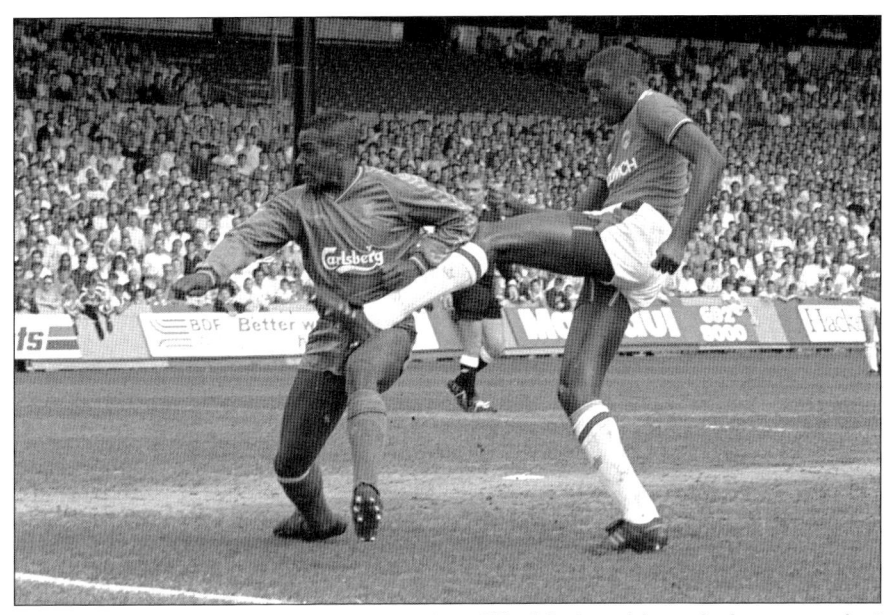

Carl Leaburn scores the winner against Wimbledon, his only home goal at Selhurst as a Charlton player

volley smashed home with his left foot from inside the penalty box. Already injured when he struck the winner, he limped off two minutes later to be replaced by Jones, whose contribution to events was unremarkable. The afternoon's other hero was Bolder, who saved a harshly-awarded Dennis Wise penalty 15 minutes from time.

It meant that Charlton had to beat Derby County in midweek at Selhurst to ensure their safety, a task they accomplished with some style, notwithstanding England goalkeeper Peter Shilton's formidable presence between the posts. Goals from Jones, Shirtliff and Williams meant that the final fixture, at Nottingham Forest, assumed the character of a party, well attended and defiantly good-humoured. It was the first meaningless fixture of the three First Division seasons and duly celebrated, despite a heavy downpour on uncovered terracing and an emphatic 4-0 defeat.

For once the gods seemed to have dealt kindly with Charlton Athletic and suddenly all was optimism both on and off the field. Even some of the estranged fans were ready to make their peace on the basis that the Addicks were going back to The Valley.

But as any Charlton supporter with a sense of history should have realised, nothing in the club's affairs is ever quite that simple.

Chapter Nine

"When the council does not listen, when the decision has already been made behind closed doors and when everybody knows it is a pretence, then democracy has been ridiculed in Greenwich."

Leader in the Eltham Times (February 8th, 1990)

Charlton's plans for The Valley, as announced at the March meeting, were both modest and sensible. Indeed, for many people, they were just about ideal, striking the perfect balance between improved facilities and respect for tradition. Only the truncated East Terrace and low capacity were controversial. If there was a question mark, it hung over how Laing's could hope to recoup the sum they had paid for Adelong from the limited redevelopment now proposed and Charlton afford to build their stand. It was a mystery that puzzled Woolwich MP John Cartwright as much as us, as he explained when Dixon and I presented him with a petition against the government's compulsory ID-card scheme outside The Valley in June.

But in fact the club's first vision of the future had already been overtaken by the tragic events at the Hillsborough FA Cup semi-final on April 15th. As the world looked on in horror through the all-seeing eyes of the television cameras, 96 Liverpool fans had been killed by crushing, innocent victims of a lethal combination of inadequate safety precautions and incompetent crowd control. Faced with a dangerous build-up of spectators outside the turnstiles, a senior policeman had ordered the opening of an exit gate, allowing hundreds of fans to make their way into an already packed enclosure with fatal consequences.

Beside such shocking and needless loss of life, the arguments about The Valley paled into insignificance. But the timing was fateful indeed. For now, just as Ibrox had begun the ground's problems with the imposition of the Safety of Sports Ground Act, and Bradford and Heysel had combined to close the East Terrace, so Hillsborough would affect the club's hopes of a return.

The awful lessons of the tragedy on the Leppings Lane terracing would be embodied in Lord Justice Taylor's commendably independent report into ground safety. Unlike the rent-a-quote politicians, Taylor listened to what he was told by supporters who had experience of the conditions in some grounds. Consequently, he attacked all the familiar targets of the still proliferating fanzines: poor toilets, inadequate refreshments and the related indignities of hostile policing, rigid segregation and spiked fences.

However, Taylor also backed the widespread demands for all-seater stadia that had come in the wake of the tragedy. Clearly, it would be much easier to identify and prevent overcrowding if every spectator had an allocated seat. But while this response was understandable in the context of the terrible disaster at Sheffield, compulsory seating addressed neither the reality of life in the lower divisions, where packed crowds were a rarity and the money was not available to upgrade stadia, nor the wishes of the customers. Most of the people calling for all-seaters did not attend football matches anyway or, if they did, preferred to sit down.

Taylor's final report demanded that First Division clubs progressively seat their

Battle for The Valley

Lights out at The Valley in May 1989 as the refurbishment programme begins

remaining terracing by 20 per cent a season, with no standing allowed from the summer of 1994. In view of their modest resources and the lack of urgency at the lower level, Third and Fourth Division clubs would have five years' additional grace. Chancellor of the Exchequer and Chelsea fan John Major was to signal the government's willingness to help meet the mammoth cost by releasing part of the levy on football pools in the 1990 budget. The game would benefit from an extra £100m over the next five years, distributed through a reformed Football Trust.

For The Valley, the immediate consequence of Hillsborough was that it rendered politically impossible the plan to restore terracing behind the goals. The disaster effectively released Michael Norris from the promise he had made in the heat of the moment at Woolwich Town Hall in March.

In the meantime, work began at the ground with the removal of what remained of the roof on the old Covered End and demolition of the west stand. Many fans were struck by the waste of the apparently sound cantilever cover erected over the old structure only ten years earlier and questioned the wisdom of simply knocking it down. But there could be no room for sentimental reservations over the fate of the stand itself, which was clearly beyond repair.

The low terracing adjacent to it on the north-west corner of the ground, which had become home to the choir in the final few years, and that on the other side of the stand was cleared away and the land filled in to provide a flat foundation for the new building. The old floodlight pylons, too, were finally dismantled.

Perhaps most symbolic was the clearing and levelling of the pitch, which proved to have a slope of 60 centimetres between one goalmouth and a corner. A wide variety of bricks, pottery and other Victoriana also had to be removed before modern drainage could be installed and the new grass seed sown, in July.

However, the summer of 1989 proved to be the hottest and driest for many years and the site still had no water supply. Supporters' club secretary Roy King, a central heating engineer by trade, was called in to help provide one, but in the meantime the local pigeon population had a field day. Fortunately, the firm tending the pitch, Anglian Sportsturf, found unlikely allies in the form of a pair of kestrels that had previously been nesting in a floodlight pylon. The birds relocated to the roof girders of one of the stands and constantly harassed any pigeons that dared to settle.

In August, five weeks after sowing, it finally rained and within seven days the new grass could be seen. To the many fans who peered through the Floyd Road gates that autumn, the pitch was a miraculous and marvellous sight. But now that the disturbance was over, back came the urban foxes that had thrived during the wilderness years. The holes they dug meant extra work for the club's New Eltham groundsman, Charlton's hugely popular former winger Colin Powell.

As The Valley came back to life, so the man who had delivered its death sentence four years before passed away. John Fryer lost his long battle against cancer in the United States on June 22nd. A memorial service was held at Shirley, in Croydon, but the death of the club's joint president was otherwise little remarked.

Unexpectedly, there was now great activity in the streets of Charlton, where the first faint stirrings of discontent were beginning to be heard. Even before the end of the previous season, Greenwich's SDP MP Rosie Barnes, a market researcher by

Last stand: The Valley's hardest-won asset is dismantled bit by bit

trade, had embarked on a major survey of local attitudes to the return. She did so by distributing a self-completion questionnaire, eventually delivered to more than 3,000 homes. The results would ultimately form an appendix to the Greenwich planning department's report into the club's application to develop the ground.

Explaining the background to the survey, the MP wrote in her submission to the council: "When it became a distinct possibility that Charlton Athletic were seriously considering a return to The Valley, I received a lot of letters supporting their return and an almost equal number opposing it. When I replied, I noticed that most of those in favour seemed to live in places far afield, such as Orpington, Gravesend, Bromley or Dartford. Most of those very worried about the prospect of Charlton's return lived in the area immediately surrounding The Valley. While I am naturally interested in everyone's views, my job as a Member of Parliament is to represent the people of Greenwich. I therefore decided to find out exactly what the people living closest to The Valley thought."

But not everyone saw Barnes as simply a dutiful MP, earnestly seeking to gauge the opinions of her constituents. Some fans interpreted her behaviour as that of a weathervane politician with no commitment to anything except her own continuing electoral popularity. Whichever description was the more accurate, her poll was to prove almost completely useless as a basis for a policy. From the very beginning, public opinion divided equally. Of the first 550 responses analysed, 42 per cent were against Charlton's return and 37 per cent in favour. By the time she made her submission to Greenwich Council six months later, the gap had closed to 42 per cent opposed and 39 per cent supporting. And she was also able to reach the staggering conclusion that opposition became stronger the closer you got to the ground.

Although the MP was lampooned in the *Mercury* by Peter Cordwell for wasting time in determining the obvious, she was not the only politician in the field. Greenwich planning chair Cllr Norman Adams had had 2,000 letters distributed over a wide area putting the pros and cons. It was his response, he said, to the "deep concern" felt by local residents. "It's our job to put people in the picture so they won't feel alienated," he told the *Mercury*. "It's council policy to support the club's return to the borough but within certain guidelines. People have a right to carry on their peaceful existence."

Whatever Adams' motives, the crucial reference here was to council policy being only to support a return to Greenwich. To judge by leader Dave Picton's performance at Woolwich two months before, the fans had a right to expect that the council now supported a return specifically to The Valley. But Picton, we would soon be told, had only been expressing his personal opinion on that occasion. In which case it might have been helpful to all concerned if he had said so at the time.

As had long been acknowledged, Charlton did not need Greenwich Council's planning consent simply to return to The Valley. The fact that it had been a football ground in the past was enough to allow them to resurrect this use. However, they would need to obtain a safety certificate, responsibility for which had now passed to the borough from the defunct Greater London Council. They would also need to remove the court order which had closed the East Terrace in 1985 and obtain permission from Thames Water if they needed to build over the troublesome sewer.

The only part of the scheme that was initially thought to require planning permission was Laing's housing development behind the west stand. An application had first been made as long ago as the summer of 1988 but it had not been progressed while Charlton's own plans remained uncertain. Comprising 54 flats and 27 two and three-bedroom houses, the development would have been separated from the remaining stadium by a new three-metre brick wall and had road access onto Valley Grove. In May 1989, it was revised to include 66 flats "to suit first-time buyers" and 12 two and three-bedroom houses at "affordable" prices.

The club's owners now attended a public meeting for local residents at the Valley Club in an attempt to calm fears, but instead seemed only to inflame them. Cordwell's warning article on the back page of the *Mercury*, "Battle stations for The Valley", brought an angry response from Floyd Road resident Andrew Marsh, alleging that Roger Alwen had dismissed local concern by saying that fans weren't the club's responsibility once they were outside the ground. In a legal, if not a moral, sense this was perfectly true, but it was hardly a statement likely to placate the worried neighbours.

The most immediate cause of residents' disquiet was the question of parking, both that of their own cars and of those that would be brought into the area by spectators on matchdays. Certainly, the roads in the immediate vicinity were narrow and inadequate for dealing with any large volume of traffic. Only fans with authority to park inside the ground would need to use them, but there was already concern about access for the emergency services. Vague promises had been made about alternative arrangements for the bulk of the cars north of the Woolwich Road, but residents wanted firmer details. In the meantime, Norris boasted that The Valley would have space for 150 vehicles, a greater number than it had accommodated prior to 1985 and

Comedian Frankie Howerd, whose performance at Dartford's Orchard Theatre in May 1989 was promoted by Charlton as a fundraising venture for The Valley

more than Arsenal, with their much larger crowds, had ever had.

But the critical development that May, although no one realised it at the time, was the publication of the new borough plan, a strategic design for Greenwich's future development which the council was legally obliged to draw up for the Department of the Environment's approval. In it the whole of The Valley, including the land which Laing's intended to redevelop, remained designated as community open space. This was hardly consistent with the "indications" that had formed the basis for the chairman's announcement at Woolwich Town Hall just two months earlier. Later Alwen would claim that Picton had shown him a draft version of the plan in which this part of The Valley was covered by housing.

May also marked a watershed for me personally. Faced with a realistic workload for the first time since I had joined the Civil Service two-and-a-half years earlier, the burden of producing *Voice of The Valley* had begun to weigh increasingly heavily. Now that we had apparently achieved our original objective, there was an opportunity to bow out and disappear onto the terraces again. But though my job was taking off, I was no more than a proficient computer programmer. Blessed with no responsibilities to anyone save myself, I determined to gamble the future on a career more to my taste and hopefully my abilities. One April afternoon, exasperated by the Civil Service's obsession with pointless bureaucracy, I scribbled my notice and walked out. A month later, I was officially unemployed.

Fortunately, this state of affairs didn't last long enough for me to trouble the government coffers. An earlier interview with Cordwell for the *Voice*, at which we

Supporters Shaun Murray and Graham Amos, who visited all 92 grounds in the autumn of 1989 to raise funds for the Valley refurbishment

had discussed the deficiencies of the *Mercury*'s coverage of the club, had yielded the suggestion that Dixon and I try to fill the gap ourselves. However, the practicality of doing so hinged on Lennie Lawrence's willingness to co-operate with us. We successfully broached the subject at the player of the year function. When I mentioned to Cordwell that I had walked out on my job, he immediately offered me the chance to take on the task. The only complication was that Dixon had been equally keen to do it. But as became clear when my involvement with the *Mercury* developed, it would simply have been impossible for him to do so while employed full-time elsewhere.

My brief was to contribute a weekly column of variable length covering team affairs. Even in spite of the political rumblings, we never envisaged for a moment that the Valley affair would erupt again in still more spectacular fashion. But when it did, I was in a key position to fight our corner. Fanzine and newspaper now began to complement each other, the former providing the detail of events, the latter giving us the ability to respond quickly to the fast-changing situation and also appeal to a wider constituency.

Cordwell's experience, commitment and, above all, flair combined with my deeper knowledge of the club and understanding of the grass roots to make the *Mercury* a formidable ally for the directors in the struggles still to come, little though they seemed to appreciate it. The paper wasn't perfect by any means, but it pushed the Charlton message through 220,000 front doors every Thursday, free publicity beyond any other private company's wildest dreams.

The relationship between the directors and *VOTV* had remained a fragile one.

Matters had not been helped by the club's abject failure, almost alone in the Football League, to oppose the government's identity card scheme, a prime ministerial whim that made even less sense than the infamous poll tax. At the root of the problem was Alwen's personal friendship with the man charged with introducing the legislation, sports minister Colin Moynihan. While Ron Noades and Reg Burr, at Palace and Millwall, were running articles in their respective matchday programmes condemning the idea, Charlton maintained an uneasy official silence. They did permit us to attack it on the newly-instituted supporters' club page, but then countered by giving Moynihan space to reply.

The theory behind the legislation, in so far as it made any sense at all, was that issuing fans with computerised identity cards which they would have to produce in order to get into matches would enable the police and the football authorities to weed out the handful of troublemakers. This would lead to an entirely new atmosphere of sweetness and light within football grounds, where family attendance would boom as a result.

More realistically, Margaret Thatcher had simply decreed that something should be done about football. For now even the most trivial hooligan skirmishes were being exaggerated out of all proportion by the army of Fleet Street news reporters sent out specifically to report on them.

Unfortunately for the government, there were grave doubts that it was possible to design a computer system capable of processing 400,000 such cards in one hour, once a week. Nor was it clear that hooligans would desist from causing trouble outside grounds just because they couldn't get in. The basis upon which cards could be withdrawn appeared to conflict with natural justice and was wide open to exploitation by overzealous police forces, or even club directors seeking to exclude fanzine editors. And most important of all, the need to obtain such an identity card seemed certain to result in much smaller crowds and an inability to recruit new fans from casual attenders. The dangers to clubs like Charlton were considerable.

Yet when we had tried to discuss the matter with Norris, a man not noted for his willingness to debate, he simply countered that the scheme was inevitable. In his view the football authorities should have been looking at ways to make it work, not trying to prevent it happening. But the scheme was not inevitable, indeed quite the reverse since it was unworkable and potentially lethal.

In the end the opposition became so overwhelming that the government was obliged to retreat. The price of victory was a dear one, however, since it was a climbdown purchased with Liverpudlian blood. Taylor's damning judgement that after Hillsborough the risk of congestion outside turnstiles would be unacceptable threatened a backbench revolt in the House of Commons that not even Thatcher would have been able to ignore.

Norris and Alwen, of course, had other things on their minds in the summer of 1989. The impending all-seater requirement meant that in the long term they had to rethink their plans for the East Terrace, as well as the stands behind the goals. They had also been informed that since the new west stand would be bigger than its demolished predecessor, they would need to obtain planning permission before they could put it up. In the event, they decided that the time was right to go for permission not just for the new west stand but also for major developments on the north and east sides of the pitch, too.

Thus it was that on August 20th, at the New Eltham open day, the club unveiled a model of how they saw the ground eventually looking which had many supporters gasping in disbelief. For it now bore a greater resemblance to Old Trafford than to the lovable old Valley to which they had been yearning to return. No one could fault the directors for their ambition, but few believed it would ever be realised.

According to Norris, the stadium would be built in three stages. The initial one was little changed from that outlined at the March meeting, except that the new stand had grown to 6,300 seats, 28 executive boxes and a restaurant, while the intention to reinstate terracing behind the goals had been dropped. There would be 6,000 standing places available on the front section of the old East Terrace and 3,300 seats for visiting fans in the south stand, giving an initial capacity of around 18,500.

But Charlton were already reluctantly conceding that it would not, after all, be possible to return during the course of the 1989/90 campaign as had originally been hoped. "Now it's entirely up to the council to see that we are able to get back in time for next season," Norris had warned at a press briefing the previous day, in the process hinting at the fact that they were already expecting trouble.

The need to pressurise the council arose, presumably, from the unexpectedly grandiose scale of stages two and three. In the second, and most controversial, the existing Covered End, the Valley Club and two adjacent semi-detached houses owned by Adelong would be demolished. In their place would be built a new north stand,

Model future: the club's vision of how The Valley would look by 1995

effectively an extension of that on the west side of the pitch but incorporating a banqueting suite and commercial office development. These elements would take the building back over the old turnstiles and previously open forecourt to the site boundary on Harvey Gardens and were said to be vital to the financing of the latter parts of the project.

Stage three was to eliminate standing at the ground by replacing the East Terrace with a new east stand, again an extension of its neighbour and virtually identical to that on the west touchline. A timescale of five years was estimated for the whole scheme, with a final capacity of 22,000-25,000. Only the south stand would have remained as it had been before Charlton left in 1985 and outside the horseshoe formation of the other three sides.

Apart from its scale, there were other controversial features to the plan. Norris announced that away supporters would be charged a "seating price" of around £10 to use the south stand. And he warned Charlton fans who wanted the East Terrace retained for standing that they would have to change their habits. But in both cases he seemed to be falling into the familiar trap of trying to reshape the customer to fit the product, rather than the other way around. Hillsborough had weakened the popular opposition to all-seater stadia, but many fans were certain to resist the imposition, particularly if it was accompanied by a substantial increase in minimum admission charges as Norris seemed to intend.

To be fair, the vice-chairman did plan to improve what was on offer. There would be better toilet and refreshment facilities, he said, while another of his early ideas was to provide giant screens upon which fans could watch the previous week's games – and no doubt advertisements – while they waited for the action to begin. The aim was to ensure that supporters would want to arrive earlier and leave later, in the process reducing congestion and presumably spending more money with the club.

But how did this address the reality of the young working-class males who largely made up the travelling fans, steeped as they were in the culture of pre-match drinking and standing on terraces? Even if Norris was able to change the profile and habits of the mass of Charlton supporters, he could hardly expect to reshape those at the other 91 League clubs. And what of people arriving from far-flung places like Newcastle and Middlesbrough, who would surely want to start their return journey as soon as possible?

The scale of Charlton's new ideas also came as a surprise to Greenwich Council officials, who received two applications from the club on August 30th, a detailed scheme for the new west stand and an outline plan for the eventual redevelopment of the north and east sides of the ground. The latter also included the construction of 24 flats at the top of the East Terrace, off Lansdowne Mews. However, this aspect was soon abandoned, perhaps because not all of the land which they had applied to develop was at their disposal. The owner of a solitary house adjacent to the Bartram Gate defiantly refused to sell up.

With that exception, Adelong and the council between them owned all the surrounding land, including a remarkable blocked-off car park at one end of Lansdowne Mews, which residents said had been constructed by the council some years before but never once used.

A fourth planning application was already in, to extend and partly convert into a souvenir shop the house at the junction of Harvey Gardens and Floyd Road that had been the club's office in the last few years at the ground. The building had been vandalised while it lay empty and the plans to renovate it did not prove contentious.

The submission of the two major planning applications for the stadium marked the first public utterances on the subject of The Valley from Cllr Simon Oelman, who had replaced Adams as chair of planning in the spring. This earnest young man, the Labour member for Eynsham ward in Abbey Wood, would now be thrust blinking into the public spotlight, an experience he was not to enjoy. "From the council's point of view, safety is the top priority," he announced in a press release. "Before any decision is taken, we must be sure that the stadium is safe."

It seemed an understandable enough public position, given the outcry over Hillsborough. Yet, on the other hand, responsibility for ground safety did not reside with the planning department. Such matters were covered by a safety certificate separately and subsequently issued, even if the planning department would need to take into account any design considerations that might be affected by it.

The council's first action was to send out 1,500 letters to residents in the immediate vicinity of the ground advising that there were now three applications pending, excluding that for the club shop. It was not until October 17th, six weeks later, that Charlton attended their first meeting with the planning department to discuss the proposals.

According to architect Michael Newberry, writing to borough planning officer Sandra Hunt on December 12th: "This meeting appeared to have the primary purpose of explaining the scheme and also to confirm that the commercial elements were an

Eve Oldham and Fritz Henning on the platform at Charlton House

essential part of the overall viability of the club returning to The Valley. We were informed that the application for the west stand could not, as we wished, be considered in advance of the overall scheme application and that all the applications, including the housing, would be considered by committee simultaneously."

The following day, a further 1,500 leaflets went out advising residents of three public meetings in the Charlton area, aimed at explaining the scheme to local people. As such, there was no attempt to attract a wider public by advertising them in the local press, although details did appear in the *Mercury* after I was alerted to what was planned by sympathisers in the streets around the ground.

The first meeting took place at Charlton House on the evening of October 25th, the attendance being put by council officers at around 100 although it looked substantially less. In any case, the majority present were Charlton fans, with Norris incongruously seated among them, alongside commercial manager Steve Sutherland and company secretary Chris Parkes.

Surprisingly, there were no politicians present. Instead, the meeting was chaired by a young Scottish woman, Eve Oldham, who was revealed to be an organiser at the North Charlton Community Project, an outfit based next to Sam Bartram's old shop at the junction of Floyd Road and Valley Grove. Established in 1973 as a neighbourhood council, its main original aim had been to reduce the flow of heavy lorries down Charlton Church Lane. The problem was eventually solved by the introduction of a width restriction that caused considerable inconvenience to football coaches. Subsequently, the North Charlton initiative had expanded and developed into an information and resource centre, for three years in the mid-1970s even publishing the coincidentally-titled *Voice of Charlton*. It had been funded by Greenwich Council since 1984.

The plans were explained by Sandra Hunt's amiable deputy Fritz Henning, the man charged with writing the officers' report into the application. But so few local residents were in attendance that it was hard to see how the meetings served much purpose. The objections that were raised were mostly to the consequences of the return of football to The Valley, rather than to the specifics of the scheme. These should have been irrelevant, since in theory the planners were only entitled to consider the effects of the rebuilding, not problems arising from the presence of a football ground and the behaviour of its customers. However, the distinction was such a fine one and the subject so emotive that it was constantly blurred by almost everyone concerned.

In simple terms, it meant that residents of Harvey Gardens could legitimately complain to the planners that the proposed north stand would blot out the sun, but not that football supporters were likely to urinate in their front gardens. In fact, they raised both objections. More contentious still was the subject of traffic and parking. If the problem had existed at least potentially to an equal or greater degree prior to 1985, which seemed fairly incontestable, then presumably no one could claim that it would be a consequence of the club building new stands. But again that did not prevent both council and residents using it as an argument against the plans and it was to prove a major sticking point.

At least the Charlton House meeting and the two which followed – attended even on the council's figures by only 30 people each – did yield some further information about what was proposed. In the first place, the initial capacity of The Valley under phase one of the scheme would have been only 17,600. The East Terrace had now been restricted to just 5,000 spectators. Secondly, the Lansdowne Mews housing development had been withdrawn. But more significant was that Charlton now intended to vary their original plan to include a new south stand, eventually revealed to be a two-tier construction with 7,300 seats. Thus the finished stadium would no longer look like Old Trafford but more like a mini-Wembley.

There was also bad news about the timescale of processing the application, which Henning confirmed would not even come to committee before mid-January. Given a 16-week backlog for orders of steel and a minimum period of four or five months needed for construction, it meant Charlton would be now engaged in a desperate rush to get the ground ready in time for the start of the 1990/91 season even if they got their permission.

Blinded by the light: Simon Oelman

In a press release, Oelman explained the delay thus: "Not all residents of the borough, and particularly some of those living in the immediate vicinity of The Valley, share the fans' enthusiasm for the club's return. The applications are not solely concerned with the rebuilding of the stadium but include a sizeable area of housing, offices and a banqueting/function room facility. Whether such activities are appropriate in the area is a major question. They also involve the erection of a far more substantial structure located closer to people's homes than were the original stands.

"In terms of timescale in dealing with the application, I feel sure no one would wish the plans to be approved until the safety of all spectators and residents has been guaranteed in the design. The club has recently changed its mind on the stadium development and the proposed housing has also been altered. A revised planning application for these alterations has only very recently been submitted and the council is also awaiting a response concerning the problems of parking which would undoubtedly arise. We are dealing with a stadium for the 21st century. Times, requirements and standards have changed since the club first came to The Valley and the council would be failing in its duty if it ignored questions of safety and of wider environmental concerns."

The fact that the detail of the planning applications kept changing was obviously a problem for Greenwich, particularly since they were concerned to keep residents fully informed lest they later fell foul of the local government ombudsman. But as to the question of whether the additional activities were appropriate for the area, it was hardly necessary to consult with the residents of Floyd Road in order to evaluate them against the council's policies. The answer, profoundly in the negative, was given in the borough plan and it was surely beholden on the politicians to point that out in no uncertain terms, not least to the anxious fans. Instead, perhaps only too aware of the local elections six months ahead, they continued to prevaricate, a mistake for which they would eventually pay a heavy price indeed.

Another potential problem for the council was the fact that a prominent activist in the campaign against the Valley proposals was one of their own planning officers. David Higham's part in the affair was unusual to say the least. Although he worked for Greenwich's planning department, he was not involved in vetting the Valley application since his job was not within the development control section. But officials were understandably surprised when he got up at one of the three consultative meetings and started questioning his own colleagues as if he was an unconnected member of the public.

Higham, who lived in Charlton Lane on the east side of The Valley, was also involved in the production of a leaflet distributed in the vicinity of the ground in November which attacked the scheme in near-hysterical terms. "Do you really know what's proposed at The Valley?" it asked. "As well as a new stadium the club want speculative offices. The stadium is massive, 60 to 70 feet high. It will dominate, overlook and cut out light to nearby houses. The whole scheme is expensive and the club are bound to want to use it as much as possible to pay for it. There won't just be football every two weeks! Find out more! Object to these crazy ideas not fit for a residential area! Object now in writing to the council – they cannot ignore all of us!"

Unfortunately, neither Higham nor his supporters chose to put their name to the leaflet. Instead, they gave as contact Eve Oldham of the North Charlton Community Project, the supposedly impartial chair of two of the three consultative meetings held around the ground. It was later claimed that Oldham's name had been used without her permission, but whatever lingering claims she might have had to neutrality were rather undermined by her subsequent appearance in a debate at Crown Woods School in Eltham as a speaker opposing the plans.

By December, the council had been aware of what Charlton were proposing for more than three months. They had known about the housing application for twice that long. And they were fully aware that both were in direct conflict with the policies detailed in their borough plan. Yet if we are to believe Newberry's letter to Sandra Hunt, it was not until December 4th that they chose to point this out to the club. At what was evidently a stormy meeting, to judge from the tone of the architect's response, they finally told Charlton that their scheme was in large part unacceptable. According to Newberry, they also seemed to have reversed their earlier insistence on dealing with all three applications together.

The overall outline scheme would be recommended for refusal because of the commercial elements and the scale of the new building on Harvey Gardens. The detailed application for the west stand would be approved, but only subject to a section 52 agreement, a legally binding undertaking which would become a condition of the planning permission. In this case, one of the things the council wanted was that the club should finance a survey to investigate and then partly fund a traffic management scheme aimed at preventing commuters from using Harvey Gardens as a rat-run. Another was that Charlton should undertake to provide parking facilities north of the Woolwich Road and a compound for residents' cars cleared from surrounding streets by the police on matchdays. Finally, there should be public access to both the gymnasium and the pitch.

Section 52 agreements (soon replaced by section 106 agreements under the Town and Country Planning Act 1990) were a common and perfectly legitimate way of requiring an applicant to make a payment to the planning authority in respect of a planning gain that would result from a permission. But Charlton argued that since no increase in spectator accommodation would result from this application, there was no planning gain against which the demand could be made.

In any case, the requirements of the section 52 were unacceptable to the club. The details of parking and street clearance were nothing to do with the planners, given that the staging of professional football was an existing use of the site. These matters, they argued, should be dealt with under the safety certificate and not set in stone as would be the case with a section 52. The legislation also demanded that any payment be reasonable and directly related in scale to the benefit derived by the applicant, but the relevance of the traffic management scheme to the club was small. The pitch was a fragile asset to which it was hardly reasonable to seek legal access without reference to its condition. As for the gymnasium, there simply wasn't one!

According to Newberry, the council had said that the application would not proceed until these conditions were satisfied and refused to offer a date for it to come to committee despite the fact that they were fast running out of the time they were legally allowed in which to process it.

None of which would probably have come to light, had not the council unilaterally decided to issue a press release two days later. "Charlton Athletic have been asked to compromise on plans to redevelop their old ground at The Valley," it announced. "At a meeting with Greenwich Council on December 4th, Charlton were urged to drop their controversial plans to include speculative office space and a banqueting suite as part of their redevelopment proposals. Instead, they have been asked to come up with a package of measures to improve the environment for those living near the ground.

"Councillor Simon Oelman, chair of Greenwich's planning and transport committee, said: 'Charlton Athletic say they want a stadium for the 21st century. But an area as congested and densely populated as Charlton is not the perfect site. The police will require streets in the area to be free of cars for long periods on matchdays. So what are local residents going to do? Parking on matchdays is not the only problem – the club have refused to rule out using The Valley for other events such as pop concerts which cause all sorts of additional problems. Greenwich Council believes Charlton need to make changes to their proposals. They need to concentrate on the football stadium, drop some of their other plans and make some compensation to local people in the way of environmental improvements. We hope Charlton can rise to the challenge.'"

The club did indeed rise to the challenge, but presumably not in the way the council had hoped. Details of the statement, "the tone of which causes us great concern", were issued as an insert to Saturday's programme for the match with Millwall. And a press briefing was called at the training ground for the following Tuesday at which the Newberry letter was released.

"I want to know if the council is putting itself in a bargaining position or if the truth is they don't really want us back at The Valley," said Alwen. "No club can survive on football alone. We must have commercial use of the stadium and the banqueting suite would be a boon to local businesses and to the community as a whole. At the moment, the ground is an eyesore. Reference was made in the statement to pop concerts but we haven't at any stage mentioned them. We have user rights at The Valley but we haven't a hope in hell without commercial use."

In order to prevent the council granting them a permission on the west stand that they would be unable to take up, the club now withdrew the detailed application altogether. They claimed it would be considered as part of the outline scheme for the rest of the ground, but since it formed no part of the application still on the table, this did not prove to be the case.

Suddenly the campaign was on again with a vengeance, but this time with one important difference. The immediate target of our activities was no longer the club, which meant that those whose sense of loyalty to the latter had constrained them in the past were now ready to act too. The supporters' club and the *Voice*, no longer two distinct entities but overlapping, were apparently fighting side by side with the directors.

Also on the team, inevitably, was Peter Cordwell. His response to the council's press release had been instant. It was to run the single word "YES" on the back of the paper in letters seven inches high. The idea was for fans to stick the page in their windows to show their support for the scheme. That flopped, but face was saved by *VOTV* printing 15,000 copies of a similar design and persuading Charlton fans to hold them up on a given signal at Saturday's Selhurst game, ironically the "home"

Greenwich MP Rosie Barnes makes a point to the Charlton reminiscence class

The Yes men: fans at the Selhurst derby make their views on the plans clear

fixture against landlords Palace. The Yes poster now became the symbol of the campaign, appearing everywhere that we did.

Meanwhile, the man who as council leader had seemed to back the club's return to Floyd Road the previous March astounded everyone by resurrecting the idea of building a new ground at the Blackwall Peninsula. This time taking care to stress that it was his own personal view, Picton now favoured building a "modest" stadium at The Valley with a view to moving out again in four or five years.

It was not the first time that the idea of a temporary return had been floated. The suggestion had emerged from the meeting between club, fans and council back in 1986 after the *Mercury* petition. But it seemed to make little financial sense to invest in restoring The Valley as a football ground if the club was soon going to leave again. And if, as Picton envisaged, the Floyd Road site was subsequently to be maintained as a community facility, how would Charlton raise the money to build another stadium, even supposing land became available? Rate-capped Greenwich Council seemed unlikely to be in a position to provide the cash.

But the biggest charge levelled at Picton by the fans was one of hypocrisy. It largely arose from statements about the best future location of the club that he was alleged to have made to Eltham Labour Party – to whom he applied without success to become prospective parliamentary candidate – and local residents around the ground. However, it was not substantiated by his comments to the *Mercury*, to whom even now he was saying: "I am not opposed to the development of part of the site as long as it is with decent housing, but I think it is the wrong place for a bigger development." That much, at least, was consistent with his behaviour the previous March. The key point is that it had never been, apparently, and certainly was not now the position of the council.

Picton's predecessor John Austin-Walker, on the other hand, took a more realistic view of the way ahead. The borough's senior Labour politician regarded the peninsula as a dead duck and urged the two sides to get together in order to sort out a compromise. Still prospective parliamentary candidate for Woolwich, where he was again due to face well-known Charlton fan John Cartwright, the Hornfair ward councillor had an interest in distancing himself from any political row with the football club. The wards directly affected by the nuisance of the crowds included his own, but with the exception of Woolwich Common, were all in Rosie Barnes' neighbouring parliamentary constituency of Greenwich. And if he had a duty to the hostile local residents in Hornfair, he would escape any retribution by moving to Slade, in Plumstead, at the following May's local election.

Of course, one shouldn't be too cynical, even about politicians. Austin-Walker had played a key role in setting up the council's £50,000-a-year grant during the negotiations to save the club in 1984. Whatever his motives, in public at least he consistently took a middle line between the warring parties and won guarded respect as a result. Just how much substance his private activities really had is unclear.

Barnes, meanwhile, was causing still more confusion at a meeting of the Thamesside Adult Education Institute's highly successful Charlton Athletic Reminiscence Class, held at Woolwich in December. She told members that although she would have preferred the club to move to the peninsula, she was prepared to back the return to The Valley providing the parking problem was solved, as she thought it could be.

However, when this appeared in the *Mercury*, the MP wrote in to the paper saying that she had changed her mind because the police planned to make residents move their own vehicles from the surrounding streets on matchdays "so that fans can park *their* cars". Of course, the police's intention was nothing of the kind. Their concern was to ensure that roads were kept clear for emergency vehicles, as the embarrassed MP was obliged to explain a few weeks later.

The fans had their first brush with the politicians on December 12th, when Norris and Alwen met council leaders and officials at Woolwich Town Hall in an effort to clear the air after the public exchanges. A more constructive atmosphere was evident afterwards, with the two sides issuing a joint statement urging supporters to avoid "precipitous action" while further meetings were held.

This did not prevent a confrontation between the small band of fans present and Oelman, who was trying to chair a special meeting of the planning and transport committee into the proposed extension of the Jubilee Line. Interrupting from the public gallery, Roy King demanded to know why such a meeting had not been called to deal with the Valley planning application, causing Oelman to suspend proceedings. To his credit, however, the councillor did emerge afterwards to answer fans' questions, explaining that the consultation process was not yet complete but a special meeting would indeed be called "in the second half of next month".

It was what he had to say about the application itself, however, that convinced

Two faces: Greenwich councillors Dave Picton (left) and John Austin-Walker

the supporters the council's position was less than straightforward. "We want Charlton back in the borough but for legal reasons I can't form a view on The Valley until we've considered all the opinions," he insisted. "If this was just about football then I'd have few qualms, but the club insist that pop concerts and other uses are essential to their finances. In my opinion, we're dealing with this application very speedily compared with other projects of similar size."

But according to Alwen, Charlton had never made any suggestion that they wanted to hold pop concerts. Oelman's press release had referred only to the club refusing to rule them out, which was something slightly different. Yet now, when pressed, the planning chair was adamant that it was the directors' expressed desire to stage pop concerts and that they had specifically said that doing so was vital to the funding of the scheme. Later, Alwen remained equally insistent that the subject had never once come up.

Understandably, pop concerts were an emotive subject in the streets around the ground. But only two had ever taken place at The Valley and the crucial point was that if the club had wanted to repeat the exercise in the future, they would have required a special licence from Greenwich, application for which would almost certainly have been refused, just as it had been in 1978. There was clearly a case for controlling the number and nature of uses of the ground other than football, and an argument for restricting those which did not require such a licence, but no particular need to specifically exclude pop concerts at this stage.

The vehemence with which the two sides protested their innocence in this matter made it difficult to believe that they were the victims of a simple misunderstanding. If Charlton had indeed introduced the subject of pop concerts, they were either extremely foolish or did not want planning permission at all. This was a belief that was strongly held in some quarters at the council, with the increasingly grandiose scale of the application cited as evidence.

One reason why the politicians were suspicious about the board's motives was the nature of some of Norris's other activities. It had long since transpired that The Valley wasn't the only football ground in which he had an interest. He had connections with League of Ireland outfit Shamrock Rovers, another club which had abandoned their traditional home and encountered a fierce backlash from supporters. And together with Jim Gilman, vice-chairman of Leeds United, he had set up Denglen Limited, a company which arranged the redevelopment of Walsall's Fellows Park by a supermarket chain and the Saddlers' relocation to nearby Bescot.

That move would take place during the summer of 1990, coinciding with the club's second relegation in consecutive seasons, this time to the Fourth Division. It was not a particularly smooth transfer, with much criticism of the obstructed view caused by the choice, on the basis of cost, of propped rather than cantilever stands at the new ground. Unexpectedly, Walsall also became tenants of Denglen rather than freeholders, as they had originally been at their former home.

Perhaps, too, old scores were surfacing in Greenwich Labour Party. Unbelievably, Norris had once been a staunch socialist and a fervent supporter.

However, in the case of The Valley, there was firm evidence that he was a genuine Charlton fan. And it was difficult to believe the directors were really capable of being as devious as the council supposed. If they did not want to return to The Valley, then why were they presently spending £280,000 on the refurbishment of the former offices and establishment of a club shop there? What were their real intentions and why had they changed since last March? Could it have been that they had realised they could not now finance the homecoming and were looking for a scapegoat, just as Fryer had used Michael Gliksten? It was possible, but difficult to believe.

On the other hand, if Oelman had invented the idea of further pop concerts then he was presumably seeking to stir up the residents, for which the only apparent motive was ideological. Certainly the council seemed unable to understand that their local football club was more than just another speculative business venture. As one fan later put it so succinctly: "They treated Charlton like it was an application for Tesco." Yet why should the politicians have needed to resort to invention? If they simply wanted to reject the remaining planning application, the borough plan already gave them firm grounds for doing so.

In this respect, the problems with the application were twofold. For a start, the bulk of the building on Harvey Gardens was deemed to be intrusive and overwhelming for a residential neighbourhood. As a result of Greenwich's objections of December 4th, Charlton made various attempts to reduce the visual impact, eventually embodied in a revised application submitted on January 9th. But the stand was still 74 feet high and 412 feet long. Its depth would be treble that of the existing Covered End and at the nearest point it would be 57 feet closer to Harvey Gardens.

It remained an imposing new structure for a quiet residential backstreet, even if all but eight of the houses directly opposite were laid out at right angles to The Valley, diminishing the immediate effect.

More controversial still were the planned offices and banqueting suite the stand was intended to include. The borough plan stated: "Public and private open space areas defined as community open space... will be safeguarded from built development. Buildings will only be permitted where they are ancillary to the existing land use, are limited in size and extent, sensitively sited, and are compatible with neighbouring development."

Of course, The Valley was not like any ordinary playing field and the council recognised that it required considerable built development in the form of spectator stands and ancillary accommodation. But how far 32,280 square feet of office space and 14,127 square feet of banqueting suite could be deemed ancillary was a moot point. Even if it could be argued that they did meet that description since they were supporting the football club financially, the building still had to meet the other requirements of the policy in terms of fitting in with the ground's neighbours.

"The council will not give consent to proposals to establish or extend buildings on public or private open spaces unless it is satisfied that the proposal is ancillary to the principal use of the open space and that it will not harm the amenity of nearby residents," insisted the policy document.

And there was another complication. The borough plan specified that office

Record signing Joe McLaughlin goes in where it hurts at Aston Villa in August

development of any type would be encouraged to locate in the centre of Woolwich. Development not exceeding 30,000 square feet would be permitted within defined town centres, but that elsewhere would be restricted to just 5,000 square feet, and then it would only be allowed where the offices provided a local service and did not conflict with residential or shopping policies. That proposed for The Valley was clearly well outside those guidelines.

Quite who Charlton expected to rent the offices also remained a mystery. Originally, there had been talk of leasing them to the council, but that idea seemed to come from the club. Greenwich consistently termed them "speculative", meaning that they had no intended occupier, but for the fans the word carried a sinister overtone of property speculation.

There was concern, too, about the traffic and parking problems that would arise from both the offices and the banqueting suite, although the parking question seemed to be answered by what were now envisaged to be 200 spaces within the completed ground. Less easily dismissed was the noise and other nuisance that would inevitably result from people leaving functions late at night, although that already occurred to some extent from the activities of the established Valley Club.

Yet another source of dispute between Greenwich and Charlton was the deadline by which the council had to reach a decision on the application. The eight-week legal time limit was regarded as unreasonable by officials because of the extensive consultation necessary and the situation was further complicated by revisions to the plans. But once the period had expired the club had the right to take the application straight to the Department of the Environment.

This would have suited the council very well, since it would have absolved them of political responsibility for the decision, something of which Charlton were quite aware. But it would have taken longer still and also removed the possibility of appeal, so it was not a course of action that the directors were keen to take. Instead, they had to wait for Greenwich to make their minds up in their own time.

And all the while, the club's First Division life was ebbing away. After making the best start of the four years back in the top flight, the side had slid down the table, hitting the bottom after the dire Boxing Day defeat at Wimbledon. Now, just when Lawrence needed funds to revive his demoralised squad, the cost of The Valley began to bite into the budget available for players. At the beginning of January, he was obliged to sell exciting winger Micky Bennett, who had only recently returned after his long injury lay-off, to neighbours Wimbledon for £250,000. The money was required to help finance the building of the club shop. Had planning permission for The Valley already been granted Charlton would at last have had an asset against which to borrow. As it was, they were struggling to pay their way.

Less than a fortnight later, new skipper Colin Pates followed Bennett out of the door bound for Arsenal. This time the picture was more complicated. The £500,000 offer was generous and provided 28-year-old Pates with an apparently outstanding opportunity. Charlton wanted the money and from that perspective were keen for him to go, but the player could not make up his mind. In the end, his decision proved to be the wrong one for everyone concerned. Charlton lost one of their most influential players, Gunners boss George Graham paid too much and Pates was left to bide his time on the fringe of the first-team squad for more than a year. He went on to make just two League appearances, one as substitute, as Arsenal conceded the championship to Liverpool in 1990 and one more from the bench before being loaned out to Second Division Brighton & Hove Albion the following March.

The effect of these departures on morale at Charlton could not have been worse. As Lawrence admitted, some of Pates' value to the side was in his partnership with former Chelsea defensive teammate Joe McLaughlin. But equally much of the latter's value to Charlton was in his partnership with Pates. The Scot had arrived from Stamford Bridge in a record £600,000 deal at the start of the season to replace the inspirational Peter Shirtliff, who had sadly left during the summer to rejoin Sheffield Wednesday, his former club, for £100,000 less.

Together Pates and McLaughlin had appeared invincible at the start of the season as Charlton drew their first three games, the opener against Derby County at Selhurst and then away at Millwall and Aston Villa. They might easily have won them all, particularly that at The Den, where Paul Williams had scored to put his side two up with just four minutes remaining. The visiting supporters were exultant, only to see their neighbours come roaring back with two late goals to equalise.

Just a week later had come the high point of the club's modern First Division career when they dismissed early League leaders Chelsea 3-0 at Selhurst Park. Williams scored twice in the first half then chested down Pates' through ball for Paul Mortimer's breathtaking late strike, crashed against the underside of the bar from the

Now you see him: skipper Colin Pates against Southampton on January 1st

edge of the box. Third in the table, Charlton that night appeared set for easily their best season since promotion. However, it was to be followed by six consecutive League defeats, ended only by a solitary 1-0 win at QPR. A point from a home game against Coventry City and the 2-0 Selhurst defeat of Manchester United on November 4th created the illusion that the corner had been turned, but a further run of 12 League games without a victory, punctuated only by an FA Cup replay win at Second Division Bradford City, confirmed the perilous position.

At least the painful "home" defeat by newly-promoted Crystal Palace, an occasion which saw Eagles' fans confined to one end of their own ground, passed with little of the crowd trouble anticipated by the club. Some Palace supporters entered into the spirit of things by setting out on a morning coach trip round London to simulate a normal away game. But Noades was jeered to his seat in the directors' box and inside the stand one man had to be physically restrained from confronting him. The Palace chairman had criticised his tenants in a string of interviews for not taking up the full benefits of groundsharing and privately Charlton officials were furious with him for inflaming the already tense situation.

Going into the derby game already badly weakened by an injury crisis that forced midfielder Mortimer to start at centre-half, Charlton lost his partner Tommy Caton with concussion at half-time. By then they were already two down, having spurned a generous penalty award when Mark Reid struck the ball against a post. Even so, Colin Walsh reduced the arrears with a spectacular free-kick and Palace keeper Nigel Martyn had to make a tremendous save from Bennett's bullet header in the final minute to prevent a largely undeserved equaliser. But despite the revival it was to prove the first of seven more consecutive League defeats.

Palace's inferior status had always been one of the sharing arrangement's few saving graces. Now they had clearly signalled that they were no longer the underdogs. The indignity was compounded by the fact that Charlton had to return three days later to play them in a Full Members' Cup match, now under the title of new sponsors Zenith Data Systems. Few Addicks fans could bear to watch the inevitable defeat of their even further depleted side in a competition that remained almost totally irrelevant.

True to Oelman's promise, the date for the planning meeting proved to be in the second half of January – on the last possible day, the 31st. The Laing's housing application had now also been withdrawn, presumably because the builders were experienced enough to know that there was no possibility of it being approved. Charlton continued to insist that the decision would cover outline proposals for all four sides of the stadium, but Greenwich remained adamant that the west side formed no part of the outstanding application.

Whatever the respective merits of the way the two sides had conducted themselves thus far, the council now made a calamitous political mistake. They announced that their verdict would be given at the end of a special meeting of the planning committee held before 600 members of the public at Woolwich Town Hall. No attempt was made to reserve admission, although advertisements inviting any interested parties who wished to speak to contact the committee clerk were placed in local newspapers.

In principle, the council's desire to resolve the issue in public was laudable, but the format of the meeting was a disaster. By failing to make admission all-ticket, they guaranteed that hundreds of anxious fans would turn up and have to be locked out. They put opposing residents in the daunting position of having to compete with the much more numerous supporters for the places in the hall. And their commitment to announce a verdict about such a complex matter on the night ensured that the consultation embodied in the speeches from the floor would be a charade.

Despite a few dissenting voices that had made themselves heard through the local press, the majority of supporters still seemed firmly behind the stadium plans. The critics wrote that they objected to their loyalty to the club being used as a cover for property speculation. But we were suspicious that such letters were being planted. After all, most of those which appeared in the *Mercury* in favour of the scheme certainly were. One week Roy King had four published on the same page!

A similar situation existed with the council's monthly propaganda sheet *Greenwich Time*, where a letter from a supposed fan called Kevin Evans appeared, accusing supporters of getting "far too emotional about the prospect of going back to The Valley". He went on: "Let's concentrate our energies on the club, not the ground. Charlton have done well at Selhurst and could do even better if supporters stopped harking back to the good old days." Shortly afterwards the same letter turned up in the *Mercury*. And then Oelman wrote in quoting it approvingly.

Whether, in retrospect, the fans' uncritical support for the board was right is questionable. My own view remained that no more than the initial stage of the scheme, the west stand, would ever be completed, so to a large extent the argument was irrelevant. What concerned me more was that the council appeared to be hostile to the club returning to The Valley at all. But I could see the need to raise income from commercial activities. The fact that those presently envisaged conflicted with the borough plan was obviously a problem, but then it had been the council's own decision to retain the site's designation as community open space the previous May.

Moreover it had been done in the full knowledge of the housing scheme that it effectively ruled out. Other London grounds were not so described in their respective borough plans and even Oelman later conceded that the designation was insufficiently sensitive to the club's needs.

Of course, the councillors could have ruled that Charlton were a special case and approved the latter application anyway. Oelman argued otherwise, claiming that this would create a precedent that would allow developers to build houses on every playing field in the borough. But quite clearly a professional football ground was not a public open space and there were grave doubts that it would do any such thing.

Oelman's stated belief was that we should have been putting pressure on the directors to submit more modest plans. But even had we been able to assess the club's true financial needs, and so been able to judge the scale of commercial development required, that would surely have been a tactical blunder. For just as when Norris had wanted to go to the Blackwall Peninsula, we could not afford to alienate the owners. They were our only hope of getting out of Selhurst Park. In any case, we owed them a debt of loyalty from the decision to return to The Valley at all. And there was a tremendous desire to believe that they were genuine.

With this in mind, the news of the decisive meeting appeared in the *Mercury* with

Battle for The Valley

A poster produced by the group of residents based around the North Charlton Community Centre in Floyd Road, aimed at increasing local concern about the scale of the proposed redevelopment at The Valley. Note the barbed wire!

an appeal from King to besiege the town hall on the evening in question. In fact, the plea was invented by me in my capacity as supporters' club press officer. It was a calculated gamble that sheer weight of numbers would put immense pressure on the councillors, but it depended upon the assumption that the fans who did turn out could be relied upon to behave themselves. For there could be nothing more likely to damage our cause than trouble in Woolwich. Understandably, the club was nervous about the behaviour of supporters. So too were some of the residents, who later claimed that they had felt intimidated even before the event. However, the more thoughtful among them knew very well that a riot would be the best possible thing that could happen from their point of view. According to one insider, they even discussed its desirability.

As it turned out, the numbers of people on either side and their opinions were of no bearing whatsoever because the issue was effectively decided by the planning officers' report. Perhaps, with hindsight, that had always been inevitable because of the complexity of the issues at stake. After all, the members of the planning committee were by and large no more expert and certainly no more intelligent than the public on whose behalf they made their decisions.

Henning's report was a damning document indeed, making all the well-rehearsed points about parking, traffic, visual amenity and council policy on office development and concluding with a firm recommendation for refusal. But confusingly, it acknowledged that the problems which arose from football had "existed when the

Roy King (left) on the steps of Woolwich Town Hall before the meeting

club were previously at The Valley. There is no reason to suppose that the situation will have changed significantly since then". In which case it begged the question of what business they were of the planning committee.

Bafflingly, the passion so evident among the fans had hardly surfaced in the council's consultation exercise. Despite all our pleas, only 246 letters supporting the application had been received by the time the report was compiled, 121 from outside the borough. But that was still more than the opposing residents' total of 83, and this despite the patronising form letter distributed around the ground in the name of the North Charlton Community Centre.

It was never very likely that the committee would overturn the report's recommendations, as Oelman insisted to me might happen when we spoke on the day before the meeting. For one thing there were still too many loose ends, with the club refusing to admit the planners' rights to restrict non-football activities or insist on the provision of a compound for those residents' cars displaced by parking controls.

Surprisingly, however, the club had appeared hopeful of success right up to the report's publication, which perhaps suggests that they were more naive than devious. Indeed, Alwen had described himself as cautiously optimistic just three days before the document landed on the desk at the *Mercury* on January 26th, based on the fact that the club shop plans had been approved and recent discussions with the council had centred on the detail rather than the principle of the north stand proposal. The report's availability also took him completely by surprise. I had to photocopy the paper's version to pass on to the Charlton chairman at the following day's fourth-round FA Cup tie with West Bromwich Albion.

In return, Alwen gave me a telephone interview at home on the Sunday evening that was to prove decidedly more trouble than it was worth. In it he described the report and the borough planning officer in terms to which she was to take great exception, for several months threatening legal action. Fortunately, his words only appeared in the *Mercury* the day after the planning meeting had taken place, so there could be no suggestion that they had influenced the outcome.

And still he clutched at the straw that a vast turnout of supporters might persuade the politicians to overturn the recommendation made by their officers. We had already urged fans to turn out on the night in a *VOTV* editorial and distributed a leaflet to our supporters at West Brom repeating the message. But apart from the expensive and therefore minority method of Clubcall, the only remaining channel through which we could impress the renewed urgency was Tuesday's *South London Press*. At my suggestion, Alwen arranged for press officer Peter Burrowes to give the rival paper the story.

Then, just two days before the meeting, came the publication of the final version of the Taylor Report. It called for more groundsharing and the relocation of existing stadia in greenfield sites where possible. But it also demanded the end of terracing and recognised the need for additional commercial activity to fund the necessary work. So its impact on the Valley application was decidely mixed. Both sides would seek to use it in their arguments, with Charlton claiming they had anticipated its findings by six months.

Wednesday, January 31st, dawned wet and blustery. Thomas Hardy himself couldn't have scripted the conditions better, but they threatened to put a big dampener on our planned march from The Valley to the town hall. Another factor was that those most determined to get into the meeting wanted to be in the queue by six o'clock in order to be sure of their place, while many more could not get away from work early enough to get to the ground. In the event about 300 made the rain-sodden trip, their chants echoing with deceptive volume through the streets of Woolwich as they arrived.

Thus far the residents and fans, and some who were both, had mingled good-naturedly on the steps of the town hall. Only a handful of locals had come to oppose the plans but they made no secret of their position. Also heavily in evidence were the electronic media. At least the local television news teams were able to spot a good story, even if London's monopoly evening paper couldn't. There was plenty for them to record. By the time the doors were finally opened, there were more people outside than could reasonably be allowed in. And as the evening wore on, hundreds more arrived to wait in the rain for the verdict. The wiser ones took cover in the nearby Director General pub pending developments, perhaps guessing that it would be some hours before the outcome was known.

Inside the hall, officials were concerned that they had admitted too many. All the available seats were taken and there was a short delay while they debated what to do about it. But their chances of persuading anyone to leave were slim.

The 14-strong, all-male committee, ten of them Labour members, two Conservative, one SDP and one Liberal, sat facing the audience at a long table which stretched the length of the crowded stage. Two Tories and Labour's new prospective parliamentary candidate for Eltham, Clive Efford, had failed to put in an appearance. Behind the main group sat two dozen more people: officials, police and fire brigade representatives, and other councillors with an interest, such as Picton and Austin-Walker. In the very middle of the front table were Sandra Hunt and Oelman. Henning was in the West Indies watching the touring English cricket team, so she had to present the report.

Immediately opposite her, on the floor of the hall, was the sparsely populated press table and behind that, centrally, stood a microphone, ready for the contributions from the applicants and the public. The Charlton officials all sat in the front row of the audience: directors Alwen, Norris, Ufton and Collins, architect Newberry, general manager Arnie Warren and even Lawrence. Hostile residents sat in two small and isolated groups, perhaps 20 of them in total.

Everywhere else there were Charlton fans, even up in the gallery, which had been draped with banners including a Union Flag emblazoned with the plaintive plea: "I wanna go home!" The scene was set for a planning meeting unlike any the council had ever known.

First Sandra Hunt introduced her department's report, announcing that since its completion more letters had been received, as well as a new petition of some 700 names opposing the scheme. She referred to the Hillsborough Report's comments about the unsuitable location of many of Britain's football grounds. But most astonishing, given the complexity of the matter in hand, was the fact that not one question was asked of her by the politicians. It strongly suggested that they had

Passing fancy: supporters eye the model nervously as they enter the town hall

already made up their minds.

For the applicants, Newberry defended the scheme. He made the familiar complaint that much of what the report contained was irrelevant. Yet his tactic of ridiculing aspects of it seemed a curiously ill-judged one. If anything, Norris and Alwen were even worse. The former was strangely ineffective, as if knocked quite out of his stride by having to appeal to the council in this way when he was used to giving the orders. The habitually nervous Alwen seemed to be on the verge of bursting into tears.

There were also contributions from the police and fire brigade, although just as Charlton had argued these seemed out of place and they could only offer vague warnings.

Next came an hour-long session of comments from the floor. There was scattered applause as the first man came to the microphone, but it was premature. Although as yet his identity was unknown to us, it was the planning department's very own David Higham. As Oelman was to imply when he called me last, this part of the meeting had been deliberately structured. But we, at least, had had no advance knowledge of whether we would be called and if so when, which made it much more difficult for us to prepare our speeches.

To be fair, the planning chair did call all the key players on our side who had telephoned the council asking to speak: relative newcomer Richard Hunt, King, Dixon and myself, even if he did appear to take great delight in announcing where we lived. This was particularly damaging in Richard's case, because he had moved out to distant and faintly ridiculous Surbiton. But there were other speakers for the cause who lived more locally, such as Charlton schoolteacher Joanna Moore and Peter Page from Greenwich Sports Council.

Some of the faces on the residents' side were soon to become very familiar. The elderly but spirited Grace Sole lived so far from the ground that the chances of her being affected by the proposed commercial activities were negligible in the extreme. But she claimed the right to speak for local people as chairwoman of Tenants Action Group 90, an extraordinary local pressure group that appeared to spend much of its time praising Greenwich Council and pointing out that any and every problem was really the fault of the nasty Tory government.

Her formidable sidekick Bob Dean was also involved in TAG90 and certainly lived closer to the ground, but he was allowed to announce unchallenged to the meeting that he represented 300 people. The audience cried in vain for an explanation of who they were. The arguments of neither were particularly impressive. But what marked the two of them out from the other opposing speakers was not so much what they said but how they said it. They were both very obviously working class. The rest of those who came to the microphone to object were equally obviously not. It was relevant, because the social composition of the part of Charlton adjacent to the ground had changed in the years the club had been away. The yuppies had moved in, bringing with them an ignorance of what football crowds were really like and a

It's a walk-out: fans leave the meeting in disgust before the vital vote

familiarity with pressure-group politics. A principal objection which was voiced to the club coming back was the effect it would have on house prices.

Of all people, Higham was surely best qualified to understand which arguments against the application were valid, but he did not confine himself to them. Instead, he claimed to have information that GM Vauxhall Conference neighbours Welling United were in discussions about sharing The Valley, something the directors vehemently denied. Another speaker made the unlikely claim that the ground was in a "delightful residential area" that would be spoiled by the return of football.

But the climax of their contribution was a fluent and apparently never-ending tirade from Floyd Road's Andrew Marsh. Oelman had announced that speeches would be limited to three minutes but Marsh, unquestionably the residents' star turn, just went on and on, until the clamour for him to be silenced by the chair grew so loud he could hardly be heard. Among his many points were that women would be frightened to venture out to the hairdresser's on a matchday and that the elderly would be prisoners in their homes.

"When people from Eltham, Blackheath, Swanley, Welling and Surbiton tell me it's their local club, I am puzzled," he added, omitting to mention that he himself came from Wolverhampton. Marsh and his wife Kate were central figures in what remained very much a minority of activists opposed to the plans.

By this time, I had given up hope of being called myself, but Oelman had decided to give me the task of summing up. Such was the hubbub caused by Marsh that I got the most tremendous reception as I approached the microphone. "What a load of rubbish!" I began, to another deafening roar.

Unfortunately, I was suffering from a streaming cold and could hardly talk. The effect of that and the anger generated by Marsh was to make my voice crack up as I spoke, with quite comical effect. My speech was also completely over the top, as I realised even in the process of delivering it. The threat of electoral retribution if the application was vetoed sounded so unlikely in practice that behind me I could hear some of the residents laughing. Luckily, the audience was on my side and generous in its applause.

Perhaps the members of the public, or most of them at any rate, could be excused for using arguments that were irrelevant in planning terms. It was more difficult to make the same excuse for the politicians, with their greater experience of such occasions. Yet their debate on the scheme was woeful. Tory leader Peter King, ironically enough the representative for Palace ward, in Eltham, brought the house down when he recalled how he had begun to support Charlton in 1948, "the year they won the Cup".

More sinister was the speech by Adams, who once again raised the question of the phantom pop concerts. Even Austin-Walker, speaking as a Hornfair ward councillor, was moved to point out the complete irrelevance of the issue. And it was "Jaws" who insisted that if the council would not permit the proposed commercial development on the site, then it was beholden on it to specify what level of such activities would be acceptable. It was not realistic to claim, as one councillor had, that gates would improve so much simply as a consequence of the club's return that no other source of income would be necessary.

No go: the planning committee vote 10-2 to throw out the club's application

But the vote was always a foregone conclusion. As the fans grew steadily more restless, Oelman had several times to appeal for quiet. People were drifting away now, shaking their heads in disbelief. Seated together on the far side of the hall, Dixon, King and I decided to seize the initiative by leading a mass walk-out.

For several minutes there was utter chaos. Perhaps three-quarters of those present got to their feet to join us, but the solitary exit could not cope with the numbers and only around half got out. As they made their way past the front of the stage, many fans threw screwed up Yes posters in the direction of the top table. One or two grabbed the microphone to tell the councillors what they thought of them and there were numerous cries of "Fix!" Amid it all, Alwen vainly appealed for calm.

Outside in the rain and wind, the crowd was hungry for news and swelling by the minute. They didn't have long to wait now. Soon the rest of the audience was streaming out to report a 10-2 defeat. Poor Bill Strong had been caught in the crossfire once again, this time as mayor. As a former director of the club, he declared an interest and did not cast his vote. Another Charlton supporter, Phil Graham, had abstained, while two Labour members, Jim Coughlan and Bob Callow, had voted in favour of granting permission. With the solitary exception of Graham's abstention, it was exactly the outcome Alwen and Norris had been told the previous day to expect.

And still the angry supporters, around a thousand of them, waited at the doors of the town hall. The opposing residents had been ushered out through another exit by the police, but the politicians who emerged were loudly jeered. Eventually, Alwen appeared on the steps and the crowd fell silent to hear what he had to say. It was to ask them to disperse peacefully, on the understanding that further talks would take place in an effort to reach an agreement. Remarkably, it was enough to bring the night's events to a peaceful close. There had not been a single arrest.

The planning refusal, however, was nothing short of disastrous. Perhaps the directors were as much to blame as the councillors, but it almost certainly meant another season at Selhurst Park, this time with the probability of Second Division football. In the confusion of the next few days, the owners even seemed to hint that they might give up the fight altogether.

For the supporters, on the other hand, that night at Woolwich Town Hall marked an important turning point. What had begun two years earlier in a Bexleyheath pub with a handful of conspirators now became a truly mass movement at last. The fans did not like being treated with such obvious contempt by their elected representatives and they would prepare a stunning response.

Councillor Simon Oelman, in particular, would soon rue the day he had come between Charlton Athletic and The Valley.

Chapter Ten

"Messrs Gliksten, Fryer and Noades may not be trade union leaders, but many of us wish they had been subject to some sort of ballot."
Peter Cordwell – *Mercury (September 12th, 1985)*

It had been Richard Redden who had first suggested standing in the local elections, back in December. The secretary of the self-styled Hayes and West Wickham supporters' group, he was then putting the finishing touches to the first complete history of the club to be published since 1949. Ironically, Redden, a failed Labour parliamentary candidate now in the SDP, would play little part in the subsequent campaign – he had an election of his own to fight in his native Bromley, where he was well beaten by the Tories.

At first the idea held little appeal for me. As a member of the Labour Party, I didn't much like the idea of running against them, although that problem was overcome by the discovery that as a Bexley resident I was ineligible anyway. More seriously, however, if we did stand and failed to get a respectable share of the vote, we might well end up doing ourselves more harm than good. That, indeed, was the prediction made by Nick Raynsford, Labour's squeaky-clean new parliamentary candidate for Greenwich, during the election campaign. It was something that continued to worry me even after the contest became inevitable.

For his part, Redden seemed to believe that there were 500 Charlton fans in each ward, a proposition which seemed a trifle fantastic. Much of the historic following in Greenwich had long since moved out and the club's own figures suggested support was now stronger in Bexley, Bromley and even Dartford, although later statistics suggested this was an overstatement of the position. Letters sent to the council backing the planning application had divided almost equally between those from inside and those from outside the borough, but given that Greenwich people were presumably more likely to write anyway, that only served to underline the point.

There was also no way of knowing how even the football fans among the electorate would respond to being asked to cast their vote for single-issue candidates. We had no coherent political programme or, for that matter, any real ambition to run the borough. Finally, there was the uncertain impact of the poll tax, an horrendous piece of Thatcherite nonsense that by March would sweep Labour a record 25 per cent clear in the national opinion polls. So we seemed certain to be swimming against a rising political tide.

Seen purely as a publicity stunt, however, the threat of standing had some potency and, after all, what harm could it do? So the prospect was duly aired in the *Mercury* on December 14th, albeit well down the copy, which is an illustration of just how seriously we regarded it. For once the *South London Press* went in harder, splashing the story in their free paper and even doing a vox pop on it with local residents for their weekend issue.

When *Thames News* latched on to the idea and I was whisked up to Euston in a chauffeur-driven limo to be interviewed on camera for the early-evening sports slot, the ploy seemed to have achieved its object. We had successfully fired a warning shot

Battle for The Valley

across the council's bows. As far as I was concerned, the only pity was that no one was around to see me arrive at my former office's Christmas party afterwards in the car.

As we waited for the planning meeting, the idea of standing for election rumbled on in the background, prompting the occasional radio interview. Then, on the morning of the day itself, came a visit to my front garden from Duncan Kennedy and a team from BBC1's *Newsroom South East*.

We were getting our publicity all right, but could we carry the threat through if it came to the crunch? By 10pm that evening we were left with no choice. Not only had Steve Dixon announced to the TV cameras outside the meeting that we would be standing, but we had little other means left by which to try to influence events.

Thus was born the Valley Party. Officially, its leader was to be 40-year-old Barry Nugent, the social secretary of the supporters' club but, more importantly, a Labour Party member in Eltham. In fact, Barry never led anyone anywhere, for such was the democratic spirit of the newly-formed party that leadership was not really a requirement. Either way, he needed little persuasion to appear on the back page of the following week's *Mercury* tearing up his party card and the battle was on.

Peter Cordwell had required no prompting from me to give this story an enormous "Vote Valley" headline, but to some senior figures at the paper the words looked dangerously like an imperative. Now that the issue had become highly political, the sports department's backing for the fans' cause threatened to disrupt the news reporters' normal working relationship with the council. Indeed, it was questionable whether the story properly belonged in the sports pages at all any more. After discussions, it was decided that I should write no more articles about the campaign

Follow the leader: Barry Nugent displays a Valley Party car sticker

201

for the duration and that my byline on anything I did contribute would be qualified with a reminder that I was the editor of *Voice of The Valley*.

In practice, this made no difference whatsoever. Cordwell and I continued to collaborate just as before, publishing a stream of thinly-disguised propaganda throughout the spring. It culminated with an outrageously upbeat back-page lead on polling day, published in open defiance of the office ban on politically contentious stories that week. Yet we did no more than much of the national press does on behalf of the Tories at every general election. And at least we were reflecting the views of a large section of our readership, rather than those of a powerful proprietor or shadowy vested interests. In any case, this sports editor would have found the role of impartial observer a difficult one to carry off.

The part played by the paper in the next three months was to be a crucial one. Without it, the Valley Party might well have been marginalised. But it was the extraordinary swelling of grass-roots support that gave the coverage credibility by generating a presence in the streets and on the doorsteps. On the second Monday in February, a dozen of us gathered at the Valley Club for what was to be the first of many long meetings. From the outset, it was clear that Greenwich had badly mishandled things. Many who had hitherto been content to watch from the sidelines were outraged by the way the planning committee session had been conducted.

When we met again, a fortnight later at the nearby Meridian sports club, numbers had more than doubled. After a 500-strong public meeting at Greenwich on March 6th, when Simon Oelman bravely tried to explain the council's position to a polite, but entirely hostile audience, the now weekly sessions began to attract between 60 and 70 people.

Early meetings were chaired by Richard Hunt, an advertising executive in his mid-30s who way back in 1985 had so outraged the CASC committee by proposing the motion of disgust at the directors' failure to attend the AGM. Little had been heard of him subsequently, however, until he was drawn back into the campaign through reading *VOTV*. His Surbiton address was to provide a frequent source of ammunition for our opponents, but in fact, and unlike many of those who ridiculed it in the *Mercury*'s letters pages, he had actually grown up in the borough.

More to the point, he had attended the same Catford school, St Dunstan's College, as Channel 4 boss Michael Grade and new council leader Quentin Marsh, something we would later turn to our advantage.

Hunt had more substantial contributions to make, however. Unlike the majority of the people involved, he could talk to the directors in the measured middle-class tones with which they were quite obviously most at ease. Yet his perspective on events was entirely our own. Furthermore, he was able to deliver a borough-wide advertising campaign of saturation proportions at negligible cost.

There were also other newcomers in the front line. Steve Reader, Alex and Danny Hayes, Dominic Crowe and Derek Woolley were all involved from the outset and went on to play prominent roles. Perry Bartlett, from Penge, in the heart of Palace country, and Paul Giannandrea each took on the arduous duties of an area organiser.

Orthodox political affiliations within the new party were varied. Some of our earliest advice came from Charlton fan Mike Moore, a rabid Tory who had once stood

No: Simon Oelman explains the planning refusal at Greenwich on March 6th

in the by-elections forced by Greater London Council leaders to protest at their authority's abolition. Another who obviously relished the opportunity to take on the Labour council was Ken Dudman, one of the candidates in Slade ward. Redden was in the SDP. Yet the overwhelming sympathy was with Labour. Two Valley candidates were expelled from that party and at least two more resigned.

The most prominent group, consisting of Roy King, Nugent, Dixon, 18-year-old A-level student Ben Tegg, Hunt and myself, contained three Labour Party members, one sympathiser, one floater and one Tory voter. So any whispers that we had some hidden political agenda were well wide of the mark. Indeed, we agreed at an early stage that in order to maintain the cohesion of the party it was essential that we offered no views whatsoever on any subject other than The Valley.

The recruitment of candidates was not at first a problem, except to King and his wife Pauline, whose telephone rang constantly. Even so, we had to turn away dozens of people because they could not meet the necessary residence or employment qualifications. Many of them would have liked to have stood in Bexley, but even though we thought at the time that we probably had more supporters in that borough, to have done so would have only served to split our resources. It's also hard to see how we could have justified standing to the voters, since neither Bexley's Tory council nor, for that matter, the local Labour party could reasonably be held responsible for what went on in Greenwich. As a result we would probably have ended up being viewed simply as wrecking candidates.

We did find it difficult to fill the last few vacancies, however, especially when it was discovered that the transfer of Inner London Education Authority responsibilities to Greenwich Council at the beginning of April prevented teachers from standing. It was only after one of our Monday meetings at the Meridian reversed a previous decision to contest the seats of the two Yes voters from the planning committee, Bob Callow and Jim Coughlan, that we reached a final list.

Politically, Greenwich was unique, with a solid Labour majority on the council, but no Labour MPs. The most affluent seat of Eltham had been lost to the Tories in 1979, while Woolwich MP John Cartwright had defected to the SDP in 1982 and managed to hang on in both the 1983 and 1987 general elections, largely as the result of his considerable personal following. Labour had lost the remaining parliamentary constituency, Greenwich itself, to Rosie Barnes in a bruising 1986 by-election and to some surprise she too had survived the ensuing poll. For all that, however, it was Labour votes we had to take if we were to make any real impact because they were certain to retain power in the town hall.

Since other parties' candidates were not disclosed by the returning officer until nominations closed, we had, at the selection stage, no clue to the strange way fate was about to conspire in our favour. For some never fully explained reason, the Conservatives failed to contest 13 of the 62 seats, although it can hardly have been a coincidence that they were largely those in which they had the least chance of winning. Presumably, they were simply unable to find the candidates in such unpromising territory. The SDP, on the other hand, fought all the wards in their two parliamentary seats, with the single exception of Slade, in Plumstead. That was held by the Liberal Democrats, who were in general contesting only Eltham wards.

There remained two places in that constituency, however, where we were effectively left to form the only opposition to the ruling party. A graphic illustration of our naivety is that not until the declaration of the result did we realise the possibilities that had existed in Middle Park, where Paul Ellis and Chris Wilkins had only a single Liberal challenger in the battle against Labour. However, the situation in Sherard, where we now had just Kevin Fox standing, was plain. The two seats were between him, Callow and the council leader, Quentin Marsh. And as if this wasn't fortuitous enough, Kevin, a middle-aged company director in the printing industry, turned out to be by common consent the best of our candidates.

The Charlton directors' attitude to us in the early stages was very positive, if vaguely incredulous. There was an early offer of funding from Mike Norris which we left open, but fortunately never needed to take up. Discussing the matter with me on a rail trip to Everton in early February, Norris even suggested that we should stand as independent socialists; an indication, perhaps, that he thought our existing platform would win us few votes. It was only when the first details of Hunt's advertising coup were explained to them that they began to take us seriously.

That began to take shape in a local Indian restaurant a fortnight after the planning committee meeting. Hunt brought in a Mancunian, Dave Buchanan, a copywriter from his agency, BMP DDB Needham. By coincidence, the latter lived in Blackheath, and together with Dixon and Nugent we spent a couple of hours tossing ideas back and forth.

There were four possible aspects to our appeal; that The Valley was the proper place for Charlton and so to prevent them playing there was wrong; that football had

The home team: prospective Valley Party candidates pictured before the match

a part to play in strengthening the community's sense of identity; that the club was an important part of the borough's history which should not lightly be allowed to disappear; and that politicians ought to keep their promises. By this stage, we were taking for granted the backing of existing Charlton fans. The task now was to enlist former or potential supporters as voters and to widen the campaign's appeal beyond our solid, but ultimately small (or so we thought), natural constituency.

It took just over a month for Hunt to reveal what his creative team had produced. There were no fewer than four 48-sheet poster designs, three of them intended to evoke nostalgic sympathy from older voters. Based around the club's most loved player, goalkeeper Sam Bartram, Cup-winning captain Don Welsh and the triumphant procession through the streets after the 1947 Wembley triumph, they were an immediate hit with the party workers.

The fourth, intended to appeal to women voters in particular, featured a young boy, whom we never succeeded in identifying, watching a recent game with Arsenal at Selhurst Park. It posed the question: "If you don't support us, who's he going to support?" Remarkably, when the posters eventually went up, local Millwall fans resisted the temptation to supply an answer. We later used the same picture on the front of the first of our three main leaflets in an attempt to give the campaign some sense of continuity.

There was also a fifth design, a third of the size, which was meant to go up on the

Battle for The Valley

corner of Polytechnic Street and Wellington Street in Woolwich, just yards from the town hall. Unfortunately, we were unable to get legal access to the site, on the wall of Flamingos night club, but its message, "Let's send the council to Croydon and see how they like it", did make a belated appearance elsewhere in the borough.

Somehow Hunt managed to use his connections to have his team's work plastered on about 25 poster sites in Plumstead, Woolwich, Charlton and Greenwich. They should have been the Labour Party's first warning to take us seriously, but unwisely they chose to ignore it, instead conducting an ill-informed whispering campaign about the effect on our legally-restricted election expenses of about £15,000. There were drastic penalties for overspending, with even gifts having to be assessed at a realistic rate for the purpose of the law. In certain circumstances, an offender could end up paying for the election to be re-run. But, in fact, by not naming candidates, our posters slipped through the same legal loophole that allows the big national parties to spend millions at every general election.

The posters were impressive in themselves, and later Hunt's team would collect advertising industry awards for their efforts, but like the *Mercury* coverage it is doubtful that they would have been effective on their own. Their main impact was to reinforce the credibility of the people on the streets. However, they were also seen far beyond Greenwich, being reproduced in *The Guardian*, *Time Out* and even the *SLP*, and they gave a focus to our official press launch on March 26th, by an unconscious irony two years to the day of the aborted boycott.

For this occasion, Albert "Sailor" Brown, a veteran of Charlton's boom years in the 1930s and 40s and a wartime international, was brought down from Norfolk to share the platform, while Cordwell obligingly asked the right questions from the audience.

Launch day: the Valley Party press conference on March 26th

Canvassing the youth vote: red, red robin Darren Risby in Woolwich

Fleet Street failed to appear – typically, *Evening Standard* sports editor Michael Herd chose instead to ridicule the campaign in his weekly column – but the interest of both TV networks more than compensated. The launch was extensively featured on each of the local news magazines that night, a considerable propaganda coup.

A notable exception to the general indifference of the nationals was *The Guardian*. Not only did it report our press conference in detail on its back page, but four days later the paper carried a lengthy piece by Michael Grade backing the campaign. Hunt had pulled off another stroke and we gleefully reproduced part of the text in the second of our main leaflets.

The same morning as the launch, King delivered the first nomination papers for the approval of the returning officer. The latter had helpfully suggested submitting them early so that there would be time to correct any mistakes arising from our inexperience – another Labour prediction – but there were no major problems and within days acceptance letters started to arrive on candidates' doormats. The die was cast.

Thus far the only extent to which we had tested the water with the electorate was in collecting nominations. This had been hard work because of the strict rules that govern it, but the response from the public had generally been very positive. Now we had to take to the streets and persuade them to vote for us. Since most Saturdays found us otherwise engaged, the only real opportunity for a concerted assault was Grand National day, April 7th, when Crystal Palace had stolen our opponents Liverpool for their FA Cup semi-final. Unfortunately, the publicity necessary to get our supporters out inevitably alerted the Labour Party, so we were also to have our first taste of political confrontation.

A slightly disappointing total of around 100 people answered our appeal to rally at the Valley Club. By mid-morning, however, all the borough's major shopping centres were covered, with the bulk of the helpers concentrated in Woolwich and Eltham. Darren Risby, the candidate in Plumstead Common, entertained the smaller children by dressing up as a robin, while Vote Valley balloons (a subject of some contention at our impeccably democratic meetings where one activist dismissed the idea as "lightweight") were given away, together with the first of our main leaflets.

At the same time, two cars toured the borough equipped with loudspeakers and another candidate set off for The Den, where Millwall were entertaining Manchester City, to distribute a special leaflet aimed at securing the votes of any of their supporters who lived in the borough.

By common assent the response on the streets was outstanding, even in such apparently barren territory as affluent Blackheath. Although one or two irate Charlton residents did make their presence known in Woolwich, we were all greatly encouraged, particularly by the backing from the older generation. The only sour note came when a good-natured tannoy contest with Labour canvassers in Powis Street briefly threatened to flare into something rather more ugly.

The following day, the mammoth task of leafleting the whole borough, some 85,000 addresses in all, got under way for the first time. The 36 wards had been divided into groups of six, each having its own organiser who was responsible for checking candidates' nominations and supervising delivery operations. Fortunately, in most cases there proved to be enough volunteers to do the work, although there were still some complaints from fans who claimed they never received anything.

Meanwhile, it was important to ensure that our efforts were not overtaken by events. We had always been concerned that further talks between the directors and the council might produce a deal based around a new stadium elsewhere in the borough which would both scupper the campaign and provoke a row within the club.

After a short period of confusion immediately following the planning refusal, Alwen and Norris had insisted that they would appeal against the decision to the secretary of state, claiming to be confident of victory. However, Greenwich officials were equally certain that the club would fail. In any case, the whole procedure would have taken another 12 months, time Charlton could ill afford with their First Division future now in grave doubt. The directors eventually agreed to stay their appeal while efforts were made to find a more amicable solution.

Despite the fact that a year had already been wasted looking for another suitable site for a ground, Oelman had made public a new possibility even in the week of the planning refusal. This was the Victoria Deep Water Terminal, a disused wharf on the far side of the Blackwall Peninsula. The fact that maintaining it as a facility for water-borne freight had been specifically identified as a policy aim in the borough plan appeared in this instance to count for nothing.

This time, however, Charlton were dismissive. The wharf did not belong to the council and neither Greenwich nor the club had the money to acquire it. In any case, its development as a football ground would have been dependent on the construction of a new road, which might have taken years. Alwen and Norris were equally unimpressed by rumours that former military land might become available at

Woolwich Common. That, they said, might not be until the mid-1990s.

Two other options that were seriously considered involved entering into new groundsharing schemes, based on the premise that the existing one had failed largely because Selhurst Park was too difficult to reach and too closely identified with Palace. According to this theory, sharing a new stadium with Millwall or Welling United might have been more successful.

There was undoubtedly an element of truth in this, although it did not address the point that many Charlton fans were only interested in watching the club play at The Valley. In any case, the idea of sharing with the Lions soon collapsed. The mooted location was Arsenal's old home district of Plumstead, but it seems that Millwall were not prepared to move out to Greenwich. Equally, Charlton were not interested in the Lions' proposed new stadium at Senegal Fields on the border between Lewisham and Southwark. Apart from the location, they didn't believe it would be viable because it was too small and hemmed in by railway lines.

A more attractive proposition would have been a move to a stadium close to the A2 motorway in Bexley, probably to share with Welling United. Charlton had already formed a close bond with their non-League neighbours, using their existing Park View Road headquarters for Football Combination matches since 1987. But this ground, inadequate for League competition, was on a short lease from the local authority and was rumoured to be a target for developers.

Certainly, a tie-up with Welling would have had some advantages. For a start, Charlton would have been back in the heart of their shifting catchment area instead of

Party activists arrive at Selhurst for the club's last First Division game there

isolated on its fringe. And many people, including some on Tory-controlled Bexley Council, would have been delighted to put one over on Greenwich. But even though there was a great deal of sympathy for the Addicks within the authority, and exploratory talks had been held in the past, the problems of finding land and obtaining planning permission would have been just as great as they were in the Labour borough.

All these possibilities were the subject of intense speculation in the aftermath of the January refusal. When we discovered early in March that the board was actively considering a return to a patched-up Valley in time for next season, a meeting to make sure the two sides understood each other became urgent.

As required by the terms of the lease, Charlton had given Ron Noades two years' notice of their intention to quit Selhurst Park. That period was due to expire in March 1991, although the Addicks had intended to leave long before then, paying the landlords compensation for the balance of the lease. An agreement had also been reached that if Wimbledon took over as tenants, the outstanding period would be waived. But now, if Charlton wanted to stay at Selhurst for another season, they would need to extend their notice until May 1991.

As an alternative, the directors looked at the option of taking on the planners from a different angle. For if they re-established football at The Valley without building anything that required permission, as the politicians agreed was their right, then the arguments about traffic and nuisance that had been deployed against the club would be redundant.

Unfortunately, the practical difficulties of preparing the derelict stadium for even the smallest crowds would have been immense, not least because of the need for new floodlights. There was no guarantee that the Dons would oblige by taking over the tenancy at Selhurst, so Charlton could have been left paying for both grounds. And once the team were back at The Valley, mass public support for future planning applications would have been unlikely. So the idea was abandoned as unworkable.

This, and the lack of progress in the new talks with Greenwich, the chairman confirmed when we met him at the training ground two days after our foray onto the streets. But from the beginning it was clear that something had changed. Alwen reacted very sharply to a question from me about the consequences of relegation, which he correctly interpreted as of journalistic origin, rather than just from personal curiosity. However, he wrongly jumped to the conclusion that it was hostile. It was, of course, wholly reasonable for him to expect that meetings with supporters would not be turned into press conferences, but both sides had previously agreed that such occasions were on the record, and as far as I was concerned that meant they could be reported in the *Mercury*. Previously, indeed, they had been. Now, however, the rules appeared to have been changed. Even so, it was a foolish attempt to exploit the occasion on my part, explained, but not excused, by the fact that I had only a couple of hours to meet an unusually early *Mercury* deadline.

No sooner had this exchange been concluded than the chairman launched into an attack on *VOTV*, which he described as "sarcastic, derogatory and not supportive of the club", adding for good measure that it made no financial contribution. "We'll have to have some control over it in future," he warned. His only specific objection to the magazine at that stage related to an obscure diary item about the management of the new club shop at The Valley, on which subject I had been genuinely misinformed. Later on, I discovered that the players had also complained to the board about a letter in the previous issue.

However, it was clear that Alwen's objections to me ran deeper, a point confirmed when he told King that if it hadn't been for my involvement with the campaign, he would have had me banned from the training ground. On the basis of the evidence, this seemed rather absurd. There were obvious complications arising from my dual role as reporter and supporter, but on balance it was hard to see how Charlton suffered from my input, which was overwhelmingly positive towards them. Certainly, if Alwen thought that because I was a fan every single article in the *Mercury* ought to be favourable to the club, they were always likely to be disappointed. Neither Cordwell nor myself were much at home with the PR school of journalism.

The inference that we were profiteering out of the *Voice* was deeply ironic, as well as untrue. One of the underlying assumptions of our campaign, after all, was that Alwen and Norris, both wealthy businessmen, were involved with the club on a primarily altruistic basis, a view which many people regarded as naive. Presumably, however, his judgement was coloured by Sandra Hunt's threats of legal action. At Alwen's insistence, talks had only been resumed between club and council on the basis that this was deferred. She continued to demand an apology and legal costs, although for their part the *Mercury* did not take the action very seriously. I had myself received a letter threatening proceedings against me as the author of the piece and also in respect of an article in *VOTV*, but decided to ignore it and heard nothing more

Getting home the message: one of Hunt's posters on display in Charlton

from her solicitors.

Fortunately, the immediate antagonism between club and fans soon died down. Although Peter Burrowes told Cordwell two days later that the *Voice* had been "banned", this rather doubtful imposition was quietly abandoned within hours when the latter pointed out that the paper might take steps of its own in support. Apart from the damage that such an edict would have done to Alwen's own reputation among the supporters, it is hard to see how it could have been made effective. Had *VOTV* ever been dependent on the directors' approval it would hardly have survived the first issue. An attempt at peacemaking led by Hunt was dismissed as unnecessary by the board.

For us to have fallen out publicly at such a stage, and on such apparently trivial grounds, would have been ridiculous, a point both sides seemed to appreciate. Nevertheless, the incident did serve to make me much more sceptical about Alwen than I had been previously. My mood was not improved when I learned that Valley Party candidate Mark Mansfield, who had set up an 0898 recorded message service, Valleycall, to keep people informed of developments, had been required to produce a letter on supporters' club notepaper stating that CASC, and by inference not *VOTV*, would receive the profits.

The whole episode was to prove no more than a rehearsal for an even sillier row six months later, but for now it appeared to have been defused. Fortunately, Alwen and I were to have little contact for the remainder of the election campaign, to which the directors were, after all, incidental.

Better news arrived in the shape of interest from *Thames Reports*, a weekly, 30-minute news magazine programme for the capital that went out on Tuesday evenings. They agreed to make a film which would eventually be broadcast just two days before polling and we privately began to refer to it as our party political broadcast. In the

The smallest of the posters, designed for a site next to the town hall

This Sam Bartram poster proved particularly popular with older voters

event, it wasn't quite that, but it certainly embarrassed and antagonised the council, as well as shedding new light on some of the activities of the local residents.

The foremost of these was planning officer David Higham, who Thames now discovered had been behind the infamous North Charlton leaflet. Earlier he had responded to a letter sent under a bogus name to the *Kentish Times* about his dual role with a particularly pompous threat of legal action. Now he refused to talk to the television company on camera, and eventually off it too, with the result that they had to station a photographer outside his house one morning in order to snatch a picture of him for the programme.

Andrew Marsh, unsurprisingly, was less reticent and claimed that he had been punched at the January meeting. Indeed, all the residents made various allegations about the behaviour of the supporters. The programme used only one of them, fortunately not that made by the highly plausible Marsh, but yet another who had moved into the area since 1985. Perhaps the only disappointing feature of the 12-minute piece was that it failed to rebut this charge of intimidation, the relevant clip apparently being cut for time reasons on the day of transmission.

Although the final version was heavily censored by Thames' legal department, the programme's impact was overwhelmingly positive. Not only was Quentin Marsh forced onto the defensive, but he came across very badly, not least when he blustered his way through a staged doorstep confrontation with a supposed Charlton supporter.

By comparison our spokesman, Kevin Fox, who provided the legally required political balance, came across as the genuinely concerned, sincere and respectable member of the public he so obviously was. For those in any doubt about the rights and wrongs of the issue, though, the clincher had to be a sound tape recording of Picton welcoming news of the return 12 months earlier. This was suddenly produced by Alwen during the production phase.

Three days before the film went out, however, we received a kick in the teeth from Norris that left many people involved in the campaign fuming. Arriving at Selhurst for the last home game of the season after a busy morning touring Greenwich in an open-top bus, we were greeted by an excited Burrowes, waving the matchday programme. In it was an extraordinary article in which Norris unilaterally announced that a return to The Valley was now unlikely, other discussions were being held and a planning application for residential development of the whole site would shortly be submitted.

In the context of the directors' previous support for the election campaign, it was an amazing thing to do. No one within the club who had seen it prior to publication had had the slightest doubt of the damage it would do us, so the subsequent claim of both owners that it was intended to "gee the council up" had few takers. Furthermore, an application for housing on The Valley would presumably have met a similar fate to that of the existing stadium scheme, because the ground was zoned as community open space. "Other discussions" could only be about temporary or permanent groundsharing with Millwall or Welling United.

On the positive side, it did seem that Alwen had known nothing about the content of the article until he arrived at the ground. So at least if this was attempted sabotage, as many people assumed, it didn't necessarily mean that the club as a whole was behind it. The chairman's gloss on Norris's comments was that it would be wise to submit a number of planning applications in order that the appeal, if it proceeded, would resolve the matter finally. However, if that had been the intention, it begged the question of why Norris hadn't made it clear. Perhaps significantly, Alwen failed to keep a local radio phone-in appointment the following night, instead answering vetted questions fed to him by commercial manager Steve Sutherland down the line.

We did have one stroke of luck over the incident, however. In order to confirm their First Division place for next season, our opponents that day, Sheffield Wednesday, needed Luton to lose at home to Palace the same afternoon. The Hatters won, but due to a mix-up Charlton's tannoy man gave out that they had lost, sparking wild celebrations. We could only sympathise with the visiting fans, particularly as exactly the same thing happened to them at Hillsborough the following week and they were indeed relegated, but all the same the story provided a first-class diversion for the press.

Inevitably, however, Norris's remarks did do us some damage. A report of them appeared on BBC TV's regional sports slot at teatime and within hours a dispirited Fox was being asked on the doorstep about the news. Helpful as ever, the *South London Press* revived the story for their midweek issue, despite the fact that they had nothing to add to the original comments aside from a snide conclusion of their own that the Valley Party's efforts might now be redundant. If Norris did hope to harm our prospects, he could hardly have been pleased at the eventual outcome, a topic upon which he remained strangely silent in the immediate aftermath. His motives remained a matter for speculation, although none of us had ever forgotten his original preference for a new stadium elsewhere in the borough. The probability, however, is that the vice-chairman did not take us or our election chances seriously enough to

Desperate men: Marsh and Callow (first and second left) await the Sherard result

concern himself about the effect of his article.

Another surprise on that final Saturday was our first sighting of what became known as "the yellow leaflet", a semi-literate and poorly argued document urging people not to vote Valley, produced by an organisation calling itself the Charlton Action Group. Supporter Paul Watts had discovered it in Charlton House, where it was apparently plastered over the noticeboards and stockpiled in large quantities. This in itself was illegal, because Charlton House was a council building, and so too, we thought, was the leaflet, if only on a technicality. The law forbids the publication of material soliciting votes without the origin being made clear. This was effectively anonymous, in the circumstances inevitably raising questions about whether it had been printed using public funds.

So first thing on Monday morning, King marched into Charlton House, slung all the leaflets into the back of his van and took them down to the deputy returning officer, George Barton, at Woolwich. He agreed that they were illegal and advised informing the police, which was done. By the following day, however, they had reappeared in Charlton House, so a further complaint was made and an instruction issued that on no account were they to be displayed or stored on the premises.

Then, on the Tuesday evening, Charlton ward candidate Dominic Crowe was alerted by a sympathetic local to the fact that a man was delivering them to houses in the area. The resident had chased his unwelcome caller, who wore a Labour Party sticker, back down his garden path. Dominic subsequently caught up with the man and questioned him about the origin of the leaflet and he would later identify him at the count. Meanwhile, another sympathiser, from neighbouring Hornfair ward,

Moral victory: Kevin Fox congratulated by Ben Tegg after the Sherard result

reported that the offending document had been delivered to him together with one from the Labour Party.

Clearly, someone was very worried about the support we were getting in the area. We had our suspicions about who it might be, and the identity of the Charlton Action Group would later become apparent when leaflets bearing that heading were distributed by some familiar faces outside the first meeting of the new council.

On the positive side, we did receive two more publicity boosts in the final week, from the *Sunday Express* and the *Daily Mail*. Unfortunately, the interest of both seemed to centre on how they could best angle the story against the Labour Party. Someone even fed the *Express* the old nonsense about pop concerts. Generally the national press was disappointing throughout, although to a large extent the aim of obtaining publicity had now been supplanted by a genuine ambition to embarrass the council by getting a significant number of votes.

On the Monday, some 250 people answered our last-ditch appeal for volunteers to come to the Valley Club and be allocated delivery rounds for the final leaflet. Distribution of the previous two had in each case dragged on for over a week, but this time we needed to complete the job in a single night, that of the eve of poll. It was a mammoth operation but by and large we accomplished it, with some people finishing the task on the morning of May 3rd itself.

However, the big question still remained. How many votes were we actually going to get? We had always carefully avoided setting a target, not least because we didn't have a clue what was likely to happen. In the same way, talk of winning seats had been played down but never completely discounted, because to have ruled it out might in itself have had a negative effect. We were encouraged that our poster leaflet, the second delivered, had gone up in a reasonable number of windows and we were running second to Labour in that respect in many places. But was that because our supporters were that much more enthusiastic? Might those anxious to advertise their backing be the only ones who would vote for us?

Our best indication should have been the canvass returns in the only two wards we had done properly, Sherard and Charlton. Unfortunately, neither was a good guide. We knew we would do very well in Sherard, but then there were no other candidates. Charlton, on the other hand, might reasonably be expected to have the most hostile electorate of all. Even so, we thought Crowe would pick up about 200 votes, a total for which I, at least, would happily have settled. Little did we know.

At least the great day dawned warm and sunny. My first task was to plaster the car with Vote Valley posters and then make my own visit to the polling station, just a few hundred yards away from the Greenwich border, in East Wickham. There I was approached by a Liberal Democrat teller, whom I expected to tell me I was in the wrong place. Instead, he confided that he had once played for Charlton himself!

Over the border, volunteers were already doing the tedious job of marking off voters in the two target wards. Originally we had intended to focus on six; in the event we had started too late and with too few people who were willing to do the necessary door-knocking. Tempers flared late in the afternoon of polling day when it was discovered that even parts of Charlton ward had not been covered and tellers in some polling stations had therefore been wasting their time.

Our base for the day, inevitably, was the Valley Club, from where Ben Tegg, by virtue of the fact that his family background had given him some experience of elections, ran the show. Complete with mobile phones, his job was to dispatch volunteers to work as tellers, organise lifts and generally act as a clearing centre for information. An early cause of aggravation was the number of people who simply wanted to ride around on the bus, back for its second tour in five days, but eventually everyone settled down to the task in hand.

One couple, hitherto unknown, turned up with a specially constructed roof-rack complete with Vote Valley posters and loudspeakers, through which they had apparently been assaulting the ears of the Greenwich population with *The Red, Red Robin* for several days.

By late afternoon new helpers were arriving almost by the minute. Returns from the polling stations were being analysed and knocking-up teams organised to get our missing voters out. We also had leaflets to distribute at all 14 of the borough's railway stations, reminding returning commuters that they had until 9pm to vote. But as the evening wore on, there was nothing left for fresh arrivals to do but savour the occasion.

Meanwhile, the battle in Sherard was reaching fever pitch. This was Labour's safest ward, a sprawling 1930s council estate of the better kind, where they were defending a majority of four figures. Yet by the middle of the afternoon, it was plain they thought that they were in trouble. As late as 8pm, Callow was touring the streets in a loudspeaker car, hotly pursued by me in another contradicting his appeals. The

Down and out: ex-councillor Simon Oelman leaves the scene of his humiliation

scene wouldn't have been out of place in a *Carry On* film.

One big problem for us was that each person supporting Fox had a spare vote, the result of that late decision not to oppose the two Yes men from the planning committee. We wanted them to cast it for Callow – or better still not at all – and had virtually said as much on the special leaflet we had produced for the ward. Every time a second vote went to Quentin Marsh, it effectively cancelled out the one for Kevin. Against that, if we had run a second person, as elsewhere, some of the electors who wanted to split their votes between the parties, and there were an unprecedented number across the borough by all accounts, would inevitably have selected the "wrong" Valley candidate.

In the event, only a handful of people actually voted Fox and Marsh, and in any case the decision not to oppose the Yes men was fully vindicated by Coughlan's narrow survival in Kidbrooke, where the other seat fell to the Tories on the back of our intervention. Our failing in Sherard was that we never at any time really believed that we could win. Afterwards, Kevin was convinced that had he personally been able to visit the remaining thousand or so homes in the ward he would have succeeded in unseating Marsh. On the basis of what he did achieve, it seems very likely he was right.

All that still lay ahead, however, as we gathered wearily at the Director General, the pub immediately opposite the town hall in Woolwich, around 9pm. Despite the very limited number of people who were supposed to have access to the count, the bar was packed to the rafters with Charlton supporters. In fact, security inside the town hall proved surprisingly lax and there were no problems getting all the fans in by one means or another. If anything, it was almost a bigger problem getting them out of the pub.

The first results were announced shortly after 10pm and once again fate had a trick to play. Avery Hill and Sutcliffe, by coincidence the only two seats to return Liberal Democrats, were first to declare and we polled just 88 and 66 respectively. They were small, single-member wards, and that still represented around 5 per cent of the votes cast, but it was a disappointment all the same. Sights were lowered accordingly, but Labour relief was premature. They proved to be our lowest percentage shares of the evening. Only minutes later a rumour swept round that in Hornfair, Les Turner, who had worked tirelessly for the cause, was in front.

It was true, but of course too good to last. As more boxes were opened, he soon fell behind. Yet as the votes piled up it slowly became clear that this was a victory nonetheless. Together with Andy Keen, Les eventually collected some 738, or 14.2 per cent of those cast. In next-door Charlton, Crowe and Brian Bird got 629 or 13.5 per cent. Discounting seats distorted by the Tories' failure to stand, these were to be our best results of the evening; tangible backing from the very streets around the ground that were supposedly up in arms against us. The pattern was repeated in neighbouring Rectory Field and Woolwich Common. In all four wards the turnout had shot up and the Labour share of the vote had crumbled.

On the basis of these results alone, the tactic of standing had paid a handsome dividend. But there was much more to come. In Sherard, a triumphant Fox fell just eight short of the thousand mark, leaving Marsh to bite his fingernails right to the last. As the returning officer gave the figures, a great roar went up from the 200 or so gathered around Queen Victoria's unamused statue, now decorated for the occasion with a red and white scarf.

By comparison, Labour could raise barely a half-hearted cheer in response to the council leader's 1,361. The tempers of the red-rose faithful had long since begun to fray. In Well Hall, sitting councillor Clive Efford had promised Dixon a pint if the latter got more votes than Charlton's meagre goal total for the season. Steve, ironically a notorious teetotaller, earned his prize with more than 300 to spare. The ward remained split, Efford's running mate trailing the successful Tory by just 35, and we tasted blood for the first time.

As dawn broke, the very last declaration of the night would see the Conservatives make their only gain. Our other, largely forgotten, friend on the planning committee, Coughlan, won his Kidbrooke seat by just 43. His running mate lost out by 13, while our solitary candidate polled 326.

In between the two came the sensation of the evening, when Oelman's 1986 majority of 450 in Eynsham somehow became a deficit of 300. The dying SDP, which won just five seats that night across the whole country and had already lost four of the six they previously held in Greenwich, were ecstatic; the Valley Party were incredulous. The former chair of planning was in tears.

Even by the standards of this extraordinary affair, it was an astonishing turn of events. Not only did Oelman's personal vote drop 300 despite the increased turnout, but he finished 200 behind his running mate, offering conclusive evidence that it was

The jubilant candidates celebrate their remarkable showing at the polls

the Valley factor which had done for him.

Yet still the drama wasn't over. As he was led away with the chants of the delirious Charlton fans ringing in his ears, Oelman spotted Valley Party supporter and photographer Andy Soloman on the other side of the road taking pictures. Finally losing control, he charged towards Soloman screaming: "You bastard, you bastard!", only to be arrested by police before he could reach him.

Back in the hall, the atmosphere now deteriorated even further. A chant of "Simon's been arrested" from the gallery did little to placate Labour activists, one or two of whom seemed to be looking for a means of levelling the score. The police presence, tactfully discreet throughout, grew steadily more obvious. But if they had come to protect the public from the football fans, the boot was now well and truly on the other foot.

It was nearly 4am before the result in Eynsham was finally declared. By then, Soloman had generously decided to spare the vanquished councillor the final humiliation and had declined to press charges. No one left in the hall really needed to be told the outcome of the ballot. The crowd had long since thinned, but nonetheless a great roar of approval greeted the final confirmation. It was a fitting end indeed to a day that had surpassed everyone's expectations and surely transformed the situation. In all, we had received 14,838 votes, 10.9 per cent of those cast, a quarter of those polled for Labour and more than half the Tory total. In the parliamentary constituency of Woolwich more votes had been cast for The Valley than for the Conservatives and across the borough around 10,000 people had given us the nod.

As I drove home through the deserted streets to the relative sanctuary of Bexley, I finally believed that the battle for The Valley would be won.

Chapter Eleven

"If you can keep your head when all around are losing theirs, you're probably Lennie Lawrence."
Voice of The Valley *editorial (December 1990)*

In the aftermath of the poll, anything seemed possible. Two days later, a joyous celebration of a football match took place at Old Trafford. It was Charlton's last in the First Division, but the delirium sparked by the election results, a fancy-dress party promoted in the pages of *Voice of The Valley* – and the fact that Manchester United were to play the loathed Crystal Palace at Wembley the following week – combined to produce an atmosphere that was truly unique.

At first scornful, United fans soon caught the spirit of the occasion, responding to our chants of "You're gonna win the Cup" with the rather less credible "You'll be back!" The Mexican wave crossed the border between home fans and visitors time and time again, while the game, in fact a dour contest won by a solitary United goal, was completely forgotten.

Unused to the phenomenon of a football crowd united in goodwill, the local constabulary insisted on keeping the Charlton supporters behind after the match. The United fans simply tried to follow suit. Eventually, the police succeeded in shepherding them away, but only to line the streets outside the ground, where badges, scarves and hats were exchanged in an unprecedented warming between two sets of supporters whose ambitions and experiences in modern times could hardly have been more different.

The harsh reality, however, was that Charlton were back in the Second Division and moreover in precisely the circumstances that had sparked the campaign in the first place – still stuck at Selhurst Park. We had now proved that we were more than a vociferous minority, an allegation Ron Noades had made against us in the *Sunday Times* during the election. But would the politicians, still nursing the wounds inflicted on them at the polls, respond positively?

Surprisingly, they would. When we met at the Valley Club 11 days after the event, Peter Cordwell was able to bring news of a fresh initiative, led by Simon Oelman's replacement as chair of planning, Norman Adams. Unusually, the councillor had approached the *Mercury* to indicate his readiness to reopen negotiations. It soon became obvious that the directors were well aware of these overtures. Indeed, they indicated a willingness to respond quickly with scaled-down proposals.

On the face of it, this was a startling development. Only a month earlier the politicians had been so keen to avoid discussing the issue with fans that they had apparently rearranged a full council meeting at short notice in order that it would clash with Charlton's home game against Liverpool. Now, suddenly, a compromise was possible. Clearly a dramatic change of mind, if not of heart, had taken place.

It is highly likely that this owed something to pressure from the Labour hierarchy. The author of one *Mercury* letter criticising our electoral activities had been exposed as a full-time employee of party headquarters during the campaign, so we knew that Walworth Road was well aware of what was happening in Greenwich. Indeed, the

Digging for victory: Roy King installs The Valley's new sprinkler system

issue was said to have been discussed at shadow cabinet level, where there was known to be concern about the damage being done to Labour's national standing by the activities of some London councils.

While many Charlton supporters had blamed the impending local poll for Greenwich's original prevarication, in the event it had proved ideally timed for us to make our point. And now, three years into Margaret Thatcher's third term, the general election was beginning to appear on the distant horizon. In a parliamentary poll, more pressing concerns would probably have squeezed the Valley vote. It is very unlikely that Hunt's agency, which ironically had close links with Labour leader Neil Kinnock's inner circle, would have wished to be involved. But party headquarters simply couldn't afford to take the risk, so we were quick to threaten that we would stand again, this time extending our activities into the three vulnerable Tory seats in Bexley and Lewisham as well.

However, if the prospect of further humiliation was a spur to the politicians, it would be wrong to pretend that all the ground was given on the authority's side. Charlton certainly showed more flexibility, particularly over the scale and nature of the commercial development. Indeed, council leader Quentin Marsh insisted in a letter to the *Mercury* that it was the club's new approach which was wholly responsible for the progress. "These issues could have been resolved by Charlton's directors through proper negotiations some time ago," he wrote.

One significant change on the club side came with the decision to dispense with the services of architect Michael Newberry, whose working relationship with borough planning officer Sandra Hunt had not been an easy one. The split was less than amicable, with Newberry threatening legal action against Charlton for the near

£100,000 balance of his £148,000 fee. He was replaced by Ray Woodward, of Richard Collins' Kennedy Woodward Partnership, by coincidence a man born in Floyd Road.

Hunt's dispute with Roger Alwen was also finally resolved, by the publication in the *Mercury* of a letter from the chairman explaining that his January comments had not been meant as criticism or to imply there had been any bias on her part.

A more significant factor, perhaps, was the end of Laing Homes' housing plans. The builders' two-year option on 4.5 acres behind the demolished west stand had lapsed at the end of February. This had the advantage of releasing the area for matchday parking again and offered the possibility of relocating the commercial aspects of the scheme well away from the Harvey Gardens boundary of the site. But it also meant that sooner or later cash would have to be found to repay the original loan with which Mike Norris had bought Adelong.

It took just two months for the club and the council to reach an agreement, one that in most respects they might easily have concluded earlier. The new west stand would now seat only 4,500, but would include a money-spinning bowling alley with its own restaurant, as well as a replacement Valley Club, a creche and day nursery facility available to local residents and a function room to accommodate 90 people, against the 400-capacity banqueting suite previously proposed.

The rest of the ground would proceed more or less as envisaged under stage one of the old scheme, except that there would be 190 car parking spaces behind the west stand and 12 "work-homes", workshops with living accommodation above, along the Valley Grove frontage of the site. Unusually, there would be only two floodlight

The Valley man: former groundsman Maurice Banham gets back to work

Got the message? Charlton fans demonstrate at the new council's first meeting

pylons, at either end of the East Terrace, with the remaining lights mounted on the fascia of the new stand.

Former groundsman Maurice Banham was recruited to help tend the Valley pitch and even the efforts of the familiar group of local residents to lobby the first meeting of the new council seemed forlorn to the fans who packed the public gallery. But there still remained the hurdle of planning permission, and further down the line the need to obtain a safety certificate, before an August 1991 return would be assured.

The new scheme had been drawn up in such close consultation with officials that there was never much chance of it being rejected. However, initial hopes of receiving permission by October were soon to be dashed by yet another setback. The outline application was not submitted until mid-September. The same week, the relevant council officers went on strike.

It was the latest twist in a six-month dispute inside Greenwich's housing department, which had begun over collection of the poll tax. But NALGO's decision to pull out their members in the development control area of planning was no accident. They knew the high profile that the Valley issue would give their action and had determined to use it for their own ends. And so began yet another seemingly endless delay.

The submission of the new Valley planning application also sparked a ridiculous row between the Charlton board and the *Mercury*. The capacity of the ground had remained a controversial point, even if it had been overshadowed by the battle to get back there at all. Now examination of the outline plans revealed the limit for the East Terrace would be just 5,000 instead of the 10,000 that had been expected. The cause of the lower figure was a wide access road for emergency vehicles, apparently to be driven through the middle. Taken with the reduction in the size of the new stand, it meant the total capacity of The Valley would fall to less than 16,000 and then to 14,500 if the terrace was seated, as envisaged, by 1994.

The future of this part of the ground was also of symbolic importance to many fans and not just as part of the opposition to all-seater stadia. It was the last distinctive feature of The Valley and as such many wanted it preserved for sentimental reasons. However, this was not the origin of the article that caused the problem. It began with a suggestion that the capacity was inadequate made to me from within the club.

The story duly appeared, under the headline "Road to ruin?", with the question mark being of particular significance. The first hint I had that there was a problem came when Norris phoned me at home on the Saturday morning to say that the piece had been "unhelpful". He was perfectly amicable and I offered him a right of reply in the following week's issue. However, it wasn't the story that he was disputing, but the headline. That wasn't my responsibility, as anyone remotely familiar with newspaper practice would readily appreciate. So I put him on to Cordwell.

Maybe the headline was a bit strong, but it was not out of character with the paper's robust style. And it had to be weighed against the countless positive stories that had appeared about the club and The Valley in the past, particularly over the previous year. Instead of letting the matter rest, however, the two owners took the argument a stage further before that afternoon's game with Barnsley, approaching new supporters' club chairman Roy King in the Selhurst car park to demand that he have me removed from the CASC committee. Having got nowhere with the bemused King, they decided to instruct club employees not to co-operate with me as a reporter in an attempt to make it impossible for me to do the job. And all this, apparently, on the strength of a headline that I hadn't even written!

Norris finally made contact with Cordwell on the Sunday morning but was given very short shrift. What the vice-chairman didn't seem to understand was that Charlton needed the *Mercury* far more than the paper needed the club. Much to his credit, the

Picture perfect: the club's 1990 vision of The Valley, with only two floodlights

sports editor then spent two days trying to persuade the directors to see reason. However, they wouldn't listen and there was no way they could be allowed to dictate who covered the club's affairs. So, reluctantly, we went into print with the row. Charlton had banned me, so now the *Mercury* would ban Charlton. There would be no match reports, team news, Valley stories or pictures until they backed down.

The paper also published a letter of complaint about the headline from Norris. "In my view this was cheap sensationalism, totally incorrect and also counter-productive to our planning application, which has now reached a sensitive stage," he wrote, along with a completely unfounded claim about what information had been contained in the club's recent press release on the subject.

There was no room for any confusion in what had passed between the parties concerned. Yet as soon as Norris realised that we had gone public on the story, he began to withdraw, telling the *South London Press* that there had never been a ban. Two weeks later, he alleged on the local radio station, RTM, that he had even told the *Mercury* there was no ban and the paper had invented it. If this was true, it was indeed curious that Alwen had felt the need to phone the deputy editor the following Tuesday in order to lift it. We had no problem with that, since we hadn't understood the basis of the dispute in the first place.

Whatever the cause of the row, it was indicative of the owners' continuing distrust of me, although I was greatly heartened by the dozens of letters of support we received from readers. Indeed, we were preparing a large number of them for publication when Alwen backed down and we had hurriedly to remake the relevant page. Perhaps just as significant was the fact that the directors were prepared to turn on the newspaper which had been their most loyal ally on the strength of a single headline. Such behaviour surely placed a large question mark over their judgement on other matters. Our story did appear to have some impact, however, since when the detailed application was finally submitted, the road in question had disappeared and the capacity of the terrace had been revised upwards to 6,000.

Of more immediate importance was the continuing frustration for Charlton fans on the foreign field. The plunge out of the First Division had looked inevitable even before the emotional scenes at Woolwich in January. Certainly the sale of Micky Bennett and Colin Pates had not helped but, as Lawrence would later argue, it had been the failure to recruit the previous summer which had been the decisive factor in the team's relegation. Although Joe McLaughlin had replaced Peter Shirtliff, the money to strengthen the squad further had simply not been available. And the blame for that lay not with the current board but with the man who had made the decision to move to Selhurst Park in the first place.

In the end, Charlton had finished next to bottom, with only the fact that neighbours Millwall were the team below them as consolation. Evidence of the side's demoralisation can be drawn from the fact that all the last six League games were lost, with confirmation of their fate arriving on a damp Tuesday evening at Selhurst. Painfully, it was a defeat by old rivals Wimbledon that sent them down, although that at least was preferable to having the blow inflicted by Crystal Palace four days later.

The prospect of playing Second Division football in exile remained an alarming one, even though the relegation season had seen Charlton record their highest average gate for 12 years. At 10,773, it amounted to an increase of more than 14 per cent on the previous campaign. There can be no doubt that the intention to play in SE7 once again was a major factor in this, but equally a new box-office admission system at Selhurst had played a part. Under the new arrangements fans had to queue up to purchase a ticket before going through turnstiles. It was less convenient and initially caused much confusion, but it meant that all cash was receipted and therefore eliminated traditional fiddles at the gate. Supporters had long been sceptical about the official attendance figures at Palace and their doubts appeared to be confirmed.

How many people would make the tedious trip for lower-grade football was an open question, however. In the event, the Charlton fans showed remarkable loyalty but the loss of the large visiting contingents brought by many First Division clubs was a hefty financial blow. Also missing from the balance sheet was much of the revenue that Charlton had received from ITV as a member of the top flight.

There were other, less obvious, consequences of relegation, too. Despite the successful launch of the subscription scheme, Valley Gold, in September 1989, the club's ability to raise money off the field through commercial activities remained severely constrained. At its peak, Valley Gold attracted around 1,800 members, but half of their £10 monthly contribution was paid out again in prizes. Even discounting the wages of the man taken on to administer the scheme, Palace supporter and former Noades employee Andy Bryant, it could not be expected to raise much more than £100,000 a year.

As for more conventional commercial activities, such as the sale of advertising space in the programme, pitch perimeter hoardings and match sponsorship, all had suffered badly since 1985 from the club's identity crisis. Selhurst Park was a long way from businesses in Greenwich and Bexley, whose owners did not necessarily appreciate the fact that Charlton fans were still their customers. In the same way, Croydon firms had no interest in an audience which lived outside their area. If neither group of potential advertisers had wanted to reach the First Division crowds, the task of attracting them would surely be even more difficult in the Second.

And there was a final complication to the bleak financial outlook. Thanks to the terms of the tenancy agreement, the exiles had to pay half the cost of seating Selhurst's Arthur Wait enclosure, although Palace did now accept a cut in their share of Charlton's gate revenue to seven-and-a-half per cent.

Together these factors had made the summer sale of players inevitable. In one case, however, the departure was determined just as much by the individual's obvious personal claim to First Division status. Right-back John Humphrey had long since assumed hero status among the fans. The skipper since Pates's departure, he had been voted player of the year three times running and had just completed a third consecutive season as an ever-present in the League side. Cool under pressure at the back and always ready to push forward down the right wing, Humphrey surely deserved consideration for the full England side but had suffered the fate of omission common to the stars of less fashionable sides.

One attempt to sell him had already been thwarted. The previous summer Queens Park Rangers had offered £1m to take both Humphrey and Paul Williams to Loftus Road, but Lawrence had pulled out of the deal at the last minute following a furious telephone protest by fans. However, few supporters seriously imagined their star defender would stay to play Second Division football. Additionally, he would be 30 during the course of the coming season. It meant that if Charlton were ever to realise his value on the transfer market, now was the time to sell.

When he did go, in June after returning from the club's close-season tour of Australia, his destination was especially difficult for his many admirers to swallow. For it was Palace, and the modest fee of £450,000 included £70,000 owing to the landlords in outstanding stadium maintenance costs.

Next to leave was Williams, the impish striker with the lightning pace who had scored 23 times in 82 First Division games and finished leading marksman in each of the previous two seasons. He went to relegation partners Sheffield Wednesday midway through Charlton's pre-season tour of the West Country. The £600,000 fee was widely criticised as too

Hero status: John Humphrey

Under fire: Lennie Lawrence shares a joke with Barry Nugent and Bill Treadgold

low, a familiar complaint where Lawrence was concerned. In fact, it was still £50,000 below the club record for the sale of a player, set by manager Andy Nelson with the transfer of Mike Flanagan to Palace almost 11 years to the day earlier. Given the inflation in the market during the 1980s and Charlton's elevated status, the longevity of this statistic was truly remarkable.

Humphrey and Williams had been among the highest wage-earners in the squad, with both having been granted expensive new contracts following the breakdown of the QPR deal. Another was McLaughlin, who had been unsettled anyway since the departure of Pates in January. For a while it looked as if Big Joe, too, would join Palace, but instead Watford stepped in with a £350,000 bid, a figure that cast grave doubts over Charlton's wisdom in paying £600,000 for his services in the first place.

Together the three deals had realised £1.4m, and allowed the reimposition of a more modest wage structure, but little of the income was to be made available for team rebuilding. Nor was the money going into The Valley, as the Charlton boss explained: "It's going to meet the horrendous losses that we are surely going to incur as a Second Division club at Selhurst Park," he insisted.

Three new signings did arrive, however. Former midfielder Alan Curbishley returned from Brighton & Hove Albion on a free transfer to take over the reserves as player-coach and two central defenders were recruited just before the big kick-off. Ex-Tottenham Hotspur apprentice Simon Webster, 26, came from Sheffield United for £120,000 and 21-year-old Stuart Balmer joined from Celtic for £100,000. As things began to go wrong, loan striker Alex Dyer arrived from Palace at the beginning of October.

Remarkably, the team won all seven pre-season friendlies, but their Second

Battle for The Valley

Golden boy: Gordon Watson briefly captured the fans' imagination

Division start proved disastrous. A run of four straight defeats meant that Charlton had lost ten consecutive League games for the first time ever. A creditable draw at Oldham Athletic ended the sequence, but by the time they went down at home to Watford in mid-October, just one of the 11 matches had been won and the side had slipped to the bottom of the table. For the first time since he had been appointed boss eight years earlier, Lawrence's future was in grave doubt.

His position had hardly been helped by the sacking of senior coach Flanagan less than a week into the new season. Comments made by the Valley veteran on RTM in which he appeared to criticise team selection and tactics were the immediate cause. It was candour more typical of Lawrence but in this case constituted disloyalty which the manager could not accept.

Off air Flanagan was far more outspoken, particularly about the signing of Balmer, which he did not support, complaining that he and not influential general manager Arnie Warren should have been sent to assess that player's potential. Whatever the 63-year-old Warren's merits as a scout – and Flanagan was not his only doubter among the coaching staff – Balmer was to have a difficult beginning at Charlton, struggling to break into the team and then scoring two own goals in his first five starts. By the end of the season, however, he had convinced most observers that he had at least been worth the fee and he went on to become a popular player.

The response to the crisis on the field from the boardroom was noticeably equivocal, with Lawrence probably owing his survival to the close relationship he enjoyed with Alwen. But he had also been at Charlton a long while, longer than any director except Richard Collins, in fact, and it is doubtful the board would have had the nerve to dismiss him. In any case, he had manoeuvred the club out of so many tight corners, few of them of his own making, that a sacking would have been outrageously harsh.

If the Watford defeat was the low point in terms of results, the crisis had been reached with Leicester City's extraordinary win at Selhurst the previous week in a game which Charlton had dominated. On the Monday that followed it, Lawrence even threatened to resign. But following talks with the board, he appeared to know he would survive the Watford result. By that stage, anyway, his supporters were rallying to the cause. He had been strongly defended by the journalist Michael Hart in a rare *Evening Standard* article the previous day and was warmly received by the Selhurst crowd.

That confidence was immediately justified because the manager took his team to Newcastle United in midweek and saw them win 3-1. It was to prove the turning point and although the rest of the season would hardly be memorable, relegation to the Third Division was only a remote possibility thereafter. Even when results suggested otherwise, the team was simply too good to go down. No member of it contributed more than Robert Lee, granted a free role up front and scoring regularly for the first time in his career, notching eight goals in 11 games in the run-up to Christmas.

Lawrence had taken over first-team coaching himself in the aftermath of Flanagan's departure, but he soon promoted Curbishley to fill the gap. That left a vacancy at reserve level, resolved by the appointment of the remarkable Steve Gritt, now 33, who had briefly left the club the previous season for Walsall but failed to settle in the Midlands. Gritt's new charges promptly won their first six games under his wing, before going down to QPR at Loftus Road. Such was the enthusiasm generated during this run that attendances for the floodlit Football Combination matches at Park View Road began to top the thousand mark, rivalling Welling United's own GM Vauxhall Conference crowds.

The veteran Gritt would also make ten appearances in the League side, having begun the campaign as Humphrey's replacement at right-back. The spirit was willing but perhaps not the legs and after the defeat at Bristol Rovers in the second game he gave way to Darren Pitcher, a former captain of the reserves. Now nearly 21, Pitcher had waited a long while for his chance but took it well and would miss only two more matches during the season.

In late November, Charlton finally clinched the permanent signing of Dyer. The Palace man had made a slow start in the Addicks colours but improved greatly as he regained full fitness. However, Lawrence had struggled to persuade the directors to part with the cash, at one stage attempting to sell the unsettled Colin Walsh to Leicester to raise it. In the event, the £100,000 fee, offset against outstanding payments on the Humphrey deal, proved something of a bargain because 25-year-old Dyer developed into an exciting force on the left side of the attack. It was also less than half the £250,000 Noades had paid Hull City for his services two years earlier.

Prior to Dyer's arrival, it had been hoped that Andy Jones would find his goalscoring form at the lower level. Instead, he had continued to struggle, memorably missing a particularly easy chance in the away game at Oldham. It was to general relief that he left for Third Division AFC Bournemouth in an £80,000 deal at the end of October.

Also gone was Garth Crooks, who retired at the beginning of November after failing to recover from a long-term back injury which had restricted him to a solitary substitute outing the previous season. Crooks' absence from the side had become something of a running joke, mainly because his injuries had not prevented him making frequent radio and television appearances.

The two departures created an opportunity for 19-year-old Gordon Watson, one that he grasped with both hands. The Sidcup-born youngster was a keen Charlton supporter who had first attracted the fans' attention two seasons earlier when he hit 45 goals for the youth and reserve teams. Blooded by the cautious Lawrence in the opening League game of the 1989/90 campaign, he had then watched impatiently from the sidelines as the team were relegated. Now he exploded onto the scene, scoring seven times in his 14 Second Division starts by the end of November, despite the initially poor form of the side as a whole. It was good enough to earn him both a call-up for the England under-21 squad and great affection from the crowd, who warmed to his obvious enthusiasm for the task at hand.

And then, in February, he was abruptly sold to Sheffield Wednesday. Including out-of-favour midfielder Steve MacKenzie, who had gone to Hillsborough on an extended loan the previous week, he became the fifth former Charlton player on the Yorkshire club's books. More significantly, he was the sixth star to leave the Addicks in just over a year. This time, however, the mood of the fans was not one of resignation but of anger and disgust, because they felt that they had been betrayed. As usual, the directors pointed to the balance sheet, yet the gates at Selhurst had exceeded their expectations and at the CASC AGM Alwen had promised no more

Back to The Valley: the opening of the new club shop in April 1990

players would be sold. The deal was a public relations disaster.

It was also a particularly poor transaction from a financial point of view. The directors tried to keep the exact fee secret and were upset when company secretary Chris Parkes revealed it to the *Mercury*. Indeed, Alwen even told me that transfer fees were "none of the supporters' business". But in fact the details were freely published in the Sheffield press and were furnished just as readily by the player himself. Charlton would get £200,000 as a down payment and a further £50,000 in the summer, with £20,000 to follow for each ten first-team appearances up to 50 and a further £75,000 if Watson made the full England team. Finally, the Addicks would receive 20 per cent of the amount above the total already paid from any subsequent transfer.

In the space of 13 months, the club had earned nearly £2.5m in transfer fees and spent just £320,000. Once more Greenwich Council were in the dock. According to Parkes, part of the problem was that the £280,000 already spent on refurbishing the offices and shop had been projected to reappear in the club's cash flow by December.

But this money was part of a larger Valley loan package and contingent on the delayed planning permission. In the meantime, the directors had failed to secure expected support from the banks to bridge the gap. Despite receiving income of over £1m from the sale of players in the eight months to the end of January 1991, Charlton had still managed to make a loss of £300,000, largely due to a wage bill of £100,000 a month and net receipts of only £10,000 per home match at Selhurst Park. In other words, the company was once again hopelessly insolvent. Perhaps the council was partly to blame, but the real villain was the man who had moved the club to South Norwood in the first place. For this, inevitably, was John Fryer's final bequest.

Fans Lorraine and Dave Pearce, from Shooters Hill, pictured in December 1990 with their six-month-old daughter Katie Valley, named in honour of the ground

Parkes believed that he had been given the authority to disclose these figures and did so purely to defend the directors. As both company secretary and a genuine supporter, he was in a unique position to see both sides of the story. By contrast, Alwen's justification of the transfer had consisted of a string of platitudes cobbled into a press release. The public surely deserved some kind of detailed explanation, yet Parkes's reward for his loyalty was to be hauled over the coals by the board.

If the fans were upset about the transfer of the young striker, so too was Lawrence. He was no great admirer of Watson, as the supporters had already detected, but he did oppose the deal on the basis that the player might yet develop into an outstanding talent and to sell him at this stage was foolhardy. Publicly, he kept his views to himself, but there can be no doubt that the incident coloured his future judgement.

He feared, too, that he might soon be forced to sell again. Apart from Lee, Paul Mortimer and Scott Minto would have looked attractive if placed in the shop window by the directors. Like Watson, Minto was a graduate of the colts team that had reached the FA Youth Cup final in May 1987, but he had first broken into the League side as early as December 1988. Unusually for a debutant selected by Lawrence, the Biggin Hill youngster was just 17 at the time, although he played with a composure that belied his years. The following season he had looked outstanding on the left side of midfield, earning an England under-18 cap on the strength of an assured performance against Arsenal at Selhurst Park and a Barclays Young Eagle of the Month award.

Down in the Second Division he marked time a little, but his form was still good enough to earn another Barclays award and then, in December, an England under-21 cap. Equally at home at left-back, a position he filled during Mark Reid's lengthy absences through injury, he looked a tempting prospect for Wednesday boss Ron Atkinson and his ilk.

Charlton's playing fortunes ebbed and flowed, but all the while the strike dragged on at Greenwich. The planning application had not even been formally registered, although Alwen observed wryly at the CASC AGM in October that the council had still managed to bank the fee which accompanied it. The new club shop, opened in April, was thriving despite the fact that the original franchise-holders, Tottenham Hotspur, had pulled out. But by Christmas, time was fast running out if the ground was to be ready for 1991/92. It looked increasingly likely that the club would have to return before the west stand was available for use and play in a three-sided stadium.

The fans were in something of a quandary over the delay. Collectively, they had no firm view on the issues at stake in the strike, although their instinctive reaction was to sympathise with any group in conflict with the council. Against this, they did not like the way they were being used by NALGO. In the end, the dilemma was resolved by the disclosure that legally it was possible for Greenwich to process the application without the officers presently in dispute. Sandra Hunt and Fritz Henning, at least, were still at work and they could set the wheels in motion. But because the issue was so politically sensitive and such activity might have led to an escalation of the strike, it would need specific authorisation from the council leader.

In a bid to pressurise Marsh into taking this action, the supporters' club committee unanimously decided to send him some Christmas greetings, in this case 5,000 letters distributed at Selhurst Park for fans to post to his home address. When news of this initiative broke the Sherard councillor got very upset, telephoning Norris to protest. Under pressure from the latter we called the exercise off, but quite clearly it had already gone some way to achieving its object.

Marsh did not immediately call for the paperwork to be processed, perhaps because the strike appeared to be moving towards a settlement. But in mid-January, when it seemed to have reached a conclusion, he issued a statement promising that the Valley scheme would be given priority over the 400 other planning applications outstanding and would reach committee in eight weeks. However, the peace talks collapsed and eventually he was forced to indicate that the council would still adhere to the newly-announced timetable despite the continuing dispute.

The first step was to get the 3,500 consultation notices delivered to local residents, a job which was normally done by the planning officers. Norris had volunteered the supporters' club for this, but it was a venture about which I had some misgivings. Having lost the argument, the residents would surely be looking for any basis to obstruct the application's progress. There was no right of appeal against a permission, but a decision could still be overturned if it could be proved that the council had not followed correct procedures. Might the residents later protest to the ombudsman that we had not delivered the leaflets properly or, worse, had intimidated them into not responding? It was a point I raised with the enormously helpful Henning, but he seemed fairly confident that we were on solid ground.

That was more than could be said for our team of deliverers, who set off on their task amid the worst weather for some years, with thick snow and dangerous ice underfoot. Norris also came out but having seen King and his team begin work, drove off to the warm comfort of home. Evidently he regarded such menial activity as beneath him. Henning, on the other hand, stayed to help.

Although Greenwich had promised to decide on the application by the end of March, the format of the committee meeting posed a major headache. All sides were agreed that there could be no repeat of the previous debacle and the council was keen that this time admission should be controlled. But the numbers to be allowed in proved a contentious point, with the politicians eventually deciding to limit attendance to 100 members of the public. This was a concession to the residents, who claimed they felt intimidated by fans. In the event, the scheme's opponents failed to take up their full allocation of tickets. When they took their places on one side of the committee room at Woolwich, there were numerous empty seats and a few interlopers, including club chaplain Steve Bridge who was resplendent in a red and white scarf.

The disposal of the rest of the tickets also proved problematic. Henning had indicated that they would be handed over to the supporters' club to distribute, but Norris and Alwen insisted otherwise, claiming the right to decide who should attend and which members of the public should speak in favour of the plans. As we tried in vain to explain to them, there was no way the applicant could be allowed to pack the meeting in this way as it would make an even bigger farce of the public consultation aspects. Fortunately, Henning agreed with us, taking the view that the supporters were an interested third party, who were fully entitled to express an opinion independently of the club.

Having been defeated on this point, Norris approached King to demand that I should

The marchers arrive at Woolwich before the second planning meeting

be prevented from speaking. Quite what he thought I might say that would be damaging, it's hard to imagine. Certainly it was difficult to have any confidence in the directors choosing the right people to contribute, given the way they had handled the council thus far. After some debate at a Valley Party meeting, Henning was duly notified that our four permitted speakers would be Richard Hunt, Steve Dixon, King and myself.

At first, Norris was also keen to head off the other major activity we had planned for the night, a repeat march from The Valley to the town hall. Quite why this should have been a problem wasn't clear. The residents had also told the council that they found this intimidating, but in fact it was about as aggressive as a primary school crocodile. The procession was simply a means of organising the fans who would inevitably turn up on the night anyway, giving their demonstration a focus. The police certainly had no objections and so well organised had been the original march that they barely controlled the second one at all, simply driving beside it in a van.

When the bulk of the supporters reached Woolwich, they were once more accommodated in the familiar public hall, their third visit in just over two years. This time proceedings were relayed from the upstairs committee room by tannoy. Oddly, the council had originally wanted to connect this live link-up to the Valley Club. We were against that idea because the whole point of having the fans turn out was to exert legitimate democratic pressure on the politicians, which would obviously be much reduced if they were far away. And it didn't seem to have occurred to Greenwich that having the fans mass at Charlton to hear the news could have led to an unnecessary confrontation with the residents.

On the night, the arrangements worked well. The march was better attended than before and all the tickets for the big hall had been quickly claimed, leaving up to 1,500 people outside. They had to rely on newsflashes, broadcast by helpful comrades armed with a loudspeaker.

Ironically, Norris had now come round to the view that a big turnout of fans was desirable, so long as they were well-behaved. For now that victory was apparently in sight, he had decided to engage in some last-minute brinkmanship.

Few people, including the residents, were under the delusion that this application would be refused. Admittedly, Richard Hunt had sent a letter to the *Mercury* and I had produced a special free *VOTV* suggesting there was a significant element of doubt, but that had been purely a tactical manoeuvre to ensure that we maximised the number of people on the streets. However, it was still important that the permission was not framed in such a way as to make the scheme unviable.

An important design feature of the new stand was the fact that the bowling alley and new Valley Club would be largely subterranean. As such, the escape of noise from within would be minimised, there was no longer any massing of buildings on Harvey Gardens and even the argument that they took up land that might otherwise be available as open space was difficult to sustain.

To combat the nuisance of fans' cars, a park-and-ride scheme had been agreed for 200 vehicles at Woolwich Common and an additional 200 parking spaces found within walking distance of the ground at the Thames Barrier. Together with 65 places behind the north stand and the 190 behind the west, the club could now offer facilities for 655 cars. There was even accommodation for 60 residents' vehicles inside the

YES! Jubilant fans celebrate their victory outside the town hall on April 2nd

ground on matchdays. Whether the fans would utilise the more distant sites seemed very doubtful, but as Charlton observed in the planners' report: "No other London League club has such a provision or indeed has been required to provide such by their local planning authority."

Now the stumbling block was the bowling alley, and more especially its opening hours. As the Valley Party's Paul Giannandrea wrote in a letter to the *Mercury* later, the residents had done themselves no favours in blocking the original scheme, for the new facility seemed likely to cause considerably more nuisance than ever the office block might have. Floyd Road's Andrew Marsh even argued that bowling would become the main use of the ground and hence could not be ancillary to the playing of football, a point which Greenwich Council would probably once have pursued.

The outstanding issue, however, was when the alley should be allowed to open. The hours, like those of the Valley Club and the function room, the parking arrangements, plans for a creche and a football in the community scheme, were all to be embodied in a legally-binding section 106 agreement. Charlton wanted the alley to open until 2am seven days a week. The planners' report, which as expected recommended permission overall, argued that such hours were defensible but was phrased loosely enough to suggest the politicians might take a different view.

Not surprisingly, they did. The fact that an amendment would be moved proposing midnight closing every night except Friday and Saturday had soon become common knowledge. In response, Norris decided to send the council a letter demanding 3am opening at weekends, with the strong suggestion that anything else would threaten the viability of the whole stand.

Quite who wanted to go bowling in South East London at 3am in the morning remained unclear. A similar facility at Bexleyheath closed at 10pm, and one at Streatham at midnight during the week. Even that at Lewisham was only open until 2am. While the activities inside the alley might cause no disturbance, the noise of people leaving late at night certainly would and for once the fans tended to side with the residents. Indeed, privately many of them thought midnight opening seven days a week would be quite reasonable.

The effect of Norris's intervention was to sour the relationship between the council and the club on the night. The politicians clearly regarded it as an act of bad faith, which indeed it was, and one articulated his suspicions that the directors were looking for a reason to back out while putting the blame on the council. Fortunately, when challenged on it by the committee, Norris withdrew the letter.

As before, the decisive meeting was an elaborate charade, with the important difference that this time the noises made by the politicians were those we wanted to hear. The make-up of the planning committee had changed, although our old allies Jim Coughlan and Bob Callow were both still there. The mood, too, was different, with John Austin-Walker teasing Callow about his allegiance to Chelsea and much stifled laughter at Ted Claridge's earnest enquiry about the lack of changing accommodation for female matchday officials.

This time the consultation process had yielded only 90 letters, 53 in favour and 37 against. As I commented in my own speech, it hardly suggested deep unrest in the neighbouring streets and had to be compared with the 2,400 votes cast in Charlton for the Valley Party the previous May. As we knew very well, the residents had gathered another petition, this time of 412 names, but they would always struggle to negate our landslide at the ballot box.

Only three aspects of the proceedings caused us any concern. The first speaker from the objectors' side, Bob Dean, called for an adjournment on the grounds that the application might be called in by the Department of the Environment. It later emerged that Greenwich MP Rosie Barnes, who had hitherto remained silent about the new scheme, had been active to just such an end. Fortunately, Greenwich had already established that the government had no plans to intervene.

Our second complaint involved the extent to which the residents were indulged in making their speeches. We had been told that there would be a limit of three minutes per speaker and consequently kept ours short, but now found that two of the objectors were allowed to go on at considerable length.

Finally, Hornfair councillor Irene Hogben, who was not a member of the planning committee, took the opportunity provided by her position as a local ward representative to launch into an outrageous and unjustified tirade about fans' behaviour at the election count.

None of it mattered. Outside the cheers of the waiting crowd could be heard above the politicians' rhetoric, growing louder by the minute as message after message of support from around the committee table was relayed by loudspeaker. At last, the permission was granted by 17 votes to one. Only Sukhdev Sanghara, the Charlton ward councillor who had spoken for the objectors throughout the meeting, stood out against the scheme. But there were amendments. The first, which would have closed the bowling alley at midnight throughout the week, was proposed by two opposition councillors and easily defeated. The second, proposed by vice-chair Tony Moon and seconded by Quentin Marsh, appeared to be carried unanimously.

As expected, the weekday opening hours for the bowling alley were cut back. Despite Norris's complaints, both the club and their operator might have lived with what was agreed. But the committee also placed the whole matter under a six-month review. It meant that Charlton might get their later hours if things went well, but the politicians would also retain the right to change their minds completely. In theory, they might wait until the spotlight had moved on and then decide the alley could not open at all. Whatever the intention, it was a ludicrous imposition from a commercial point of view. For what bank would lend money to build a facility that might be compulsorily shut down six months after it was completed?

Not that the gleeful fans downstairs knew or cared about any of that. The 600 in the hall had made confetti of the 60-page planning documents and now threw it deliriously into the air, filmed by the TV cameras. Then it was out into Market Street to merge with the waiting crowd and salute an historic night.

"Back to The Valley, we're going back to The Valley," they sang, the words of triumph booming once more round the streets of Woolwich. At length, a hesitant Alwen came out to speak to them from the town hall steps. They cheered him to the echo, but did not fully comprehend his words.

It was exactly two years since the day of the emotional Valley clean-up, when he had addressed those same happy faces from the foot of the doomed main stand. Once more they celebrated victory together. And once more their celebrations were hopelessly premature.

Here we go: Roger Alwen addresses the delighted crowd at Woolwich

Chapter Twelve

"I feel a tremendous exhilaration. It's been a huge challenge but we've got through it. I'll be able to look back and say I achieved something."
Mike Norris – Mercury Valley Special (August 1991)

By the time Greenwich Council finally gave what seemed to be the green light for The Valley, Charlton had just four games left to play at Selhurst Park. They were meaningless, mid-table fixtures and attracted little euphoria. The only sign of celebration was the release of balloons at the match against Ipswich Town on April 6th as part of a Valley Gold promotion, but somehow it was appropriate that the six years of exile should end in anti-climax.

Lennie Lawrence's ill-advised comments about the superior atmosphere of Selhurst rang very hollow now. With the installation of seats in the Arthur Wait enclosure the previous summer, the noisier Charlton fans had been pushed out onto the high, open banking at the Holmesdale Road end of the ground, leaving the team to perform in what seemed a largely empty arena. In fact, the average attendance that year was 6,547, just about respectable in the circumstances and higher than in the first season there, when the club had won promotion. But the dispersal of the home supporters into four isolated groups meant that most games were watched in near silence, an unnatural state of affairs which the manager admitted his players found disturbing.

Even the last League fixture at Selhurst, against Second Division championship contenders West Ham United, somehow fell flat. It had been approached with much trepidation, both police and clubs fearing damage to the ground. At one stage, there was even talk of switching it to another venue to avoid the possibility of trouble, a prospect made credible by the revelation that Charlton had never obtained the short extension required to their lease. But in the event the game went ahead without a hint of a problem.

Hammers fans made up half the 16,137 crowd, undoubtedly reduced by the panic imposition of an all-ticket ruling, and unusually the visitors were allocated the whole of the Arthur Wait Stand as well as part of the Holmesdale Road terrace. It meant the Charlton faithful were crowded into the remainder of the ground, but even so their efforts to raise a farewell chorus in the closing stages did not really succeed.

Few would have disagreed that the 1-1 result was a fair reflection of an even contest, with Scott Minto claiming the honour of scoring Charlton's last "home" League goal at Selhurst Park. The giant electronic scoreboard erected at the supermarket end in 1989 bade the weary travellers goodbye and this time few lingered for a last look around. The Palace stadium had claimed a place in the club's history, but never the affection or respect of the fans.

For real enthusiasts, however, there was one last trip round the South Circular to be made. Five days later, little more than 100 people saw the Addicks' reserve side run out to play Millwall in a game switched from Park View Road because of work on the Welling United pitch. Steve Gritt's men won 3-0 and youngster Rossi Franco earned a footnote in history by netting the final goal late in the game.

That season, with the office staff based back in Greenwich, the club's only presence at the ground had been on matchdays. Within an hour of the reserve match

Signing off: one way of celebrating the final game in London SE25

ending, there was nothing left to say that the Addicks had ever been at Selhurst Park except the presence of the perennial Portakabins, which had been taken over by Palace the previous summer.

Ron Noades was strangely silent about Charlton's departure. Maybe it was diplomatic on his part not to highlight the failures of the previous six years with Wimbledon already preparing to move in as replacement tenants. Instead, the papers were soon full of the same fatuous optimism about the Dons' move as the incredulous Addicks fans had read in September 1985. Unless the two chairmen had some hidden agenda, it seemed that they had learned little if anything from Charlton's depressing experience.

This time, Noades argued, the two sharing clubs would have a true partnership. Perhaps he didn't realise that a corpse is not an ideal bedfellow. Certainly it was relatively easy for Wimbledon fans to reach Selhurst, but there were few enough of them already. And if Plough Lane was inadequate, at least its 4,000 regulars could generate a decent atmosphere in such a tight enclosure. Predictably, the Dons' tenure in London SE25 would commence with a string of record low First Division crowds.

Charlton, meanwhile, wound up their Selhurst years 16th in the Second Division table, a position which did not quite reflect the talent still in the squad. Indeed, until a crazy last ten minutes at Hull City the day before the planning meeting, it had not been entirely impossible that they might yet make the promotion play-offs.

Such optimism had seemed unlikely when Gordon Watson was sold, but the emergence of another outstanding youngster, 18-year-old Ghanaian-born Kim Grant,

Rossi Franco gets up to score Charlton's last "home" goal at Selhurst Park

had quickly banished much of the fans' disappointment. Two stylish goals from him in the space of four March days suggested that youth-team coach Colin Clarke had produced another unexpected gem.

A further popular newcomer in the side towards the end of the season had been Paul Gorman, a prolific scorer in the GM Vauxhall Conference with Docklands-based Fisher Athletic. The 22-year-old was signed for £15,000 late in March on the recommendation of groundsman Colin Powell, who was a part-time Fisher coach, and soon won the fans over with his raw enthusiasm.

Before the transfer deadline, Steve MacKenzie's move to Hillsborough had been made permanent and Charlton had also taken young Manchester United midfielder David Wilson on loan. But of all the new faces in the side that spring, one was to play a fateful role in the club's history, a part completely out of proportion to his contribution to the team. Middlesbrough central defender Alan Kernaghan had arrived in South East London in the middle of January on a month's loan, to deputise for the injured Tommy Caton. In exchange, the unhappy Colin Walsh moved to Teesside to play for his former Nottingham Forest teammate, Colin Todd, and at Selhurst in February the two loan signings had the novel experience of lining up against their usual teammates.

Out of favour at Ayresome Park, the 23-year-old Kernaghan was looking for a permanent move, although initially the prospects of him finding a long-term berth at Charlton seemed remote. In Caton, Simon Webster and Stuart Balmer, the club already had three capable players in his preferred position and two more, Steve Brown and Linvoy Primus, were on their way up through the ranks. However, Kernaghan's impact on the side was immediate and obvious, and his commanding presence at the back appeared to inspire his new colleagues.

Lawrence called the defender "his best-ever loan signing", but the fans soon wanted this stylish recruit made a permanent member of the squad. Given the circumstances of the Watson transfer, it seemed unlikely that Charlton could find the money, but strangely they did. When Middlesbrough recalled Kernaghan on the day of the planning meeting, the Addicks twice tried to buy him, offering around £250,000. But Boro were adamant that they would not sell while they remained in promotion contention, which they did until they were eliminated from the play-offs by Notts County in May.

Now Second Division rivals Barnsley entered the market for him, tabling a £300,000 offer which Middlesbrough accepted. Charlton matched it, but then Kernaghan got married and set off on three weeks' honeymoon. By the time he came back, events had moved on.

Moving out: Paul Pace packs up

Despite leading the Teessiders to seventh spot in the table in his first season at the helm, Boro boss Todd had alienated many of the Ayresome Park players and at the end of June he was abruptly dismissed. A fortnight later, on the morning of Wednesday, July 10th, the club announced to widespread disbelief that his successor would be Lawrence.

It was just five weeks to the opening day of the season, and apparently the historic return to The Valley, the dream for which so many had laboured so long. Almost in spite of himself, no one had done more to keep it alive than the manager. And now, suddenly, he was gone. Directors, players, staff and fans were stunned. Even the local reporters, who just the previous day had watched him endure a ridiculous publicity stunt designed to sell more Valley season tickets, were more than a little amazed.

The story was broken overnight by the nationals and never was the back page of the *Mercury* remade at the last minute with more urgency or such a sense of shock. Owing to ridiculous deadlines that demanded the paper was put together on a Tuesday afternoon, we had to scramble from our beds to change the existing lead, with frantic phone calls being made to stall the printers. Initially, Peter Cordwell began to write an emotive piece imploring Lawrence to stay. But it soon became clear that it was much too late for that. The element of surprise had caught us all out.

Inevitably, it was the Kernaghan saga which had led to Lawrence's departure. The persuasive skills which the manager had used to bring so many players to Charlton had finally impressed one man too much. Middlesbrough chairman Colin Henderson had determined to recruit them for his own club's cause.

Sadly, there were sour aspects to the affair. In the days that led up to the move, Lawrence had been close to finalising the Kernaghan deal for Charlton, prompting grave suspicions among the Addicks fans that the transfer had been deliberately stalled. The manager's official line was that he had known nothing of the approach until Tuesday morning. Few were buying that version of events, although certainly the first the defender knew of the changed circumstances was when he walked into Ayresome Park on the Wednesday morning to find Lawrence on the pitch being introduced to the media as his new boss at Boro.

Roger Alwen, too, felt betrayed. He had granted his manager permission to talk to the Teesside club, but apparently expected the courtesy of further consultation before a decision was reached. Instead, Middlesbrough presented Charlton with a fait accompli, staging their press conference to announce the news before notifying the Addicks chairman.

Now it was revealed that Lawrence had signed a two-year extension to his existing contract on July 1st, just nine days before his departure. There was also an undignified wrangle about compensation, which continued even after the manager revealed that he had cannily insisted upon a clause that ruled it out.

The Charlton directors were left clutching at air, their naivety exposed for all to see, and the anger surfaced in a press release, issued after a nine-hour board meeting

Last man in: Lennie Lawrence (right) with his final signing, John Bumstead

the following Monday. "Although Lennie Lawrence has been an extremely good servant to the club, we are very upset at the manner of his departure and the fact that he effectively walked out leaving a substantial debt and has failed to make any contact with the club," it claimed.

Unfortunately, two aspects of the statement were simply nonsense and served only to diminish the directors' credibility further. The debt in question was a £50,000 personal loan, a sum which Lawrence had already told the *Mercury* that the Middlesbrough chairman had agreed to repay. As for the former manager having made no contact with the club, he had been at the training ground on both Thursday and Friday and was known to have spoken to Mike Norris at some length about the circumstances of his move.

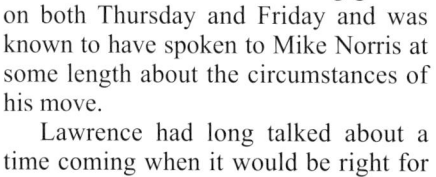

The ill-fated publicity stunt

Lawrence had long talked about a time coming when it would be right for him to leave Charlton, but few had imagined it would be on the brink of such a highlight as the return to The Valley. Yet there was a kind of logic to it. For the manager had increasingly resented the extent to which the campaign to move back to SE7 had overshadowed and restricted his team's achievements on the field. He recognised the importance of going back, and had made a very personal appeal to fans to back his team-building plans by purchasing season tickets, but somehow it had always seemed that he did not quite believe it would work out.

Had the directors been more staunch in their backing during the crisis of the previous October then perhaps he might have shown more loyalty when put to the test. As it was, he was highly conscious of the fresh cash constraints that might be imposed in the autumn as the bills for The Valley fell due. It made him wary of a repeat of the previous season's poor start, this time ending in his dismissal. To that extent, the board was reaping a harvest of distrust that it had itself sowed.

Something else which surfaced again in his valedictory remarks were the familiar slights upon Charlton that had so infuriated fans over recent years. His main reason for accepting Boro's offer, he said, was their status as a "big club". In evidence, he cited their attendances the previous season, which had averaged 17,000. Perhaps he had a point. But those Charlton fans with long memories could remember him being similarly enthusiastic about their own outfit when appointed manager at The Valley by Mark Hulyer way back in 1982.

Had Lawrence shared that length of recall, he might have noted that three of his first four visits to Ayresome Park with the Addicks had been watched by fewer than 4,500 people. Such gates were no more indicative of a "big club" than Charlton's in the last years at Floyd Road. He might have realised, too, that whereas his former employers had won the FA Cup and been beaten finalists, Middlesbrough had never got past the sixth round. Nor could they match Charlton's achievement of finishing second, fourth and third in their initial three First Division seasons. Boro's highest-ever League placing was third, and that was before the First World War.

If Middlesbrough were a bigger club than Charlton in 1991, which seemed beyond dispute, the disparity was not as great as Lawrence imagined, nor necessarily as irreversible. The real and growing distinction within the League was that between the biggest five or six and the remainder. Below the elite level, the North East giants of Newcastle United and Sunderland dwarfed Middlesbrough. Had it been any other manager, it would probably have been safe to assume that he was engaged in a public relations exercise aimed at winning over the fans of his new club. However, such behaviour was hardly in Lawrence's character.

But if the circumstances of his departure were not particularly creditable, his achievements at Charlton cannot be forgotten. No one will ever know what might have happened had the club not abandoned The Valley, but his feat of getting the Addicks back into the top flight and keeping them there for four years on Third Division support stands any critical examination. In the end, the inevitable price of moving to Selhurst had to be paid, but it was no reflection on a truly great manager.

His was an awesome act to follow and there was much speculation about who might be given the task. The playing staff, who had returned for pre-season training just two days before Lawrence's departure, were sent home as soon as it became clear he had gone. When they reported back, it was left to the two player-coaches, Steve Gritt and Alan Curbishley, to assume temporary charge.

The favourite for the top job had to be Keith Peacock, the club's former skipper and longest-serving outfield player, with 591 appearances to his name between 1962 and 1979. Peacock had long been regarded as the heir apparent to the Charlton managership and had served a six-and-a-half-year apprenticeship at Kent neighbours Gillingham, where such was his popularity that fans demonstrated on the pitch when he was sacked.

He had led the Gills as far as the Third Division promotion play-offs in 1987, and most regarded his dismissal in January 1988 as unreasonably harsh. More recently, he had spent 18 months as boss at League newcomers Maidstone United, who were playing inside the Addicks' catchment area at Dartford following the sale of their former ground for redevelopment. There, too, he had been sacked, in January 1991, a poor reward after he had taken the Stones to the Fourth Division play-offs in their debut season. The timing, however, appeared to be fortuitous, for that spring he had been a familiar figure at the Charlton training ground, putting his knowledge of the lower divisions to work for Lawrence as a scout.

Had the identity of the new manager been decided by a poll among supporters, there would have been no need to count the votes. But inside the club there were other forces at work. One was Arnie Warren, the general manager who had steadily accumulated more and more power since his arrival on the scene as chief scout in 1984. Although strongly disliked and distrusted in some quarters, Warren had the ear of the chairman and thus was able to exercise considerable influence.

The initial indications which came out of the club were that Warren was saying

Men at the top: new bosses Alan Curbishley (left) and Steve Gritt

Lawrence's successor should not be a former Charlton player. This would have ruled out another contender, former manager Mike Bailey, who was known to have some support among the directors, but it seemed to make little sense as a proscription. If a better candidate was available so be it, but the club surely needed the lift that a man such as Peacock's appointment would have provided. Mindful of the vibes from the training ground, Cordwell and I decided to throw the paper's weight fully behind the longer-serving former captain.

It took the board a fortnight to reach a decision, announced late on the afternoon of Wednesday, July 24th, and it appeared to amount to the worst kind of muddle-headed compromise. Gritt and Curbishley would continue in charge as joint coaches, with Peacock getting responsibility for the reserves as a consolation prize. But Warren would look after transfer negotiations, contracts and other matters off the field.

The fans divided between those who thought it was a joke and those who were horrified. It was not so much the separation of football and business elements, which was not that unusual, but rather the people involved and the proposed equality of the two team bosses. Neither Gritt nor Curbishley even had much experience as a coach. Both had applied for the manager's job and each had thought he might work as assistant to the other, but no one had expected this. As for Warren's further elevation, that was simply staggering. Small wonder that the board had not been unanimous.

Unfortunately, the decision about the managership was not the only eccentric one the directors reached during the summer of 1991. The longer-running farce over the future of The Valley took a further series of twists that left fans gasping.

Back at Woolwich in April, Norris had been deeply unhappy about the restrictions placed on the bowling alley. While Alwen was outside addressing the crowd on the steps of the town hall, he had been far more subdued. "I've just told the local authority, thank you very much indeed, we'll go back to a three-sided stadium. That just about sums it up," he had explained to a press conference. Indeed, such was his dissatisfaction with the terms of the planning permission that the section 106 agreement upon which it hinged had still not been signed six months later.

For the present, however, the board proceeded with plans for the return. It was now inevitable that the new stand would not be ready for August, so they decided to restrict away fans to 1,000 places in the Jimmy Seed Stand, reached via a corridor from Valley Grove just as Michael Gliksten had envisaged in 1985 and John Fryer had proclaimed impossible. It left standing room for 6,000 and around 5,000 seats for Charlton fans, although Norris indicated privately that he hoped to renew more of the East Terrace than expected during the summer, boosting the capacity further.

The original plan had been to relay the terrace to a seating specification, to save further expense later on. Now he announced that this would not be possible because there wasn't sufficient time. There would, however, be a row of temporary executive boxes built on stilts at the back. Not surprisingly, this idea, too, was soon scrapped as impractical.

Work on the £5m new stand, it was said, would begin in September despite the continued rumblings about the bowling alley. The Football Trust indicated it would give a maximum £1m grant towards the cost, subject to receiving certain assurances about Charlton's security of tenure at The Valley, a condition Norris laughed off as unnecessary. But the club still faced playing a whole season without the ground's most important facilities, both in terms of accommodation and ability to earn additional revenue.

A more immediate obstacle for the Charlton board, however, was a storm of protest over the proposed Valley admission prices. As expected, season-ticket rates soared because the club had previously held them down in order to attract people to Selhurst Park. More controversial were anomalies within the prices and plans to make all applicants pay a further £20 membership fee unless they were already in Valley Gold. Pensioners, in particular, were badly hit, with some of their season-ticket rates being trebled.

Perhaps the biggest cause of complaint were the prices at the top and bottom ends of the market. The imposingly-titled vice-presidents and members of the executive club found their charges doubled to £1,000 and £700 respectively, while at the same time the facilities offered were sharply cut back.

General manager Arnie Warren

Instead of an exclusive bar at Selhurst, they would have access to a refurbished Valley Club while the new stand was being built. Their seats would be virtually the same as those of the ordinary season-ticket holders at the front of the old Covered End, which had never offered a particularly good view. And for the coming season they would have nowhere to park their cars.

Not surprisingly, they baulked at this package and one of three meetings held in the Valley Club at the end of the season to explain the directors' plans for the ground became an acrimonious showdown between supporters and board. Eventually, Charlton were obliged to scrap their vice-presidents' section because nobody was prepared to join it.

At the other end of the scale, the club had tried to counter the loss of revenue caused by the low capacity figure by pushing up the minimum admission price, apparently on the assumption that demand was inelastic. Fans who joined the membership scheme could sit for £10 or stand for £7, which in itself was a big increase on prices at Selhurst. But casual supporters would have to pay £10 to use the East Terrace and £12 to sit, with all away fans expected to pay the latter price.

The need for money was understandable, but these rates appeared fanciful and unlikely to maximise receipts. A £10 minimum standing price would be the dearest in the League and the board's retort that the team's success was the sole criterion in determining crowd levels seemed ill-considered. For six years the journey to Selhurst Park had acted as a block on generating new support. Now Charlton were coming home, they seemed intent on erecting another obstacle.

Despite the prices, or perhaps in part because of them, season-ticket sales did moderately well, ending close to the 3,000-mark, which was nearly double the

Coming down: a bulldozer moves in on the old Harvey Gardens turnstiles

previous year's total at Selhurst. Among the applicants were many returning fans who had defiantly refused to make the trip. But there were also many who had attended regularly at Palace and now simply wanted to ensure that they could get into The Valley despite the low capacity.

Quite when they would need to do so, however, remained to be seen. The League computer threw out an attractive home fixture against highly-fancied Newcastle United for the opening game, but by then there were already grave doubts that the ground would be ready in time for the start of the season.

The first blow had fallen in June with a leak to the *Mercury* that the safety authorities had rejected the use of the old Bartram Gate because the access to it was too steep. It meant that the limit for the East Terrace would be revised yet again, down to 3,000, and since the police demanded that Valley Grove be kept as a dedicated exit for away fans, no Charlton supporters would be able to use the south stand. So now the capacity was down to 9,300, of which more than a third would be reserved for visitors, who in many cases would number only a few hundred fans.

The sensible solution would have been to impose a temporary ban on away supporters, but mindful of the way Luton Town had been stigmatised for their attempt to do the same, albeit with a different motive, the Charlton board was reluctant to embrace the idea. Instead, the directors opted for the construction of a temporary west stand, intended to cost around £130,000.

This quickly began to look like a mistake. When work got under way the price of it rocketed, not least because the council's building control officers took a very dim view of the proposed foundations. Despite Alwen's insistence to the contrary, the club needed to obtain planning permission for this and all the other temporary

Going up: the temporary west stand at The Valley under construction

Back home: the first team picture taken at The Valley for six years

accommodation. And although it was claimed that the permanent west stand could be built around the short-term structure, by the time the council was satisfied the latter looked as substantial as Fort Knox. Now construction of the vital bowling alley would not begin until the following summer at least, even supposing that an agreement could be reached with the proposed operator.

If this development was an error, Charlton also remained dogged by extreme bad luck. The main contractors for the Valley refurbishment, G Percy Trentham, did not come on site until the beginning of June and almost immediately they went into receivership. Fortunately, the firm that bought them out, Beazer Construction, was happy to take over the job, but precious days were lost while the company's affairs were sorted out. Then the weather made a malign intervention. It rained almost every day in June, making it difficult to mix concrete and proceed with the work.

At the beginning of July came the extraordinary news that there was no longer time to relay the East Terrace and consequently the club would erect a framework over the bank upon which to provide 3,000 open-air seats. Ten years on, Gliksten's crackpot all-weather seats plan was set to be made reality. There was also to be further work at the demolished Bartram Gate, where an elaborate steel staircase was built to provide an alternative emergency escape route from that corner of the stadium.

It was becoming increasingly difficult to take the board's announcements seriously and the continued assurances that the ground would be ready by August 17th, the scheduled date of the first match, had very little credibility. By the end of July, the club was obliged to admit that the contractors could not meet the deadline. The first three matches of the new season would take place at West Ham, with the happy return now set for Portsmouth's visit on September 14th.

Battle for The Valley

The news did not impress the League, partly because the two Second Division matches involved clashed with the Hammers' schedule and would therefore have to be played on Sundays. Eventually they agreed to the switch, but issued a stern warning that they would expect Charlton to be back at The Valley in time to entertain Portsmouth.

Upton Park had not been the first choice as the alternative venue. Despite a repeated and very public offer from Fourth Division Gillingham to share their Priestfield Stadium, 25 miles south-east of The Valley, the directors' initial thought was to move in at The Den. Lions chairman Reg Burr had told the *South London Press* as long ago as the previous August that if the situation did arise "we would be happy to help out". Since then, however, relations between the clubs had been soured by a dispute over the way Charlton fans were treated when they visited Millwall for the local derby. Burr was still willing to co-operate, but the Addicks' approach was blocked below board level.

Another possibility would have been to reverse the early games, or simply postpone them as Liverpool had done previously during work on the Kop at Anfield. But distorting the fixture programme might have had negative consequences for the team and everybody was agreed that a successful season was essential if the impetus derived from the return to The Valley was to be maintained.

Although Lawrence had touted Welling United as an option, and Gillingham might have had the advantage of reviving some of the dormant Kentish support, the only real choice now was to cross the river. Leyton Orient was the closest ground, and their early fixtures did not clash, but instead Charlton had opted for Upton Park.

Take your seats: work under way on the East Terrace in September

In many respects it was a wise choice, a traditional stadium with good facilities and unlike Selhurst a pleasure to visit. Unfortunately, for most fans it could only be reached through the bottleneck of the Blackwall Tunnel, a handicap that should not have been underestimated. It was also expensive. Charlton had agreed to pay the Hammers a fee of £10,000 per match. On top of that there were heavy stewarding costs needed to satisfy the Upton Park safety certificate and they initially faced an extraordinary police bill of £9,000 for each game, because the force insisted upon treating the fixtures as if West Ham were at home.

None of which would have mattered much, except that it was apparent to all concerned that The Valley would no more be ready for September 14th than it had been for August 17th. Just in case there was any doubt, only two days after the Addicks had kicked off their season with an impressive win over Newcastle, most of the sub-contractors packed up their plant and walked out. It soon emerged that they hadn't been paid.

Thus far the stands behind the goals had been stripped of seats ready to receive replacements and the cladding over the frame of the Covered End had been renewed. The Valley Club, found to be insufficiently sound to be worth refurbishing for even nine months' use, had been demolished, as had the old turnstiles and urinals. Impressive modern floodlights, four of them as it turned out and none yet with planning permission, had been erected, but now work ground to a halt. Only on the two sides of the pitch, where other contracts were involved, did the men remain on site and by the middle of October they too would have gone.

Matters were not much helped by the lack of information coming out of the club through official channels. It was somewhat ironic, therefore, that my erstwhile colleague Steve Dixon had been hired that summer to oversee communications. Roy King, meanwhile, had been appointed Charlton's stadium manager, although many were beginning to doubt that he would ever have a stadium to manage.

Whatever happened in the long term, the latest developments obviously meant that Charlton would have to continue playing at Upton Park for some time. Apart from disappointing the fans, the news upset the League, who called a summit meeting with the club and council in an effort to find out what was going on. In theory, they could have fined the Addicks or deducted Second Division points, but there seemed little purpose in doing so. The directors had declined to set a new target date but they plainly needed no greater incentive to get back to The Valley than the amount of money they were losing on the other side of the Thames.

Just to complicate matters, fans were extremely suspicious about the attendance figures being returned at West Ham. The Newcastle gate had been announced as 9,322, but to many it had looked more. By the time Charlton played Norwich City at the end of September, the club was sufficiently concerned to put a watch on the turnstiles. At the end of the evening, six operators were sacked. It suggested the supporters had been right to some extent, but there was no real way of knowing the extent of the fraud.

At the same time, the transport problem was beginning to bite. Despite the best efforts of Chris Parkes, now the club secretary, the Blackwall Tunnel authorities had not proved particularly accommodating. Charlton's first expedition through it had been obstructed by workmen cutting back trees on the approach road and it seemed that each fresh match brought a new, unexpected obstacle. By October, Parkes had resorted to spending £1,200 on hiring an extra Woolwich Ferry in a bid to ease congestion. For even the players were finding that it could take up to two hours to get to the ground from south of the river.

Once again, however, it was the heroics of the team that were coming to the club's rescue by maintaining morale. To general astonishment, Gritt and Curbishley were proving an outstanding success. Despite an indifferent pre-season and losing the services of Warren, who had to undergo triple-bypass heart surgery after collapsing in August, Charlton lost only three of their first 14 League games. It was exactly the form that would have been required to ignite the passion generated by the return to The Valley. At Upton Park, it at least provided the incentive necessary to keep the loyalists going.

What made the feat all the more remarkable was the fact that it was achieved with hardly any spending. The cash apparently available for Kernaghan had disappeared and with it £350,000 received for out-of-contract Paul Mortimer in July.

The loss of the latter to Aston Villa had been a blow, although not an unexpected one. As usual, the chief criticism was of the fee, but this time Lawrence could not be blamed and nor could his successors, because it had been agreed while the manager's job was vacant. What made it bitter was that three months later, Villa boss Ron Atkinson sold him on to Palace, of all clubs, for £500,000.

Gone, too, was Mark Reid, the last survivor of the seven summer signings in 1985. Now nearing his 30th birthday, he had been allowed to leave for Scottish

A red and white elephant: the temporary west stand nears completion

Premier League St Mirren on a free transfer, a just reward for six years' loyal service.

Three players did come in, however. Chelsea's veteran midfielder John Bumstead, 32, had been Lawrence's last signing, on a free transfer just days before the manager left. And in the week before the opening League game, Curbishley took advantage of Warren's absence to acquire two experienced men from his former club Brighton & Hove Albion, 30-year-old striker Garry Nelson and 32-year-old central defender Steve Gatting, the latter without a fee.

Nelson's value was assessed at £50,000 by a transfer tribunal, but it was money well spent for he proved to be just what was required up front. The autumn's other success story, however, was a quite remarkable one. Carl Leaburn, with four goals to his credit in exactly 100 games, had further improved his overall contribution the previous season but offered little threat to opposing goalkeepers. Now he more than doubled his goal tally of over four years in the space of less than two months.

It was hard to escape the conclusion that this was linked to the departure of Lawrence. Indeed, the new managerial duo had brought an unexpected breath of fresh air to the whole club. The cultured Walsh, whose relationship with the former boss had all but broken down, was thriving in the new environment and young talents like defender Anthony Barness were blossoming. Perhaps more by luck than judgement, the board appeared to have found a winning combination. Lawrence, too, had reason to be satisfied, for Middlesbrough led a mediocre Second Division.

By late October, Charlton had begun to look like serious promotion contenders. The side was brimming with confidence, but if the challenge was to be sustained it was imperative the club got back to The Valley in order to generate income.

Change of venue: Charlton's first "home" game at Upton Park, in August 1991

Part of the problem, as usual, was Greenwich Council, although this time there could be no suggestion that they were being deliberately awkward. The Valley was the first football ground to be built since Taylor had reported into the Hillsborough disaster and inevitably some of the procedures and rules laid down in the new safety regulations were open to interpretation. In his own interests, the council safety officer had to be sure he followed them correctly. No one could fault him for that, but it meant the estimated cost of the refurbishment alone had soared to £1.8m.

Fortunately, Charlton had come into a windfall from the old Football Grounds Improvement Trust. When the club left The Valley in 1985, they had already claimed £319,000 for safety work on the ground, close to the maximum allowed. However, in the time that they had been away, the rules had changed. FGIT had in fact been incorporated into an expanded Football Trust, but happily for the Addicks any money paid out for work on Selhurst Park had been credited to Palace's account. Hence, Charlton could now claim another £800,000.

The problem was that the Trust was not allowed to pay out until Beazer's bill had been met by Charlton. And the club could not do that until they received the cash from the Trust. Moreover, if they tried to square the circle by borrowing the money from a bank, there was a danger that Beazer might take the £800,000 in part settlement of the £1.2m already outstanding and decline to do any more work.

Meanwhile, Norris, the man overseeing the whole operation at The Valley, was quietly sinking into a financial morass of his own. Just as the club's finances started to unwind, so his private property interests began finally to drag him down, leaving debts which ran into millions of pounds.

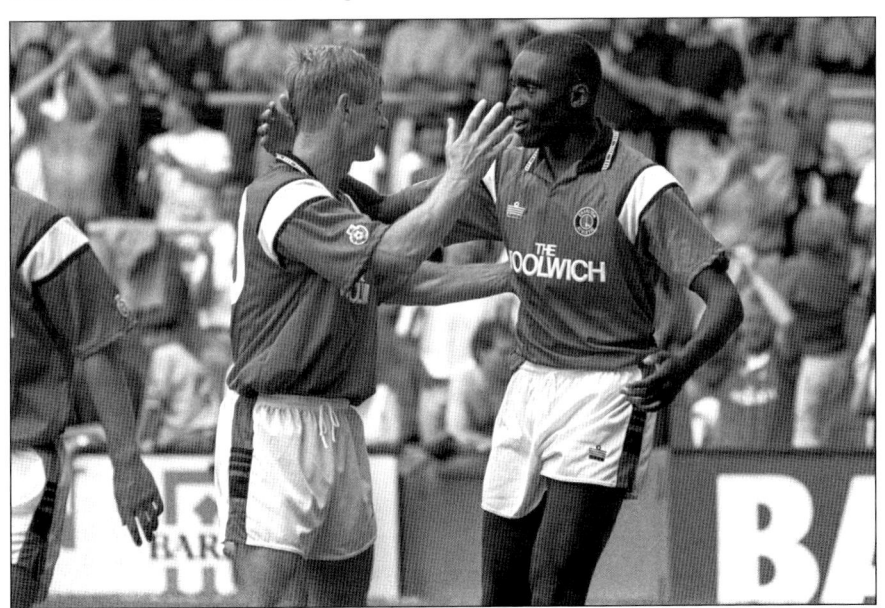

New boy Nelson (left) congratulates Leaburn on his goal against Newcastle

New directors Martin Simons (left) and Richard Murray

It came as some surprise, for throughout the summer a buoyant Norris had persistently been linked with taking over as chairman, a prospect which he took no trouble to deny. Indeed, his unlikely partnership with Alwen had been a strained one for some time. The pair had had an agreement that the chair would rotate after two years, but in the event the prevailing circumstances had allowed Alwen to retain it.

The major business deal which might have allowed Norris to take over and solved his other problems did not go through. By the end of September, he had lost control of both his 50 per cent shareholding in the club and Adelong Limited, the company which owned The Valley and which it soon emerged was legally responsible for the refurbishment costs. For Norris it was the end of the line. A terse two-sentence statement claimed that he had "resigned" from the board "for personal reasons to pursue other activities". In fact, he had been given no choice.

Pessimism hung over the club once more and there were even genuine fears that the newly-erected floodlights would be taken down by the sub-contractors. The inevitable Richard Collins took charge of The Valley and the business of sorting out the still unresolved question of the various planning applications. But the task of funding the building work to completion, recovering Norris's £175,000-worth of share capital in the club and resolving the matter of who would own the former vice-chairman's half of the training ground remained to be sorted out.

Fortunately, two newcomers with money to invest now came to the fore: Richard Murray, 41-year-old chairman of Avesco, a company with interests in the TV and video industry, and 42-year-old Martin Simons, a retired oil executive from Blackheath. The two friends had joined the board in April and Murray, who had only become a supporter during the exile, had impressed fans with his interventions in the close-season argument about pricing. Simons had hitherto remained fairly anonymous, but when he did come forward it was immediately apparent that the club's affairs were at last coming under the supervision of businessmen of a different calibre. Just by the fact of his public intervention, the gloom began to lift.

As Adelong headed into liquidation, the whole question of the ownership of The Valley was once more thrown open. Laing Homes, who had put up the money to purchase the company in 1988, were the chief creditors, but the ground was next to useless to them. And the crowning irony was that Greenwich Council was the party responsible for that, through their unwillingness to grant planning permission for redevelopment. Seemingly, the door had opened at last for the club to reclaim its rightful property at an affordable price.

How the money might be found was a hot topic for discussion on a new Sunday night radio programme that had taken to the local airwaves on the second weekend of the season in less than harmonious circumstances. It abruptly replaced the *Charlton Chat* programme hosted by the club's ex-commercial boss Steve Sutherland – who had joined the Football League – and fellow supporter Clive Richardson on former cable station Radio Thamesmead, now simply known as RTM and available across a wider area of Greenwich, Bexley and north Kent, albeit via what was then a notoriously unreliable signal.

The previous presenters only learned from station management at the end of their final show that their services were no longer required, leading studio guest Dixon to claim that the club would not co-operate with the new set-up. No doubt it didn't help that they were led to believe I would be taking over the show. In fact, I would play a supporting role in the studio over the following years. However, the driver for the change had been the results of a survey carried in the free issue of *Voice of The Valley* the previous April, which suggested 60 per cent of the 1,000-plus respondents would listen to a matchday radio station. The behind-the-scenes coup had been orchestrated with boardroom support by the survey's author Richard Hunt, like Dixon a key figure in the Valley Party, along with Arsenal ward candidate Mark Mansfield. The latter already provided home-match commentaries for Clubcall and would now deliver them, initially only for away games, to a local radio audience. For most listeners this was bound to trump any concerns about the inelegant way the change had been handled and for many of the supporters able to receive it the extended coverage would become an essential part of their weekly routine for the next ten years.

Another fracture in the relationship between fans and club appeared three weeks into the season when the latter announced that it had "taken over" CASC's away travel service. Long-serving supporters' club coach organiser Bill Treadgold stood down on the basis that he could not cope with a barrage of telephone bookings triggered by inadequate facilities to handle them on matchdays at Upton Park. However, it immediately became clear that he had agreed to work instead with Valley shop manager Chris Tugwell, who was already running Wimbledon's away coaches. Tugwell told the *Mercury*: "A decision has been made and we're doing it. We've spoken to the police and we'll be the only official travel, although we don't want a price war."

The remaining supporters' club committee voted unanimously to give them one, with acting chairman Barry Nugent retorting: "There has been no dialogue with the supporters' club committee about this matter. Charlton have simply announced that they are taking travel over, which is not acceptable to us."

One undercurrent was a bogus claim that the supporters' club was refusing to make donations to the football club, in particular regarding a request to finance the replacement of a minibus that the staff had managed to lose. The reality was that CASC did not have the money, having struggled to meet its costs from the Valley Party. More recently it had had to cover a heavily loss-making supporters' tour of Scotland to see the team in pre-season, a venture which ironically had been organised by those who had now switched camps.

The away travel story ran on the back page of the paper under the headline "Hijack!" – immediately next to an advert promoting the new service. Charlton claimed that part of their purpose was to ensure that everyone could travel, not just supporters' club members, but they compromised this by admitting that their eventual intention was to force passengers into the club's own membership schemes. By using paid staff to take the bookings and in their inevitable pursuit of profit from running the operation, however, they would always be at a competitive disadvantage. What's more they clearly reckoned without the determination of fans still energised by the success of the Valley Party.

Married couple Steve and Wendy Perfect, with strong family and personal ties to Labour, had been among the last to sign up as election candidates the previous year. But accountant Steve was the new supporters' club treasurer and better placed than anyone to know the effect that losing the travel service would have on the organisation. Just as big a factor in the fans' resistance, however, was indignation at the apparent lack of respect being shown to them only a year after they had changed the local political landscape in the club's favour.

Using Greenwich-based Lewis Coaches, who had previously provided supporters' travel for many years, CASC aggressively undercut the football club's offer, underpinned by allowing passengers to book out of hours through the Perfects' home phone line and to pay on the coach instead of in advance through the Valley shop. It also opened a second front by operating an alternative service to one already being provided by the club to home matches at Upton Park.

In mid-November commercial manager Andy Bryant, egged on by Sutherland, wrote to advise me that the Charlton badge was "under copywrite" (sic), claiming that if I was "considering" using it in this book the club would require a licence fee of £500 plus an eight per cent royalty on all sales. Apart from the fact that Colin Cameron's *The Valiant 500* had already been published that year with the logo on the front without any such stipulation, the enforceability of which was dubious, the club knew that the book had already gone to print. In any event, I had always been aware of potential issues around the badge so hadn't used it. I simply published the correspondence in the next *Voice of The Valley*.

Despite these squabbles, the more substantive cause of friction was the continuing failure to make any progress towards the return home. The club's position remained that there were six to eight weeks' work still required, but the picture was complicated by the fact that Norris's 50 per cent shareholding in the club was now in the hands of merchant bank Hill Samuel. Murray and Simons had never received shares they had been promised when they joined the board in the spring, although this was eventually resolved by means of a rights issue, giving each of them an initial 12.5 per cent stake in the club.

Speaking to fans at the supporters' club AGM at the end of October, which saw former Valley Party candidate Steve Clarke elected as the organisation's new chair, Alwen said: "We are now at the stage where we are seeing a little bit of light at the end of the tunnel. We are looking at three or four avenues, some more hopeful than others. We have certainly got to know where we stand by the end of the year. We've got to do whatever we can to be playing at The Valley as soon as we possibly can. We have to solve the problem of Mike Norris's shareholding before bankers and funders will talk to us and I believe that will be resolved quite quickly."

Striker Paul Gorman celebrating his goal at Bristol City in November. He had a good rapport with fans

When Charlton travelled to face Lawrence's high-flying Middlesbrough side in mid-November, losing 2-0, it was the former boss's post-match remarks that sparked a debate about the further contribution supporters might make: "If I was at Charlton now it wouldn't matter if we were ten points clear of the Second Division. The thing with The Valley would be driving me mad," he said. "I would be saying to myself, what's it all about? How can they run out of money after I've sold all those players. What's going on? I don't want to be critical of individuals. I think Roger Alwen's a marvellous man and he's done everything he possibly can. But what is it all about?"

The theme was taken up the following evening by callers to RTM and then to the *Mercury*, urging that supporters be given the opportunity to contribute. The paper's back-page headline asked the question: "One more mile?" The hesitation was born out of the modest response to the Mercury Trust Fund four years earlier. This time there would need to be a more substantive offer on the table.

"We're not talking fivers and tenners, but hundreds and thousands," I wrote. "And this time it wouldn't be a donation. We'd want season-ticket credits, or even shares in the club. That would give people a real incentive to take part and the new-look supporters' club has all the accountants and lawyers it needs to work the details out."

However, the board's response was muted. It was felt the sum involved in completing the work would be too substantial. Fans were already contributing via Valley Gold and Simons told me that the club would be "embarrassed" to go back to them for the money. He believed at the time that the solution was more likely to lie with "blue-chip investors". In the meantime, Gritt and Curbishley eased the immediate financial situation when they picked up 30-year-old midfielder Alan Pardew on a free transfer from still First Division Crystal Palace and almost immediately sold skipper Andy Peake, also 30, to Middlesbrough for a surprising £150,000, which turned out to be good business for everyone concerned.

Pardew was quickly on the scoresheet, along with Paul Gorman, as the Addicks ended a run of seven matches without a victory by winning 2-0 at Bristol City on November 30th, but was then dismissed ten minutes from time for spitting at an opponent. But it was the unorthdox Gorman, soon to be sidelined by a cruciate ligament injury, who stole the headlines and captured the fans' immediate enthusiasm, although it was already clear that the 23-year-old was somewhat less popular with his teammates.

Gorman was out of the side by the time Charlton travelled to Newcastle on January 18th for the reverse fixture from the opening day. It looked like an afternoon to be forgotten when the Magpies struck three times in quick succession midway through the first half to assume an apparently unassailable 3-0 advantage, with 21-year-old striker Andy Hunt – later to enjoy a memorable spell at The Valley – claiming their second goal. Not even an immediate long-range riposte from 18-year-old left-back Barness was enough to give the travelling supporters much cause for optimism

Revenge: Walsh scores Charlton's second goal in the 4-3 win at St James' Park

Boardroom invitation: new investor Mike Stevens (front row, standing) joins the celebrations of existing directors Derek Ufton (seated), Richard Murray, Martin Simons, Richard Collins and Roger Alwen (seated) against Southend in February

as they enjoyed a warming drink at half-time.

Confidence was fragile in the home ranks, however, and when, 17 minutes from time, the home side failed to clear Darren Pitcher's free-kick, Walsh further reduced the arrears in front of a suddenly anxious Gallowgate End. Just over three years earlier its inhabitants had pelted him with rubbish as he lay in front of them with a broken leg. Now he exacted more retribution with a second goal three minutes later after keeper Tommy Wright had dropped Bumstead's cross. If 3-3 had been the final score it would still have been a fine fightback. But incredibly Charlton were not finished and in the 89th minute a goalline clearance saw Pardew's follow-up effort deflect off Liam O'Brien for a remarkable winner.

It was the Addicks' fourth win in five visits to what remained one of English football's iconic venues, but never before had they come back from three goals down to win any away fixture. It demonstrated Newcastle's fragility under Ossie Ardiles, soon dismissed as manager and replaced by Kevin Keegan, who narrowly saved them from relegation to the third tier. But the victory was also a tribute to the battling spirit that Gritt and Curbishley had engendered in their own ranks, and the fans had now begun to wonder what they might be able to achieve. The following week Charlton held First Division Sheffield United to a goalless draw in the fourth round of the FA Cup, although the replay at Bramall Lane proved to be a step too far and was lost 2-0.

Meanwhile, the club had still not given up on returning to The Valley before the end of the season. Now confident that they could retrieve Norris's shares from the bank, the board was hoping that contractors Beazer would be back on site at the start of February, allowing the team to return for at least the final three matches of the season, beginning with Watford's visit on April 18th. Part of the reasoning was that

Fundraisers: Martin Simons, general manager Jonathan Fuller and Richard Murray address fans at the Meridian on April 2nd about the proposed debenture scheme

getting home was seen to be key to making a credible season-ticket offer for the 1992/93 campaign, having failed to deliver on the promises of the previous summer. The cost of playing at Upton Park was also punitive. But making it back at all depended on retrieving ownership of the ground. It was hoped that this might be achieved by transferring the freehold to contractors Beazer and the club leasing it back, thus providing the builders with security against which the cost of the work – now estimated at £3m – could be deferred.

Instead the saga dragged on. Work did not resume at The Valley and by the middle of March the club was finally forced to concede that the team would see out the season at Upton Park. Now everything would be focused on getting the ground ready for August. And by this point they were ready to turn again to the supporters for help. A letter was sent to the 5,500 people on the club's membership mailing lists canvassing support for a debenture scheme, which would provide ticket discounts according to the level of investment, the right to elect a representative to the board, and ultimately a full refund after ten years.

The rationale behind the idea was that the club's long-term business plan, including the bowling alley, remained sound. For example, the directors believed that they could generate £500,000 a year in additional commercial revenue from the permanent west stand. Simons suggested that a German trust fund might be willing to put in as much at £9m. But the whole project would only become sufficiently attractive to such investors once there was enough other capital in the club that the gates were open and football was being played. To achieve this they set the ambitious target of raising £1.5m from supporters.

On April 2nd, exactly three years after fans had helped clear the ground of weeds, around 250 attended a public meeting at the Meridian Sports and Social Club to hear more about the scheme. Simons now put the cost of re-opening The Valley at £3.75m, including purchase of the freehold. As well as the contribution from supporters, there would be £1m from the Football Trust, with the remainder being borrowed commercially. The new target for the contractors to be on site in order to get back for the start of the 1992/93 season was June 16th, with the promise that fans who committed to the debenture scheme would be offered their money back if this was not achieved. To assess the plan's viability supporters were invited to pledge their level of financial support using pre-paid reply cards. By the end of the month, the total promised had already reached £1m. Meanwhile, the temporary seating decks were being removed from the west stand for use elsewhere.

The club had also gained a new director. Chicago-based Mike Stevens had grown up locally as a Charlton fan, but made his fortune as the owner of the American Nameplate Company. He flew in to meet the board at the beginning of February and saw the team beat Brighton on what proved be the Addicks' last-ever visit to the Goldstone Ground, then defeat Southend United 2-0 at Upton Park. He soon agreed to invest an initial £250,000 in return for a 10 per cent shareholding, but would also be the source of other loans as the club struggled to meet its commitments in the months that followed.

Leaving the scene, meanwhile, was the Woolwich Building Society, which announced that it would not be renewing its £75,000-a-year shirt sponsorship deal after eight seasons. It seemed a strange time for them to sever the link, and one suspicion inside the club was that it might be a consequence of the relationship between Norris and the society's chief executive Donald Kirkham. Eight months earlier, the Woolwich's marketing services manager Roger Ham had told the *Mercury*: "We've done very well by Charlton. The position now is that we will be with them for as long as they want us." Yet by December they had been looking to back out of the existing contract. Now they offered the meaningless comment that "all sponsorships, even the most successful, have to come to an end eventually". But set against any conspiracy theory was the backdrop of a housing-market collapse and a general increase in mortgage defaults, which was bound to have impacted on their business. The timing at least meant that the potential media exposure around the return to The Valley could be offered as an incentive to their successors.

If fans were disappointed by the lack of progress towards a return home, they were feeling far from let down by events on the pitch. A first victory over Millwall in 14 years, courtesy of loan signing John Hendry's 84th-minute strike before an 8,167 crowd at Upton Park on March 7th, proved to be the start of a ten-match unbeaten run that carried Gritt and Curbishley's team up to a tantalising sixth place in the table, having been as high as fourth in early April. The 2-1 victory at Sunderland on April 11th equalled the club record of 11 away wins in a season, established by Mike Bailey's Third Division promotion side in 1980/81. Given both

Loan star: David Whyte rounds Leicester City's Kevin Poole to put Charlton 2-0 up at the end of April. It left them sixth with two matches remaining

the inexperience of the joint bosses and the club's very limited ability to invest in the playing squad, it was a considerable achievement even to be in contention and probably also helped to contain criticism of the board over the continuing uncertainty off the pitch. If Charlton succeeded in gaining an improbable promotion it would be to the inaugural season of the new FA Premier League.

With three matches to play, the penultimate weekend of the season brought second-placed Leicester City to Upton Park. Victory for the visitors would see them promoted automatically – if Lawrence's fourth-placed Middlesbrough side, just three points ahead of the Addicks, failed to beat Bristol Rovers at Ayresome Park. An estimated 10,000 Leicester fans turned up, overwhelming the south stand accommodation set aside for them. Police and stewards struggled to cope, as many as 2,000 were admitted without paying and the usually empty Chicken Run terracing opposite the main stand had to be opened to relieve the congestion. The official attendance of 15,357 was easily Charlton's biggest of the season, although still a considerable underestimate of the real number in the ground.

The match eventually kicked off 15 minutes late, but it was the minority Charlton supporters in attendance who would find it worth the wait. Five minutes before half-time their team went ahead. The goalscorer was Robert Lee, who received the ball from a short corner taken by Walsh and drilled home from the edge of the penalty area. It was the 26-year-old's 12th goal of the season, making 25 in the past two years, and capped a fine campaign in which his talent had fully flowered for perhaps the first time. Remarkably, considering their League position, it was also the first time the Addicks had scored in the opening half at Upton Park for 14 matches, dating back to the end of October.

Four minutes later, they were two up. Greenwich-born David Whyte, 20, was on loan from Crystal Palace and made an enduring impression when he received the ball from Pardew, beat the last defender and then drew keeper Kevin Poole before slotting home from six yards. Half-time brought news that not only were Bristol Rovers leading at Middlesbrough, but fifth-placed Cambridge United were behind to Port Vale and seventh-placed Blackburn Rovers trailed to Millwall. As it turned out, all those other scorelines were reversed as the afternoon wore on, but crucially there would no further goals at Upton Park. Bob Bolder even saved a weak 89th-minute penalty from Gary Mills, after Balmer had been penalised for holding Ian Ormondroyd, to stall any fears of a late comeback by the visitors.

Charlton's fate was in their own hands. If they won both the midweek home fixture against mid-table Tranmere Rovers and the final-day visit to Bristol Rovers' lodgings at Bath City's Twerton Park then they would certainly be in the play-offs. There was even a very remote chance they could squeeze into second place. That was to reckon without the former Liverpool striker John Aldridge, however. There was some doubt that he even touched Kenny Irons' low cross ten minutes before half-time the following Tuesday, but Aldridge claimed the goal and with it went the points. The Addicks were crestfallen, although the game ended with a rousing ovation for a squad that had exceeded every expectation. And there was still a slim chance they could make the play-offs, if other results went in their favour.

Blackburn could only manage a point at home to Sunderland the following evening, but it was enough to take them above Charlton on goal difference and into the crucial sixth position. Their final fixture was away to Plymouth Argyle. Cambridge would only come into the equation if they lost at Roker Park.

A travelling contingent officially restricted to just 900 supporters at Bath was actually supplemented by a few more who had obtained tickets for home areas of the ground, while another 1,000 watched the match for £8 a head via closed-circuit link to Erith Sports Centre, with commentary from Dixon and Colin Powell. Fighting broke out in the crowd at Twerton Park in the second half when inspirational skipper and recently voted player of the year Simon Webster appeared to have headed the visitors in front, only for Whyte to be judged offside. It was a game that Curbishley felt his side had done enough to win, but instead Andy Reece's 25-yard effort flew back off the bar with 11 minutes left and David Mehew nodded the only goal past a stranded Bolder.

At the end there were tears from striker Nelson, firmly established as a fans' favourite. He had given his all for the cause, despite the last of his six goals having come as long ago as December. Runner-up in the player of the year by just six votes, Leaburn had notched 11 in the League and three in cup competition, but missed the last four matches through injury, which may have been a factor in the team failing to

Disappointed: an emotional Garry Nelson receives commiserations as Charlton miss out on a play-off place after losing 1-0 to Bristol Rovers at Twerton Park

get over the line. But the defeat by Bristol Rovers was irrelevant. Cambridge had drawn and Blackburn won, leaving the Addicks stranded in seventh regardless.

It was Kenny Dalglish's Rovers side who eventually won the play-offs, while Leicester had been beaten at home by Newcastle on the final day and finished fourth, behind Derby County and Lawrence's Middlesbrough, who were promoted as runners-up to Ipswich Town.

For Charlton, the 1991/92 season had been a case of so near and yet so far, both on and off the pitch.

Chapter Thirteen

"People thought the Valley saga was going to outlast The Mousetrap. But I think we've finally reached the end."

Roger Alwen – *Mercury (September 3rd, 1992)*

Charlton ended the 1991/92 season still hopeful that they would begin the following campaign at The Valley. Sharing Upton Park on a temporary basis had been much less traumatic than being at Selhurst Park, notwithstanding traffic difficulties. Average home attendances had increased by a modest 3.6 per cent to 6,786, although this remained disappointing in the context of the team's results. It was estimated that 500 of the 3,000 season-ticket holders had typically been absent at any particular match. But a key consideration for the board was the cost of staging fixtures at West Ham United's ground, with ticket receipts barely enough to cover matchday expenses, never mind player wages. The club had lost a record £1,013,000 over the year.

The team's record suggested the continuing exile was having another impact, with Steve Gritt and Alan Curbishley's side having collected 37 points from away matches, against 34 in their nominal home fixtures. Indeed, Charlton had scored just 25 goals in their 23 League matches at Upton Park, with only bottom club Port Vale getting fewer on their own turf.

While both men continued to be on playing contracts, Curbishley had made a solitary appearance on the pitch, starting the 2-0 home defeat by Wolverhampton Wanderers in January, whereas Gritt had begun five games in all competitions and featured in 12 more as a substitute. He had even got on the scoresheet to secure an important point with a late equaliser at Port Vale in April.

More importantly, the duo had overcome what might have been a confusing division of responsibility. The job share was wide open to ridicule by the media, not least in respect of the pair's sensible practice of taking alternate post-match press conferences, which avoided the possibility of conflicting opinions being expressed. Indeed, the risk of mixed messages was managed very effectively by not allowing any hint of disagreement between them to reach the players, never mind the outside world. However, as Curbishley remarked in a *Voice of The Valley* interview looking back at their first season in charge, the most likely cause of contention was over team selection, but that had rarely been a problem because it was in the nature of the club's resources that they didn't have too many choices to make.

There had also been the potential difficulty of off-field matters being separately overseen by general manager Arnie Warren, the explanation of which showed how brief their tenure might have been had results gone differently. "There weren't any problems as such," said Curbishley. "But we do feel that if you're working with the players then you need to do the other side of the job as well. We understood the reasons behind the separation. The thinking was that it would be wrong for us to have privileged information about our fellow players if we were going to be moved aside after a couple of months. We could have started causing problems over contracts."

Recognition that this was no longer a consideration came in June, when they were handed new two-year deals with full control on the football side, including scouting,

In control: joint manager Curbishley (right), with Keith Peacock, Steve Gritt and Colin Powell to help promote the launch of the Valley Investment Plan

following Warren's retirement. Henceforth they would be called joint managers, not first-team coaches. Gritt explained: "From now on we'll be much more involved in transfer deals and with everything that goes on at the training ground."

Amid much speculation about interest from Chelsea in England under-21 left-back Scott Minto the two bosses were sanguine about the club's priorities, with Curbishley having already acknowledged in the aftermath of the Bristol Rovers defeat: "We've got two or three players in our sights and we'll be asking the directors where we stand. But if there's a choice between spending money on the team and getting back to The Valley, it's got to be the latter."

By the middle of May, however, doubts were already surfacing about the club's ability to get home for the start of the season. Despite the fact that the economy was only beginning to emerge from a deep recession, 2,400 fans had pledged £1.08m to the debenture scheme. But the target had increased from the original £1.5m to £2.2m, because of the cost of insuring the supporters' money. The original plan had been to buy capital bonds in order to generate funds to repay fans after ten years. However, this had raised issues about whether there would be enough cash available, especially if the club was to go bust in the meantime. The latest idea was to insure the sum with Legal & General, which would also give some protection in the event that the work began at The Valley and for some reason was not completed. But the cost was substantial. "The extra will have to come out of our own pockets and some short-term borrowing," said Simons, who also admitted that legal complications arising from the need to comply with the Financial Services Act were slowing matters down.

The original scheme had been drawn up with little wider consultation, prompting new supporters' club committee member and former Valley Party candidate Craig Norris to put forward an alternative in *Voice of The Valley* under which fans would create a separate company to buy shares in the football club. However, a closer relationship was now being established between CASC and directors Martin Simons and Richard Murray than there had ever been with Roger Alwen and Mike Norris, reflecting the fact that the supporters' club had itself moved on under the influence of those brought in through the election campaign.

This emerging partnership was further cemented at the end of May when the debenture scheme collapsed. Ultimately, it had not proven possible to underwrite the fans' investment to the point where they could be guaranteed to get their money back. With the existing pledges now based on an undeliverable premise and the prospect of institutional funding for the building work finally discounted, Simons turned to the supporters' club to help put together a replacement plan.

There were at least two good external examples why the board should have valued the public support of the fans. Bond schemes at Arsenal and West Ham had proven highly controversial over the previous year, as these and other clubs grappled with ways to find the money to make their stadia all-seater in line with the Taylor recommendations. Both London clubs had proposed schemes under which fans would pay for the right to buy a season ticket over the following 150 years, in the Gunners' case to fund the seating of the North Bank at Highbury and in West Ham's to build new stands behind each goal. At Arsenal, with the price of a bond up to £1,500, the club had been accused of social engineering to exclude poorer supporters. At Upton Park, the cost was lower, ranging from £500-£950, but the response was equally angry, with sit-ins and pitch invasions at matches in the early part of 1992. Arsenal sold only a third of their 16,000 bonds, while West Ham managed 800 out of 19,000, despite eventually softening the scheme to include season-ticket discounts for ten years. Charlton had the advantage that their objective was entirely shared by the club's supporters, but in view of the failures of the recent past it was important to present a united public front.

The *Mercury* played its part too, donating free of charge a colour wraparound cover to its issue of June 11th to announce what had become the Valley Investment Plan, under the banner headline "NOW or NEVER?". The main story began: "It's time to go that extra mile for The Valley", a deliberate echo of the question the paper had asked six months earlier. Alongside it was an application form and on the inside back page the full terms and conditions. As the news hit the streets, so the directors staged a press conference to brief the rest of the media, while Curbishley, Gritt, reserve-team manager Keith Peacock and groundsman Colin Powell posed on the pitch for pictures.

Richard Hunt had been called in to help market the revised scheme, based on his poster success with the Valley Party. He told the paper: "The plan has two great advantages. First, it's not a bond scheme, where you pay for the privilege of being able to buy a season ticket. And with this scheme, there's no messing about. The more you put in, the more benefits you get. And, second, everyone who invests £50 or more has a say in electing a new director. This will pull the club and supporters together in a way that has never been seen in British football before."

Hunt remembers being asked by Simons if his agency could devise promotional material and then liaising with general manager Jonathan Fuller, who had stepped up from assistant on Warren's retirement, over the content. A proposed flyer with the catchline: "Believe us, Robert Lee can really move!" proved a sticking point with Fuller, who understandably saw a completely different connotation to that intended by the creative team. Instead, the late Sam Bartram reprised his role in the election campaign, this time under the slogan: "The most important save you'll ever make."

In the light of the events of 1985, the supporters' club attached particular weight to the offer of representation on the board, even though it had been clear that Greenwich Council's director at the time, Bill Strong, had been sidelined over the decision to leave The Valley. Craig Norris, in particular, had argued that it would be a selling point to fans, albeit minor in relation to the return home itself. In the short term, supporters' club chair Steve Clarke was co-opted on to the board to represent the investors' interests, along with Bill Jenner, who had served as a director under both Michael Gliksten and Mark Hulyer and was thought to be closer to potential high-value investors.

The crucial difference from the abandoned version was that fans would no longer get their money back after ten years, although they would benefit from a 2.5 per cent discount on ticket prices over the life of the scheme for each £50 invested. At £1,250 they would qualify for a ten-year season ticket on the uncovered East Terrace, at £1,500 they would get a seat in the Covered End and at £2,000 a top-price season ticket. Each £50 put in would also give the investor one vote in the election of a member of the scheme as a director. The removal of the refund offer also meant the target amount was back down to £1.5m.

Clarke summed up: "We've worked closely with the club in coming up with the plan and we believe it will be a model for other clubs in the future. This is the only practical way of raising the money to get back to The Valley, but we also think supporters get a fair deal with the discounts and the opportunity of getting their own representative on the board. The Valley is not a dream. It is there, with a perfect playing surface, just waiting for us to go home. All we need is one more push."

Money raised would be paid into a ringfenced account and only released once the club was confident that it had enough to complete the work. Having lost a further month in launching the revamped scheme, however, the board had to concede that it would no longer be possible to return for the start of the following season. A decision had already been taken to commit to Upton Park until the end of October, although it was hoped that work would be able to resume in late July.

Even so, it was still unclear exactly how The Valley would take shape. It was suggested that the team might return with just the two stands at either end of the pitch in use, should it not be viable to reopen the East Terrace. Once again, faraway events had affected Charlton's intentions. On May 5th, three days after the Bristol Rovers match, a temporary stand built at short notice on the Mediterranean island of Corsica for the French cup semi-final between Bastia and Olympique Marseille collapsed

Planning ahead: Martin Simons, Richard Murray and Derek Ufton at the VIP launch

after kick-off, killing 18 and injuring more than 2,300. Suddenly the international football authorities were unwilling to allow temporary structures at all.

With the seats placed on the former terrace a year earlier no longer an option, the club now proposed to construct a new concrete terrace with modern crush barriers to accommodate 6,000, but raked for the possible future installation of seats under the requirements of the Taylor Report. Beazer put the cost at £500,000. However, it was the lowest priority within the £1.5m the club hoped to raise through the VIP scheme. And the situation was further complicated by the temporary stairway that had been built to allow fans to leave via the Lansdowne Mews exit. If utilising that emergency route was no longer permissible, the club might be limited to just 3,000 on the terrace, which made the viability of the work more marginal. On the other side of the pitch the board was keen to preserve the option of moving quickly to build the permanent west stand, with its greater potential to drive commercial revenue.

The VIP scheme got off to a flying start. There were three public meetings at which fans could ask questions, two at the Meridian Sports and Social Club in Charlton and the third at Crayford Town Hall, all paid for by CASC. The club also set up a marquee inside the Valley gates over a weekend in order that fans could drop in and sign up. Speaking at one of the meetings, chairman Alwen told supporters that just over £1m had already been spent on refurbishing The Valley, of which £208,000 had been raised via Valley Gold, with the final bill to complete the work on three sides of the pitch now expected to reach £3.1m. Beazer had agreed to defer £600,000 for two years on an interest-free basis and there would be £1m in grants from the Football Trust.

If Charlton stayed at Upton Park they stood to lose £750,000 over a full year, whereas the directors estimated the club could break even on a 6,700 average crowd

Alex Dyer leads the Charlton charge in the 1-0 away win over West Ham United

in SE7. "We feel we can quite easily average 8,000-9,000 at The Valley, in which case we can generate an extra £200,000-300,000 a year," said Murray.

Four weeks after the launch, more than 1,100 supporters had already stumped up £600,000, including one *Mercury* application form with a cheque for £2,000 that had been posted in Caracas, Venezuela. But there was already some nervousness about whether the target would be reached. Simons told the *Mercury* on July 9th: "The amount coming in seems to be accelerating as people get their funds out of building societies or whatever. We're now hopeful of reaching £1m, but it remains to be seen how much above that we will get."

The wider uncertainty about where Charlton would be playing also took its toll on season-ticket sales, which had not begun until the start of June. The club had learned some of the lessons of the previous year, dropping the requirement for applicants to pay an additional membership fee and introducing big reductions for pensioners and teenagers. There was also a new Primary Junior Reds ticket offering free admission to U11s in exchange for a £10 registration fee, an idea credited to Alwen. However, the directors were resigned to the fact that they could not expect to match the previous season's figures. By the eve of the opening Upton Park fixture against Grimsby Town, on August 15th, the total including 500 "free" season tickets provided through the VIP scheme only narrowly exceeded 2,000.

Confusingly, for those who had qualified for a season ticket, the board still felt unable to make a final decision about accepting the VIP cash. With the total funds received standing at £940,000, provided by 1,500 people, the scheme remained £260,000 short of the sum now reported to be necessary to open just the two end stands. Meanwhile, contributions had all but dried up, despite efforts to provide additional incentives including cup matches for a larger contribution and for fans introducing their friends, as well as a telephone marketing campaign targeting those who had pledged to support the original debenture scheme but had not come forward for the VIP.

"What we're trying to do is close that gap," said Alwen. "We've got two or three irons in the fire, but unfortunately bankers are very nervous and I can't see that changing in the near future. What frightens me is starting and not being able to finish. We can't do that with supporters' money."

The looming problem was less the prospect of yet another delay, but rather the August 31st deadline the club had imposed on making a decision. At that point it was due to hand the money back, but having raised so much this never seemed a realistic possibility. Finally, with three days to spare and having negotiated the cost of the works down with Beazer, now rebranded as Kier as part of a corporate demerger, the board called a press conference and gave the go-ahead. The scheme had narrowly topped £1m and the directors themselves would help fund the gap. Clarke and Jenner indicated their consent to the release of the money. The return would now be on Saturday, December 5th, and the first visitors would be Portsmouth, but unless there was a further influx of funds to pay for the work on the East Terrace, the capacity would be barely 6,000. The scheme was duly reopened with a minimum contribution of £250 in the hope that the commitment being made would encourage additional investment, but to little avail. The fans had done what they could and the rest was now up to the board.

Three days later the directors confirmed that they had finally acquired the freehold

Ready to go: chairman Roger Alwen announces that the board has agreed to proceed with the remaining work at The Valley and the date for the first match

of The Valley from the receiver of Adelong for £1.25m, via a loan from Simons secured on the ground, although Laing Homes retained an option over part if it was ever sold for redevelopment. It had been the separation of the ownership of club and ground ten years earlier that had been the trigger for so many of Charlton's problems in the intervening years, so the moment was more than symbolic. Kier also took a legal charge over The Valley, while a raft of other related debts moved from Adelong to the football company. Behind the scenes, Peter Tegg, father of the Valley Party's Ben and previously financial adviser to Mike Norris, had been a key player, along with Murray and Simons, in unpicking the financial tangle.

In the meantime, the Charlton board also had to shoulder the cost of continuing to play at Upton Park and there was considerable speculation that Robert Lee, Scott Minto or even Simon Webster would be sold to keep the club in business. It was no surprise that Gritt and Curbishley had to soldier on with much the same squad, especially given its success in the previous campaign. In practice the Addicks made a blistering start, winning their opening four fixtures for the first time, including the away game against West Ham, and earning the duo a third Barclays Manager of the Month award to add to those they had received the previous October and in March.

Going out: Anthony Barness

Alan Pardew scored the only goal against the Hammers on August 22nd, taking Charlton to the top of the Football League for the first time since September 1937. The more meaningful comparison, given the rebranding of the divisions following the launch of the Premier League, was with their last spell as the top of the second tier in 1968. Although they lost first place on September 12th to Kevin Keegan's Newcastle United, who began the campaign with a startling 11 consecutive victories, Gritt and Curbishley's men went unbeaten for their own first ten matches, before a sequence of three consecutive defeats in October.

For the first time the Addicks supporters had the use of the Chicken Run along the opposite side of the pitch to the main stand at West Ham, in an effort to improve the atmosphere. However, attendances remained poor, with the opening two home matches failing to attract 5,000 people. Something had to give, but there was general surprise that it was Anthony Barness – not Minto – whose departure to Chelsea was first to be announced in mid-September. Unusually, the £350,000 basic fee was all to be paid up front, an indication of the financial stress the club was under.

When the signing of Brighton & Hove Albion winger John Robinson was confirmed the following Monday and he went straight into the side for the Anglo-Italian Cup tie against Portsmouth at Upton Park the next night, few were taken in by the management's claim that Lee had a slight groin injury. It was inevitable that the latter had played his last match for Charlton and so it proved, although his destination would not become clear for several days.

Initially, it appeared that Lee would rejoin his former manager Lennie Lawrence at Middlesbrough and he travelled there to discuss the move. The deal appeared to be done, but instead Keegan made a last-minute intervention to take him to St James' Park for £700,000, the same price agreed with Boro and again all was to be paid immediately. However, Simons explained to the *Mercury* that none of either fee was going towards The Valley: "This money takes care of the Inland Revenue, the VAT man, other outstanding debts and wages for the rest of the season," he said. "At long last we're on an even keel. We did need to sell and I don't think we did a bad job in holding off previous bids."

The fact that Lawrence's initial offer for Lee was now disclosed to have been £250,000 caused some bad feeling among Charlton fans, who felt the club's former manager had been attempting to exploit the Addicks' financial weakness. It was something that as Middlesbrough manager he was entitled and perhaps bound to do, but that didn't stop it leaving a bad taste for some. Lee's contract had been up the following summer, but it was a stark illustration of the task facing Gritt and Curbishley that they were forced to sell their best player to what seemed to be their main promotion rivals. It was also a somewhat difficult introduction for 21-year-old Robinson, who was injured on his debut and could not really hope to step into Lee's boots. An orthodox winger, rather than an attacking midfielder, he would go on to become a popular and successful figure in his own right and play more than 350 games for the club, including at the top level, winning 30 caps for Wales. The fee for Robinson was eventually set by a transfer tribunal at a modest £75,000.

In other circumstances, either of the player sales might have sparked protests. Indeed, there were some complaints that the pair had been sold too cheaply. But

Stepping in: John Robinson on his Upton Park debut against Portsmouth

Volunteers at work at The Valley in mid-September. They would play a key role in helping the club prepare the ground in time for the opening match

generally the supporters accepted that these departures were the painful price that they had to pay to see the club return home. As Simons put it starkly in the matchday programme: "No player sales – no club." It was some irony that the final man out was Lee, who had made his first senior appearance immediately after the 1984 winding-up crisis, scored the last goal at The Valley, the first in the top flight for 29 years and even the first as the home side at Upton Park. It seemed to break the playing link with the squad that had left in 1985. Still only 26, Lee had amassed 65 goals in 343 appearances and would go on to play 21 times for England. But the bigger prize was finally looming large on the horizon and everything else was now secondary.

The same week some work finally began again at The Valley, fully a year after the contractors had withdrawn from the site, but significant progress was held up until the end of the month by delays around an initial £450,000 payment from the Football Trust and issues with a sub-contractor. It meant the club was already eating into the timescale allowed to hit the December deadline. But once the work began there was a steady stream of visitors to Floyd Road and Harvey Gardens to see for themselves the evidence that this time Charlton really were going home. Indeed, much of the tidying up required around the ground as a consequence of the year's interruption was accomplished by a group of volunteer supporters. One aspect that had not been neglected was the pitch, which had been lovingly tended by groundsman Colin Powell with some help from his predecessor Maurice Banham.

Fortunately, British clubs had gained exemption from the FIFA ban on temporary structures, opening the way for more than 2,000 seats to be reinstalled under the west stand roof and lifting capacity for the opening game to a still inadequate but somewhat more manageable 8,000-plus. One of the first projects was to lay the foundations of the new police control room, which was expected to take eight weeks to fit out, while the two remaining stands had to be made ready for new seats to meet the more stringent safety requirements since the Taylor Report. The ever-rising bill for returning to The Valley was now put at £4.4m, broken down in the matchday programme as £1m from the VIP scheme, £1m from the Football Trust, £0.9m deferred by Kier and £1.5m in directors' loans. This wasn't quite the full story, however. Although it wasn't yet ready to concede the point, the club would ultimately have to hand over a percentage of the VIP funds as VAT.

In the meantime, the supporters' club was making good use of the spare capacity at Upton Park, bussing in four coachloads of new supporters from Maidstone to see Charlton beat Swindon Town 2-0 on September 26th. The Kent county town's own club had been wound up in controversial circumstances following three Football League seasons at Dartford's Watling Street. More than half the 200 passengers, who paid £5 a head for adults and £2 for children, identified themselves as former Stones fans, with Simons and Murray assisting the success of the exercise by arranging free match tickets. The next week there were five coaches for Southend United's visit. This followed the establishment of a Medway branch of CASC by Gillingham-based book rep Mick Everett over the summer and would mark the first of many similar initiatives over the following seasons to help rebuild the club's support after the years of exile. Presciently, *Voice of The Valley* commented: "Ultimately, we ought to aim at running coaches from every significant population centre in the county."

In October the supporters' club celebrated victory in the travel war, with the football club bowing out in return for a £1 levy per passenger, provided in exchange for booking facilities in the club shop. Negotiations the previous season had led to Charlton agreeing to publicise the CASC service in the programme, but relations with the staff behind the club's coaches remained fraught. The supporters had then introduced a further element of farce by returning their business to Redwing Coaches, meaning that the two providers would run identical vehicles to matches at different fares. However, it was the incongruity of continuing the competition while at the same time the supporters' club was increasingly working with the directors to rebuild support that finally led to a resolution. The agreement could easily have been reached a year earlier. The fact it was now was further evidence of the extent to which Murray and Simons were in the ascendancy.

Charlton had also prepared for the return home with the appointment of their first community officer, Jason Morgan, the 22-year-old son of former Queens Park Rangers and Tottenham Hotspur winger Roger, whose role was supported financially by the Professional Footballers' Association. A fundraising night for his work was scheduled for December 3rd at Catford greyhound stadium, just two days before the return to The Valley. But as the autumn wore on it was never certain whether the ground would be ready in time. Despite working weekends to make up lost time, the contractors only began to install the first seats with four weeks remaining, the turnstile units had just arrived and there remained considerable groundworks to be done around the boundaries, with temporary fences still running the length of the Harvey Gardens frontage.

End game: Garry Nelson scores Charlton's final "home" goal away from The Valley in the 3-1 defeat by Newcastle United

The club needed planning permission for the raft of temporary and minor structures that were necessary for the reopening of The Valley, including the floodlights, turnstiles, dressing rooms, toilets and the small village of Portakabins that would house the ground's hospitality facilities. None had been part of the scheme approved the previous April. More urgently it needed to satisfy Greenwich's building control team and to obtain a safety certificate for the stadium, which meant a great deal of discussion with the emergency services, as well as the council, and frequent changes to the plans. There was still a monumental amount of work required to get everything in place for the big day, and to many observers it did not seem possible. In truth, the club could not be confident of meeting its deadline, but it was determined that the last day of exile would be Saturday, November 14th. If the Portsmouth game could not be played on December 5th then they would risk the wrath of the Football League by asking for it to be postponed.

Meanwhile, the board was looking further ahead by meeting builders John Mowlem with the intention of developing a new east stand. Simons and Alwen had travelled to Notts County's Meadow Lane, which had been impressively transformed over the summer by the firm, who had demolished two stands and built three new ones in the space of 17 weeks. Altogether they had provided 13,500 seats at a cost of £3.3m, less than £250 per seat. With revised grant rules being put in place following the establishment of the Premier League, Charlton believed they could build an east stand much quicker and more easily than their more ambitious scheme for the west side of the pitch, despite the challenges posed by the sewer, with the mooted £2m cost met entirely by the Football Trust. Now, even if they had been able to find the money to relay the East Terrace for standing, work which would not in any case attract a grant, it made no sense to do so.

Despite beating Leicester City 2-0 on November 4th in their penultimate outing at Upton Park courtesy of two Garry Nelson goals, the first of which brought up his career League century, Charlton's form had slumped alarmingly. There was little doubt that this was related to the loss of Lee. In the ten League matches played in October and November just five points were gained. They also went out of the Coca-Cola Cup to Third Division Bury, whose single goal of a two-legged second-round tie was seen by just 2,083 in East London.

Fate had decreed that League leaders Newcastle would be Charlton's final opponents at West Ham, just as they had been the first. The symmetry continued with the return of Lee in unfamiliar black and white stripes. This time he did not score, but Keith Peacock's son Gavin did, twice, as the visitors won 3-1 in front of a crowd of 12,945. The Addicks only slipped from sixth to seventh as a consequence, but their direction of travel was clear. The team was heading down the First Division table. For once, however, the prospect was almost irrelevant to the fans in red and white who slipped back across the Thames that evening. After 182 matches in exile at Selhurst Park and Upton Park, they were going home.

Chapter Fourteen

"Paddy's starting to behave like a normal groundsman. He's moaning every time we go near his pitch."

Alan Curbishley – Mercury (December 3rd, 1992)

There were still three weeks between Charlton's final match at Upton Park and the scheduled date for their first home game at The Valley in seven years, which inevitably proved too long for many to wait. The club soon had to make an appeal via the media for the public to stay away. The arrival of too many cars in Floyd Road and Harvey Gardens was obstructing the path of the construction vehicles, while some of the more inquisitive fans wandered recklessly into what was still a building site.

The club had originally hoped to complete the work with a week to spare to allow plenty of time for the safety certificate to be issued, but that margin was soon eroded by bad weather and multiple changes to the specifications imposed by Greenwich Council and the emergency services. It was frustrating for all concerned, but the fact that The Valley was being reconstructed under new safety rules was simply an unfortunate accident of timing.

The variations helped push the final bill up to £4.5m, but stadium manager Roy King would pay tribute to the co-operation from the professional team that enabled the project to proceed in the special 72-page *Valley Review* that his former supporters' club colleague Steve Dixon produced for the opening game: "They've been here from seven in the morning to eight or nine at night," he said. "Bearing in mind the conditions, which have been awful, with rain every day and mud up to your knees, they have done us proud. When you find a problem on a normal building site, the architect comes in, looks at it, redesigns the drawing and then you continue. What's happening here is that they are redesigning things as they stand, then going back and drawing it afterwards. They've done a fantastic job."

Some of the difficulties arose from the way the ground had been built originally, including the inconsistent make-up of the soil. The Covered End had been found to be sinking at its northern end, requiring extensive shoring up and reconstruction of two of the internal stairways. A massive toe bar with foundations 15 feet below ground level had had to be built along the east side of the pitch to prevent the old terrace sliding down on to the playing surface over time. New perimeter railings along the Harvey Gardens frontage also required unusually deep concrete foundations because of the unreliable terrain.

Necessarily, The Valley that took shape in those final weeks was very different from the much-loved but ultimately scruffy arena that had been abandoned in 1985. The sides of the pitch were now dominated by a range of temporary structures, very different from the new grounds that would open elsewhere over the following decades. Yet the two end stands were both instantly recognisable and clearly improved by their refurbishment, which in each case included new plastic seats, only a dozen years after the previous installation. The originals had been too close together to comply with the latest regulations. The new ones in both cases had the letters "CAFC" picked out in white, with a black border, but it wasn't until the final month that they

Back at their posts: groundsmen Colin Powell and Maurice Banham (standing either side of the upright) with volunteers at the re-erection of the north goal

began to appear in position.

Of all the parts of The Valley, the Covered End was the one that looked most improved, with the original 1934 frame completely reclad and repainted. Gone was the security fencing at the front, no longer acceptable in the aftermath of Hillsborough, and with it the familiar red railing and low wall on which generations of children had perched. Instead, there was a new and more substantial retaining wall, with seven gated emergency stairways down to the pitch. The seating deck was now interrupted by a new horizontal gangway to serve the rear access points. This both obstructed the view for some and was itself narrowed by a further railing in order to achieve a uniform width – examples of the safety adaptations required by the council.

To the rear the Valley Club was no more, while the former turnstiles had benefited from a wide forecourt. The consequence of bringing this land inside The Valley was the creation of useful additional space that could be divided between car parking and temporary refreshment and toilet facilities for spectators.

Previously, these services had been in the voids beneath the stand and a new water main had been laid so that this could soon be the case again. However, both the funding and the timetable had been too tight to do this for the return to a standard that would comply with fire regulations. In the meantime, the voids were sealed off, with the exception of the one nearest Floyd Road, where a water tank and computer-controlled sprinkler system for the pitch was already in place. A side door also gave access to a new electricity switch room for the stand, which had been completely rewired.

For the time being, Harvey Gardens would provide the entrance for all home spectators. Indeed, while the club's address remained Floyd Road, the main point of vehicle access was now on the other side of the club shop, with three sets of red fibreglass units providing ticket offices and turnstiles for each self-contained home area. Those furthest from the shop were ultimately intended to serve the new east stand, but for now they led on to one of the strangest structures The Valley had ever seen, a huge scaffolded walkway with no view of the pitch that traversed the width of the East Terrace to give access to the Jimmy Seed Stand at the other end of the ground.

Just as the giant terrace had been a silent witness to the final match in 1985, so it would remain almost empty for the return. This time, however, the London Weekend Television cameras would be there, perched on an open-fronted Portakabin, to record proceedings for the following day's *London Match*, together with veteran commentator Brian Moore. The ITV company had opted not to televise the fixture live, perhaps because of the doubts about whether it would happen, which at least meant that football could resume in its traditional Saturday afternoon slot. Otherwise the terrace remained blank, weeded by the volunteers and stripped of its crush barriers. The club had said that it had to leave The Valley because this area could not be used and now it would return without being able to use it either.

The emergency stairway leading to Lansdowne Mews was gone, a wasted investment the previous year along with the temporary seats on either side, and the buildings that had been clustered at the old Bartram Gate had been demolished. This meant that for the remainder of the 1992/93 season the Jimmy Seed Stand would be reserved entirely for home supporters, since everyone using the stand would need to be able to leave together via Valley Grove.

Whereas the capacity of the Covered End had risen marginally to 3,019 with the installation of the new seats, at the opposite end it had fallen slightly to 3,072. Otherwise the major change here was simply the counter-intuitive narrowing of the central and rear walkways with waist-high red railings to meet the requirement of uniform width, and as at the north end the bright yellow paint now used to demarcate the aisles. Each led to one of five gated emergency stairways down to the pitch, projecting on to the familiar red track. In the south-west corner was a double-decker Portakabin, the top part housing the safety control room and the lower half the club's public address room and forward reception for the police.

For now the visiting supporters, just 495 of them for Portsmouth's visit, would gain admission via a fourth set of turnstiles with accompanying ticket office in Valley Grove. Ultimately, these were designed to serve the Jimmy Seed Stand, via a segregated corridor along the site's southern boundary. Initially, however, the away fans would turn sharply left through a gate, down steps and into the two end blocks of the temporary west stand, with adjacent segregated services. With the gate reversed the same route could provide an emergency exit route for home fans in the south end. But crucially for the police and council, they need never mix. These were precisely the turnstile arrangements that fans had been told in 1985 were an obstacle to remaining.

Arguably the temporary stand provided another link to The Valley's more distant past, echoing the interim structure that had been erected by Humphreys to welcome

Plenty to do: work continues on the temporary walkway linking Harvey Gardens and the Jimmy Seed Stand on November 19th

the club to the Football League in 1921. However, by the time the safety experts had done their work this one was considerably more formidable. Multiple roof props obstructed the view, but it did have the advantage of an elevated perspective because even the front rows were eight feet above pitch level. There was no internal concourse and all facilities had to be provided in temporary buildings to the rear.

To the north-east corner of the pitch, where the terrace had once been dug out to improve the sightlines from the main stand, was a gap into which the most incongruous cabin of all was eventually lifted into place. This was to provide temporary dressing rooms giving immediate access on to the pitch.

Behind a hoarding to the rear of the west stand was another sprawl of interconnected Portakabins, with sufficient bars and lounges to hold 800 people, including the directors, players and officials, hospitality guests and sponsors. Beyond that, fronting Valley Grove, was a residents' parking compound large enough to accommodate 65 vehicles on a first-come, first-served basis from 9am on matchdays. This had been a key aspect of the planning application for all the new structures, which was heard on November 17th. Of itself that consent was not a potential stumbling block to the timetable. Having applied, the club was quite within its rights to proceed in anticipation of it. The council, however, was anxious to ensure that it included some of the street-cleaning and parking conditions that had been part of the extant permission for the west stand.

Battle for The Valley

Only one feature of the original Valley survived in the vast area behind the west stand. This was the electricity sub-station built in 1961 to power the new floodlights. Remarkably, it had now emerged that it also served part of Charlton village, effectively demolishing another argument used to justify the departure in 1985. It would have had to be retained or replaced in any event.

The floodlights themselves, with swan-neck stems and lamps accessed by the intrepid from a platform lift, were much brighter than their predecessors and computer controlled. They had stood unlit for more than a year, but were put to good use as November became December and contractors, staff and fans alike worked long hours on some of the shortest days of the year to ensure that everything would be ready.

The final weekend of November saw the team beaten at Barnsley – a fourth consecutive defeat – but an army of volunteers was also in action at The Valley painting the new perimeter fence red. The following Monday, chairman Roger Alwen and director Martin Simons were to be found putting numbered stickers on the seats.

The players had already trained on the pitch. Striker Garry Nelson, meanwhile, had come perilously close to missing the homecoming after being sent off for dissent at Wolverhampton Wanderers. Fortunately, the fact that the Wolves match had been televised meant it had been moved to the Sunday and with the Portsmouth game not scheduled for live coverage it fell inside the 14-day interval before his suspension took effect: "The first thing that came into my head was that I would miss the opening game," admitted Nelson, in the *Mercury*'s preview issue. "I'm really looking forward to it. We've been training there since last week and being there has really given us a bit of a buzz. When you walk in and see the building work still going on, you have to wonder whether it will all be ready on time, but I'm sure it will be. Mind you, I'll

The temporary west stand (far side) under reconstruction with 16 days to go

Chairman Roger Alwen formally receives The Valley's new safety certificate from Greenwich Council on Thursday, December 3rd, two days before the first match

have to wait and see if I'm selected. I'm not counting any chickens."

Joint manager Steve Gritt, the man on the playing side with the strongest emotional connection to The Valley, meanwhile confided to the *Daily Mirror*: "I'm frightened, apprehensive. I'm not sleeping at night and I've got butterflies in my stomach. To see the ground full again is an ambition come true. It will mean so much to me. The players mustn't let down all the people who have believed in Charlton. I hope whoever has written the script has got the ending right."

It was already known that those who did take part would be wearing a new red shirt introduced for the occasion by replacement kit supplier Ribero. However, the club was still without a shirt sponsor and had also become embroiled in a messy dispute about sponsorship of the first match, which had been promised to the Petts Wood-based *News Shopper* in exchange for advertising space, a decision ridiculed by the *Mercury* with more justification than would have been the product of normal commercial rivalry. Eventually the club covered its embarrassment by naming London Electricity, which opened a new Powerstore in Charlton the same weekend, as "floodlight sponsor", while the *Mercury* had its own full-page advert in the programme. The *Shopper*, meanwhile, blotted its copybook by publishing an advert touting tickets for the game.

Allocating the 8,337 seats, inevitably, had been fraught and left many disappointed, with few available for general sale after accounting for the club's season-ticket holders, members and guests. Nobody could yet know how far the exceptional demand would be replicated over the following weeks and months, and whether in fact the hope that the return home would improve attendances would eventually be borne out.

Cabin fever: hospitality arrangements in place behind the west stand

One journalist, however, was prepared to venture an opinion. Sounding a typically negative note amid overwhelmingly positive press coverage of the impending return, the *Evening Standard*'s resident curmudgeon Michael Herd predicted a return to 5,000 gates once things settled down. "Even in a week when there is saturation sympathy for Charlton fans, there is a need for the truth," wrote the paper's sports editor on December 1st. "Men of fewer emotions, fans who read balance sheets as well as programmes, know that had they stayed, Charlton Athletic would have remained insolvent, and that, inevitably, would have ended in bankruptcy. Football likes to pretend it is part of the fabric of our society, the presence of a League ground, its sense of purpose, enough to tantalise the public. Perhaps it was 50 years ago but no longer."

Nobody could accuse Herd or London's monopoly evening paper of inconsistency. His commentary on the club's exile ended in the same disparaging tone that supporters had come to expect. Yet his argument was flawed because those who could read balance sheets knew as well as anyone that returning to The Valley – "the biggest gamble that the club have ever made" – was the only hope of survival. At both Selhurst Park in 1990/91 and at Upton Park in 1991/92, Charlton had made operating losses equal to three quarters of turnover. The club was only afloat at all because there had been a £3.5m profit on transfers since 1989. Herd was simply wrong about the crowds and the general futility of the return, and eventually had the good grace to admit it.

Getting the pitch ready had never been a problem, despite the bad weather. But it had to be set further away from the Jimmy Seed Stand than before for safety reasons, because of the way the new emergency stairways protruded on to the track behind the goal. Then the directors had discovered that the view of the near goalline from the rear seats remained unsatisfactory. Aside from further training, during which inexperienced young defender Steve Brown caused much amusement when he managed to break the north stand guttering with a misdirected shot, there was one other significant ceremony to take place on the pristine playing surface before the weekend. On the Thursday morning the Mayor of Greenwich, Cllr Brian Sullivan, arrived to present the safety certificate formally. It was another major hurdle negotiated, but even so the work continued right up to the morning of the game.

Back in Welling, my phone had been ringing relentlessly all week with reporters looking for fresh information or new angles on the homecoming. I'd written preview pieces and interviews for the *Mercury* and an article for the *Valley Review*. There would be no *Voice of The Valley* to mark the occasion, because none of us wanted to have to sell it on the day. But now even I was finally lost for words.

Many who had been involved in the campaign spent the Friday evening at the Meridian Sports and Social Club, where the supporters' club had arranged a celebration disco. It was premature in a way, but somehow right that supporters came together to share their excitement. They knew that tomorrow the dream would be made real.

Battle for The Valley

Chapter Fifteen

"We've not heard that noise for seven years. Today we became a club again."
Alan Curbishley (December 5th, 1992)

If there was one risk in the return to The Valley that only divine intervention could manage, it was the weather. Rain had been an unwelcome complication to getting the stadium ready and while all spectators would be under cover – itself a first for the ground – poor conditions on December 5th could have detracted from the celebrations, if not the match itself. The previous fortnight had been almost unremittingly wet. So the first sign that the gods were finally smiling on Charlton Athletic came when the great day turned out to be dry, sunny and crisp. In SE7, predictably, workers were still laying tarmac at 10am.

For all that the day's events would ultimately mark the resumption of normality and the reinstatement of pre-match routines and habits forcibly abandoned seven years earlier, this could never be an ordinary afternoon. Charlton's first team had returned to The Valley in 1924, as we have seen, but in that case the club had never really left it and the change of venue had been brief. Whatever happened in the future, we all knew that there could never be another day like this one and fans and officials alike were determined to celebrate the achievement, both together and in smaller, more personal ways.

My own day began at Steve and Wendy Perfect's house in Welling, with a champagne breakfast among fellow campaigners. Then it was off to Woolwich, where the supporters' club had arranged for a symbolic march of the 1.8 miles back to The

End of the road: the march from Woolwich reaches Charlton Lane as the return to The Valley becomes a reality on December 5th, 1992

Programme panic: souvenir hunters snapped up an amazing 15,000 copies of the bumper *Valley Review* produced to mark the first match back home

Valley to leave General Gordon Square at midday. It was a reversal of the route followed before the two big council planning meetings. Hundreds, perhaps a thousand, gathered there for the 40-minute walk, up past the town hall in Wellington Street, along Artillery Place and Hillreach, then Little Heath and Charlton Park Road, before turning left down Charlton Lane to Harvey Gardens, all to the beat of a solitary drum. For some reason, perhaps by now obvious, I had charge of the supporters' club's megaphone and was able to announce our final mission to residents and waving passers-by. A number of marchers carried banners and placards, several again prepared by Valley Party candidate and 1985 protestor Dick Ayers. The mood was uniformly buoyant. At Harvey Gardens we met a police line checking tickets and then the party began.

Dedicated home and away supporter Les Turner, the hardworking Valley Party candidate in Hornfair ward and a fan since 1949, had eschewed the march because the timing meant that participants could not be at The Valley for the opening of the turnstiles, which was also due to take place at midday. He wanted to savour every moment. In the event there was a short delay because the key to unlock the gate to the compound was apparently missing, but Roger Alwen was soon able to lead the way. The chairman and his wife Heather were also celebrating their 28th wedding anniversary. Never could they have imagined it would be marked by such extravagant festivities.

Special destination: this group of supporters from Bromley had particular reason to be grateful for the improvement in the weather

Pre-match entertainment on the pitch was due to begin an hour later. But for many the immediate opportunity was to linger in Harvey Gardens and soak up the atmosphere. A jazz band played *The Red, Red Robin* on the corner opposite the club shop, some fans had come in fancy dress, and shortly after one o'clock an open-top double-decker bus negotiated the awkward bend in Floyd Road to deliver a contingent that had been touring Bromley borough.

Inevitably, the extraordinary demand for the special programme had been underestimated, despite a mammoth print run of 15,000, with most people buying multiple copies to keep or pass on as souvenirs. The shop, too, had a huge queue and reported record takings, with many fans snapping up the new replica shirts, even though it had been made clear they would have a life of just six months.

Unable to take my favoured place on the East Terrace, I'd opted instead for a seat in the Jimmy Seed Stand, although notably the club did not give it that title. It was argued, implausibly, that this might confuse the emergency services, despite the names given to other football stands up and down the country, but that was a quibble for another day. The great metal walkway shimmered in the weak winter sun as we made our way along it to our seats at the rear of the front section, where a group of around 20 of us had arranged to sit together.

Out on the pitch the Boys' Brigade Band entertained the growing crowd, much of which was in the ground by 2pm. High above The Valley even those without tickets were gathering in back gardens, behind high mesh security fences and even in the branches of trees in order to gain any glimpse of the scenes about to unfold below.

Ten past two brought a repeat parade of past heroes, including a number who thought they had taken their final bow in the same event seven years earlier. Among the group was Sailor Brown, who had helped launch the Valley Party in 1990; a veteran of the 1947 FA Cup campaign, Charlie Revell; and Peter Croker, who had played in the final that year. There were more modern heroes too, like Colin Powell, Keith Peacock and Mike Flanagan, and each received a respectable roar of appreciation. There was an even bigger cheer for Charlie Wright, popular goalkeeper and more recent Greenwich cafe proprietor. But the loudest reception, inevitably, was reserved for the old Valley's last great hero, Derek "Killer" Hales. On cue out of the Covered End sprang well-known supporter Vince Nieszwiec, who sprinted half the length of the pitch to welcome Hales home with a personal embrace. In any other circumstances this might have seen him ejected, but the police too had caught the mood and allowed him to return to his seat amid more cheers and laughter.

Meanwhile, the team news soon confirmed a rumour that had begun to circulate the previous evening. Joint manager Steve Gritt had made just three substitute appearances so far that season, the latest two months earlier, and hadn't started a game since February. Yet now he was restored to the side as one of the three changes from the 11 beaten at Barnsley. The man he replaced in midfield, Alan Pardew, was so upset by the decision that he later admitted to having tried to injure Gritt in training as payback. The joint bosses would always stick doggedly to the line that it had been a purely football decision with no element of sentimentality. But whether that was true or not, Gritt's inclusion did resonate deeply with the supporters. He had not

Musical welcome: a jazz band entertains returning supporters in Harvey Gardens

Point of entry: chairman Roger Alwen, who had first steered the board back towards The Valley, opens the turnstile compound gates shortly after midday

played in the final match at The Valley, but had been a regular in the team there for eight years prior to that. The link that had seemed to be lost with Robert Lee's departure was now restored.

At the other extreme, 20-year-old Norwich City striker Lee Power, signed on loan the previous day, would make his Charlton debut. But even he had local links, having been born in Lewisham. Of the team beaten at Barnsley a week earlier, the reliable John Bumstead also missed out, while Kim Grant dropped down to substitute. The line-up that would immediately be etched into so many memories would be Bob Bolder, in goal; Darren Pitcher, Simon Webster, Stuart Balmer and Scott Minto at the back; John Robinson, Gritt and Colin Walsh in midfield; Power, Carl Leaburn and Garry Nelson up front. Apart from the joint manager, only Bolder had played at The Valley before in a senior match, conceding three goals for Sheffield Wednesday in October 1981. Ironically two of them had been scored by 18-year-old Paul Walsh, who would feature as a Portsmouth substitute. The following year, however, Bolder had returned to take part in the Owls' 3-0 win.

Whether the team could summon a performance worthy of the occasion appeared doubtful, given that Charlton had taken just five points from the previous 30 available. The result had barely been discussed, because simply seeing the players take the field again was always likely to provide the emotional crescendo for the day. But it did matter and not just because of the team's declining League position.

First, however, there was more symbolism as young supporters from the Junior Reds, each representing groups who had played a part in the return, such as the Valley Party, Valley Gold members and contributors to the Valley Investment Plan, collected

Battle for The Valley

scarves from the centre circle, reversing the gesture of those placed there by protesting supporters in 1985.

There was the formal presentation of a large cheque to the directors by the Football Trust. It had mistakenly been made out for £2,078,000, £1m more than was actually due, but unfortunately it wasn't in a form that the club could take to the bank. Then came the switch-on of the floodlights, each set of bulbs revealing a letter to make up the initials "CAFC".

Finally, almost three hours after the gates had been opened – and seven years, two months and 14 days after they had been closed – the stage was set. Five to three. A large net containing 2,632 red and white balloons, one for each day of the exile, had been positioned in the centre circle. Now every seat was occupied and every eye was trained on the north-west corner of the pitch.

All Hales: Vince Nieszwiec (left) greets his hero following a one-man pitch invasion

Yesterday's men: former Charlton stars parade on the pitch prior to kick-off, just as they had at the "final" match seven years earlier

Wrong number: the six Charlton directors receive an over-large cheque towards the work at The Valley from the Football Trust

The club seemed to have played every popular hit with the slightest possible association with homecoming in the build-up to kick-off, but only one familiar refrain could signal the end of the exile. With so little else by way of identity to cherish in the years away, *The Red, Red Robin* had become more than a tradition for Charlton. It had represented continuity at a time when so many other matchday rituals had had to be discarded. Never had the lyric "I'm just a kid again, doing what I did again" been better suited to the occasion. But as for there being "no more sobbin'", that was hopelessly premature. Instead, Billy Cotton's cheerful rendition was precisely the signal for tears, from young and old, male and female, as the doors to the dressing rooms opened at last, club captain Webster and the rest of the team emerged, and up and over the East Terrace went the balloons.

All the protests, marches and meetings, all the passion, determination and ingenuity of so many supporters, all the financial and emotional commitment of the directors, had led to this moment of catharsis. It had been a monumental investment of time, energy and money. Yet here we were, not only back home, but also surfing a wave of optimism and self-belief that now the club could move forward again. Together we had not just opened the gates of The Valley, but surely laid to rest the legacy of apathy that had brought Charlton so low in the first place.

Alan Curbishley would call it the day we "became a club again", but the miracle ran deeper than that. Ten or 20 years later, we could look around the rebuilt ground

Battle for The Valley

Magic moment: skipper Simon Webster leads the Charlton team out for the match with Portsmouth to the familar refrain of *The Red, Red Robin*

Rising to the occasion: 2,632 red and white balloons were released as the teams took the field, one for each day of the club's absence from The Valley

297

and firmly conclude that John Fryer's "impertinent assumption" – and the reaction it eventually provoked – had been the catalyst that transformed the Addicks. Curbishley, along with Richard Murray as chairman, would be a huge contributor to the success that followed, but it remained the revolt that had slowly taken shape in the South London traffic jams of the late 1980s that had made it possible.

For now, for most of us, The Valley was enough. I'd only gone on to the pitch at the end of the game in 1985, but this time I was due there at half-time, to make a symbolic presentation of a framed photograph of the ground to Alwen on behalf of the supporters' club, and another with Steve Clarke and the Perfects to representatives of the Portsmouth fans. Steve Dixon was already out there with a microphone. But all I really wanted to do was watch from the stand.

The game began and was played throughout to a huge roar of encouragement such as never had been heard at Charlton matches at Selhurst Park and Upton Park, or indeed for many years before that.

There was only one remaining question and that was whether the team would be overawed by the occasion. The answer came less than seven minutes in and seemed to arrive in slow motion. Gritt chipped the ball forward from inside the Charlton half towards the edge of the penalty area, where Leaburn, with his back to goal, drew two defenders and laid it square to Pitcher. The full-back pivoted and with his second touch played the ball into the path of Walsh, 20 yards out in a central position.

And then we all looked on with gleeful incredulity, as the Scot's low, first-time, left-foot shot eluded the outstretched hand of Portsmouth goalkeeper Alan Knight and rolled, unerringly, into history.

First strike: Colin Walsh scores the only goal against Portsmouth, despite debutant Lee Power (nearest camera) being in an apparently offside position

Battle for The Valley

Looks familiar: surprise starter Steve Gritt in the thick of the action

Packed out: Charlton fans in the south stand and a long line of photographers wait to see if the home team can add to the scoreline in the second half

Appendix One

The following is a statement issued by Michael Gliksten on September 20th, 1985.

It will be the saddest day for me if Charlton abandon their traditional home at The Valley. And it would be totally unreasonable if the blame was laid at my door. For as far as I am concerned, I have leaned over backwards to help the club since stepping down as chairman in 1982. But at every crisis I am made the scapegoat by the management – small thanks for the support my family have given Charlton, both in time and money.

Imagine my horror at reading of how I was held up as the culprit for forcing the move to Crystal Palace in leaflets handed out at the match a fortnight ago. This is totally untrue. So I want to set the record straight.

First of all, let me state unequivocally that I have never entertained the notion of putting the club out of business so that I could develop the Valley ground. On a number of occasions offers have been made to me, some of which had been acceptable, both by the former chairman, Mark Hulyer, and at the time of the rescue in March 1984, to acquire all my interests, and I have been prepared to consider them. But in the event, none were proceeded with.

Let me describe specifically the situation regarding the two acres of land with the car park and turnstiles. In March last year, as everybody knows, Charlton were in severe financial difficulties. They owed considerable sums of money to a number of creditors including myself. The money owed to me was over £600,000, including unpaid rent and a loan.

A winding-up order was made on the club, but at the eleventh hour a rescue attempt was mounted with new financial backing and the club approached me to negotiate new arrangements. As a result, I agreed to write off the £600,000 owing and to let The Valley to a newly-formed Charlton 1984 at a reduced rent. Hardly the actions of someone who was out to do Charlton down.

The new lease was in most respects identical to the old one with three exceptions – the rent was reduced, the period of the lease was reduced and the area of land and buildings included in the lease was reduced.

The exclusion of the two acres was specifically at the club's suggestion and request. They actually said that they did not want this land. At the meeting where the deal was struck, it was the club who produced a drawing showing the boundaries of the land they required and the two acres were outside it.

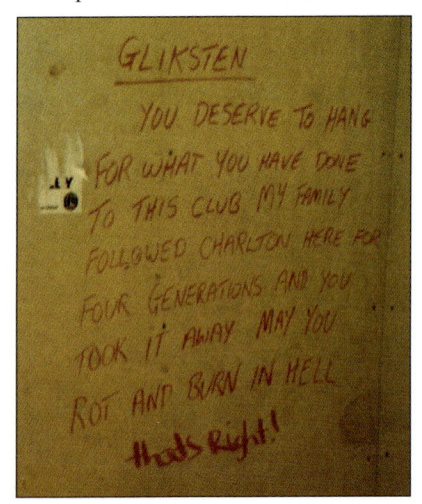

Strong words: a message left on an inner wall at the empty Valley

300

Overgrown and abandoned: The Valley as it looked by March 1989

It is totally untrue that I refused to agree a lease unless this land was left. My advisers and I clearly recall the directors producing the plan and suggesting to me that I might be able to carry out some development on this land as a way of recouping some of my own losses in due course. This I agreed to. I also agreed that the club could continue using the land free of charge until such time as I might require it and that they would vacate it on request.

Now, you might think that knowing about this situation since March 1984, the club would have made appropriate alternative arrangements, particularly on the question of turnstiles. Perhaps some of the money spent on players since that time could have been used on this project.

In the meantime, I have been involved in negotiations for the possible disposal of the land and as part of this have asked for it to be vacated as provided for under the terms of the agreement.

I regard all my actions as having been honourable and straightforward. Some people may say that I have been overgenerous in my attitude to successive managements, bearing in mind the sums of money involved. But I am still very committed to the history and footballing achievements of Charlton Athletic.

You can be sure that if the club abandons its traditional home, it is not me who has blown the whistle.

Footnote: Michael Gliksten passed away early in 2009. In October 2007, he had returned to The Valley for the first time in more than 24 years as a guest of the club's Former Players' Association at the Championship fixture against Barnsley and was greeted by chief executive Peter Varney, who gave him a tour. The ex-chairman was moved to tears by the welcome he received, particularly from players who had been at the club in his time, and the sight of the redeveloped stadium.

Appendix Two

Charlton fans contested the local elections in the London Borough of Greenwich on May 3rd, 1990, as the Valley Party, standing on the single issue of the council's refusal to approve the club's planning application to redevelop the ground. They stood in 60 of the 62 seats, leaving only the two members of the planning committee who voted in favour of Charlton's scheme, Bob Callow and Jim Coughlan, unopposed. Although failing to win a seat, they received an incredible 14,838 votes, 10.9% of those cast, helped remove the chair of planning, Cllr Simon Oelman, and shook the political establishment in the borough to its foundations.

Election results

LABOUR	59,372	43.6%
CONSERVATIVE	28,689	21.1%
SDP	20,670	15.2%
VALLEY	14,838	10.9%
LIBERAL DEMOCRAT	6,381	4.7%
GREEN	4,372	3.2%
OTHER	1,793	1.3%

ABBEY WOOD (12.2%)
LEWIS (SDP) 1418
MALONE (SDP) 1411
Wakefield (Lab) 1050
Minhas (Lab) 910
Gwen King (Valley) 347
Alex Hayes (Valley) 341
Weston (Green) 170

ARSENAL (15.2%)
MULCAHY (Lab) 575
Costello (SDP) 290
Mark Mansfield (Valley) 162
Cannon (Green) 40

AVERY HILL (5.3%)
RANDALL (Lib) 1042
Walker (Lab) 304
Spooner (Con) 236
David Fox (Valley) 88

BLACKHEATH (5.6%)
BRIGHTY (Con) 1127
HENDERSON (Con) 1116
Ramsey (Lab) 655
Madaugwu (Lab) 644
Stone (SDP) 603
Abbott (SDP) 573
McCracken (Green) 382
Pat Bristow (Valley) 152
Chick Fowles (Valley) 151

BURRAGE (10.5%)
DUVALL (Lab) 697
Gilbert (SDP) 232
Shaun Edwards (Valley) 125
Bynorth (Green) 91
Sidhu (Asian) 42

CHARLTON (13.5%)
PICTON (Lab) 1288
SANGHARA (Lab) 1136
Lines (SDP) 433
Bertram (Con) 353
Brian Bird (Valley) 352
Miah (SDP) 326
Jagusiewicz-Haines (Con) 279
Dominic Crowe (Valley) 277
Cunliffe (Green) 216

COLDHARBOUR (11.5%)
JEAVONS (Lab) 1150
CHALLIS (Lab) 1108
Parrett (Con) 1004
Rutt (Con) 949
Robert Weeks (Valley) 296
Wendy Perfect (Valley) 290
Churchill (Lib) 278

DEANSFIELD (10.5%)
MILES (Con) 743
Draper (Lab) 496
Victor Skinner (Valley) 163
Broad (Lib) 145

A Valley Party poster on display in the middle of Woolwich during April 1990

ELTHAM PARK (8.2%)
MITCHELL (Con) 1412
KEAR (Con) 1290
Harrington (Lab) 981
Slater (Lab) 887
Guthrie (Ind) 490
Hagyard (Lib) 337
Andrew Crouch (Valley) 297
Thornley (Green) 255
Steve Perfect (Valley) 211

EYNSHAM (7.1%)
SDP gained 2 from Lab
RASTALL (SDP) 1115
GROVES (SDP) 1102
Fitzpatrick (Lab) 1037
Oelman (Lab) 851
Chris Budgen (Valley) 195
Sinfield (Con) 159
Barry Nugent (Valley) 139
Mutimer (Green) 83

FERRIER (11.1%)
GILLMAN (Lab) 860
McPARLAND (Lab) 827
Fletcher (SDP) 369
Antcliffe (Con) 311
Millson (SDP) 301
Campbell-Smith (Con) 294
Kevin Merrick (Valley) 199
Nigel Taylor (Valley) 182
Caliendo (Green) 170

GLYNDON (12.4%)
Lab gained 1 from SDP
CRONIN (Lab) 1210
RAI (Lab) 910
Newton (SDP) 579
Jahans (SDP) 548
Craig Harwood (Valley) 303
Cooper (Con) 267
John Morris (Valley) 226
McPhee (Green) 180
Pindoria (Asian) 39

HERBERT (13.2%)
COKER (Lab) 1019
PATEL (Lab) 833
O'Brien (Con) 702
Garth (Con) 665
Barnett (Green) 336
Dick Ayers (Valley) 334
Ottery (Lib) 259
Nick Bullen (Valley) 248

HORNFAIR (14.2%)
HOGBEN (Lab) 1261
LEWIS (Lab) 1241
O'Keeffe (SDP) 474
Lamb (Con) 462
Ross (SDP) 435
Stirling (Con) 429
Andrew Keen (Valley) 404
Les Turner (Valley) 334
Reeves (Green) 133

Battle for The Valley

KIDBROOKE (5.8%)
Con gained 1 from Lab
COUGHLAN (Lab) 1033
BRENNAND (Con) 990
Rogers (Lab) 977
Harris (Con) 967
Mallone (Fellowship/Anti-poll tax) 415
Hegg (SDP) 400
McNeill (SDP) 357
Robert Taylor (Valley) 326
Caliendo (Green) 160

LAKEDALE (8.9%)
FRANCIS (Lab) 1105
JAWAID (Lab) 1033
Smith (SDP) 438
Wilson (SDP) 419
Bennett (Con) 233
Brian Smart (Valley) 178
Roger Taylor (Valley) 174
Master (Asian) 165
Kaur (Green) 124
Singh (Green) 93

MIDDLE PARK (24.2%)
GRAHAM (Lab) 1338
HARRIS (Lab) 1283
Paul Ellis (Valley) 576
Shayler (Lib) 422
Chris Wilkins (Valley) 398

NEW ELTHAM (10%)
MEPSTEAD (Con) 1341
GOODING (Con) 1238
Harrington (Lab) 976
Stratton (Lab) 973
Nicklin (Ind) 506
Jon Bangs (Valley) 370
Hurren (Lib) 325
Eve Waterman (Valley) 224

NIGHTINGALE (12.9%)
GORDON (Lab) 683
Peter Finch (Valley) 133
Mapes (Con) 126
Wilkins (Lib) 96

PALACE (8.2%)
KING (Con) 673
Carter (Lab) 408
MacQueen (Lib) 122
John West (Valley) 116
Pridham (Green) 90

PLUMSTEAD COMMON (8.1%)
MORSE (Lab) 762
Horne (SDP) 269
Frost (Con) 221
Darren Risby (Valley) 118
Cowdell (Green) 82

RECTORY FIELD (12.7%)
FAIRLIE (Lab) 1016
ADAMS (Lab) 1005
Hewson (SDP) 529
Wright (SDP) 462
Cummins (Con) 382
Martinez (Con) 323
Sandra Pace (Valley) 286
Paul Messeter (Valley) 285
Sharman (Green) 192

ST ALFEGE (9.1%)
GORDON-PEINIGER (Lab) 966
SMITH (Lab) 937
Binstead (Con) 539
Martinez (Con) 489
Marcus (SDP) 461
Stuart (SDP) 367
Pearson (Green) 214
Brian Smith (Valley) 198
Adam Beales (Valley) 198

ST MARY'S (18.5%)
FAHY (Lab) 952
O'SULLIVAN (Lab) 934
McElroy (SDP) 436
Morgan-Welldone (SDP) 343
David Long (Valley) 329
Danny Hayes (Valley) 315
Brown (Green) 168

ST NICHOLAS (10.1%)
HOOK (Lab) 1072
PURCELL (Lab) 949
Carter (SDP) 582
Martin (SDP) 488
Harvey-Bailey (Con) 391
Manns (Con) 359
Scott Forrest (Valley) 239
Clive Collett (Valley) 218
Baines (Green) 211

SHERARD (24.2%)
CALLOW (Lab) 1744
MARSH (Lab) 1361
Kevin Fox (Valley) 992

SHREWSBURY (7.4%)
SERGEANT (Con) 559
McManus (Lab) 387
Blade (SDP) 375
Tinsley (Green) 153
Colin Holland (Valley) 117

SLADE (10.1%) Lab gained 2 from Lib
AUSTIN-WALKER (Lab) 1081
BARRATT (Lab) 1019
Woodhead (Lib) 961
Mitchell (Lib) 949
Bowe (Con) 514
Salter (Con) 511
Stavros Demetriades (Valley) 292
Ken Dudman (Valley) 275

Battle for The Valley

SUTCLIFFE (4.0%)
Lib gained from Con
WOODCRAFT (Lib) 674
Glover (Con) 531
Shlackman (Lab) 378
John Biggs (Valley) 66

TARN (10.0%)
RICHARDS (Con) 691
Willsman (Lab) 431
Stephen Clarke (Valley) 138
Carter (Lib) 117

THAMESMEAD MOORINGS (5.4%)
Lab gained 1 from SDP
CLARIDGE (Lab) 926
CLARIDGE (Lab) 810
Austen (SDP) 759
Kennedy (SDP) 627
Fieldgate (Con) 173
Wignall (Con) 142
Simon Caddock (Valley) 112
Bernie Taylor (Valley) 93
Stott (Green) 90
Du Sauzay (Ind) 45

TRAFALGAR (11.2%)
FARMER (Lab) 1203
TAYLOR (Lab) 1161
Elliott (SDP) 375
Browne-Clayton (Con) 347
Casey (Con) 300
Thomas (SDP) 299
Dave Archer (Valley) 285
John Stickings (Valley) 218
Sewell (Green) 196
Renouf (Lib) 101

VANBRUGH (7.6%)
BIGWOOD (Lab) 1049
MOON (Lab) 921
Blackaby (Con) 702
Vickery (Con) 648
Grylls (SDP) 354
Newman (SDP) 310
Plummer (Green) 244
Gary Hannant (Valley) 196
McGinty (Lib) 191
Craig Norris (Valley) 184
Stride (Lib) 129
Allman (Anti-poll tax) 51
Fay (Ind) 40

WELL HALL (11.2%)
EFFORD (Lab) 1344
DEAN (Con) 1295
Hayes (Lab) 1260
Clark (Con) 1238
Steve Dixon (Valley) 372
Keith Crowhurst (Valley) 305
Wilkins (Lib) 233

Not amused: Queen Victoria's statue at Woolwich during the count

WEST (6.4%)
STRONG (Lab) 1101
SHAHZAD (Lab) 1012
Caslake (SDP) 401
Kemshell (SDP) 338
Gough (Con) 262
Wise (Con) 249
Bull (Green) 190
Rosina Larking (Valley) 122
Marlon Seton (Valley) 119

WOOLWICH COMMON (11.5%)
Lab gained 1 from SDP
DHILLON (Lab) 965
PIKE (Lab) 887
O'Brien (SDP) 544
Slavin (SDP) 528
Richard Grove (Valley) 246
Salter (Con) 230
Magonigle (Con) 227
Terry Lloyd (Valley) 209
Hodgson (Green) 109

305

Acknowledgements

I should not, of course, have been able to write this book without the backing and encouragement of the numerous friends and fellow supporters who made possible the campaign to return Charlton Athletic to The Valley. To each and every individual who played a part in that endeavour, however minor their role, I express my thanks.

In particular, I acknowledge the various efforts of Peter Cordwell, Steve Dixon, Richard Hunt and Roy King. Hopefully their roles are sufficiently highlighted in the text. While I had many differences with them, I cannot omit to mention Roger Alwen and Mike Norris. We shared a common goal and each side needed the other's support. In the later stages the contribution of Richard Murray and Martin Simons was crucial and I don't believe the club would have got home without it.

Former club photographer Tom Morris supplied most of the pictures from the 1960s onwards for the book in 1991, as he has for the second edition 23 years later. The fact that he was present at so many important junctures illustrates his own sympathy with our ultimate aim and I am under no illusions about the extent to which his work contributed to *Battle for The Valley*'s original success.

In preparing the story for publication, I was lucky enough to enjoy the generous assistance of two Charlton historians whose knowledge of the club, I freely admit, was much deeper than my own. These were the late Colin Cameron, author of *The Valiant 500* and *Home & Away with Charlton Athletic 1920-2004*, and Michael Whelan. The historical chapters would have been impossible to compile without their support and Colin was enormously helpful in supplying hard facts about the development of the ground to flesh out my original assumptions and guesswork.

His sudden death on Christmas Day 2012 was a heavy blow, not just in respect of the gap it left in recording and safeguarding the club's history, but also to the many of us who were proud to call him a friend. He was rightly accorded the rare tribute for a supporter of a minute's applause by the Valley crowd the following day, and his work lives on in this book as well as in his own.

I am grateful to Mike for his tolerance of the degree to which I drew on his published articles in 1991 and for being so obliging, in 2014, when I needed to locate some of the historical pictures again.

Richard Redden, author of *The Story of Charlton Athletic 1905-1990* (later updated and reissued as *Valley of Tears, Valley of Joy*), was also most co-operative, and I found his explanation of the complexities of the 1984 winding-up saga helpful.

Roy King was the conscientious archivist of the Valley Party phase of the campaign. Candidate Colin Holland, who sadly passed away early in 2013, alerted me to the existence of some useful additional material.

Steve Bridge, Colin Cameron, Steve Dixon, Dave Hales, Dave Sturge and Michael Whelan provided extra pictures, as did the *Mercury* and Andy Soloman. I was grateful to the late Mike Loveridge for permission to reproduce his spectacular aerial view of the ground (inside front cover), taken from a helicopter in 1974. Ron Hooper and Terry Stevens generously volunteered additional pictures for this edition, while the 1944 image of The Valley in wartime appears by agreement with Mirrorpix.

Patrick Collins gave permission for material from his *Mail on Sunday* reports to

Credit where it's due: board members Martin Simons, Richard Collins, Roger Alwen, Mike Stevens, Richard Murray and Derek Ufton on December 5th, 1992

be used and Simon Inglis kindly agreed to allow me to quote from the first edition of his stadium book, the *Football Grounds of England and Wales*.

Terry Bushell, Colin Cameron, Peter Cordwell and Richard Hunt read the original proofs and offered advice, not all of which I was able to follow up in the time available, but I thank them nonetheless, as I do Corinna Huxley and Matt Wright, who have stepped into their shoes two decades later. Matt's attention to factual detail has proven particularly invaluable, but any remaining errors are mine.

Finally, I wish to record my appreciation of the work done by the various journalists and authors who compiled the sources upon which I have drawn in my research. The main newspapers used were the *Kentish Independent*, the *South East London & Kentish Mercury*, the *Lewisham Borough News*, the *Kentish Times*, the *South London Press* and the *Croydon Advertiser*.

I am obviously biased, but the *Mercury* – reliable ally of the fans for all the seven years of exile and longer, as well as home to my own ramblings for nine – must be singled out for particular praise due to its role in the campaign.

I drew heavily on Anthony Bristowe's then rather obscure 1949 history of the club, issued by Convoy Publications. I subsequently reproduced it for the supporters' club and commend it to any future historians for its accuracy and attention to detail.

The feedback to the original edition, its 3,000 copies long sold out, was generous and gratifying. I thank readers past and present, and am grateful to have had this opportunity after so many years to complete the story. I hope I have done it justice.

Rick Everitt

Battle for The Valley

Heroes one and all

Article by Rick Everitt published in the Valley Review on December 5th, 1992

If you were handed that shameful piece of paper at the Valley turnstiles on September 7th, 1985. If you stood, with me, on the Valley pitch a fortnight later and shouted defiance. If you signed the *Mercury* petition in October 1986 and protested to the directors when they came to the Valley Club to receive it. If you never went to Selhurst Park or Upton Park on principle.

If you gave or raised cash for the Mercury Trust Fund. If you are that paper's sports editor, Peter Cordwell, so obviously the right man in the right place at the right time. If you came out on that rainy Sunday morning of April 2nd, 1989, to help clear the ground of weeds.

If you protested inside and outside Woolwich Town Hall on January 31st, 1990, when the council rejected the club's planning application. If you delivered leaflets in the local elections of May that year, or simply cast your vote for the Valley Party. If you posted planning department letters through Charlton street doors when the snow was six inches deep under foot. If you marched and assembled and cheered at Woolwich Town Hall on April 2nd last year, when the council granted permission for the second planning application.

If you trudged, loyally from London SE25 to London E6, even when you didn't really want to go. If you joined Valley Gold, or put your money into the VIP scheme when the directors could not find the cash themselves. If you bought another season ticket this year, even after the club had let you down so badly last summer. If you answered Roy King's appeal for painters to help with the final refurbishment work.

If you are Roger Alwen, Martin Simons or Richard Murray. Or even if you simply cared with the same relentless passion about the fate of this plot of land in London SE7.

Then this is your day. And I salute you.

For when, in years to come, you bring your children and grandchildren to watch our team, you can honestly tell them that you helped save The Valley. Nothing less.

Just as much as did the

308

pioneers of 1919 who toiled to make a football ground out of a derelict chalk pit, you have breathed life into the club.

Words on this affair have been cheap, but none are adequate for what we are to witness today. The prospect is simply mind-boggling. What I do know is that when we walk away from Floyd Road this afternoon – win, lose or draw – we will at last be a proper football club again. Next time we play at home, we'll once again have time to watch *Football Focus* over lunch and not face the prospect of an hour or more stuck in traffic. And when we get to the game, we won't have to listen to the taunts and ridicule of opposing fans.

The very idea of Charlton Athletic without The Valley always was nonsense, as many of us took the trouble to point out in 1985. There is scant consolation in having been right all along. But there is much to be drawn from what has happened since.

For the experience of exile has changed the club immeasurably for the better. Just look at the board, the training ground, the supporters' club – even, dare I add, the local media. The roots of all these transformations lie in the campaign and the skills and passion which it uncovered.

The question now is whether or not we finish the job by using those precious resources to make this club the roaring success that it always should have been.

I know we can do it, I just hope that when you've dried your eyes this afternoon, you'll find the strength to join me in making sure we do. This time we may not get another chance.

Volunteers who had worked on the ground in the run-up to the return to The Valley were recognised by the club on the day with individual plaques

The last word

Front-page article by Rick Everitt, in the Mercury, December 10th, 1992

Shortly after one o'clock on Saturday, a red, red bus bob, bob, bobbed its precarious way down Floyd Road and into a sea of smiling faces.

The milling crowd of fans raised a hearty cheer and waved their welcome to the latest arrivals. Like so many kids again, doing what they did again, they could hardly contain their glee.

Outside the club shop, the Pope conversed with a skeleton, TV boss Michael Grade puffed on a huge cigar and Valley Party candidate Gwen King posed for photographers in a robin's nest hat.

And from behind their net curtains, one set of Harvey Gardens residents peered suspiciously at another.

For this was the tearful, magical, engagingly nutty and ultimately thrilling day when Charlton Athletic finally came home. Home to SE London. Home to Charlton. But most of all home to The Valley.

Before the kick-off, a parade of more and less distinguished names from a proud past strode out from the touchline. Each received a respectable roar. Then out came Derek Hales. So too did a male admirer, from the Covered End, to deliver a kiss. And the ground simply erupted.

And then it was five to three. Time for normality. Moment of dreams. Now the dreams came true. Balloons drifted skywards from the centre circle, one for each of the 2,632 days of exile.

And the ghosts of Sam Bartram, Stuart Leary and Don Welsh stood shoulder to shoulder on the vast, condemned East Terrace with those of the pioneers who built the ground in 1919.

The first secretary, Bert "Fatty" Heath, was there. Arthur Brandon, the pre-League chairman. And Edwin Radford, who invited the directors to return from their other foolish expedition, to Catford, in 1924.

Their successors in the three open stands had not betrayed their memory, after all. And the modern players did not let down their illustrious predecessors, either. The Valley had found its voice again. And the editor of *Voice of The Valley* lost his. Portsmouth never stood a chance.

And afterwards, as the ground's first-ever sell-out crowd saluted the club's first home win for seven years, you wanted to linger among the ghosts. But you knew you could come back to see them again on Monday. And the next week. And the week after that…